WOMEN AND MARRIAGE IN GERMAN MEDIEVAL ROMANCE

In contrast to the widespread view that the Middle Ages were a static, unchanging period in which attitudes to women were uniformly negative, D. H. Green argues that in the twelfth century the conventional relationship between men and women was subject to significant challenge through discussions in the vernacular literature of the period. Hitherto, scholarly interest in gender relations in such literature has largely focused on French romance or on literature in English from a later period. By turning the focus on the rich material to be garnered from Germany – including *Erec*, *Tristan* and *Parzival* – Professor Green shows how some vernacular writers devised methods to debate and challenge the undoubted antifeminism of the day by presenting a utopian model, supported by a revision of views by the Church, to contrast with contemporary practice.

D.H. GREEN is Professor Emeritus in the University of Cambridge and a Fellow of Trinity College.

CAMBRIDGE STUDIES IN MEDIEVAL LITERATURE

General editor
Alastair Minnis, *Yale University*

Editorial board
Zygmunt G. Barański, *University of Cambridge*
Christopher C. Baswell, *University of California, Los Angeles*
John Burrow, *University of Bristol*
Mary Carruthers, *New York University*
Rita Copeland, *University of Pennsylvania*
Simon Gaunt, *King's College, London*
Steven Kruger, *City University of New York*
Nigel Palmer, *University of Oxford*
Winthrop Wetherbee, *Cornell University*
Jocelyn Wogan-Browne, *Fordham University*

This series of critical books seeks to cover the whole area of literature written in the major medieval languages – the main European vernaculars, and medieval Latin and Greek – during the period c.1100–1500. Its chief aim is to publish and stimulate fresh scholarship and criticism on medieval literature, special emphasis being placed on understanding major works of poetry, prose, and drama in relation to the contemporary culture and learning which fostered them.

A complete list of titles in the series can be found at the end of the volume.

WOMEN AND MARRIAGE IN GERMAN MEDIEVAL ROMANCE

D. H. GREEN

CAMBRIDGE
UNIVERSITY PRESS

CAMBRIDGE UNIVERSITY PRESS
Cambridge, New York, Melbourne, Madrid, Cape Town, Singapore, São Paulo, Delhi

Cambridge University Press
The Edinburgh Building, Cambridge CB2 8RU, UK

Published in the United States of America by Cambridge University Press, New York

www.cambridge.org
Information on this title: www.cambridge.org/9780521513357

© D. H. Green 2009

First published 2009

Printed in the United Kingdom at the University Press, Cambridge

A catalogue record for this publication is available from the British Library

ISBN 978-0-521-51335-7 hardback

Contents

Preface

In the preface to *Women Readers in the Middle Ages* I wrote that the present companion volume was under active preparation. I was able to say this because the research and collection of material for both volumes were conducted at the same time and with an eye to what I originally, and optimistically, thought might be their joint appearance. If I have been able to complete the present book so relatively soon after its predecessor this is also because, when one has advanced well into one's eighties, one is more than ever conscious of the pressure of time exerting its own urgency. The converse of this is that retirement gives one the freedom for uninterrupted research which our political masters, for all their talk of research assessment exercises, are loath to grant to academics, especially in the humanities, before they retire.

As previously, I owe a number of debts of gratitude. Foremost amongst these I thank Mark Chinca and Nigel Palmer for reading through the chapters of this book in their first shape and for giving me their detailed comments, most of which I have accepted. I have made considerable demands on the patience and readiness to help of members of the Cambridge University Library, which they have uniformly met with courtesy and efficiency. It is also a pleasure to thank once more Laura Pieters Cordy, and assisting her Hansa Chauhan, for transposing my handwriting into a print-ready text and for the helpful suggestions on style and wording which this elicited. Further, I acknowledge with gratitude the financial support from my University and my College which made a number of research stays in Germany possible.

My greatest debt is to Sarah, for her unflagging help, encouragement and willingness to talk over my many questions with me. Without her this book would not have been written.

Abbreviations

AASS	*Acta Sanctorum*, J. Bolland *et al.* (eds.), Antwerp 1643ff.
ABäG	*Amsterdamer Beiträge zur älteren Germanistik*
AfK	*Archiv für Kulturgeschichte*
BMZ	G. F. Benecke, W. Müller and F. Zarncke, *Mittelhochdeutsches Wörterbuch*, Leipzig 1854–61
CCM	*Cahiers de Civilisation Médiévale*
CN	*Cultura Neolatina*
DVjs	*Deutsche Vierteljahrsschrift*
EG	*Études Germaniques*
Ep.	Epistola
FMLS	*Forum for Modern Language Studies*
FMS	*Frühmittelalterliche Studien*
FS	Festschrift
GRM	*Germanisch-Romanische Monatsschrift*
HRG	A. Erler and E. Kaufmann, *Handwörterbuch zur deutschen Rechtsgeschichte*, Berlin 1971–8
IASL	*Internationales Archiv für Sozialgeschichte der Literatur*
LiLi	*Zeitschrift für Literaturwissenschaft und Linguistik*
MÆ	*Medium Ævum*
MF	*Minnesangs Frühling*
MGH	*Monumenta Germaniae Historica*
MHG	Middle High German
MIÖG	*Mitteilungen des Instituts für Österreichische Geschichtsforschung*
MLR	*Modern Language Review*
MSt	*Mediaeval Studies*
NML	*New Medieval Literature*
OL	*Orbis Litterarum*
PBB	*Paul und Braunes Beiträge*
PL	J. P. Migne, *Patrologia Latina*

PMLA	*Publications of the Modern Language Association*
RBPH	*Revue Belge de Philologie et d'Histoire*
RG	*Recherches Germaniques*
RPh	*Romance Philology*
RR	*Romanic Review*
SG	*Studia Gratiana*
SMRH	*Studies in Medieval and Renaissance History*
ZfdA	*Zeitschrift für deutsches Altertum*
ZfdPh	*Zeitschrift für deutsche Philologie*
ZfRG (GA)	*Zeitschrift für Rechtsgeschichte (Germanistische Abteilung)*

Introduction

This book is conceived as a companion volume to *Women Readers in the Middle Ages* (Cambridge 2007), but with a double change of focus. In the earlier book I attempted to give a selective survey of the various classes of women in three countries (Germany, France, England) throughout the Middle Ages who were active as readers or engaged in other ways in literature, and also of the kinds of text they read, whereas now my question is more what appeals their reading made to them and how they may conceivably have reacted to it. Whereas the first book ranged over the whole span of the Middle Ages, from the seventh to the early sixteenth century, this one concentrates on the years before and immediately after 1200, above all because the wonderfully innovative force of the twelfth century promises illumination in regard to our question and because of the disturbances in the gender system which have been registered in that century. Focusing on the earliest German romances has the added advantage that they were written by authors of the highest rank and can be compared with French counterparts of similar quality.

The title of this book refers specifically to women alone. The reason for this is to provide continuity with the earlier volume, of which this one was at first conceived to form a part, but also because medieval misogyny felt the problem to lie more with women than with men, just as its modern successors coined a term for this (*Frauenfrage*) without feeling the need for a corresponding *Männerfrage*. Writing this book after its companion volume means that certain problems discussed earlier are not taken up again. These include the importance of women's literacy and their reading practice (especially of romances), but also their activity as sponsors and patrons of literature in the vernacular. As a consequence, authors addressed not merely a lay audience, but more specifically a female audience, to whose interests they made special appeal.

In Part I one chapter gives a brief, but purposely general sketch of views about women commonly held in the Middle Ages and a second chapter prepares the ground for what is to follow by narrowing its focus down to feminisation in the twelfth century. Part II is devoted to a more detailed discussion of three of the earliest romance themes in European literature: Erec, Tristan and Parzival. It is not difficult to justify the choice of these romances, for they are historically important as the first examples of the 'matter of Britain', the first works to engage in vernacular fictional writing, and they were also in the lead in treating lay themes for a lay audience. Above all, they are works of high literary quality, of European rank. English speaking medievalists may perhaps know the works of Chrétien de Troyes, yet few outside the dwindling band of Germanists in English speaking countries are acquainted with his German colleagues. This is regrettable, not simply because of the quality of these German works (no mere copies of French originals), but also because they provide rich evidence of value for a gendered approach to the medieval period.

As a Germanist my main concern is with the German versions of these three romance themes, but their French counterparts are also taken into account. To assist English speakers, quotations from medieval works are translated, either where my text introduces them or in brackets after the actual quotation. Those who, it is hoped, wish to explore the works in their entirety are well served by English translations. Chrétien's *Erec* and *Perceval* are available in translation in W. W. Kibler, *Chrétien de Troyes. Arthurian romances* (London 1991). The *Erec* of Hartmann von Aue has been rendered into English by M. Resler, *Erec, by Hartmann von Aue* (Philadelphia *c*.1987), Gottfried's version of the Tristan story by A. T. Hatto, *Gottfried von Strassburg. Tristan* (Harmondsworth 1960), who has also translated Wolfram's version of the Parzival theme, *Parzival. Wolfram von Eschenbach* (Harmondsworth 1980). Hatto's translation of Gottfried also includes a translation of the fragments of *Tristran* of Thomas of Britain.

Although medievalists have learned much from the new questions raised by women's studies in particular and by gender studies at large, I seek to qualify what may be termed an extreme feminism, the reluctance of some to recognise that, however dominant misogyny may have been in the Middle Ages, we cannot talk of a universal antifeminism in this period. If in A. Blamires's anthology of texts, *Women defamed and women defended* (Oxford 1992), the defence seemed to fall markedly short, this was soon more than made good by the same scholar's monograph, *The case for women in medieval culture* (Oxford 1997), in which the detailed and far-ranging case was argued by an impressive number of male as well as female authors. In the pages that follow I attempt to show that the case was also presented by the earliest authors in the romance genre in Germany as well as France. Medieval women were not entirely without sympathisers and allies amongst men.

PART I

The role of women

Introduction

In the two chapters that make up Part I the argument operates with a double time-focus. The first chapter ranges over the medieval period at large, discussing selectively views held about women, largely negative but sometimes positive. Given its importance for clerical views we start with authoritative biblical evidence, but also consider ways in which it was developed throughout the Middle Ages, and include occasional significant qualifications or divergences from its implications. This theological testimony is then supplemented by what light the practices of feudal society may throw on secular attitudes towards women and their position in the world, sometimes in agreement with ecclesiastical views, sometimes deviating from them.

In Chapter 2 we narrow our range down to the twelfth century in considering what I term 'feminisation' in this restricted period. The justification for this closer focus is the important changes in the relationship between the sexes which have been registered for this century, but also because this sets the scene for Part II with its treatment of vernacular romances dating from before and just after 1200.

Both chapters provide a background for the works discussed in Part II and are meant to contextualise them. They cover a broad range of social and ecclesiastical issues relating to women, deliberately broader than those treated in Part II, in order to illustrate the extent of the debate into which vernacular authors then insert their literary contributions. This breadth of range is also meant to highlight the ambivalence of traditional views which lie at the heart of such a prolonged debate.

CHAPTER I

Women in the Middle Ages

The difficulty facing Eileen Power in her *Medieval Women* – how to treat a large subject in a short book – is even more acute in the case of a short chapter such as this. My first task is to present an abbreviated survey of the range of topics concerning women commonly discussed in the Middle Ages, providing the wider background for the more restricted number of themes taken up in the romances to be considered. Secondly, I focus on the variety of opinions, divergent and even contradictory, that could be held, thus preparing the way for the discussion or debate about women, love and marriage which the authors of these romances hoped to encourage in the vernacular amongst laypeople. The highly selective evidence presented in this chapter covers first the authoritative opinions voiced in the Old and New Testaments, with echoes and deviations in medieval discussion, and secondly the extent of agreement and also opposition between ecclesiastical views and the secular practices of feudal society in the Middle Ages. If this double perspective means omitting other contributory factors, such as medical views about the differences between the sexes,[1] my excuse must be that we thereby move more in the mainstream of medieval thought on these matters.

By talking of a variety of opinions and an opposition between views I have already suggested the core of what follows, namely that it is a mistake to regard the Middle Ages, as has long been done, as being characterised by a monolithic antifeminism. Misogyny may well pervade the whole period (and beyond) and may even be predominant, but not to the exclusion of other opinions questioning it from many points of view. Two scholars in particular have performed yeoman service in questioning the assumption of an unrelieved misogyny in this period. In England, Blamires gave markedly more space in his anthology of medieval texts to antifeminism than to defensive responses to it, but this impression of imbalance was redressed by

---

[1] On these see Bullough, *Viator* 4 (1973), 485–501, and Cadden, *Meanings*.

his monograph on the case for women in the Middle Ages.[2] Whereas most earlier work in this direction had concentrated on isolated and relatively late examples of profeminine attitudes (e.g. Chaucer, Christine de Pizan) Blamires covers a much wider range. He thereby establishes a tradition in defence of women, existing alongside and in answer to the misogynous tradition, from the early to the late Middle Ages, but also drawing on support from the examples of a number of biblical women.

In Germany this argument has been reinforced by Schnell in two monographs.[3] He argues that scholarship on medieval views on women has largely depicted them as uniformly misogynous because it has been based too narrowly on evidence taken from Latin clerical writing for 'internal' consumption, which has been wrongly held to represent the only view of women in the Middle Ages. In taking other discourses into account Schnell differentiates the picture and argues, like Blamires, that women could be defamed, but also defended against such attacks. Against the assumption of an all-embracing medieval misogyny Schnell stresses the interdependence of what is said and the conditions under which it is said, including such varying factors as oral or written communication, discourse amongst men alone or including women, Latin (for clerics) and vernacular (for laypeople), learned or pragmatic function, different social groups addressed for whom the issue works out differently. Schnell also makes a fundamental distinction between discourse on women (*Frauendiskurs*) on the one hand (scholarly, androcentric and a vehicle for misogynous views) and discourse on marriage (*Ehediskurs*) on the other (pastoral in intent and stressing the shortcomings of men as well as women).[4] He emphasises the relevance of various types of discourse meant for laypeople in the vernacular. To these belongs, as the argument will show in Part II, court literature treating themes such as the relationship between men and women in love and marriage.[5] This literature may reflect misogynous opinions deriving from clerical discourse as well as patriarchal attitudes to women at home in feudal society, but it would be rash to assume that the employment of such topoi necessarily implies an acceptance of them, rather than including them as a subject for discussion and debate. Finally, Schnell also maintains that the divergence of views can imply the contrast between imperfect reality and a utopian project, stressing that such utopianism can be detected in clerical views as well as in court literature.

---

[2] Blamires, *Woman and Case.*   [3] Schnell, *Frauendiskurs* and *Sexualität.*
[4] On some of these distinctions see also Schnell, *FMS* 32 (1998), 307–64.
[5] Treated with relative brevity by Schnell in chapter VII of *Sexualität.*

We may sum up these varying attitudes to women by applying to them what Bond, in another context, maintains of the conception of the private secular self in the high Middle Ages: the images 'which began to appear are neither uniform nor coherent; they represent instead contested positions within an arena of ideological controversy'.[6] More specifically with regard to the manifold depictions of women in medieval literature we must reckon not merely with differences between genres (which is Schnell's main concern), but also within a given genre, within one author or even within one work. To look for a unified picture of women under such conditions and to expect that picture always to be essentially negative does little justice to the intensity of a debate on their nature which persisted throughout the medieval period.

We start by considering what first the Old Testament and then the New have to say about women, including also some selective references to how later authors reduplicated or qualified such statements. My main purpose is to illustrate the undoubted antifeminine current throughout these examples, but also to point to occasional, but persistent deviations from this tradition.

OLD TESTAMENT

For the Old Testament we may begin by quoting what Blamires says of the scriptural background in his anthology, that 'ideally one would need the complete stories of Samson, Judith, Esther, etc., as well as extensive readings in Proverbs, Ecclesiastes, and Ecclesiasticus, the three books in which the most damaging assertions are made about women'.[7] Such an undertaking is clearly out of the question as much for us as for Blamires, so that we must confine ourselves to selected passages from these books, but also considering the two episodes in Genesis, the Fall and the creation of man, on which misogynous tradition drew so persistently.

Solomon, or the gnomic sayings attributed to him, is our leading Old Testament misogynist. Ecclesiasticus 25, 33 begins at the beginning with its claim that from woman arose sin and through her we all die, but surpasses this in extremism when it says that the iniquity of a man is better than a woman who does good (42, 14) and gives warning that there is nothing worse than the anger of a woman (25, 23). This warning recurs in Proverbs 21, 19 with a shift from misogyny to misogamy in the statement that it is better to live in a desert than with a quarrelsome and irascible woman. The

---

[6] Bond, *Subject*, p. 1.   [7] Blamires, *Woman*, p. 31.

same book also refers misogynously, in a manner not made clear in the Authorised Version, to the insatiability of women when it includes the mouth of the vulva, alongside the grave, parched earth and fire, amongst the four things that can never be satisfied (30, 15f.). Such categorical statements, enjoying biblical authority, seem damning enough, but that does not protect them from later qualification, however discreetly. Schnell draws attention to two admittedly early modern modifications of this kind. Where according to Solomon's saying only one good woman was to be found amongst a thousand (Ecclesiastes 7, 29) João de Barros (1540) makes the minor adjustment of talking about one good human being amongst a thousand, thereby involving both sexes, not women alone.[8] The other example concerns Ecclesiasticus 42, 14 (the iniquity of man preferable to a good woman), as interpreted by Nicolas l'Archevesque as late as 1638.[9] Whereas the biblical saying was meant misogynously, the French author converts this into one critical of men instead. He does this by arguing that the biblical text does not mean that the virtue of a woman is of less value than the offences of a sinful man, but rather that the man is morally so weak that, on seeing a woman, he lusts after her and commits sin. What brings about his sin is therefore not the beauty, let alone the virtue, of the woman, but the man's desire ('mais c'est sa propre concupiscence'). We shall see in what follows that the modification of the antifeminine thrust of the biblical argument brought about in these two examples of Schnell is not without parallel in the Middle Ages.

More important for the development of medieval misogyny than such sayings, however frequent and categorical, are two episodes in the Bible: the Fall and the creation of man. Both are recurrently used to establish woman's proneness to sin and her inferior status, but both call forth attempts to rectify such interpretations.

In the biblical account of the Fall (described by Blamires as the 'front-line weapon of misogyny')[10] the serpent's tempting of Eve and her subsequent tempting of Adam are enough to bring down on Eve, and through her on all women, the punishment of the pain of childbearing and subordination to man (Gen. 3, 16: 'in dolore paries filios, et sub viri potestate eris, et ipse dominabitur tui' you will bring forth children in pain and be under the authority of your husband, who will rule over you). Paul makes reference to both these points as part of his argument that women are not to teach, for that would amount to authority over man and also because it was not the man, but the woman who was first seduced (I Tim. 2, 12 and 14). The

---

[8] Schnell, *Frauendiskurs*, p. 233.   [9] *Ibid.*, p. 202.   [10] Blamires, *Case*, p. 32.

apostle is followed by fathers of the Church on this, as when Tertullian, quoting Genesis on woman's subordination, refers to her as the gateway of the devil, the first to go against divine law and the one who persuaded him whom the devil could not seduce,[11] or when Ambrose likewise quotes Paul to the effect that the woman, but not Adam, was deceived as the justification of women's subjection to the stronger sex.[12] The weakness attributed to women in this connection can be interpreted in various ways, as naive simplicity (*simplicitas*), softness (*mollities*) as opposed to firmness of character, short-sightedness or intellectual inferiority, but in any case explaining why the devil was able to tempt Eve as more vulnerable than Adam.[13]

The history of the exegesis of this doctrine, however, reveals a number of significant variations which lessen or question the antifeminine implications seen in it. Blamires has pointed out that, as part of the hierarchical relationship which demoted women, men were conceived as active and women as passive, but that as a result men must be more guilty than women, so that scrutiny of responsibility affects all areas of the debate.[14] An example of how the antifeminine exegesis of the Fall, placing the blame squarely on Eve, can be adapted to involving Adam as well occurs in the Middle English *Dives and Pauper*.[15] This text castigates Adam for the sin of blaming Eve, attributing his fault to her when God rebuked him, an evasion of responsibility by the 'stronger' party which amounts to a *fals excusacioun*. A similar strategy (undercutting misogyny by extending the criticism to embrace men as well) is employed by the author of the Anglo-Norman *Bounté des femmes* in insisting on Adam's share of responsibility because of his own folly.[16] Nor do we have to wait for late medieval texts in the vernacular for the articulation of such criticism. As early as with Chrysostom Adam can be condemned since, if he is to be seen patriarchally as the 'head' of his partner and Eve as the 'body', then his responsibility is all the greater.[17] That is a very condescending mitigation of Eve's responsibility and it lurks within a pronouncedly antifeminine context, but it does point the way to a later possible exculpation from an explicitly misogynous charge. Insofar as Adam is involved as well, the fault lies with human nature itself and is not gender specific, a defence of woman which as we shall see plays a prominent part in vernacular literature around 1200 with critical generalisations which are not restricted to the female sex alone, but extended to males too. The logical force of this strategy has been summed up well by Blamires as a refusal 'to let

---

[11] Quoted by Blamires, *Woman*, p. 51.   [12] *Ibid.*, p. 61.   [13] Blamires, *Case*, p. 113.
[14] Blamires, *Woman*, pp. 14f.   [15] *Ibid.*, p. 265, and *Case*, pp. 118f.
[16] Blamires, *Case*, p. 28.   [17] *Ibid.*, p. 114.

misogyny get away with a view of woman as a being of congenital un-responsibility on the one hand who is simultaneously, on the other hand, held profoundly responsible for sin'.[18] Behind the claims for female or male responsibility which such examples illustrate we may detect traces of reflection on how to reconcile traditional biblical exegesis on the Fall with what was provided from other sources: hagiography (women saints), scripture (the women disciples' loyalty to Christ) and everyday experience.[19]

The other episode in Genesis, the creation of man, was also exploited misogynously, as a means of establishing woman's secondary, derivative and hence subordinate status. Material for debate, if not always used for that end in the Middle Ages, was present in the Bible in that Genesis incorporates two different accounts of creation difficult to reconcile.[20] The first version (1, 27), in biblical scholarship known as the 'priestly' one, implies the creation of man and woman at the same time, equal in their common designation as a human being (*homo*), but differentiated by terms denoting their sex ('Et creavit Deus hominem ad imaginem suam; ad imaginem Dei creavit illum, masculum et feminam creavit eos' And God created man in his own image, in the image of God he created him; male and female he created them). This version was largely ignored in exegetical tradition (until modern feminist criticism) in favour of a second ('Yahwist') account followed by patristic and medieval commentators. According to this version God first created man (Adam) from the slime of the earth (2, 7) and only subsequently took Eve from one of Adam's ribs (2, 7 and 21f.), whereupon Adam, because she had been formed from his bones and flesh, called her *virago*, woman, taken from *vir*, man. (The Latin word play follows the model of Hebrew and has a fortunate parallel in English *man* and *woman*, just as Luther employs *Mann* and *Männin* in this passage.) This version of creation therefore sees woman formed after man and deriving from him, a sequence Paul sums up in saying that man was not created for woman, but woman for man.[21]

As with exegesis of the Fall there are a number of variant interpretations of creation which, without reference to the first version of Genesis, attempt to rescue some equality for both sexes. The chronological sequence which was used to give man priority over woman was reinterpreted, for example, in a response, possibly by a woman author, to Richard de Fournival's *Bestiaire d'amour* by the simple, but effective means of arguing that, although man had been fashioned well by God the artisan, this was with the lowly material of slime, whereas woman was created from nobler material, the result of

---

[18] *Ibid.*, pp. 238f.   [19] *Ibid.*, p. 239.   [20] Discussed by Bloch, *Misogyny*, pp. 22–5.   [21] I Cor. 11, 9.

God's handiwork.[22] It is no surprise that this argument also recurs with Christine de Pizan in her *Livre de la Cité des Dames*.[23] This view that woman, formed from Adam's bone, was made of better material than he and therefore occupied a superior position in creation could be strengthened by developing corresponding privileges of women in post-creation history,[24] which suggests a sustained need to rectify Eve's bad press concerning her supposed guilt for the Fall. Blamires points out the weakness of this argument (in attempting to convert disadvantages of sequence into advantages it remains tied to the concept of sequence present in the Yahwist version, but not in the first), but we break away from this with Hugh of Saint-Victor who uses details of the creation story for another purpose. With him the rib cliché, used traditionally to demonstrate woman's secondary status, acquires a novel function when applied to the relationship of man and wife. Had Eve been created from Adam's head she would have been intended for dominion, if from his feet for subjection, but in being formed from his side she was meant for companionship, so that equality of the sexes, at least in marriage, has been retrieved from inferiority.[25]

The idea of man's dominion and woman's subjection which was derived from the Yahwist version of Genesis also found concrete expression in the equation of man with the head and woman with the body.[26] This is brought out in the injunction of Eph. 5, 22f. to wives to submit themselves to their husbands, as if to the Lord, on the grounds that the husband is the head of the wife, just as Christ is the head of the Church (cf. the hierarchical arrangement in I Cor. 11, 3). This paradigm of head and body was acceptable because it lent itself to various interpretations: the head controls the body while the body serves the head; the head is superior and the body inferior; the head leads or goes 'ahead' while the body takes its place behind.[27] All these interpretations contributed to a reinforcement of gender hierarchy, even to the point of gaining entry into ecclesiastical law in the twelfth century in Gratian's *Decretum*, in which the paradigm is quoted as a demonstration of woman's servitude to man in all things.[28] In making this point Gratian refers to Augustine's commentary on Genesis, but Blamires has shown that paradoxically Augustine also illustrates some reluctance concerning woman's place in this paradigm,[29] especially since, basing himself on Gal. 5, 13, he enjoined married couples to serve one

---

[22] Quoted by Blamires, *Woman*, p. 243.   [23] Christine, *Livre* I 9 (pp. 22, 23).
[24] Blamires, *Case*, pp. 96, 105f.   [25] See below, p. 68.
[26] On this doctrine see Blamires, 'Paradox', pp. 13–29.   [27] *Ibid.*, p. 17.
[28] Quoted by Blamires, *Woman*, p. 84, referring to Gratian, *Decretum*, Part II, *causa* 33, *quaestio* 11.
[29] Blamires, 'Paradox', p. 28.

another, but not to exercise authority.[30] It was also he who raised the crucial question whether the paradigm could function for the wife whose husband is sinful and cannot truly lead, and answers by recommending her to regard Christ, no longer her husband, as her head.[31] This transfer of authority or 'headship' from husband to Christ still leaves the woman in a subordinate position, but as a 'solution' it illustrates the difficulty of always maintaining the paradigm on the human level. It suggests an evasion by the woman of the husband's authority, just as the woman who became the bride of Christ as a nun or recluse could regard this freely chosen spiritual marriage, as did Christina of Markyate, as an escape from the 'headship' of an earthly husband.[32]

NEW TESTAMENT

The biblical evidence for an attitude to women passed on to the Middle Ages has so far come from the Old Testament, mainly from Genesis. To the extent that Christianity incorporated the Old Testament as proof that what the prophets foretold had come to pass, it could easily adopt its predecessor's written views on women. However, this is not as straightforward as it seems, for the New Testament also grants a role to women, especially those who surround Christ or come into contact with him, which would be unthinkable in the Old. This is best summed up by the new religion's view that the sexes are equal concerning grace and salvation (Gal. 3, 28), for there is neither Jew nor Greek, neither bond nor free, neither male nor female. Although this declaration comes from Paul it is by no means typical of him, because in his epistles he largely continues what we have hitherto seen as characteristic of the Old Testament, and any amelioration of the position of women promised at the beginning by Christianity seems largely to have vanished after him. This means, however, that not even Paul himself presents a unified view of women and that there is a similar potential discrepancy between what Christianity promised and what it inherited from Jewish tradition, enough to provide material for exegetical debate in the following centuries.

Although most feminists nowadays would presumably regard Christ's views on gender relations as more acceptable, it is striking that medieval discussion of women concentrates less on what he says than on Paul. Our

---

[30] Schnell, *Frauendiskurs*, pp. 262f.
[31] Blamires, 'Paradox', pp. 24f. See also Schnell, *FMS* 32 (1998), 321, 333.
[32] On Christina see Head, 'Marriages', pp. 116–37.

starting point must therefore be Paul, whose epistles exercised as profound an influence on the Christian view of the relationship between the sexes as did the passages from Genesis. They also contributed to 'the enduring ambivalence in the Christian tradition between the teachings and actions of Christ regarding women and the currents of antifeminism that often flagrantly opposed them',[33] not least in the discrepancy between Paul's declaration of equality between the sexes in his epistle to the Galatians and what he says elsewhere.

It is apposite to begin with Paul's interpretation of Genesis, where from the chronological sequence of creation in the Yahwist version he derives a hierarchy of the sexes, in which man is fashioned directly in the image and glory of God, but woman only indirectly, in the glory of man (I Cor. 11, 7). Given this starting point (in every sense of the word) most of what Paul has to say on man and woman follows self-evidently. He therefore maintains man's superiority, as we have seen, by asserting that the man was not created for the woman, but the woman for the man, as his helpmate (I Cor. 11, 9). (Hildegard von Bingen changes Paul's actual wording away from male authority and in the direction of reciprocity, so as to read that in marriage woman was created for the man and from the man, man for the sake of woman and from woman.)[34] Women are to be subject to their husbands in all things, since the husband is the head of the wife (Eph. 5, 22–4). Paul also follows convention in instructing women not to speak in church: if there is anything they wish to learn, they are to ask their husbands at home (I Cor. 14, 34f.). However, he goes even further, for woman is forbidden not merely to speak, but also to teach, on the grounds that by doing that she would usurp authority over man (I Tim. 2, 11–13). Paul expressly justifies this by reference to the sexual hierarchy established by the chronology of creation. The prohibition on women, however learned and holy, teaching men in public could even acquire the force of ecclesiastic law,[35] but against this exceptions can be quoted with women such as Hildegard von Bingen preaching to the clergy with papal permission.[36] Justification for what had to be regarded as an exception could be found in her case in the concept of a womanish age (*muliebre tempus*) in which the lethargy and decline of men (the clergy) made it necessary for women to take on pastoral tasks which men were neglecting.[37] A parallel exception, involving teaching rather than preaching, is proposed by Bernardino of Siena. He refers to

---

[33] McLaughlin, 'Abelard', p. 296.
[34] Hildegard, *Scivias* I ii, 11f. (p. 21). See Cadden, *Meanings*, p. 193; Ferrante, *Glory*, p. 159.
[35] Dinzelbacher, 'Wirken', pp. 268f.   [36] Newman, *Sister*, pp. 11f.   [37] *Ibid.*, pp. 238–40.

Paul's injunction that women should be instructed by their husbands at home, but argues that times have changed for the worse since the apostle's day, since men are now ignorant and incapable of teaching, but are rather in need of being taught by their wives.[38]

In this last feature the subordination of women to men advocated by Paul on other scores was called into question (but with the safeguard that this was to be regarded as an exception) at later points in the Middle Ages. With Paul himself, however, we also find traces of a more tolerant attitude towards women which can only have prompted debate as to how they were to be reconciled with his statements in other contexts. One example concerns the marital debt (*debitum*), the readiness for intercourse which one marriage partner owes the other, implicitly conceding the same right to both or the equality of the woman with her husband. Although the wording smacks more of a binding obligation than of loving affection, I Cor. 7, 3 treats each partner equally in saying that the husband is to render his wife her due (*debitum*) and likewise the wife in return. The reciprocity of this relationship is emphasised in the following verse, for the wife has no power over her body, but the husband does, and he has no power over his body, but she does. Baldwin has pointed to the symmetry of this reciprocity: in the first verse the wife demands and he satisfies her, but in the second the converse is the case, with the husband having rights over the woman.[39] Marie de Champagne, according to Andreas Capellanus, may reject such an element of obligation in marriage in favour of the freedom of lovers,[40] but this does nothing to diminish the equal reciprocity recommended by Paul. If we combine this with the Pauline declaration that the new religion knows neither male nor female the implications are disturbing for a patriarchal view of woman's place, including the opinions expressed by Paul on Genesis and by others who agree with these opinions throughout the Middle Ages. Such ambivalence precluded any monolithic view of women and instead called forth a prolonged debate on the relationship between man and woman.[41]

What Paul had to say in his epistles with regard to man's dominion and woman's submission was repeated in patristic exegesis as part of a gender hierarchy passed on as a doctrinal heritage to medieval commentators. The tendency of this heritage was to strengthen the assumption of male

---

[38] Schreiner, *FMS* 24 (1990), 348.   [39] Baldwin, *Language*, p. 192.
[40] Andreas, *De amore*, p. 153. See below, p. 104.
[41] The outlines of this debate have been traced in the works by Blamires and Schnell mentioned above in fn. 2 and fn. 3.

superiority and to deny women any authority, apart from the exceptional cases (arising mainly from men's deficiencies) which could not be denied, but which prompted worrying questions how far doctrine conformed to reality. These were growth points for a possible defence or rehabilitation of women, the first suggestions of which are already present in Paul.

The fathers of the Church inherited from Paul not merely his negative views on the place of women in Christian society, but also the discrepancy we have seen in his views, so much so that discussions on them have been said to be 'shot through with a fundamental ambivalence about the place of women in the scheme of salvation'.[42] Two examples must suffice.

That Augustine had a negative view of woman is clear from what he says in his work on Genesis on the companionship which Hugh of Saint-Victor felt she offered her husband, for Augustine holds that another man would have made a better companion, concluding that the only irreplaceable value women possess lies in childbearing.[43] As for the affection of a married couple for each other, Augustine stands far removed from the twelfth-century theologian, in that he recommends the man to love his wife insofar as she is a human being, but to hate what is feminine in her.[44] Against the unpromising tone of such remarks, however, must be set other observations which qualify them to some extent. Like Jerome and others, Augustine had no truck with the double moral standard that allowed men the sexual licence which they would not tolerate in women.[45] Although he condescendingly bases his objection on what he sees as the man's task to set a good example, at least his unmasking of male hypocrisy assisted the defence of women. Augustine disagreed, however, with Jerome's extremism in condemning women and marriage. He does this in a programmatically entitled work *De bono conjugali*, but perhaps felt reassured that his praise of matrimony would not be taken at face value since he addressed it to nuns.[46]

Jerome, too, illustrates a similar dichotomy of attitudes. One of his more extreme statements is to claim that all evil comes from women ('omnia mala e mulieribus')[47] and his treatise against Jovinianus became a veritable source-book for antifeminism in the Middle Ages. How far he could go in his subordination of woman to man is seen in his argument that a wife not subject to her 'head' (husband) is guilty of a crime as great as that committed by a man not subject to his 'head' (Christ).[48] The sexual hierarchy of antifeminism extends so far with Jerome that woman, as long as she is

---

[42] Brundage, *Law*, p. 85.   [43] *Ibid.*   [44] Schumacher, *Auffassung*, p. 203.
[45] Blamires, *Woman*, p. 78.   [46] Brooke, *Idea*, p. 61.   [47] Horowitz, 'Diabolisation', p. 241.
[48] Quoted by Blamires, 'Paradox', p. 27 and fn. 48.

there for birth and children, is as different from man as the body is from the soul. If she should wish to serve Christ more than the world she will cease to be a woman and will be called a man.[49] Uncompromising these observations may be, but alongside them we must set what is known of Jerome's personal relations with women. The misogyny of his writings in general did not prevent him from praising the spiritual dedication of women in ascetic communities which he supervised, he devoted much helpful, even affectionate correspondence to pious aristocratic Roman women.[50] This correspondence was known in the Middle Ages and provided a model for male-female friendships in the religious world. The contrast in Jerome's life between the antifeminism of his more theoretical discourses and the warmth of the letters he addresses specifically to women confirms Schnell's argument that by taking the context of writings into account we are led to abandon the idea of an invariable and all-pervading misogyny. However dominant it may have been, the voices which diverge and dissent from it deserve to be listened to.

MIDDLE AGES

The medieval period had its own contributions to make to the discussion about the relationship between the sexes and although, as with what it inherited from biblical tradition, the dominant attitude may have been antifeminine and in favour of marginalising women, there are still alternative voices to be heard. In the second part of this chapter we move more decisively into the Middle Ages, looking first at what theologians, commentators and canonists have to offer, and then at the inbuilt patriarchy of feudal society. Although there is a measure of agreement or overlap between these two, their opposition on important points is undeniable, contributing still further to the debate on what the nineteenth century misogynously called the *Frauenfrage*.[51]

Fundamental to the clerical view of women and persistent throughout the Middle Ages, even when account is taken of Schnell's genre qualifications,[52] is an undeniable traditional misogyny which drew much of its strength from Jerome's *Adversus Iovinianum*. Writing against the idea that marriage could be put on the same level as sexual abstinence, Jerome

---

[49] Quoted by Bullough, *Viator* 4 (1973), 499 and fn. 65.   [50] Ferrante, *Glory*, pp. 26f.

[51] McNamara, '*Herrenfrage*', pp. 3–29, polemicises against this, but commits a linguistic solecism in her title: the contrast is not between *Frauen* and *Herren*, but between *Frauen* and *Männer*.

[52] See above, p. 7.

advocated misogamy as very close to misogyny, so much so as to alarm Augustine, but also to provide ammunition for later antifeminists.[53] These views reach a particular highpoint as a result of the Gregorian reform of the eleventh century, whose campaign for universal clerical celibacy likewise moves from misogamy to misogyny.[54] Although this is not the place in which to rehearse these arguments, a few specimens may illustrate how critical, even vitriolic they could be throughout the Middle Ages. The preacher Bromyard (early fourteenth century) castigates a woman whose bare neck incites lust, saying that the fault is hers, not men's, so that the object of temptation has become its cause.[55] Osbert of Clare in the twelfth century admonishes a nun to subdue her flesh and its desires by conquering the woman within ('Vince mulierem, vince carnem, vince libidinem'), while the Premonstratensian Konrad von Marchtal argues against the inclusion of women in his order on the grounds that the wickedness of women exceeds all others and they are to be shunned like poisonous animals.[56] For Arnulf of Orléans it is almost axiomatic that women are more given to lechery and vice than men, but Bernard of Cluny preaches contempt of the world more extravagantly. For him woman is 'a guilty thing, a wickedly carnal thing, or rather all flesh', and that is only the start of his diatribe.[57] Less extravagant, but still betraying a distance from the female sex is the opinion of Thomas Aquinas, in which he echoes Augustine that, apart from the bearing of offspring he can see no positive function for woman and that a man would find better companionship with another man than with a wife.[58]

Rather than continue this dismal litany it is better to turn to cases where, still within a dominant negative tradition, examples can be found pointing in a positive direction. We find these first in the medieval view of the physiology of the sexes in which views inherited from antiquity combine with others of biblical origin in such a way as to provide various contrasts to explain the difference between the sexes.[59] One such contrast was between man as constituting the form or cause and woman no more than the raw material (thus Isidore of Seville sees an etymological link between *mater* and *materia*),[60] but this demotion of women could also be used in reverse to condemn male failure (if women can nonetheless worship Christ, how

---

[53] Blamires, *Woman*, pp. 63f.   [54] Barstow, *Priests, passim.*
[55] Blamires, *Woman*, p. 4, quoting Owst, *Literature*, p. 395. See Ferrante, *Woman*, pp. 20f.
[56] Osbert: Newman, *Woman*, p. 23. Konrad: Southern, *Society*, p. 314.
[57] Arnulf and Bernard: Minnis, *Magister*, pp. 166, 95.
[58] See Bumke, *ABäG* 38/39 (1994), 116, fn. 19.
[59] A general survey is given by Cadden, *Meanings*.   [60] *Etymologiae* IX 5, 5f.

much worse is clerical corruption?).[61] Another contrast was between reason and flesh, where unsurprisingly the former is frequently equated in exegesis with Adam and the latter with Eve.[62] Here too the denigration of woman can be undercut by the argument of the joint nature of all human beings (*sensualitas* in men, *ratio* in women)[63] or, more decisively, with the rise of what has been termed incarnational theology with its stress on Christ's humanity, by the association of woman with Christ's humanity (as, for example, with Hildegard von Bingen).[64] A third contrast was between active and passive, where the woman is seen as a passive, receptive vessel (*vas*), but again it is a woman, Dhuoda, who avoids the passive implications of *mater* by calling herself *genitrix*, thereby feminising the term for the active male partner, *genitor*.[65] The physiological contrast between the sexes reaches perhaps its peak in the opinion that woman is in fact a male *manqué*, a *mas occasionatus*. This can be traced back to Aristotle ('the female is as it were a deformed male') and recurs in medieval learned discourse, but not without being contested by Aquinas with the clear statement to the contrary ('Femina non est aliquid occasionatum').[66] In this, as in other cases, discordant voices point to lasting discussion from differing points of view and undermine any simplistic view of an unqualified denigration of women.

The reservations such as those we have mentioned, however significant from our point of view, are not frequent enough to undo the overall picture of a marginalisation of women in clerical thought, at least in those genres not covered by Schnell's warning against generalisations. From its view of women's physiological inferiority the medieval Church extracted a functional inferiority,[67] allowing them on principle no public or legal role. An edict of a ninth-century Council of Nantes condemns women who impudently offend both divine and human law in attending public meetings to discuss the affairs of men and usurp the authority of senators.[68] In the twelfth century Gratian states categorically in his *Decretum* that woman is subject to man's authority and has none herself, that she may neither teach nor give evidence, neither pledge her word nor dispense justice.[69] This exclusion of women from public activity applies even more to the

---

[61] Bynum, *Feast*, p. 262.   [62] Schnell, *Andreas*, p. 147; *Frauendiskurs*, pp. 197f.

[63] Schnell, *FMS* 32 (1998), 313–16.

[64] Incarnational theology: Watson, *NML* 1 (1997), 85–124. Hildegard: Cadden, *Meanings*, p. 191 ('femina vero humanitatem Filii Dei significat' woman indeed signifies the humanity of the Son of God).

[65] Thiébaux, *Dhuoda*, p. 28.

[66] Aristotle: Blamires, *Woman*, p. 40. Aquinas: Gössmann, 'Anthropologie', pp. 291f.; Schnell, *Frauendiskurs*, pp. 94, 148f.

[67] Bynum, *Feast*, p. 217.   [68] Schulenburg, 'Sanctity', p. 116.   [69] Stadler, 'Sünderin', p. 206.

institution of the Church, where they are forbidden to hold any office. In this Christianity followed Hebrew practice and derived support from what Paul had laid down, even if in its early period the new religion allowed deaconesses to perform a number of non-priestly functions together with deacons. However, the order of deaconesses merged over time into monastic orders and disappeared as such, although significantly Abelard, as part of his upholding of the dignity of women, pays attention to these earlier deaconesses.[70]

The minimal qualification of women's exclusion which this represents is taken noticeably further, however, with regard to the Pauline injunction that women should not speak, or more explicitly teach or preach, in public.[71] The apostle's prescription had been clear enough and was largely followed, even embellished with stock misogynous arguments,[72] especially when women presumed to speak on matters of religion, thereby daring to instruct men. Such exceptions must have come to loom large, for they were called forth by a variety of causes, passing well beyond the important, but rare case of Hildegard von Bingen embarking on preaching tours with ecclesiastic sanction on which she addressed clerics.[73] The fact that recourse was had to hagiographic models such as Mary Magdalene and Catherine of Alexandria, both of whom were held to have evangelised amongst the pagans, and that Eustace of Arras knew of different opinions about this question ('circa istam quaestionem sunt variae opiniones') suggests that it was controversial and a matter for debate.[74] The need for this was topical in view of the rise of various heresies in the high Middle Ages in which women were suspected of preaching, but apart from that a special case was made of what might be called the metaphorical preaching of wives to their (pagan or sinful) husbands. Thomas of Chobham states the case for this, saying that a wife can soften a man's heart where many a priest fails and using the uncommon term *predicatrix* (woman preacher) for her in that function.[75]

MARRIAGE

It is in fact with regard to marriage that the tendency to move from a hierarchical relationship between the sexes towards one closer to a form of

---

[70] Shahar, *Estate*, pp. 22f.; Fenster, *Debate*, p. 50; McLaughlin, 'Abelard', pp. 298–301.
[71] Green, *Women*, pp. 229f.   [72] See d'Alverny, 'Théologiens', pp. 25f. for an example.
[73] Newman, *Sister*, pp. 11f., 27–9. On this question see also Blamires, *Viator* 26 (1995), 135–52.
[74] Blamires, *Viator* 26 (1995), 147f.   [75] Sheehan, *SMRH* 1 (1978), 24; Schnell, *Sexualität*, pp. 361f.

equality is most marked, calling into question any extremist view that medieval theology acknowledged only a subordinate position for women in marriage. This shifting of views came about largely in the twelfth century and is therefore particularly relevant for us because it is in this period that the Church attempts to take control of marriage and impose its views on laypeople, calling forth debate with the lay world and also within the Church itself.[76] An objective purpose served by marriage was derived from Gen. 1, 28 (the procreation of children for the increase of God's kingdom: *generatio prolis*), but to this two further purposes came to be added: marriage as an escape from fornication (*remedium concupiscentiae*) and as involving a reciprocal marital duty for both partners (*debitum*).[77] From the twelfth century theologians more realistically acknowledged the existence of other motives with laypeople, such as the reconciliation of warring families, the accumulation of wealth and power, and even the beauty of a prospective partner.[78] The inclusion of this last, more personal motive amongst the 'secondary causes' (*causae secundae*) of marriage is in agreement with what Schnell has postulated as the causes of love (*causae amoris*)[79] and opens the way for more personal considerations, less dominated by collective or legal implications. Against this background must be set what we shall later see with Hugh of Saint-Victor,[80] for whom marriage was not merely a mutual love of souls, essentially reciprocal, but was based on the companionship (*societas*) between the partners, not on hierarchy. (This he established from his interpretation of the creation of Eve from Adam's side, rather than from his head or feet, which would have implied domination or subjection.) In this deviation from Paul's interpretation of Genesis (the man is master in marriage) Hugh does not stand alone, but is followed by other thinkers such as Peter Lombard, Bonaventura and Humbert of Romans.[81]

   This means that the concept of man's dominion (as the head) and woman's subjection (as the body) can be questioned from two flanks. On the one hand, as we have just seen, from the view that woman is neither above nor below man, but stands beside him as his companion, which could lend further support to Paul's own emphasis on the reciprocity of the marital *debitum*. On the other hand, the relationship between head and body can be turned upside down once it is acknowledged that a man's shortcomings may mean that, contrary to Paul's view of things, it is he who

---

[76] Schnell, 'Frau', pp. 121, 169f.   [77] Schumacher, *Auffassung*, pp. 194f.
[78] *Ibid.*, p. 197. Cf. Schnell, *Sexualität*, p. 236.   [79] Schnell, *Sexualität*, pp. 228f., and *Causa*, pp. 322–4.
[80] See below, pp. 67f., and also Schnell, 'Frau', pp. 125–7, 140.
[81] Schnell, 'Frau', pp. 124f. (Peter Lombard), 129f. (Bonaventura), 150f. (Humbert of Romans), but also p. 127, fn. 21 (Abelard).

stands in need of instruction from his wife.[82] This is the point made by Bernardino of Siena who justifies his disagreement with Paul by arguing that times have changed.[83] No matter whether wives were presented as the companions of their husbands or as in some way superior to them, questions are raised as to whether they may always be considered as subordinate to men.[84]

By contrast with these movements in clerical thought the attitude to women and their place shown in feudal society, insofar as we have access to its views, remains almost unchangingly ready to marginalise and subordinate them. Feudal society, allied with the still dominant conservatism of the Church on this issue, therefore represents the opposition against which the new ideas advocated by Hugh and others have to pit themselves.

That women were granted no social position of their own is clear from what became common practice from the eleventh century, the theoretical division of medieval society into three estates: those who pray, those who fight, and those who till the soil ('oratores, bellatores, laboratores').[85] All three Latin nouns (not just the second) denote men and are not meant as the common gender, as is clear from a vernacular rendering: 'gebûre, ritter und pfaffen' (peasants, knights and priests).[86] To this differentiation of men according to their social function there corresponds no equivalent for women, who are defined instead in terms of their relationship, or lack of relationship, to men,[87] as virgins, wives, widows or prostitutes. This implies that women were not perceived in their own right, but only with regard to men, without the opportunity to play an independent role in life, and that, whereas men lived in a variety of different contexts, women were restricted to their relationship with men. This distinction is made clear numerically by Bonizo in his *Liber de vita christiana*: to thirteen male ranks in the ecclesiastical world there correspond but two female, virgins and widows, and to six male ranks in the lay world only two female, *mulieres imperantes* (women who rule) and *mulieres*.[88] Women are seen more pointedly as functions of men by Gilbertus Lunicensis (of Limerick) who acknowledges that it is not the role of women to pray, toil or fight, but adds that they are married to those who pray (at a time when clerical celibacy was not universal), toil and fight.[89]

---

[82] Schnell, *Diskurs*, p. 270.   [83] See above, pp. 14f.

[84] Arguing along quite different lines for the period around 1200 Baldwin, *Speculum* 66 (1991), 619, concludes: 'In the balance, however, the vectors converging towards gender equality and reciprocity probably outweighed those supporting male superiority'. That may be an exaggeration, but it points in the same direction as my argument.

[85] Duby, *Orders, passim.*   [86] Freidank, *Bescheidenheit* 27, 1.

[87] Schnell, *Sexualität*, p. 76.   [88] Berschin, 'Herrscher', p. 129.

[89] Gilbertus, *De statu ecclesiae*, PL 159, 997 (quoted by Duby, *Orders*, p. 287).

This marginalisation of women finds expression in numerous ways in secular society. Sons were valued more than daughters – property generally passed from fathers to sons, whereas daughters required dowries for marriage, thereby depleting the family's wealth, so that material benefits for the family were to be expected more from sons than daughters.[90] In law, too, women were disadvantaged. In a trial involving a woman the oath-helpers (*compurgatores*) had to be men; on marriage a woman in effect abrogated her legal rights to her husband; how much less value attached to her by virtue of her sex emerges from the stipulation of the *Sachsenspiegel* that only half the wergeld or compensation paid for the killing of a husband may be allotted in the case of a woman.[91] That as a woman she had no legal standing is clear from the same source, according to which she had to be represented at a court of law by a guardian, normally her husband.[92] In this respect marriage brought no change in a woman's legal position, for she moved from the guardianship of her father to subordination to the authority of her husband, whom it was her duty to obey as her lord, again as laid down in the *Sachsenspiegel* and also by Gilbertus Lunicensis.[93] In such a patriarchal society it is no surprise that in Chaucer's *Man of Law's Tale* Constance, married off after political negotiations without apparently being consulted herself, should be resigned to her fate as the lot of women (286: 'Wommen are born to thraldom and penance, / And to been under mannes governance').[94]

Nor should it surprise us that, in a society in which the dice were so weighted against women, a double standard could prevail in sexual matters, granting men a licence, before and in marriage, unthinkable in the case of women if their virginity and the certainty of rightful heirs were to be guaranteed. Despite the Church's attempts to impose the same standards of morality on both sexes the pragmatic needs of feudal marriage politics, with its wish to keep property within the family's blood, meant that a woman's extramarital affair was viewed much more harshly than a man's.[95] Inevitably, it is difficult to be sure about such matters, but it is suggestive that the love-poet Albrecht von Johannsdorf should talk about permitting things to men, but not to women (*MF* 89, 20: 'wan solz den man erlouben unde den vrouwen niht') and that the didactic poet Freidank should

---

[90] Cadden, *Meanings*, p. 256; Schmid, *Familiengeschichte*, pp. 24f.; Schulenburg, *Forgetful*, pp. 124, 240f.

[91] *Compurgatores*: Shahar, *Estate*, p. 14. Legal rights: Labarge, *Women*, p. 27. Wergeld: *Sachsenspiegel*, *Landrecht* III 45, 2.

[92] *Sachsenspiegel*, *Landrecht* I 46; II 63.

[93] *Sachsenspiegel*, *Landrecht* III 45, 3. Gilbertus, *De statu ecclesiae*, *PL* 159, 997 (quoted by Duby, *Marriage*, p. 6).

[94] Mann, *Feminizing*, pp. 100f.   [95] Bumke, 'Liebe', p. 31.

criticise the double standard of a man boasting in his case about what would be accounted a disgrace for a woman (*Bescheidenheit* 102, 24: 'daz ist ein ungeteilet spil' that is an uneven game).[96] With this point we have reached the question which was central to a woman's social position in the Middle Ages and which will occupy us in the rest of this book, namely her relationship to a man in the form of marriage. We may consider this under three headings: arrangement of the marriage, conditions in married life, and the woman's position after marriage, as a widow.

The aims of feudal marriage, arranged between two families, were pragmatic and hard-headed. They have been summed up by Wiegand in the titles to sections of his opening chapter as serving dynastic and alliance policies, an instrument of conquest, a means of establishing peace between warring houses, and often involving the engagement or actual marriage of young children in order to safeguard these ends.[97] Feudal marriages were therefore meant to ensure the succession of heirs, to initiate or strengthen alliances, to bring about peace, so that against these overriding considerations there was little room for the personal inclinations of the two individuals involved as an aim of marriage, as distinct from what might be hoped for as a result.[98] Given these aims, it is self-evident that the choice of a partner for a daughter was a matter for her father and other males in the family or court and it has been said that women did not marry, but were given in marriage.[99] How little the consent of the woman counted against the plans of father or guardian is clear from the biographies of Christina of Markyate and Iolande von Vianden, both of whom defeat parental intentions by escaping to an anchorage or convent.[100] The authority giving a woman in marriage can even be more remote at times, for rulers can also act as wife-givers, so much so that often 'a father took the earliest opportunity of marrying his child so that the right of marriage might not fall to the lord'.[101] The feudal lord might wish to exercise this right in the case of a widow or daughter who inherited a fief so that, if she were married, the man could supply military service, or in order to reward a vassal with wife and land.[102] In such cases the lord supplanted the woman's father or other male relatives and himself chose her husband in accord with his own interests.

---

[96] Quoted by Bennewitz, 'Literatur', p. 35.   [97] Wiegand, *Studien*, p. ix.

[98] See Wenzel, 'Fernliebe', p. 195; Shahar, *Estate*, p. 131.

[99] Wiegand, *Studien*, p. 26. Cf. Duby, *Knight*, pp. 104f. and also the observation by Lot-Borodine, *Amour*, p. 18, that marriage took place not between two individuals, but between two fiefs.

[100] Christina: Head, 'Marriages', pp. 116–37. Iolande: Bürkle, *Literatur*, pp. 95–7.

[101] Power, *Women*, p. 31.

[102] Shahar, *Estate*, p. 132; Duby, *Knight*, p. 236. In a lai by Marie de France King Arthur distributes lands and wives to ensure the loyalty of vassals thus rewarded (*Lanval* 13–17).

In either case, whether from father to husband or from lord to vassal, the woman was passed, together with her land, from man to man with little regard for her own wishes.

It is clear that the dynastic-political considerations dictating such arranged marriages are highly impersonal, leaving the individual preferences of the partners very much on one side. This absence of personal attachment is frequently suggested by the way in which one potential wife can be seen very much like another, for example a sister if the intended bride were to die before the marriage.[103] In the case of the Hohenstaufen Konrad III the arrangement for his marriage to a niece of the Byzantine emperor was left open between either of two women, whose exchangeability underlines political interests rather than individual preference.[104] The emperor Otto I sought a political alliance by offering his widowed sister Gerberga to Duke Berthold, but alternatively Gerberga's daughter, almost of marriageable age.[105] To the same Otto Athelstan of England sent his half-sister Edith in marriage, accompanied by her sister as a possible substitute.[106] In all such cases the woman is seen not as an individual, but in second place to the territory or other political advantage she brings with her. This is not to deny that an arranged marriage could at times issue in affection or love, even if these feelings played little part at the beginning. The best-known example is the surprise detectable in what Gislebert of Mons regards as the rare case of Baldwin of Hainaut's love for his wife alone, to the exclusion of affairs with other women.[107] In cases like this, marriage does not follow on love (as it does in the romances to be considered later), but love is rather a possible consequence of marriage, an order confirmed by the remark of Hugh of Saint-Victor about the love of man and woman proceeding from the companionship of marriage ('amicitia viri et mulieris ex societate procedens conjugali').[108] Although Gratian has little to say about love as essential to marriage, he does call marriage a school for love, thereby possibly implying that 'love could grow out of marriage, rather than that love ought to precede the marital relationship'.[109]

This last possibility, rare in Gislebert's view, should not be allowed to colour our picture of what married life meant for most women in patriarchal society. The primary purpose of a feudal marriage policy – to maintain property within the family by an unquestioned succession – meant that the

---

[103] Wiegand, *Studien*, p. 24.   [104] *Ibid.*, pp. 17f.   [105] Leyser, *Rule*, p. 54.
[106] Hrotsvitha, *Gesta Ottonis* 98–120.   [107] Gislebert, *Chronicon Hanoniense*, p. 192.
[108] *Summa sententiarum* VII 4, *PL* 176, 157; Kullmann, 'Hommes', p. 126. Cf. Weigand, 'Liebe', p. 49.
[109] Brundage, *Law*, p. 239.

wife's duty was to provide children as heirs, not so much females as males, as we have seen, but in large numbers to counteract infantile mortality and the potential loss of an elder son in knightly combat. One might say that the higher the aristocratic rank and the greater the wealth involved, the heavier the burden of continuous childbearing placed on the woman with all its attendant dangers and physical exhaustion. Blanche of Castile and Margaret of Provence, for example, each produced twelve or eleven children within a span of fifteen years,[110] but the woman who could not match this ran the risk of being divorced, a danger which faced any wife if the prospect of a materially more advantageous union presented itself to the husband.[111] The relative ease with which a husband could do this, despite objections from the Church, shows us where the authority lay in a patriarchal marriage. Whereas for a man marriage meant control of his own property, for a woman it meant guardianship by her husband, who controlled her property, expected obedience from her and could impose punishment.[112]

From this hierarchical relationship within marriage there follows what could be called the asymmetry of adultery, the double standard that allowed the man to get away with what was forbidden to the woman (Gratian comments on the injustice of this differential view of men and women).[113] One reason for this lay with the primary purpose of feudal marriage, for the woman's adultery had consequences different from the man's infidelity, since any conception by her of an illegitimate child was a threat to lawful succession, which was not undermined by the man's bastards.[114] How androcentric the legal view of adultery could be is seen in the fact that it was not so much actively committed by a woman as through her: she was the object through which one man committed a crime against another man.[115]

Given the legal, physical and emotional disadvantages of feudal marriage for women, it is no surprise that widowhood could be seen as an escape from oppression, as when Chaucer's Criseyde, conscious as a young widow of what marriage involves, scorns the idea of love as jeopardising her new-found freedom (*Troilus* II 771: 'allas! syn I am free, / Sholde I now love, and putte in jupartie / My sikernesse, and thrallen libertee?').[116] In reality, however, the choices open to a widow and therefore the degree of liberty she might expect were rather more restricted, amounting chiefly to

---

[110] Fossier, 'Femme', p. 7. Cf. Stafford, *Queens*, pp. 88f.
[111] Bumke, 'Liebe', pp. 30f.; Brooke, *Idea*, p. 120; Stafford, *Queens*, pp. 74–7, 83, 86f.
[112] Gold, *Lady*, pp. 124f.; Duby, *Knight*, p. 102.   [113] Elliott, 'Marriage', pp. 51f.
[114] McCracken, *Romance*, p. 18.   [115] Shahar, *Estate*, p. 107.
[116] Mann, *Feminizing*, p. 81. See also Schulenburg, 'Sanctity', p. 109.

re-marriage (more out of necessity than for preference) or a religious life, whilst the third possibility, continued secular life without a husband, had its dangers in patriarchal society,[117] as Criseyde's life demonstrates and as is illustrated in Wolfram's *Parzival*. A wealthy widow attracted men who saw marriage as a means of acquiring her lands, as in Duby's account of the widow married by Count Raoul de Vexin, passed to and fro like a shuttle-cock between men all anxious for the same thing.[118] In a society where power rested in land few noblewomen had a long shelf-life as widows: for them, as for Chrétien's and Hartmann's Laudine in their respective romances *Yvain* and *Iwein*, remarriage followed 'so fast on the heels of bereavement that widowhood scarcely became a reality'.[119] Even without such dangers from outside, a widow could come under conflicting pressures from both her families: the natal family seeking to regain her dowry for a second marriage and her conjugal family just as stubbornly anxious to retain it in their own hands.[120]

Whereas Wiegand in his monograph focused on feudal marriage policy and Schnell on ecclesiastical views,[121] this unavoidably compressed opening chapter has included both, since they provide the background for the vernacular romances to be considered. This presentation of two models does not imply wholesale agreement with Duby's theory of two models in medieval marriage,[122] but is meant to contextualise what we shall find in vernacular literature around 1200. Both models were present in the Middle Ages, with some degree of shared views and also mutual opposition.[123] Common to both the ecclesiastical and feudal models is the inferior position which both allot to women by comparison with men, but also their marginalisation of women in society, and the importance they attach to woman as a bearer of children. Opposition between the two models arose from the Church's criticism of the double standard in sexual behaviour, its attempt to exclude or limit the man's possibilities for repudiation or divorce of his wife, but above all its struggle throughout the twelfth century against arranged marriages involving parental compulsion in favour of the freely given *consensus*, especially of the woman, to the marriage bond. It is with this

---

[117] Stafford, *Queens*, pp. 145f.; Wogan-Browne, *Lives*, p. 152.
[118] Duby, *Knight*, p. 125, but also p. 128.   [119] Stafford, *Queens*, p. 50.
[120] Newman, *Woman*, p. 95.   [121] Wiegand, *Studien*; Schnell, *Sexualität*.
[122] Duby, *Marriage*, pp. 1–22 ('Two models of marriage: the aristocratic and the ecclesiastical'); *Knight*, pp. 216–26. Like Brundage, *Law*, p. 194, I recognise that the term 'model' could imply a simplified construct, but I employ it in response to Duby's usage and also to show in Part II how vernacular literature develops a counter-model, differing from what the aristocratic and ecclesiastical models have in common.
[123] Bumke, *Kultur*, pp. 544–7.

decisive feature that we conclude this chapter.[124] I term this feature decisive, not merely because it promised potentially the greatest amelioration of women's position in medieval society, but because, as our argument will show, it recurs repeatedly in the vernacular works we have to consider.

One of the aims of the Gregorian reform was to bring marriage under the control of ecclesiastical law, and amongst the principles which it sought to establish the indissolubility of marriage and the free choice of each partner told in favour of the woman (against repudiation by her husband and compulsion by her family). The indissolubility of marriage, in effect achieved by the time of Innocent III,[125] imposed constraints on society's behaviour, but compensation was provided by insisting on freedom at the point of entry into marriage.[126] A third principle, exogamy (against inter-marriage within closely related families) helped the Church to free itself from control by feudal lords ruling over contiguous blocs of land. It also provided further protection for wives against being divorced by husbands who availed themselves of what had been an escape route from an unwanted marriage by conveniently discovering a forbidden degree of kinship.[127]

For us the most important of these principles was free *consensus* of the woman as against a choice made by others for collective, impersonal and material reasons.[128] For Gratian two steps were necessary for the completion of a marriage: the exchange of words by both parties expressing their willingness to marry and physical union. Since both are necessary, sexual consummation without freely given *consensus* was no valid marriage, nor was the exchange of words of consent without physical union (although some decretists had difficulties with this).[129] Elsewhere greater weight is attached to *consensus* alone. With Alexander III (pontificate from 1159) the principle that *consensus* makes a marriage was firmly established. In the Anstey case (England, twelfth century) the decision was reached that present *consensus* alone suffices for a valid marriage.[130] In the fourteenth century William of Pagula maintained equally that marriage is contracted by *consensus* through words in the present tense, as when a man says: 'I take you to be my wife' ('Contrahitur matrimonium solo consensu per verba de presenti').[131] All this confirms Gregory IX's statement that marriages should

---

[124] On this subject see Noonan, *Viator* 4 (1973), 419–34; Sheehan, *SMRH* 1 (1978), 3–33, and especially, in greater historical depth, Brundage, *Law*, pp. 176–416. Cf. also Bloch, *Misogyny*, pp. 184f. and Gaunt, *Gender*, pp. 120f.

[125] d'Avray, *Marriage*, pp. 99–108.   [126] *Ibid.*, pp. 74f., 124f.

[127] Brundage, *Law*, pp. 183, 192–4.   [128] *Ibid.*, pp. 187f., 268, 414.

[129] *Ibid.*, pp. 235f. On Gratian's view of *consensus* see also Noonan, *Viator* 4 (1973), 420–7.

[130] d'Avray, *Marriage*, p. 184.   [131] *Ibid.*, p. 117.

be free ('matrimonia libera esse debeant'),[132] a principle that struck at the heart of feudal marriage policy. One of the most influential theologians upholding the consensual theory of marriage in the twelfth century was Peter Lombard, whom we have encountered before, together with Hugh of Saint-Victor propounding the view of marriage as companionship (*societas*), likewise working against a hierarchical relationship in which the woman is deprived of any say in matters.[133] Of Alexander III's marriage decretals Brundage has said that they 'reflected a dawning consciousness of the importance of individual choice, coupled with a new awareness of marriage as a personal relationship'.[134] Brundage also sums up his survey of the development of consensual marriage around 1200 by saying that the focus of marriage law shifted dramatically from family concerns and parental compulsion to the wishes of the two individuals concerned, a change of view which we shall also see reflected in vernacular romances written about the same time.[135] It is hardly likely to be by chance that these romances, in contrast to the social practice of the day, depict the *consensus* of the woman at the same time as ecclesiastical law stipulates the validity of marriage by *consensus* alone.[136] It is important to register this last fact for, although these romances were composed by clerics (or by men with a clerical education), they were addressed primarily to lay men and women. As regards the principles about marriage which the Church sought to carry into effect, it is from laymen, from feudal families whose political and dynastic strategies in arranging marriages were threatened by the Church's strengthening hold on marriage that marked opposition came. Although these families saw an advantage for themselves in the Church's clear definition of marriage, guaranteeing the legitimacy of heirs, they also had to defend their dynastic interests against attempts to deprive them of freedom of action. In the consensual theory and in romance literature that accepted it they faced a challenge and a subject for argument and debate.

We have come across a number of significant features in this chapter: the tentative reciprocity of the Pauline conception of the marital *debitum*, the Church's insistence on the woman's freely given *consensus*, the views of Hugh of Saint-Victor and others on companionship rather than hierarchy in marriage, the indications that love or affection could sometimes find a place in a marriage arranged for utilitarian ends. If we now correlate these points we obtain a composite picture of marriage which, unlike the

---

[132] *Ibid.*, p. 128.   [133] *Ibid.*, p. 264; Sheehan, *SMRH* 1 (1978), 13f.; Schnell, *Frauendiskurs*, pp. 40f.
[134] Brundage, *Law*, pp. 331–7 (quotation p. 333).
[135] *Ibid.*, p. 414. Cf. also Noonan, *Viator* 4 (1973), 429f., 433f.   [136] Donahue, 'Policy', p. 127.

dominant conservative attitude of Church and feudal society, was more favourable to women and their interests and on which vernacular literature around 1200 could build in presenting its own counter-model. Whereas Duby as a historian confines his presentation of marriage in medieval France to two models (the ecclesiastical and the feudal), this book extends the discussion to a counter-model provided by literary texts.[137]

---

[137] Duby, *Knight, passim*. Sheehan, *SMRH* 1 (1978), 19, acknowledges the evidential value of literature, but leaves its establishment to others. Schnell leaves literature disappointingly to the last chapter of his book *Sexualität*, treating it with relative brevity, but discusses the relevance of vernacular literature to our problem in 'Literatur', pp. 225–38. As a historian of marriage Brooke, *Idea*, p. 176, at least recognises that, given the paucity of our evidence, it would be 'an act of austerity or even blindness' to close our eyes to what literature may tell us of the inwardness of marriage in the Middle Ages.

CHAPTER 2

Feminisation in the twelfth century

In this chapter we sharpen our focus in two respects. The first of these is suggested by the word 'feminisation' in the title. In Chapter 1 we were concerned with a predominantly antifeminine tradition in the Middle Ages, denigrating and marginalising women, and with possibilities of defending them which, however, rarely went beyond suggesting that men were similarly faulty and were therefore on an equal footing. Now we go an important step further by considering ways in which, in religious life as well as in literature, women could be regarded as playing a positive role for which they were especially fitted and in which they could serve as examples for men. The part they played in the life of the Church now became far greater and had to be taken into account, both institutionally and spiritually. This feminisation found expression in the growing cult of Mary and in incarnational theology, but also extended, especially with the Cistercians, to the application of feminine imagery to Christ. In literature disquiet was voiced over fluid boundaries between the sexes, particularly the attribution of feminine qualities to men. The fear that this might be taken as effeminacy could render courtliness suspect as opposed to knightly manliness, a suspicion which the romance sought to remove by suggesting that 'feminised' was not synonymous with 'effeminate'. In this sense, the view that a human being was made up of some qualities conventionally regarded as male and others as female was made acceptable by demonstrating that the bestowal of feminine features on a man was not detrimental to his masculinity. In sum, the greater attention paid to women, their nature and concerns, provides the general setting for the ways in which romance authors show a perceptible awareness of women's interests and of the need to appeal to them.

The second change of focus is our concentration on one specific period of time. Whereas in Chapter I we used evidence from the Middle Ages at large, here we pay particular attention to the twelfth century, testimony from which has hitherto been deliberately short (apart from the concluding pages on *consensus*). The reason for concentrating in the present chapter on this period (which I understand in the sense of the 'long twelfth century', comparable to modern historians' 'long nineteenth century') is twofold: first, because of the importance for our problem of the changes introduced in this period, and secondly as a preparation for Part II, in which we consider romances composed on either side of 1200. However, in what follows I do not regard the 'long twelfth century' as a straitjacket which cannot be discarded at times if the argument warrants it, so that occasionally evidence is taken into account from the fourteenth century (Seuse, Eckhart, Ricardian literature in England).

From the point of view of his subject matter (five authors, Latin and vernacular, from northern France engaged in gender discourse) Baldwin has spoken of the years around 1200 as 'a privileged moment of gender symmetry in Western thought'.[1] Against Dronke's denial that a new conception of love arose in this century Gillingham argues that the real question is whether love now came to play a greater role in aristocratic marriage than before.[2] He answers this in the affirmative, so that for him, as for Brundage from quite a different angle,[3] this can be called a century of love, not merely in literature, but also in the inquiries of theologians and canonists into the place of personal emotions within marriage. Viewing this place positively was not always plain sailing (the debate these questions sparked off is evidence enough), with the result that this same century sees a marked increase in misogynous literature, calling forth in turn occasional explicit defences of women (e.g. Marbod of Rennes, Abelard).[4] The late eleventh and early twelfth centuries (considerably earlier than Baldwin's privileged moment) have been identified as initiating disturbances in the gender system,[5] brought about by such factors as the Church's insistence on clerical celibacy (accompanied by clerical misogyny) and on clerical control of the married life of laymen.

As part of its programme to abolish laymen's interference with the affairs of the church the Gregorian reform of the late eleventh century had also insisted on the celibacy of priests. Although certainly not condoned, clerical marriage or concubinage was common before this (and also subsequently), but the aim of the reform movement was to 'liberate' clerics from their wives (and hence to put an end to the inheritance of benefices) as much as to liberate Church property from control by laymen.[6] Although fiercely

---

[1] Baldwin, *Language*, p. 234.   [2] Gillingham, *FMLS* 25 (1989), 292.
[3] Brundage, *Law*, p. 323. See also p. 414.
[4] Blamires, *Case*, p. 9. Marbod: *ibid.*, pp. 17, 19f., 59f.; *Woman*, pp. 228–32. Abelard: McLaughlin, 'Abelard', pp. 287–334.
[5] McNamara, '*Herrenfrage*', pp. 3–29.   [6] Brundage, *Law*, pp. 214–23; Duggan, 'Equity', pp. 63, 67.

resisted because it threatened a long-existing practice, clerical celibacy was firmly established before the end of the twelfth century. Unsurprisingly, the move to bring this about was accompanied by a flood of antifeminine treatises (in Latin and meant for the clergy) arguing against marriage by the traditional means of arguing against women.[7] Jerome's *Adversus Iovinianum* and Seneca's *De matrimonio* come into their own in this context, are copied out and quoted whenever a warning against marriage is voiced. Jerome's quotation from Cicero to the effect that one cannot devote oneself equally to a wife and to philosophy ('non posse se uxori et philosophiae pariter operam dare')[8] shows how adaptable this misogynous tradition was to the ends of the Church, for the troubles of marriage (*molestiae nuptiarum*) were shown to afflict the medieval cleric in his task as much as they had the classical philosopher. Whether there is a causal connection or not, the reform movement's concern with unmarried clergy is coterminous with a debate within the Church on women and marriage.

This debate also pervaded the Church's relationship with the laity, for its reforming zeal embraced the marriage practices of secular society. In origin Christianity inherited marriage as a secular institution of the society into which it was born, but in the twelfth century (although some attempts had been made before) it became a sacrament and fell under the jurisdiction of the Church.[9] By the middle to late twelfth century the Church reform had gained effective control of all the major aspects of marriage practice after a drawn-out struggle with feudal families that saw their freedom of action circumscribed, but also as the result of a continuing debate within the Church.[10] Control of marriage was taken from the family circle to the church door and the proceedings were now conducted by the priest.[11] All this required a legal underpinning, so that the twelfth century stands out as one of the most creative periods in canon law, specifically with regard to marriage. In becoming involved in what had once been a secular institution the Church had to make its position clear on yet another front, for in this same period it confronted the danger posed by Catharism. The radical dualism of this heresy regarded the created world and the human body as evil, so that the Church, in defending the orthodox view of Genesis that God's creation was good, was forced to walk a tightrope, condemning those

---

[7] Schnell, *Andreas*, p. 169; *Frauendiskurs*, pp. 15, fn. 14, 176. Cf. Elliott, *Marriage*, pp. 98–104.
[8] Jerome, *Adversus Iovinianum*, *PL* 23, 278; Roth, *AfK* 80 (1998), 43.
[9] Brundage, *Law*, pp. 269f.
[10] *Ibid.*, pp. 223, 225, 319; Rassow, *MIÖG* 58 (1950), 310–16; Schnell, *ZfdPh* 101 (1982), 357; Head, 'Marriages', pp. 126f.
[11] Sheehan, *SMRH* 1 (1978), 28.

who condemned the flesh without itself condoning the pleasures of the flesh.[12] Theologians and canonists had no choice but to establish in what ways marriage and the relationship between the sexes were acceptable. It is this necessity which underlies the ecclesiastical debate on what precisely constitutes a marriage, whether it rested on *consensus* or on consummation (*coitus, copula*). The debate on this question ran through the twelfth century and if it was eventually decided in favour of the first alternative, this was largely because of the problem posed by the virginal marriage of Mary and Joseph.[13] By placing such stress on *consensus*, which has to be freely given to be valid, to come from the heart as well as the mouth ('corde tamen et ore consentit'),[14] the Church sharpened the terms of its disagreement with feudal society's arranged marriages and proposed a theory of marriage, the implications of which were of immense social importance.

Heavily compressed though this introduction to the chapter has had to be, it should suffice to show how, as in so many other respects, the twelfth century was one in which fundamental changes took place in how women's position in society and role in marriage were regarded. By granting them a greater space as a theme in its debates and by paying more attention to their concerns the way is prepared for what we shall observe in the vernacular romances. Before that, however, we must consider the growing importance of women in religious life and in literature in general.

RELIGIOUS LIFE

The feminisation of religion with which we are dealing in this section was already remarked upon in the twelfth century. Hildegard von Bingen was aware of her time as a 'womanish age' (*muliebre tempus*), even though by that she meant something peculiar to her own situation (she argues, as do other women visionaries, that God has chosen to act through her in condemnation of male shortcomings).[15] In one sense her age is effeminate (clerics are too weak and lethargic), but in another 'womanish' is a positive attribute, for women are capable of taking on the responsibility. In quite a different context (knowledge of the biblical languages at the Paraclete) Abelard encourages Heloise's nuns in similar terms: 'Let us recover in women what we have lost in men'.[16] Modern scholarship comes close

---

[12] Leclercq, 'L'amour', pp. 106f.; Brundage, *Law*, p. 186; Cadden, *Meanings*, pp. 219f.
[13] See below, p. 67.   [14] Weigand, 'Liebe', p. 42.
[15] Newman, *Sister*, pp. 239f.; Blamires, *Case*, pp. 7f. See Bynum, *Fragmentation*, p. 37.
[16] Ep. IX (*PL* 178, 336): 'Quod in viris amisimus, in feminis recuperemus'. See McLaughlin, 'Abelard', p. 331.

to this in seeing a feminisation of spirituality when the twelfth-century emphasis on the weakness, poverty and humility of Christ describes him with attributes commonly equated with women, but now given a positive valuation, and allowing women a privileged closeness to Christ in his *humanitas*.[17] This feminisation embraces also the metaphors used in religious speech, above all but not only by women, as when childbirth, marriage and love, seen from the woman's point of view, are adduced to express union with God.

That this period witnessed an upsurge of feminine piety was also clear to contemporaries. Women can be praised for their greater religious devotion: none other than Robert Grosseteste recognised the sanctity of women in the beguines, who led a perfect form of religious life, and Jacques de Vitry, writing the *vita* of Marie d'Oignies, praised in similar terms the holiness of many women (he refers to semi-religious women) in the diocese of Liège.[18] The fact that Jacques has to defend these women against those who attack them like barking dogs confirms male suspicion of them and their spirituality. This is borne out at about the same time by Lamprecht von Regensburg who in his German verse allegory *Tochter Syon* pours scorn on what he dismisses as the religious pretensions of these women or much later by Jean Gerson's opposition to the harm done by what he regards as the excessive, undisciplined piety of women (he has above all Bridget of Sweden in mind).[19] Such criticisms imply a widespread female spirituality which called forth this suspicion. The beguines, who were the first to attract opposition, have indeed been identified as the first women's movement in the history of Christianity, not simply part of a movement run by men. It allows us from now on to 'speak of specifically female influences on the development of piety'.[20] That this movement represented something new was clear to a critic such as Lamprecht von Regensburg, but also to an admirer such as Matthew Paris who, looking back in 1250 at events over the last half century, commented on the semi-religious life led by women in Cologne whom he called beguines. He sees it as a novel development, consisting of men and women laypeople, but especially women.[21] This development, studied in detail by Grundmann in 1935 (he describes it as a 'religiöse Frauenbewegung'),[22] was certainly not confined to beguines. Women were also attracted to charismatic preachers like Robert of

---

[17] Peters, *GRM* 38 (1988), 49; Bürkle, *ZfdPh* 113, Sonderheft 'Mystik' (1994), 134.
[18] Leyser, *Women*, pp. 196f.; Southern, *Society*, p. 320; Dinzelbacher, 'Rollenverweigerung', pp. 10f.
[19] Lamprecht, *Tochter Syon* 2838–43; Green, *Women*, pp. 156f., 158. Gerson: Bynum, *Fast*, p. 315, n. 43; Leyser, *Women*, p. 205.
[20] Bynum, *Fast*, p. 14. [21] Southern, *Society*, pp. 319f. [22] Grundmann, *Bewegungen*.

Arbrissel and Norbert von Xanten, who founded monasteries to incorporate them.[23] The flood of women seeking to join orders such as the Premonstratensians and Cistercians was so great as to be alarming, leading some in these orders to advocate closing their ranks against them until they were eventually forced by Rome to incorporate them, for fear that they be diverted into the ranks of the heretics.[24] For Grundmann the historical moment was the encounter between the mendicant orders and the religious enthusiasm of these women in north-western Europe. How ready the women were for the preachers' message has been well captured by Bruder Hermann in his life of Iolande von Vianden: a tinder that immediately caught fire ('ein zunder, dat al zc balde vûr entfeit').[25]

The greater prominence of women in religious life is also reflected in hagiography. Subject to all due caution about the mendacity of statistics and to the proviso that the numbers need to be large enough to be statistically meaningful, this has been suggested numerically for the period between the second half of the eleventh century through to the fifteenth century. At the beginning the proportion of saints who were female was approximately ten per cent, in the twelfth century it rose to nearly fifteen per cent, by the end of the fourteenth century it was twenty-four per cent and by the close of the fifteenth century it was twenty-nine per cent.[26] When these figures are broken down still further they reveal that the proportion of women amongst laypeople canonised in the thirteenth century was fifty per cent, rising to just over seventy per cent after 1305.[27] The result was that by the end of the Middle Ages the male saints canonised were almost always clerics (the male lay saint having virtually disappeared) and the 'model of holy behaviour offered to the Catholic laity was almost exclusively female'.[28] (This correlates with Hamburger's observation that lay piety was largely female piety and that women provided models of religious behaviour not merely in hagiography, but also in the home.)[29] In this connection Gaunt makes the significant point that, although hagiography is an androcentric genre, a saint's life can be devoted to a woman as its principal subject,[30] in contrast to the male-centred heroic epic and even the romances to be considered below in which a woman can act together with a man. In the woman saint's *vita* the woman can even act against male opponents, whether in the form of pagan persecutor or patriarchal parent, and rise superior to them.

---

[23] *Ibid.*, pp. 40–50.   [24] *Ibid.*, pp. 175–98, 203–8.
[25] Hermann, *Leben* 530f.; Grundmann, *Bewegungen*, p. 229.   [26] Bynum, *Jesus*, p. 137.
[27] Bynum, *Fragmentation*, p. 137 (quoting Vauchez, *Sainteté*).
[28] Bynum, *Fast*, p. 21.   [29] Hamburger, *Visual*, p. 18.   [30] Gaunt, *Gender*, pp. 185, 187.

This feminisation of religion did not stop short of depicting Christ with feminine imagery, a feature which has been analysed in depth by Bynum. Behind recent stress on this feature lie feminist dissatisfaction with a paternal image of God and the assumption that seeing Christ in feminine terms must have appealed to women and been developed by or for them.[31] Bynum, however, resists such easy explanations, drawing attention to works in which, after the fathers of the Church, the devotional image of Christ as mother first occurs. These works are by men, all of them Cistercian monks of the twelfth century, apart from the Benedictine Anselm of Canterbury, from whom the Cistercians may have derived the idea.[32] Bynum seeks to explain why these Cistercians described Christ in maternal terms. (That this imagery could later be adopted by women such as Marguerite d'Oingt and Julian of Norwich is for her strictly a secondary feature.) Her answer is to emphasise (within the context of incarnational theology and its picture of Christ's suffering humanity) three stereotypes of the female or maternal, with their parallels in this view of Christ.[33] First, a mother gives birth and is sacrificial in her birth pangs, as Christ's Passion generated redemption. Secondly, Christ's love for the individual soul was regarded as the tenderness of a mother towards her child. Thirdly, a mother feeds her child with the milk of her body, as Christ feeds the believer with his body and blood in the eucharist. The force of these parallels, for Cistercian monks or for women mystics alike, was that 'what medieval authors assume the female to be coincided with what they increasingly wished to emphasize about God the creator and about the Incarnation'.[34]

The image of Christ as a birth-giving and feeding mother raises the question of his own mother, Mary, and any role she may be said to play in the feminisation of religion. From the second half of the eleventh century, but increasingly throughout the following centuries there dates an upsurge of interest in Mary that has too readily been related to what has been seen as a reverence for women in secular love poetry.[35] What is beyond doubt is that as a woman Mary is a focus of devotional literature in twelfth-century Germany, frequently connected with women's convents, in the form of prayers and songs addressed to her (including, to give them the place-names by which they are known, texts from Arnstein, St Lambrecht, Melk and Muri).[36] Rupert von Deutz is also significant as the first exegete

---

[31] Bynum, *Jesus*, p. 111. [32] *Ibid.*, p. 112. [33] *Ibid.*, pp. 131f.; *Fragmentation*, p. 158.
[34] Bynum, *Jesus*, p. 134. [35] Gold, *Lady*, pp. 43f.
[36] Kesting, *Maria-Frouwe*, p. 42; Küsters, *Garten*, p. 173.

(after occasional references by Ambrose) systematically to interpret the bride in the Song of Songs in terms of Mary.[37]

Yet to see the growth in the cult of Mary, the woman who undid the work of Eve, as reflecting (or contributing to) a more positive attitude to her sex at large is not without its problems. It may well be that Mary can be put forward as a model for female behaviour. She came to be presented as a reader, especially in the Annunciation scene, who promoted and justified the reading activity of laywomen in the late Middle Ages; her instruction by her mother Anne served as an incentive for women to teach their young both to read and to learn the elements of the faith;[38] her virtues served as a model for women to practise virginity and humility. Behind these obvious parallels, however, there lurked a fundamental dissimilarity which told against Mary's virtues speaking in favour of all women. This is because of the asymmetry between Eve and Mary, for whereas all women are daughters of Eve and take after her in nature, Mary is unique and without parallel amongst women. Her singularity is summed up in an early hymn, perhaps by Ambrose, for she stands alone in her sex ('Sola in sexu femina'),[39] and in Anselm of Canterbury's description of her as wonderfully singular and singularly wonderful ('O femina mirabiliter singularis et singulariter mirabilis').[40] Where this singularity of Mary lies is clear and made explicit by Anselm, for she was a virgin and yet a mother ('Virgo sancta mater Christi').[41] It is because of this that modern feminists have expressed dissatisfaction with the cult for setting a standard which no women could possibly attain, thereby if not actually promoting misogyny, at least confining women to an inferior position.[42] This is brought out tellingly by a thirteenth-century clerical author, Heinrich der Klausner, critical of the secularising use of mariological imagery by love poets praising their ladies in the same terms. He concludes by stating that for Mary alone any eulogy falls short which exceeds the merits of all ladies (542: 'Unser vrowen al eine / Ist daz lop zu cleine / Daz allen vrouwen ist zu grôz').[43]

Even so, isolated attempts, referring to one particular woman in each case and not to all her sex, could be made to bridge the gap by showing that an *imitatio Mariae*, even in her singularity, was conceivable in a particular sense. As an example I take Hildegard von Bingen, for whom a parallel with Mary could be drawn in the claim that in both women God formed his

[37] Kesting, *Maria-Frouwe*, pp. 30–8.   [38] Green, *Women*, pp. 87f., 120f.
[39] Hymn 57, *PL* 17, 1202; Kesting, *Maria-Frouwe*, p. 16.
[40] Gold, *Lady*, p. 70 (quoting Barré, *Prières*).   [41] *Ibid.*   [42] Newman, *Sister*, p. 181.
[43] Heinrich der Klausner, *Marienlegende* 542–4; Kesting, *Maria-Frouwe*, p. 112.

word in order to convey it to mankind (Christ as Logos, or word, in the incarnation and the words passed to Hildegard by divine inspiration). Guibert de Gembloux, her redactor, legitimised her prophetic role by addressing her in terms deriving from Gabriel's address to Mary at the Annunciation: 'Hail, full of grace after Mary, the Lord is with you, blessed are you amongst women, and blessed the speech of your mouth'.[44] Guibert protects himself by inserting the words *post Mariam*, and by replacing the biblical 'fruit of your womb' with the 'speech of your mouth' he implies a similarity of roles for both women, the one giving birth to Christ or the Logos, the other giving expression to the word of God. With regard to our particular problem, however, Hildegard as a nun vowed to virginity, but giving birth to the words of her vision, comes figuratively close to Mary as virgin mother.

The image of Hildegard giving birth to the word of God can be taken a stage further in the mystical concept of the individual soul giving birth spiritually to God. In the twelfth-century *Speculum virginum*, written for nuns, the concept is understandably used of nuns only, in the sense that Christ who was physically born of Mary on one occasion can be spiritually conceived, born and formed time and again by nuns ('Christus semel a Matre Virgine natus est corporaliter, portatur, nascitur a virginibus sacris semper spiritaliter' Born physically of his virgin mother on one occasion, Christ is carried and borne spiritually by holy virgins time and again; also 'Equidem in virgine sacra Christus semper concipitur et formatur' Indeed, on each occasion Christ is conceived and formed in a holy virgin).[45] Here, too, the nuns, vowed to virginity, give birth spiritually: just as Mary is *Mater Virgo*, so is the nun a holy virgin who conceives, whose pregnancy is seen expressly as an imitation of Mary ('Hanc [= Mariam] si volueris imitari, conceptu et partu spiritali eris mater Christi' If you wish to imitate Mary you will be the mother of Christ by spiritual conception and child-bearing).[46] A variation of this spiritual conception of Christ by a nun is reported of Adelheid Langmann, with whom it takes place after receiving the eucharist, the body of Christ, and to whom Christ says that she has conceived him spiritually no less than Mary did physically and spiritually ('du host nit minner geistlichen an mir enpfangen denn mein mueter het, do si mich leiplichen enpfing').[47] Such spiritual pregnancies also

---

[44] Guibert, *Epistolae* 22, 18–20; Ferrante, '*Scribe*', pp. 123f.; Green, *Women*, p. 237.
[45] Bernards, *Speculum*, p. 189, fns. 179, 180.   [46] *Ibid.*, p. 189, fn. 181.
[47] Adelheid, *Offenbarungen* 26, 7–11. That Mary conceived both physically and spiritually is said at 82, 3–7. See Thali, *Beten*, p. 198 and fn. 104.

take physical shape, if we are to believe the women in question as well as those whom they call on as witnesses, in a number of cases listed by Dinzelbacher.[48] The physical symptoms of pregnancy claimed by and for these women include the swelling of breasts, the first flow of milk and the movements of the foetus within their bodies. The women listed by Dinzelbacher include Bridget of Sweden, Mechtild von Hackeborn, the Viennese beguine Agnes Blannbekin, Lukardis and Gertrud van Oosten, with all of whom the symptoms are significantly dated at about Christmas, bringing them closer to Mary as their model. Also listed are Christine Ebner and Margareta Ebner as well as Dorothea von Montau, for whom no Christmas dating is given.

At this point it is instructive to refer to a later example (1325), to what Meister Eckhart says of the birth of God in the soul in a sermon significantly entitled *Ave, gratia plena*. The preacher says that if Mary had not first born God spiritually (thus recalling what we have just seen with Adelheid Langmann) he would never have been born physically of her, but goes on to say that God prefers to be born spiritually of any virgin, that is of any good soul, than to be born physically of Mary.[49] By the equation of 'virgin' with any good soul, the implication is made that either sex, male or female, is capable of giving birth spiritually. This is relevant to what we learn from the nuns' convent Engelthal of the chaplain Friedrich Sunder of whom it is reported that at Christmas time and in connection with communion he underwent the same experience otherwise attributed to women.[50] In his *Gnaden-Leben* the Christ child informs him that he has been born spiritually of him, so that he now has two mothers, Mary his physical mother and Friedrich, his dear soul (*liebe sel mine*), his spiritual mother.[51] The reference to Friedrich's soul ties up with Eckhart's view of the birth of God, but also, because in German the word for soul, like Latin *anima*, is feminine, provides some cover for the unusual image. This is taken further in what follows, for Christ says that just as he has fed Friedrich (with the eucharist), so must Friedrich give Christ his breast and feed him spiritually. With that image feminisation affects the male believer as much as the female.

That can be confirmed with other men. The fourteenth-century Dominican mystic Heinrich Seuse, like Friedrich Sunder at Engelthal, was concerned with the supervision of religious women who were the

[48] Dinzelbacher, 'Gottesgeburt', pp. 118–24.
[49] Eckhart, *Die deutschen Werke* I 375, 10f.; Ruh, *Eckhart*, p. 137; *Geschichte* III 325.
[50] Thali, *Beten*, pp. 139–41.
[51] Sunder, *Gnaden-Leben* 848–57. See Palmer, *PBB* 107 (1985), 470 (review of Ringler, *Offenbarungsliteratur*).

most important part of the audience he addressed as preacher. His identification with the feminine underlies his rejection of the name of his father,
whom he describes as a child of this world ('der welt kint') in favour of the
maiden name of his mother, who for him is a saintly person through whom
God worked wonders ('Sin heilgú múter, mit der herzen und libe got wunder
wúrkte').[52] Hamburger has traced Seuse's feminisation in other details
observable in the drawings in the earliest illustrated copy: the head-dress of
roses he is shown wearing, the sway of his stance reminiscent of Mary's
gesture of humility at the Annunciation. By thus crossing gender boundaries
Seuse identifies with his mother and with Mary, but also allows the women in
his pastoral care to identify with him as a model.[53] At a moment of spiritual
despair in the *Büchlein der ewigen Weisheit* he sees himself expressly in
feminine terms: formerly God's tender and loving bride ('ze einer zarten,
minneklichen gemahel'), but now no more than his washerwoman ('sin ârmú
wôscherin').[54] In the same work, addressing Eternal Wisdom, he calls himself
her poor serving maid ('ze diner armen dirnen') and in her reply she addresses
him as daughter ('min tohter').[55] Bynum has observed a similar feminisation
in Francis of Assisi: winning his first disciple is like giving birth to his first
child; three women he meets address him as 'Lady Poverty'; he sees himself as
a mother labouring for her children, suffering birth pangs.[56] These men go
much further than the Cistercian monks of the twelfth century who put
forward the idea of a feminised Christ. Seuse and Francis do not draw back
from feminising themselves.

Underlying what we have seen in the last few paragraphs is what has been
termed incarnational theology, the emphasis on the humanity of Christ in
all his weakness and suffering, a doctrine which from the twelfth century
on claimed attention alongside the view of his kingship and authority. Its
importance for us is that it grants a special place to women. Hildegard von
Bingen states this expressly: man signifies the divinity, woman the humanity of the Son of God ('Et vir divinitatem, femina vero humanitatem Filii
Dei significat').[57] At a time when Christ's humanity attracted more attention this gave a positive turn to the traditional contrast between man and
woman. To stress the physical nature of women now brought them closer

---

[52] Seuse, *Exemplar* 23, 21 and 24, 3f.   [53] Hamburger, *Visual*, pp. 243–5.
[54] Seuse, *Büchlein* 211, 16 and 212, 12f. See also Bynum, *Fast*, p. 103.
[55] Seuse, *Büchlein* 223, 18 and 20. To Seuse's feminisation corresponds the fact that Eternal Wisdom,
    although grammatically feminine, is gendered masculine and addressed as *herr(e)* (223, 3, 10 and 15),
    presumably as a personification of God.
[56] Bynum, *Fragmentation*, p. 35.
[57] Hildegard, *Liber divinorum operum*, p. 243; Cadden, *Meanings*, p. 191.

to Christ in his humanity and qualified them to act as channels for his communication with the world. If women were patriarchally expected to be submissive this now made them akin to Christ's *humilitas* in the incarnation, known theologically as kenosis, the self-emptying and self-limitation of divine power.[58] The bearing this has on women is well expressed by Mechthild von Magdeburg, wondering why God has granted her, a wretched uneducated woman, such visions instead of a learned cleric. She is told by God that grace flows downwards to the lowest and least regarded places, not to the highest mountains unable to receive the revelation of grace.[59] With that, what was traditionally regarded as the lowest, carnal level of spirituality acquires a new importance, not least for women.[60]

To Bynum's work on the theological importance of Christ's humanity in the late Middle Ages we owe the identification of three strands that underlie this doctrine's association with women.[61] The first, the association of woman with flesh, we have just mentioned in the case of Hildegard von Bingen's association of women with Christ's human nature. The second strand draws on physiological theory deriving from antiquity, according to which the father provided the spirit or form of the foetus, while the woman was associated with the unformed physical material.[62] A third strand linked Christ's flesh with woman on the grounds that his body came from Mary since he had no human father. These theories all associate woman with the body of Christ. 'Not only was Christ enfleshed with flesh from a woman; his own flesh did womanly things: it bled, it bled food and it gave birth'.[63] These views had devotional and ecclesiastical consequences. Nicholas Love in his *Mirrour of the blessed lyf of Jesu Christ* recommends focusing on Christ in the eucharist because 'contemplacioun of the manhede of Christe is more lykynge more spedeful and more siker than is hiȝe contemplacioun of the godhede',[64] and amongst the various readings of the eucharist Christ's suffering humanity looms large.[65] Juliana of Cornillon was largely responsible for promoting the feast of Corpus Christi in the Liège area early in the thirteenth century as a celebration of the humanity of Christ, and was supported by a beguine campaign in favour of it.[66] In this respect, too, women were closely bound up with the humanity of Christ.

---

[58] Green, *Women*, p. 38.   [59] Mechthild, *Licht* II 26 (pp. 136, 138).
[60] Watson, *Exemplaria* 8 (1996), 6f. (talking of Julian of Norwich).
[61] Bynum, *Fragmentation*, pp. 98–101.   [62] See above, p. 18.   [63] Bynum, *Fragmentation*, p. 101.
[64] Love, *Mirrour*, p. 8; Rubin, *Corpus*, p. 330.   [65] Rubin, *Corpus*, pp. 302–16.
[66] *Ibid.*, pp. 164–76; Bynum, *Fragmentation*, pp. 122–5.

LITERATURE

What has been seen as disturbances in the gender system in the twelfth century is reflected in examples of cross-gendering which caused repeated disquiet.[67] This disquiet was felt to be far-reaching, for disorder in sex functions could be seen as social disorder (endangering patriarchy within the family) or religious disorder (jeopardising the exclusively male role of priesthood).[68] What for us might seem the trivial fashion of men shaving off their beards could have worrying implications, for they thereby discarded what distinguished them both from women and from clerics.[69] The spread of courtliness and the taming of the warrior class which it promulgated is coterminous with a concerted criticism of the effeminacy of so many contemporary knights.[70] Cross-gendering implies the presence of fluid boundaries between the sexes, recognised in the Middle Ages, above all in medical theory, but also in theology, in the concepts of the masculine female (*femina virago*) and the feminine male (*vir effeminatus*), with a number of other intermediate possibilities suggesting that 'male' need not be applied to men only or 'female' to women.[71] The uncomplimentary idea that women who excel in virtue, intellect or any form of praiseworthy activity are really men at heart goes back long before the twelfth century in hagiography. It was applied to martyrs, saints and abbesses, but was used to praise outstanding laywomen. Thus queen Bertha, the wife of Heinrich IV, is said to have a man's heart within a woman's body ('regina vero sub femineo corpore cor habens virile').[72] In agreement with the antifeminine prejudice of such praise the reverse possibility, praising men for their female qualities, has a much weaker tradition,[73] but the fact that it occurs at all is significant and is what concerns us now in a chapter dealing with feminisation. Examples already mentioned, such as Friedrich Sunder at Engelthal or Francis of Assisi, can be supplemented by others. 'To call monks women, as Bernard [of Clairvaux] does, is to use the feminine as something positive (humility) but also to imply that such is *not* the opinion of society'.[74] In what follows we shall be dealing with other such cases, present in medieval society, but in conflict with its conventional opinions.

To attribute feminine qualities to men is not necessarily to regard them as effeminate if we take account of the view (opposed to any binary construct

---

[67] Schnell, *FMS* 39 (2005), 82–5.   [68] Cadden, *Meanings*, p. 213.
[69] Putter, 'Literature', p. 36.   [70] Jaeger, *Origins*, pp. 176–94.
[71] Cadden, *Meanings*, pp. 201–27; Schnell, *Sexualität*, pp. 64, fn. 210, 340.
[72] Schnell, *ZfdPh* 103 (1984), 17f.   [73] Cadden, *Meanings*, p. 206.   [74] Bynum, *Jesus*, p. 144.

of the sexes) that features commonly regarded as characteristic of one sex may be found in both sexes and that each sex is therefore a composite. Schnell has quoted the otherwise antifeminine argument of Bruno to the effect that, although *ratio* dominates in man and *sensualitas* in woman, both qualities are to be found in both sexes ('utrumque sit in utroque').[75] A combination of both sexes is likewise found in a prayer of Anselm of Canterbury addressed to Christ, but also Paul, in which both are seen as 'fathers by result, mothers by affection; fathers by authority, mothers by kindness; fathers by protection, mothers by compassion'.[76] Both series of positive contrasts, male and female, are found in both.

We start our discussion of feminisation in literature with a temporary jump in time and space from our present concern to two romances from the Ricardian literature of England in the second half of the fourteenth century. To make this jump in time from 1200 and into romance tradition in another language is justified for the light it throws on our problem and because it shows that the feature of feminisation was latent within the romance genre. Furthermore, with one of these English romances, Chaucer's *Troilus and Criseyde*, a parallel can be drawn with Wolfram's *Parzival*,[77] and for the other, *Sir Gawain and the Green Knight*, a link has been suggested with Chrétien. In his *Ricardian poetry* Burrow discusses the 'image of man' projected in these works and sees in it a diminution (but not exclusion) of heroic feats of arms in favour of a greater interest in personal relationships and feelings, especially to do with love, a move from the battlefield or lord's hall to the chamber in the company of women.[78] This shift of attention, a civilising impulse towards greater sensitivity and ethical awareness, did not go unchallenged by those such as Thomas of Walsingham who remained true to the conservative view of a knight's essentially warlike function: 'These were more knights of Venus than of Bellona, more valiant in the bedchamber than on the field, armed with words rather than weapons, prompt in speaking, but slow in performing acts of war. These fellows, who are in close association with the King [Richard II], care nothing for what a knight ought to know'.[79] What Walsingham had in mind are the courtier knights whom we must now consider, but what he stands for in literary terms is the opposition faced by those authors who promote no longer the hero of epic tradition in his exclusive concern with combat, but

---

[75] Schnell, *ZfdPh* 103 (1984), 11. See below, p. 150.   [76] Bynum, *Jesus*, p. 114.
[77] See below, pp. 54f.   [78] Burrow, *Poetry*, pp. 94f., 100. Cf. Putter, *Gawain*, pp. 7f.
[79] Putter, 'Literature', p. 37; Riddy, 'Nature', p. 220. On the historical context of Walsingham's criticism see Ormrod, *MÆ* 73 (2004), 290–305.

rather one whose activity, even at times inactivity or passivity, lies in other fields.[80]

Chaucer illustrates this ideal in the hero of *Troilus and Criseyde*. With him Hector and the other warrior heroes of the Trojan War take a back seat[81] and although Troilus himself is still active as a fighter he is far from his counterpart with Konrad von Würzburg, advocating warfare for its own sake and rejecting the counsel of reason because it comes from a priest who knows nothing of knighthood.[82] For Chaucer Troilus is more a lover than a fighter, as he makes clear from the beginning (I 1; 'The double sorwe of Troilus to tellen / … In lovynge how his aventures fellen'). Here he goes much further than Benoît de Sainte-Maure in his twelfth-century *Roman de Troie*, in which he introduces the figure of Briseida (= Criseyde) and the love affair with her, together with other love-stories woven into the account of warfare.[83] Whereas the theme of love occupies only a fifth of the French work, otherwise taken up with battle, Chaucer makes it explicit that love is the theme of his work. He emphasises this in his opening lines, but also towards the close by saying that he has not recounted Troilus's brave feats of arms and that anyone wishing to learn about these, rather than his love, should turn to Dares (V 1765–71).

By stressing that he chose not to tell us about Troilus's bravery in the field Chaucer makes it explicit that his hero, although for him a lover, was also a warrior. He can refer to this role of Troilus in passing, saying for example that he acted as a lion on the field of battle (I 1074) or that in his time he in no way stood second to anyone in daring to do what becomes a knight (V 835–7). What is revealing about Chaucer's depiction of Troilus's knightly heroism is that it is not described in action. Instead it is merely reported to us concisely by the narrator, saying that his deeds were such that it was a marvel to think of them (I 475f.) and that he was the first to be armed and, apart from Hector, the most feared (III 1772–5). His bravery can be conveyed indirectly by what others say about him, as in what Pandarus (who has his own motives) reports to Criseyde (II 190–203) or in what the Trojans shout on seeing Troilus put the Greeks to flight in a skirmish (II 610–13). Central to our impression of Troilus's warrior status is that it is earned off-stage, as when we are shown no more than the result in his helmet hacked to pieces and shattered shield (II 638–42). Troilus's knighthood, distanced from us by indirect reporting rather than first-hand presentation, is further

---

[80] Putter, *Gawain*, p. 185.   [81] Brooke, *Idea*, p. 221.

[82] *Trojanischer Krieg* 19132–65; Reuvekamp-Felber, *Volkssprache*, pp. 323f.

[83] Nolan, *Chaucer*, pp. 75, 96.

qualified as a heroic aim in itself by being shown as performed on behalf of Criseyde, to please her (I 477–81, III 435–41, III 1776f.).

Feminisation goes much further than playing down the man's chivalry and subordinating it to love of a woman, for Troilus is shown, frequently and at first hand, to possess a number of qualities which in the Middle Ages were regarded as characteristically female. Above all, as a result of our not witnessing him in battle, the impression he conveys is of extreme passivity. Traditionally Troilus had been a hero because of what he accomplished as a fighter, but with Chaucer his role as hero is a new one: it includes his knighthood, but it is also drastically extended to embrace passivity off the battlefield in his dealings with a woman. His inexperience (by contrast with the worldly-wise Pandarus and the widow Criseyde) means that, since he lacks any sense of active initiative in this field, the affair is taken out of Troilus's hands and arranged for him by Pandarus, even to the point of his having to be thrown in a swoon into his lady's bed. Windeatt argues that behaviour like this 'which is not conventionally masculine raises questions about the values of traditional sexual stereotypes', that sexual possession in his instance results from his extreme humility, meant as 'a deflation of male stereotypes of sexual conquest and mastery'. He concludes that Troilus is 'understood to be a better man because his "manhood" includes some of the qualities of "womanhood"'.[84] But Troilus, for all his feminine qualities, retains his manhood and can be described expressly as manly (III 113, 428f., IV 154, 1674), so that his character may be termed feminised, but not effeminate. This feminisation is meant as a positive feature (in his humility he rejects Pandarus's advice to solve his problem by simply abducting Criseyde) and serves as a striking contrast with the aggressive assertiveness of Diomede, who eventually wins Criseyde from him. In the *Frigii Daretis Ylias* of Joseph of Exeter, on whom Chaucer's picture of Diomede is based, this rival is described as fierce, massive, violent and foursquare, an extreme depiction of unqualified masculinity, out for the sexual possession of his prey which plays no part with Troilus.[85] We are left implicitly to draw a contrast between the two men, but are in no need of the equation of Diomede with a wild boar in a dream of Troilus (V 1237–41) to see with whom our sympathies are meant to lie.

Our second Ricardian work, *Sir Gawain and the Green Knight*, presents in Gawain another example of a feminised hero.[86] Again, this involves a re-definition of what is meant by knighthood, an innovation which has

---

[84] Windeatt, *Chaucer*, pp. xxvif.   [85] *Troilus* V 799–803. See Windeatt, *Chaucer*, p. 183, n. 135.
[86] So described by Putter, *Gawain*, p. 228, and Riddy, 'Nature', p. 220.

been analysed for this work by Putter and traced back to Chrétien de Troyes, especially his *Lancelot* and *Yvain*. Putter sums up the nature of this re-definition: 'What these writers demand from the knight is that he internalize some of the violence he directs on to his surroundings in the form of critical self-scrutiny; that his action should be matched by reflection'.[87] He stresses, for example, that Lancelot is often passively self-effacing rather than aggressively assertive, just as in the English romance, in a manner reminiscent of Troilus, Gawain's achievement lies in this commitment to an ideal behaviour involving passivity and humiliation.[88] We may also invoke another literary parallel (with no conceivable possibility of influence) in recalling Burrow's point that Gawain's test should require him to be 'disarmed', metaphorically and literally,[89] and should take place in a bedroom in the company of his host's wife, just as Wolfram's testing of Gawan demands that he abandon his knightly steed on entering Schastel Marveile and is to be accomplished on a bed, Lit Marveile, of all places.[90] In *Sir Gawain* a test which takes the shape of one knight's combat with another has been replaced by one which involves a woman and in which the danger lies in verbal, rather than armed, combat.[91] Putter suggests that in their re-definition of knighthood both Chrétien and the *Gawain* poet introduce clerical ideals into their romances,[92] but this clericalisation can also be seen as a feminisation if we recall the extent of common ground shared by clerics and women at court. Neither clerics nor women bear arms, so that both have an interest in taming or domesticating the warrior by teaching him self-restraint and a re-direction of his violence. The widespread literacy of women is another link between them and clerical *litterati* who, whether in orders or as beneficiaries of a clerical education, composed many of their works with women recipients specifically in mind.

To show that these features from fourteenth-century England have a bearing on our concern, the earliest romances composed on the continent in the twelfth century, we have to go further than the parallels suggested between *Sir Gawain* and Chrétien. We can do this first in a negative way by considering the frequent clerical criticisms levelled against what was impugned as the effeminacy of courtier knights in their day.[93] These knights are criticised for a variety of points in their dress and appearance: for their dragging clothing sweeping the ground, the style of their long haircut

---

[87] Putter, *Gawain*, p. 221.   [88] *Ibid.*, pp. 159, 185.   [89] Burrow, *Reading*, p. 56.
[90] Emmerling, *Geschlechterbeziehungen*, pp. 120–4.
[91] Spearing, *Gawain*, pp. 190f.   [92] Putter, *Gawain*, p. 222.
[93] Platelle, *RBPH* 53 (1975), 1071–96; Jaeger, *Origins*, pp. 176–94; Schnell *FMS* 39 (2005), 81–3.

and for being beardless. As a result they are reproached for being like 'little women' (*mulierculae*) or even prostitutes (*meretrices*).[94] For Ordericus Vitalis the root cause of this lies with women, or rather with the wish of such courtiers to please women and make themselves attractive to them, thereby proving themselves effeminate ('Femineam mollitiem petulans iuuentus amplectitur, feminisque viri curiales in omni lascivia summopere adulantur' Impudent youths embrace feminine softness, men of the court devote themselves to flattering women with every kind of wantonness).[95] A few examples of criticism on this score occur already in the eleventh century (Radulfus Glaber in France, who puts the corrupt fashion down to imitation of Provence, or Siegfried von Gorze in Germany, who sees it as coming from abroad).[96] However, it is in the twelfth century that such clerical voices become more frequent, even strident, no doubt in connection with the rise of the courtly ideal and the disturbances in the gender system in that period. On the brink of that century Eadmer complains that all the young men at court have their hair long in the manner of young women and walk with a mincing gait.[97] Bishop Godfrey of Amiens takes offence at knights who have long hair like so many women (*instar muliercularum*).[98] Ordericus moves from a perverse detail of dress (shoes with pointed, turned-up toes) to the assumption of homosexuality and contrasts the practice of such catamites of the present with the traditions of warrior men ('Ritus heroum') in the past.[99] William of Malmesbury criticises similar fashions, imported from abroad and equated with effeminacy because of the wish to compete with women in softness of body ('mollitie corporis certare cum foeminis').[100] He also refers to the hairstyle of men who, forgetful of the sex in which they were born, willingly transform themselves in adopting feminine appearance ('qui obliti quid nati sunt, libenter se in muliebris sexus habitum transformant').[101] In his satire on the court John of Salisbury sees it as a place where effeminate men are deprived of the nobler sex and are changed into women.[102] In this observation, as in others, the tone of antifeminism is unmistakable, but the object of criticism in these examples is not primarily women, but rather men who behave as if they were women.

---

[94] Platelle, *RBPH* 53 (1975), 1071, 1087.   [95] Ordericus, *Historia* IV 188; Jaeger, *Origins*, p. 180.
[96] Radulfus, *Historiae* III 9, 40 (p. 89). Siegfried: Giesebrecht, *Geschichte* II 718.
[97] Eadmer, *Historia*, PL 159, 376; Platelle, *RBPH* 53 (1975), 1078 (whose reference is wrong).
[98] *Vita*, p. 926; Platelle, *RBPH* 53 (1975), 1081f.
[99] Ordericus, *Historia* IV 188; Jaeger, *Origins*, p. 180.
[100] William of Malmesbury, *Gesta* IV 314 (pp. 369f.); Jaeger, *Origins*, pp. 180f.
[101] William of Malmesbury, *Historiae*, PL 179, 1396f.; Platelle, *RBPH* 53 (1975), 1082.
[102] John of Salisbury, *Policraticus* V 10 (p. 329).

The examples so far considered come from clerics writing in Latin, but court authors using the vernacular a little later also voice similar criticism of what they regard as womanish ways in men. In his *Liet von Troye* Herbort von Fritzlar is so suspicious of the attribute beauty applied to a man rather than a woman that his description of Paris's beauty (2513–20) is concluded with the remark that he seemed to be a young woman ('Als er ein iunc-frauwe were').[103] In this implication of Paris's unmanliness Herbort stands in a long tradition attested already by Virgil's reference to 'that Paris with his effeminate crew' ('ille Paris cum semiuiro comitatu').[104] A narrative about the Trojan War in which military exploits predominate is an obvious occasion for satirising anyone who appears not to conform to masculine conventions and the same is true of the *Nibelungenlied.*[105] During a tournament before battle begins in earnest the Burgundians at Etzel's court catch sight of one Hunnish participant in particular, standing out from the others by riding about in a dandified manner (1885, 1: 'Dô sâhens' einen rîten sô weigerlîchen hie'), wearing clothing fine to the point of effeminacy, as if he were the bride of a noble knight (1885, 4: 'er fuor sô wol gekleidet sam eines edeln ritters brût'). In fact, this Hun takes part as a lover (1885, 3: 'jâ moht er in den zîten wol haben herzen trût'), a point which is clear to the Burgundian Volker, who sees in him a ladies' man (1886, 2: 'jener trût der vrouwen') and, livid at the spectacle before him, rushes forward and kills him. Love-service of a lady, expressed in foppish clothing, is tantamount to effeminacy in the eyes of Volker, whose warrior ideal is untouched by such courtliness. A similar contrast occurs in another work in heroic tradition, Wolfram's *Willehalm*, between Rennewart and the French knights to whose flight from the battlefield he is to put a stop. The deserters are explicitly called dandies (322, 21: *hârslihtaere*, a derisive term in MHG commonly used of an effeminate man)[106] and their distance from the heroic ideal upheld in extreme form by Rennewart is made clear by the wish of some of them to see the ladies (323, 17: 'eteslîcher wolde sehen wîp') and of others simply to take their ease after hardship (323, 18: 'sô wolde der ander sînen lîp / eysiern mit maneger sache / nâch dem grôzen ungemache').

The contrast between knightly manliness and courtly qualities which come under suspicion[107] is not confined to literature in the heroic tradition, as can be shown by two examples from the Tristan story. In the version of

---

[103] Herbort refers to Paris expressly as beautiful (2514: *schone gefar*), but also as *reine* (2518), an adjective commonly used of noblewomen with meanings inclusive of beauty (BMZ II 1, 659). On the gender-specific attribution of beauty to women see Schnell, *FMS* 39 (2005), 87–95.

[104] *Aeneid* IV 215f.; Bond, *Mediaevalia* 13 (1989), 112, n. 22.   [105] Jaeger, *Origins*, p. 191.

[106] BMZ II 2, 396.   [107] See Schnell, *FMS* 39 (2005), 80–3.

Thomas of Britain it is the figure of Cariado, a knightly member of Marc's court in love with Ysolt, who exemplifies this. He is summed up briefly, but tellingly, as a fine knight (Sneyd[1] 811: *molt bels chevaliers*), but does the adjective *bels* cast suspicion on his beauty, as was the case with Herbort von Fritzlar? He is also courteous and proud, a good conversationalist, full of pleasantries, gallant with the ladies, but he is not to be praised when it comes to bearing arms (812–16). We are not meant to conclude from this thumbnail sketch that Thomas criticises courtly attainments as such (Tristran himself incorporates them in full measure), for his target is rather this one person who, unlike Tristran, has accomplished nothing in Ysolt's eyes (800–10). The other Tristan example, from Gottfried's German version, concerns the steward at the Irish court, a figure to whom we shall return later.[108] In the present context he is introduced to us as one who hoped to be Isolde's lover (8954: 'der was ouch unde wolte sîn / der jungen küniginne amîs'; cf. 9097–9), he charges on horseback crying his devotion to her in modish French (9164–70) and Isolde's mother sees him very much as a lady's knight (9909: *frouwen ritter*). All this is reminiscent of the Hunnish dandy in the *Nibelungenlied*, even down to the negative assessment of this figure. This is conveyed to us from the beginning by the narrator's addition to the steward's hope to become Isolde's lover, saying that this was entirely against her wishes (8956: 'wider ir willen alle wîs'), by his turning tail on catching sight of the dragon (8957–66) and by his mounted charge against the monster only once he knows that it is already dead (9159–73). That such cowardice amounts to effeminacy on his part is made clear by the accusation by Isolde's mother that he knows too much of the ladies' chamber and that this has robbed him of his manhood (9910: 'du weist der frouwen art ze wol: / du bist dar în ze verre komen, / ez hât dir der manne art benomen'). Accordingly she recommends him to remember his manly disposition and abandon womanish ways (9922: 'sô dir got, du bist ein man, / lâz uns unser frouwen art').

If we are to uphold the difference between 'effeminate', judged negatively in the examples adduced so far, and 'feminised' we need to focus on evidence where the latter is assessed positively. In expecting to find this we may be encouraged by Jaeger's remark: 'It was the great accomplishment of the courtly romance that it resolved the differences between the two [courtesy and warrior valour], subordinating the warrior to the lover and courtier and producing a heroic type that could inspire admiration in more liberal and refined factions of the lay nobility'.[109] We may be encouraged still further by

---

[108] See below, pp. 146f.   [109] Jaeger, *Origins*, p. 193.

one simple observation on the negative cases so far discussed. The behaviour and appearance of men who could be condemned as effeminate are attested over a wide spread of evidence throughout the twelfth century, in France, England and Germany, and in texts meant for lay and clerical consumption. In the eyes of these critics such features were negative, as we have seen, but their objections testify a widespread fashion which must have been regarded positively, worthy of cultivating by those who followed it. Putter sums up these two sides of the debate: 'It will be apparent that the vehemence of the effeminacy rhetoric suggests that many knights were no longer of the belief that manliness should be made manifest in acts of aggression. The complaints about effeminacy thus yield a picture of a period which, so far from agreeing on what male heroism consists of, is divided over the question of whether arms or culture make the man'.[110]

The two sides of this debate find an echo in modern scholarship. When the young boy Parzival first encounters knighthood in the shape of Karnahkarnanz the knight is shown as magnificently attired, his surcoat reaching to the ground and with rings on his limbs which the young boy can only compare with the rings worn by the women in his mother's service (121, 30–122, 12; 123, 28–30). These details have led Urscheler to detect vanity in this knight's get-up, even made ridiculous (or effeminate?) by the comparison with the rings worn by women.[111] Doubts may be entertained about this negative interpretation. This knight's appearance is calculated by Wolfram to make the strongest possible impression on the boy, sending him out on what becomes his knightly quest. The task on which Karnahkarnanz is engaged, the rescue of an abducted woman, is meant equally positively.[112]

The suspicion of male beauty voiced by Herbort von Fritzlar finds an echo in Walther von der Vogelweide's statement that, unlike the case with women, praise of a man for his looks is unbecoming, making him too soft and despicable (35, 27: 'An wîbe lobe stêt wol daz man si heize schoene: / manne stêt ez übel, ez ist ze weich und ofte hoene').[113] Although Walther's view may be dictated by the lyric genre in which he works and in which conventionally it is women who are to be praised, his attitude, like Herbort's, raises the question how Wolfram's praise of Parzival's beauty is to be judged.

From Jaeger's work on the origins of courtliness we know that beauty plays an important role as an internal, non-physical attribute of courtly virtue, expressed in Latin, for example, as beauty of manners and virtues

---

[110] Putter, 'Literature', p. 39.   [111] Urscheler, *Kommunikation*, p. 182.
[112] See below, pp. 190–2.   [113] Hahn, 'Schönheit', p. 204, fn. 5.

('morum et virtutum pulchritudo' or 'venustas morum'),[114] with counterparts in German such as 'schoene site' or 'schôn' unde reine gemuot'.[115] In addition, physical beauty can be seen as the outward expression of virtue, as when Isolde's beautiful and pure temperament is made manifest in fine gestures and elegant bearing ('ir gebaerde süeze unde guot').[116] It is with beauty as a physical attribute that we are now concerned in *Parzival*.

It need not surprise us that Wolfram should often say of his women characters that they are beautiful (e.g. Belakane, Herzeloyde, Condwiramurs). He may not describe their beauty in detail (Jeschute is an exception for which there is a special explanation), but at least he refers to the fact of their beauty.[117] Comparable with this, as we shall see later, is his employment of the epithet *kiusche* (meaning 'chaste' or 'modest', but much more besides) of women in particular.[118]

What concerns us more, however, is the frequent mention of beauty as an attribute of men, too, in *Parzival*[119] (just as *kiusche* can also be applied to them). Examples of masculine beauty are Gahmuret (especially his splendid appearance on riding into Kanvoleis) and Vergulaht (so strikingly beautiful that he could possibly be taken for Parzival),[120] but they also include male members of the Grail community. In his youth Trevrizent was of surpassing beauty, and Wolfram achieves a *tour de force* in describing the miracle of Amfortas's restored beauty, excelling even Parzival's, towards the close of work.[121] Despite this last example (meant more to underline the wonder of God's intervention than to undermine Parzival) it is on his protagonist that Wolfram lavishes (about forty times) hyperbolic praise of his male beauty. It must suffice here to point out that Parzival's beauty is alluded to already in the prologue in its attraction for women (4, 20: 'er wîbes ougen süeze / unt dâ bî wîbes herzen suht' sweet in woman's eyes, yet woman's heart's sickness), that in another passage long before his birth his beauty is invoked as superior even to Kaylet's (39, 22–8) and that in the young boy's first encounter with the knightly world, his meeting with Karnahkarnanz, the supreme prize is expressly awarded to him alone as 'the crown of flowers of

---

[114] Jaeger, *Origins*, pp. 135, 139. Schnell, *FMS* 39 (2005), 1–100, criticises Jaeger's theory of the Ottonian origins of *curialitas*, but not the relevance of Latin terminology.

[115] Thomasin von Zerclaere, *Der Welsche Gast* 679; Gottfried, *Tristan* 8029.

[116] Gottfried, *Tristan* 8030.

[117] Belakane: 24, 6–11; 54, 23. Herzeloyde: 64, 4–8; 84, 13–15. Condwiramurs: 188, 6–14; 224, 11–14. Jeschute: 130, 3–25 and below, pp. 192, 209.

[118] See below, p. 180.   [119] Hahn, 'Schönheit', pp. 203–32; Johnson, 'Beauty', pp. 273–94.

[120] Gahmuret: 63, 16–19; 400, 15–18; 795, 23–8. Vergulaht: 400, 4–15; Johnson, 'Beauty', pp. 285f.

[121] Trevrizent: 497, 28f.; Green, *Art*, p. 200. Amfortas: 795, 30–796, 16; Johnson, 'Beauty', pp. 289–91.

all manly beauty' (122, 13: 'Aller manne schoene ein bluomen kranz').[122] So great is this man's beauty that it surpasses that of beautiful women, as when on awaking in Gurnemanz's castle he is said to outshine not merely the sun, but also the second daylight emanating from the beautiful maidens sent to serve him (167, 17–20). In this surpassing of women in a field where they might be taken to have an inborn advantage another parallel can be drawn with the quality of *kiusche*, for Belakane's lover Isenhart is described as more modest than a woman (26, 15: 'er was noch kiuscher denne ein wîp').

In highlighting the beauty of men as well as women Wolfram makes a point of not differentiating between them, just as he avoids doing this with regard to *kiusche*. Pérennec has shown that the epithets 'sweet' ('süeze') and 'lovable' ('minneclîch'), used conventionally and also by Wolfram of women, can be applied to Parzival (on one occasion in emphatic combination: 139, 26f.).[123] How far Wolfram stands from distinguishing between masculine and feminine beauty can be seen in the episode of the young Parzival's arrival at Arthur's court, where the author's neologisms render translation difficult, but underline what is his concern. Those at court press around him, admiring his looks which, as they see with their own eyes, are such that no more lovable offspring was ever sired or ladied[124] (148, 22: 'sie nâmen sîner varwe wâr. / diz was selpschouwet, / gehêrret noch gefrouwet / wart nie minneclîcher fruht').[125] A similar gender-transcending effect can be seen in Cunneware's greeting on Parzival's return to the Round Table, for his countenance is fair as if dew-covered roses had flown there (305, 23: 'als touwege rôsen dar gevlogen'). With this image Wolfram does not hesitate to apply to his protagonist the combination of roses and dew otherwise used to describe feminine beauty, as with Parzival's wife Condwiramurs (188, 10–13). Pérennec calls this undifferentiated view of male and female beauty audacious,[126] but that is another measure of the importance which Wolfram attached to it.

If we bear in mind Herbort's criticism of male beauty, Wolfram's descriptive practice faced the possible criticism by male listeners of his day who might regard his protagonist (and other male characters) as effeminate.[127] He meets this possible charge in two ways. His first method is to depict in his work a number of male characters who differ from Herbort and

---

[122] On this line see Green, *Art*, p. 18; Yeandle, *Commentary*, pp. 149–51.

[123] Pérennec, *Recherches*, pp. 247f., 456, n. 115.

[124] I follow here the wording of Edwards, *Wolfram*, p. 48.

[125] See Pérennec, *Recherches*, pp. 246f.   [126] *Ibid.*, p. 247.

[127] Pérennec rightly denies, *ibid.*, p. 248, that Parzival is therefore shown to be effeminate, but I should rather state the matter positively by saying that he is feminised.

Walther in acknowledging Parzival's beauty entirely positively, seeing in it a sign of his noble birth, his kinship with others and his future destiny.[128] This positive function of Parzival's beauty is made clear from the beginning in his encounter with Karnahkarnanz, who sees in the young boy's outstanding good looks the hallmark of knightly birth (123, 11: 'ir mugt wol sîn von ritters art') and later when Gurnemanz concludes for the same reason that the boy is born to be a ruler (170, 21f.). The same is true of another crucial point in the young Parzival's career, his encounter with the knight Ither, whose admiration of his beauty leads him to bless the mother who bore him and, with no hint of criticism, to foresee that women will love him for it (146, 5–12). Other men who react similarly include such disparate characters as the fisherman who guides the boy to Arthur's court (143, 12), Arthur himself (149, 19–21), a follower of Gurnemanz (164, 11–20) and Clamide's followers who see in the beauty of Condwiramurs's husband a token of his knightly quality (209, 11–14).[129] He is the most handsome man who ever took on service as a knight ('den schoensten man / der schildes ambet ie gewan') and incorporates all knightly honour ('aller ritter êre ist zim bewart').

This last example may serve as a bridge to Wolfram's second method, more frequently used and more important, consisting in the explicit conjunction of beauty with a demonstration of Parzival's manliness and knightly excellence. One example of this method has already been touched on, for the passage describing the Round Table's admiration for the young Parzival on first beholding him (148, 22–5) is significantly concluded with a pointer in another direction, to the effect that he feared no terror (148, 28: 'der vreise wênec vorhte'). This inclusion of a quality becoming a knight occurs elsewhere. For Karnahkarnanz, the young boy's beauty is proof enough of knightly birth (123, 11) and, on a higher social level, the same is true of Gurnemanz's estimation (170, 22) that Parzival is born to be a ruler, with all the military obligations of that office in the Middle Ages. These prophecies are borne out in the narrative action. Clamide's men are quick to see, as a result of combat with him, that Parzival's beauty is no impediment to his knightly prowess (209, 11–14). The feminine effect of the dew-covered roses with which Parzival's face is described is combined with the masculine detail of the marks of iron rust from his helmet (305, 22: 'durch îsers mâl'). Between them, *rôsen* and *îser* sum up the two gendered aspects of his nature.[130] The same is suggested when Parzival obtains leave to clean

[128] Johnson, 'Beauty', pp. 278, 281.   [129] *Ibid.*, p. 279.
[130] For a similar effect with Rennewart, replacing the helmet with dust, see Schmid, *Wolfram-Studien* 17 (2002), 112.

himself on arrival at court (306, 21–8), for the removal of rust reveals his beauty. Here the combination is of rust ('râm') with a beauty ('bî rôtem munde liehtez vel' fair skin against the red of his lips) which is compared with flowers ('gebluomt für alle man' the flower of all men). Later on, Sigune is able to recognise Parzival by his beauty despite the rust from his helmet (440, 27: 'durch îsers râm vil liehtez vel: / do erkande si den degen snel' fair skin through the rust of iron, she then recognised the brave warrior). Elsewhere, the same two aspects can be conjoined without recourse to the knightly attribute of a helmet. Beauty and manliness in the person of Parzival form no contradiction in the eyes of the queen of Janfuse (329, 9: 'liehter varwe und manlîcher site' fair looks and manly behaviour) or for Arthur (717, 26–30: 'helt so manlîch' hero so brave; 'lieht gemâl' of handsome looks). Once more, the conventionally feminine attribute *kiusche*, when applied to men, can likewise be seen as reconcilable with the manly qualities of daring and bravery.[131] This is true of Gahmuret (5, 22: 'der kiusche und der vreche' modest and brave), of Isenhart, whose *kiusche* is accompanied by *vrecheit und ellen* 'daring and bravery' (26, 16), and Parzival himself (437, 12: 'der kiusche vrävel man' the gentle yet bold man). It is above all in the person of Parzival that this reconciliation is incorporated: he is essentially *kiusche*, and his beauty surpasses that of all other men, but none of this diminishes his knightly wish for continuous combat.[132]

This feature of Parzival can be paralleled with what we have seen of Chaucer's Troilus, whose 'feminine' qualities in no way operate against his manliness on the field of battle at Troy. Like Chaucer, Wolfram depicts a feminised hero whose manly qualities remain unimpaired. So far from losing them, they are enriched by the addition of a wider range of attributes.

The debate over whether arms or culture make the man can also take personal shape in medieval literature. In his *Partonopier und Meliur* Konrad von Würzburg depicts a difference of opinion in military tactics between two brothers.[133] Walther, the younger son, has undergone a clerical educa-tion, is therefore a *miles litteratus*, enjoying the culture which Putter locates on one side of the debate (19622–7). On tactical grounds he recommends a retreat because conditions are not favourable (19628–31). For this he is immediately taken to task by his elder brother Alius, accusing him of cowardice and attributing this not to his womanish, but to his clerical ways (19635–55). This is the conventional contrast between the impulsive warrior and the reflective cleric, but Konrad makes it clear where his sympathy lies by describing Walther's suggestion as prudent and therefore

[131] See below, p. 179.   [132] See below, p. 172.   [133] Reuvekamp-Felber, *Volkssprache*, pp. 318–21.

justified (19629: *wîse lêre*). He underlines this further by having the brothers' father settle the dispute, calling his elder son foolish and praising the
younger's plan (19674–89). Konrad achieves his effect by confronting two
opposing attitudes with one another (as we have seen already in the persons
of Volker and the Hunnish knight, Rennewart and the French knights), but
heightens it by introducing the verbal discourse of those involved.

We find this personal debate at the very beginning of Arthurian literature
in the vernacular. In the Latin text of Geoffrey of Monmouth's *Historia
regum Britannie* there is no such dispute when, after Arthur decides on
war against Rome, Cador speaks up in delight that the long period of peace
in which men fell victim to women (*mulierum inflammationes*) and other
pleasures has given way to an opportunity to show the prowess of former
times.[134] That is the voice of the old-style warrior, contemptuous of new-
fangled modes, but with Geoffrey there is no other voice opposing Cador.
The position is different with Wace's vernacular adaptation of Geoffrey. He
reproduces Cador's argument, emphasising more pointedly that idleness
lessens prowess and inflames lechery and love affairs (10744: 'Uisdive ame-
nuse prüesce, / Uisdive esmuet les lecheries, / Uisdive esprent lé drueries'), but
against this Walwein (Gauvain) speaks out. He praises the attractions of peace
after war, the occasions for merriment and love affairs, adding that it is for
love and their beloved that knights perform knightly deeds (10769: 'Mult sunt
bones les gaberies / E bones sunt les drueries. / Pur amistié e pur amies / Funt
chevaliers chevaleries'). Against Cador's fears of an effeminate weakening of
warriors[135] Walwein argues if not for a feminised knight, then at least for a
knight whose life at least is feminised, but still conducive to chivalry, as
Chaucer was later to show with Troilus. Coming from the leading knight of
the Round Table, Walwein's words carry more weight than do Cador's, who
stands more for the traditional vocation of warriors.

Whether or not inspired by this scene from Wace, Chrétien depicts a
similar dispute in *Perceval* between Gauvain and Keu. The occasion is the
episode when Perceval is lost in a love trance, but is mistakenly held to be
challenging Arthur's court camped nearby. Saigremor (the 'Impetuous')[136]
and after him Keu are quick to take up arms, but are defeated, whilst
Gauvain approaches Perceval in a pacific manner, attempts to see things
by empathy through Perceval's eyes (4360–3), and successfully brings him
back to Arthur's company. Keu will have none of this, accusing Gauvain of
getting away without a fight, without even drawing a sword, as he has on

---

[134] Geoffrey, *Historia* 158 (p. 113).   [135] Putter, 'Literature', p. 44.
[136] *Perceval* 4220: 'Saigremor, qui par son desroi/Estoit Desreez apelez'.

other occasions (4370–6, 4390–3). On Gauvain's return with Perceval Keu launches into a second tirade against him, ironically suggesting that the fight must have been dangerous and that Gauvain is coming back just as bold as when he set forth, without a blow having been struck (4517–25). Whereas Saigremor and Keu saw the situation in terms of combat and failed, Gauvain proceeds diplomatically and imaginatively, putting himself in the other's state of mind to bring about a peaceful resolution. In equating these two approaches with failure and success Chrétien takes the side of the courtier-knight against the warriors[137] (even though all three may be members of the Round Table).

Although with Chrétien Gauvain considers in advance the possibility that Perceval may be musing over the loss of his lady by abduction and, on learning the facts from him, praises him for his courtesy, there is no mention of a woman in the encounters of Saigremor and then Keu with the hero. This is not the case in Wolfram's version, whose introduction of a woman (Condwiramurs) into the dispute between two conceptions of knighthood is one of the changes brought about by the German author. The pacific intentions and empathy of Gawan, already present in the French text, are heightened when, contrary to the source, Wolfram has him ride out unarmed to deal with an apparently dangerous opponent (299, 29f.)[138] and entertain the possibility that, as has happened in Gawan's own case, Parzival may be lost in a love trance (301, 22–5). By acting in accordance with this insight and throwing his cloak over the drops of blood in the snow, thus jerking Parzival out of his reverie, Gawan is more actively in control of a peaceful solution than in the French romance, where the drops of blood simply melt in the sunlight (301, 26–30). From our point of view, the decisive novelty in Wolfram's presentation of this episode comes early, before Gawan rides out to meet Parzival, in Keie's jeering words to him. With Chrétien Keu had likewise jeered at Gauvain, but Wolfram has given his words a special twist, for Keie accuses Gawan of unmanliness in being no more than a lady's knight.[139] He pours scorn on him, since a single woman's hair, however thin and fine, is strong enough to hold him back from combat (299, 3: 'Och enist hie ninder frouwen hâr / weder sô mürwe noch sô clâr, / ez enwaere doch ein veste bant / ze wern strîtes iwer hant'). A man of so gentle a disposition is an honour to his mother, for on his father's side he should be courageous (299, 7: 'swelch man tuot solhe diemuot schîn, / der êret ouch die muoter

[137] Putter, 'Literature', pp. 46f.
[138] With Chrétien Gauvain obeys Arthur's order to arm himself when going out to Perceval: 4413–21.
[139] Garnerus, *Begegnung*, pp. 170f.

sîn: / vaterhalp solter ellen hân'). Where Wolfram stands in this dispute between two members of the Round Table should be clear not merely, as with Chrétien, from the contrast between Keie's ignominious failure and Gawan's diplomatic success, but also from the role attributed to Gawan throughout the work, incorporating a new conception of the knightly hero in which combat for its own sake, as demonstrated by Segramors and Keie, comes under critical scrutiny.[140]

That Wolfram attached importance to such a disputation can be seen from his return to it, diverging from Chrétien, in a scene at Schampfanzun played out between Kingrimursel and Liddamus. Kingrimursel upholds the need for combat with Gawan, not least because he had issued the challenge to him in the first place,[141] and accuses Liddamus of effeminate cowardice, retreating like a woman whenever it came to fighting (417, 27: 'swâ man ie gein strîte dranc, / dâ taet ir wîbes widerwanc'). For his part, Liddamus says that women may thank whoever wins renown in combat, but he will not be misled for anyone's sake into great suffering (420, 18–21). With these opposing views we confront the same situation as with Cador and Walwein or with Keie and Gawan, but the narrator's dice are not loaded so heavily against Liddamus as it might seem. In the first place, it has already been made clear that the accusation against Gawan, and therefore the justification of combat with him, is unfounded.[142] Moreover, Liddamus's reluctance to fight echoes Gawan's similar attitude, especially in the Schampfanzun episode,[143] and his refusal to fight on behalf of a woman agrees with what we shall see later of Wolfram's reservations about *amor et militia*,[144] knightly combat to gain a woman's favour.

Liddamus strengthens his case by intertextual references (and one intratextual allusion) that are also significant.[145] With an eye to Veldeke's *Eneasroman* he allows Kingrimursel to play the role of Turnus, keeping that of Drances for himself (419, 11–13). These equations derive their force from the way in which Veldeke's Turnus, pressing for battle and accusing Drances of cowardice,[146] plays a negative role in his opposition to Eneas, whilst Drances is depicted positively,[147] advocating a prudent plan of single combat to avoid mass slaughter.[148] In his intratextual reference Liddamus sets himself apart from the headstrong thirst for violence of Segramors (421, 21f.), which thereby places him for Wolfram's audience alongside

---

[140] This aspect of Gawan has been brought out in detail by Emmerling, *Geschlechterbeziehungen*.
[141] *Parzival* 324, 19–24.   [142] *Ibid.*, 413, 13f.   [143] Emmerling, *Geschlechterbeziehungen*, pp. 51, 53, 55.
[144] See below, pp. 216–25.   [145] Draesner, *Wege*, pp. 321–35.
[146] Veldeke, *Eneasroman* 8633–9, 8644–54.   [147] *Ibid.*, 8528–37.   [148] *Ibid.*, 8612f., 8619–21.

Gawan's pacific tactfulness.[149] The other intertextual references made by Liddamus are to well-known figures from heroic tradition. For example, he rejects for himself the role of Wolfhart (420, 22), a counsellor whose advice and thirst for combat had catastrophic results in the *Nibelungenlied*,[150] but on the other hand he is prepared to act as did Rumolt, whose advice would have proved its value, if only it had been followed (420, 26–8).[151] For Liddamus it makes good sense to quote these figures (and others) from a heroic tradition from which he diverges radically, leaving to Kingrimursel, in his insistence on vengeance by combat, a role akin to that tradition.[152] Mohr's contrast between these two (one a 'reckless warrior' and the other a 'hero in peacetime')[153] echoes what we saw of Wace's contrast between Cador and Walwein. This series of literary allusions is meant to make it clear to the informed recipients of Wolfram's work that Liddamus's position is to be judged favourably and that Kingrimursel is in the wrong.[154]

The evidence we have considered shows that there were two conflicting attitudes towards feminisation. For some, conceivably the conservative majority amongst men, it meant a danger to masculine values and was equated with effeminacy. For others it amounted to an enrichment of traditional warrior virtues by the addition of qualities such as courtesy, breeding and sensitivity, in short the view that the knight was also to act as a courtier. The contrast between these attitudes is particularly marked from the rise of courtliness in the twelfth century, in society as well as literature. This has consequences for the authors whom we shall consider in Part II, for whom the concept of a feminised man is not the same thing as an effeminate man. We may now understand that these authors, in presenting such an idea, were best advised to proceed indirectly and by implication, for to have done otherwise could have accentuated the opposition which their views already faced.

In her discussion of Chaucer, Mann pays particular attention to what the author presents as the womanly ethos of pity, applied to Troilus, for example, so as to make of him a feminised hero,[155] as can also be said of some male characters in earlier romances. She goes further, however, in the case of the *Legend of Good Women*, suggesting that by permeating the reader with female responses this ethos also extends to the reader, so that not only the hero, but also 'the reader is feminized, as it were, by the process of

---

[149] Draesner, *Wege*, p. 330, points out that from what we already know of Wolfram's work, Liddamus's refusal to be a Segramors speaks in his favour.
[150] *Nibelungenlied* 2249, 2250; Draesner, *Wege*, pp. 325, 327, fn. 73.
[151] Draesner, *Wege*, pp. 325, 330. [152] *Ibid.*, p. 331.
[153] Mohr, 'Kyot', p. 160 ('heroischer oder ritterlicher Draufgänger' as opposed to 'Held in Friedenszeiten').
[154] Draesner, *Wege*, p. 327. [155] Mann, *Feminizing*, p. 129.

reading'.[156] If we apply this suggestion to the works which concern us two qualifications are called for. The first is that 'reader' must be understood in the two senses of reading distinguished by Hugh of Saint-Victor: reading for oneself, but also indirectly by hearing someone else read to listeners, so that a wide range of recipients could be covered by the term.[157] Secondly, two uses of the word 'feminised' need to be distinguished. It obviously cannot be used literally of women readers, but only in the applied sense of addressing their concerns or interests, so that what is feminised in their case is the literature composed with them in mind and with the intention of appealing to them. In the case of men, however, 'feminised' can be meant literally, inviting them to consider things also from a woman's point of view without detriment to their specifically male qualities so that, as both Gawan and Troilus demonstrate, feminisation cannot be belittled by an equation with effeminacy.

[156] *Ibid.*, p. 33. See Mann, *Apologies*, p. 27.   [157] Green, *Women*, p. 6.

PART II

Marriage and love

Introduction

In the two chapters of Part I we considered the different ways in which women were regarded in the Middle Ages in ecclesiastical and lay circles and feminisation in religious life and literature. If turning now to women in the context of love and marriage seems to exclude any public role and confine them to a restricted, even domestic function, my answer must be that this does no more than reflect their position in the Middle Ages. Women were frequently defined only as functions of men and in terms of their relationship (or non-relationship) with men: as virgins, married women, widows or prostitutes. To look at them in terms of love and marriage is one facet, albeit an important one, of the medieval conception of women's roles.

Marriage was a way of life theoretically for laypeople alone, so that in the following chapters we shall be concerned with literature in the vernacular (in the form of the romance) intended for the laity. Before this, however, we must recall that love and marriage were also a concern of the Church, either devotionally (love between man and God) or regarding the institution of marriage, where throughout the twelfth century the Church sought to impose its views on laypeople. Some of the attitudes illustrated in romance literature can therefore be paralleled, if under very different auspices, in clerical literature, whether in Latin (for clerical use) or in the vernacular (when addressing laypeople).

In this respect we may agree with Brooke, who in his history of medieval marriage includes literary evidence in his remit as a historian on the grounds that we cannot afford to ignore any evidence at all, especially that touching on the inwardness of marriage. He readily concedes that literature 'opens our eyes to a world which would be unimaginable if we read only the theologians' (celibate males without experience of marriage). But this observation loses none of its validity if, like Brooke, we turn it round, for if we never read the theologians (or the canonists) we would not be fully able to understand the imaginative literature of their

63

day.[1] With this in mind, we must now briefly consider some examples from clerical literature from around the time when our romances are dated. Unlike the discussion of clerical views on women in the Middle Ages in Chapter 1, what follows is geared to the twelfth century in particular and is expressly concerned with the theme of marriage (and women's position in it). The clerical views now to be considered show women in a very different light from those discussed earlier. With this Introduction to Part II we therefore approach more closely the problems that are treated in our chosen romances. The features of love within marriage which will engage us are suggestions that marriage was concluded for reasons of love (as opposed to the utilitarian family interests of an arranged marriage), that the partners freely chose each other (and were not subject to parental or other pressure) and that there was a mutual bond of affection and erotic attraction between them. Although Gislebert of Mons mentions the fervent love of Baldwin of Hainaut for his wife alone (and for no other woman), he adds that this was very rare amongst men.[2] Rare it may have been, but it could be found and vernacular literature was not alone in propagating the idea even in the face of feudal marriage policies.

We turn first to the evidence provided by canon law, hardly a branch of intellectual endeavour which one would readily associate with love, romantic or otherwise. As a long-term result of the Gregorian reform Gratian and the twelfth-century decretists debated and codified an ecclesiastical conception of marriage which, as an ideal model, contrasted in many respects with feudal marriage practice and hence met with opposition from laymen. In several respects the canonists' proposals potentially benefited the position of women, although this was more the result than the intention of the lawyers, whom we should not necessarily regard as concerned with female emancipation. The views they put forward struggle to assert themselves in the twelfth century, with some, but only partial success. We start with the canonists' thesis of the indissolubility of a legally contracted marriage, obviously of advantage to women by making it difficult for them to be divorced or cast aside, with little redress, if the husband later found a more attractive or politically profitable opportunity elsewhere. However, in also insisting on exogamy (as opposed to endogamy which allowed feudal families to concentrate their possessions) the Church unwittingly provided feudal families with a weapon which they did not fail to use, for the law of

---

[1] Brooke, *Idea*, pp. 176, 201f.
[2] Gislebert, *Chronicon Hanoniense*, pp. 191f.; Baldwin, *Life*, p. 32.

consanguinity could be 'imaginatively' used to discover a forbidden degree of kinship in a marriage which could now be dissolved.[3] With the need for *consensus* or the free choice of partner in marriage we take up what was earlier referred to as a decisive feature in the Church's teaching on marriage in the twelfth century.[4] It was also of benefit to women as a defence against being married off, without taking personal inclination into account, in order to benefit family or dynastic interests. In theory, this requirement meant that the use of force or pressure to win assent might invalidate a marriage and, if carried out thoroughly, *consensus* would have limited the degree of patriarchy exercised by a family. In the face of this threat feudal families devised indirect ways of compulsion to bring about an arranged marriage, such as the prospect of disinheritance of a daughter who refused to fall into line.[5] Nor was it difficult to convince the Church of the advantages of such a marriage if it was presented as a means of sealing peace between two warring families, just as there are cases where powerful families could intimidate the Church into compliance. An example of this is found with Christina of Markyate for, although her parents admit that they have forced her into marriage against her will, the prior Fredebertus nonetheless urges her to accept the situation.[6] A similar position is reflected in literature in Hartmann's *Erec*, where the compulsion, even violence, used by Oringles to force Enite into marriage with him against her manifest opposition (6346–50) meets with no protest from the assembled bishops, abbots and priests mentioned in the same context. Whereas Chrétien mentions only the count's chaplain (4762), Hartmann piles on the number of ecclesiastical dignitaries to underline the enormity of their omission.

Although Gratian acknowledged the reality of his day in seeing that woman was powerless and subject to the control of the husband ('Nulla est mulieris potestas, sed in omnibus uiri dominio subsit' Woman has no power, but let her be subject to the authority of her husband in all things), he made an exception of the sex life of a married couple, 'an island of comparative privacy where equal rights prevailed, within a larger society where women's rights were severely curtailed'.[7] This equality of responsibilities and rights meant that both parties (not just the woman) were to refrain from extramarital affairs and that the wife was as entitled as the husband to claim the marital *debitum*. That may indeed have been a move towards equality between the sexes by Gratian, but in other respects

---

[3] Brundage, *Law*, pp. 193f.; d'Avray, *Marriage*, pp. 91–8.   [4] See above, pp. 27f.
[5] Brundage, *Law*, pp. 265, 275f.   [6] Head, 'Marriages', pp. 122f.
[7] Brundage, *Law*, p. 255 and fn. 158.

he regarded the woman as subordinate to the man, and twelfth-century decretists at large were ambivalent about equality in a couple's sex life, imposing the conventional restraints on women, but allowing latitude to men. Although in theory the consequences of adultery were the same for men as for women, things were different in practice.[8] A further respect in which reality did not always conform to canonists' principles lies in their extension of the concept of marriage to include the emotional bond of marital affection.[9] They may have agreed with some of the considerations important in feudal practice (marriage as a legal contract, a union for producing heirs, transmitting property and establishing alliances between families), but in addition they saw in marriage an essentially personal relationship. Stressing this emotional, not necessarily sexual bond had the further advantage of explaining the nature of Mary's chaste marriage with Joseph, as against those who maintained the coital theory, who had difficulties in saying how these two could have been truly married. That even this advantage failed to settle the issue is clear, however, from the conflict between the schools of Bologna and Paris on whether *coitus* was essential to the creation of marriage.

In practice, as my qualifications have been meant to show, in each case the rights of women were restricted and conditional (the canonists were aware of the continuing bias in favour of men),[10] but at least possibilities radically different from what was found in feudal marriage practice are aired in theoretical argument, if not carried out in reality. It is important to stress that these possibilities (including freedom of choice of partner, the questioning of parental control in deciding on marriage, mutual affection as a conjugal bond) were actively discussed by canonists in the twelfth century (and also, as we shall see, by authors of vernacular literature), in other words long before what, in ignorance of medieval developments, has been argued as their emergence only in the early modern period.[11]

Canon law did not develop in the abstract, without contact with the Church whose theological doctrines it codified. Three of these theological thinkers must now be mentioned briefly for their attitudes to the questions that concern us: the function of love and marriage in religious thought and any similarity to what finds expression in vernacular literature. In his differentiation between *timor* and *amor* as religious experiences Bernard of Clairvaux regards the former as hierarchical and asymmetrical, whereas the latter, especially in the soul's bridal relationship with God, is reciprocal and

---

[8] *Ibid.*, pp. 198, 242 and fn. 58, 284, 306f.   [9] *Ibid.*, pp. 273f., 323.   [10] *Ibid.*, p. 484.
[11] *Ibid.*, p. 586, on Stone, *Family*. See the similar criticism of Ketsch, *Frauen*, by Schnell, *Frauendiskurs*, pp. 168–70.

symmetrical ('Nam cum amat Deus, non aliud vult, quam amari' For when God loves he wishes no more than to be loved).[12] The essential reciprocity of such mutual love (loving in order to be loved in return) grants it a special importance, since it is the only emotion in which man, in his relationship with God, can repay like with like. We move from reciprocity in *amor* to another feature of the bridal relationship in what Rupert von Deutz has to say of Mary as the bride not merely of Christ, but also of God the Father. In the former function she is *sponsa et mater* (wife and mother), but in the latter she is described as *vera sponsa principaliter amici aeterni* (above all, true wife of the eternal lover).[13] The conjunction of two terms (Mary as wife, *sponsa*, and God as her lover, *amicus*) brings together two concepts, marriage and love, which were more frequently kept apart and even seen as contradictory, and this conjunction, effected here in a religious context, will concern us shortly in secular literature when we consider a similar linkage as a central problem of *Erec*, the first Arthurian romance.

The views of a third theologian, Hugh of Saint-Victor, on love and marriage have come to the fore over the past decades on a number of occasions as presenting a parallel to what is illustrated in court literature, the possibility of diverging from contemporary practice by showing marriage to be an emotional bond of reciprocity and equal companionship.[14] He describes marriage as a mutual love of souls ('dilectio mutua animorum'), based on a reciprocal compact ('ad invicem' and 'foedere sponsionis mutuae'), but passing beyond a mere compact by including love and companionship ('societatis ... vinculo').[15] The essence of marriage for Hugh is love by which man and woman are joined together in their souls ('dilectio, qua masculus et femina in sanctitate conjugii animis uniuntur'),[16] but his stress on love and companionship no doubt derives from his developing his argument in two works, in one of which (*De B. Mariae virginitate*) he encountered the same problem and found the same answer as the canonists when dealing with the marriage of Mary and Joseph. He therefore states unequivocally that marriage is made by *consensus*, not by consummation ('matrimonium non facit coitus, sed consensus').[17] To the extent that reciprocity involves a degree of equality between the partners Hugh differs (without naming him) from Paul's doctrine of the man's

---

[12] Langer, *Mystik*, pp. 202, 247.   [13] *De glorificatione*, PL 169, 155; Ohly, *Hohelied-Studien*, p. 128.
[14] Bumke, *Willehalm*, pp. 177f.; Schumacher, *Auffassung*, pp. 211–17; Pérennec, 'Fautes', pp. 87, 100f., n. 38; McCash, 'Love', pp. 429–38; Quast, *ZfdA* 122 (1993), 162–80.
[15] *De sacramentis*, PL 176, 482, 485. I render *societas* by 'companionship', rather than literally as 'society' (McCash, 'Love', p. 430).
[16] *PL* 176, 482.   [17] *PL* 176, 858.

supremacy in marriage. He does this by demonstrating that Eve was given to Adam neither as a servant nor as a mistress, but as a companion ('Quia enim socia data est, non ancilla, aut domina'). His argument follows the Genesis account of Eve's creation from Adam's rib. If she had been made from his head she would have been created for domination, if from his feet for subjection, but in being made from the middle she was meant for the equality of companionship ('ad aequalitatem societatis facta').[18] Hugh thereby develops a theological argument for equality between man and woman in marriage which goes beyond Gratian's acceptance of equal rights only in the sex life of a couple.

Bumke brought forward the views of Hugh (together with those of Abelard and Albertus Magnus) when dealing with Wolfram's presentation of marital love in *Willehalm*, and Hugh is also discussed at greater length by Schumacher, above all with regard to *Parzival*. Both compare Hugh's theological views on marriage with what is found in these two vernacular works, even though they differ (Bumke sees Wolfram more in a line from Abelard to Albertus Magnus, whereas Schumacher stresses more what separates Wolfram from these theologians, above all his inclusion of sexual love alongside emotional attachment in his picture of marriage). What interests us at the moment, however, is not the extent to which Hugh may or may not be compared with Wolfram, but rather the fact that the very possibility of a comparison arose from Hugh's inclusion of a bond of affection and companionship in marriage, contracted not merely as a mutual legal obligation, for the procreation of offspring or as a salutary *remedium fornicationis*. The fact that Hugh has also been adduced in connection with the marriage problem discussed in *Erec*[19] suggests further that this thinker sketched a view of marriage which, no doubt incompletely because of his theological approach, nonetheless was of interest to authors of secular literature engaged in the problem of reconciling love and marriage.

Further discussion of this problem, significant because it bridges the gap between the Latin of canonists or theologians and the vernacular of laypeople, is conducted in devotional literature, frequently addressed to laywomen and dated both before and after the romances to be discussed. This literature conveys a picture of spiritual marriage (between a woman, whether a nun or not, and God or Christ) as an ideal model, contrasting it with its adverse picture of secular marriage and putting forward a counter-model against which the bleak realities of many feudal marriages could be seen as deficient. It is no argument against the attractions of a spiritual

[18] *PL* 176, 485.   [19] See fn. 14 (Pérennec, McCash, Quast).

marriage to say that in heeding the call of her heavenly bridegroom to abandon earthly marriage the woman shows herself to be as obedient and submissive to him as to any husband in the world, for against this has to be set the really troubling fact for feudal families, namely the recurrence of the theme of the woman's disobedience to their marriage plans for her. This disobedience to family within obedience to the woman's heavenly bridegroom is well illustrated, for example, in the adventurous escape of Christina of Markyate from enforced marriage in Huntingdon in order to remain true to her marital vow to Christ and is not to be dismissed as no more than a hagiographic topos (it may be that, but it is also more than that).[20] Also from England (soon after 1200) comes the testimony of *Hali Meiðhad*, addressed to women recluses. It argues likewise from the contrast between the freedom of spiritual marriage (the woman has chosen Christ as a lover of her own accord) and servitude to a man in earthly marriage (4, 11–35). In *Seinte Margarete*, belonging to the same group of works, a similar contrast is invoked between the woman's free choice (46, 8–10) and the tyrannical opposition of both father and would-be husband (56, 26–8; 46, 24f.). In Germany the *Speculum virginum* works with a similar opposition between the slavery (*servitus*) of earthly marriage and the freedom (*libertas*) of a virginal life and draws the same conclusion (*Melior est plane libertas expedita quam servitus in coniugio velis nolis necessaria* Clearly, unhampered freedom is preferable to imposed slavery in marriage).[21]

Christina's fortunate ability to remain true to her earlier vow means that she reserved for herself a sphere of action against her parents' wishes and retained freedom of choice as to her marriage partner. This is an advantage of spiritual over secular marriage which clerical propagators of the virginity ideal were not slow to point out, as already with Ambrose in *De virginibus*, promising the woman freedom ('sola virginitas libertatem dare') and hence a privileged position ('feminei principatus') not otherwise available.[22] A similar argument is used in Priester Wernher's *Maria*, in which Mary, just as emphatically but just as unsuccessfully as Christina of Markyate, announces her intention to remain unmarried.[23] She sees this as an affirmation of freedom against subjection to an earthly husband (D 1486: 'daz si gerne friliche/lebet ane mannes gebende' that she might gladly live freely without subjection to a husband) and an act of personal choice of heavenly husband exercised by herself (1489: 'got einen haete sie erwelt' she had chosen God alone). That in itself echoes Ambrose and Christina, but

---

[20] See Head, 'Marriages', pp. 116–37, as against Fanous, 'Christina', pp. 53–78.
[21] Bernards, *Speculum*, p. 49 and fn. 141ᵃ.   [22] Keller, *Secret*, pp. 85f.   [23] *Ibid.*, pp. 81f.

Wernher goes much further, for with him Mary sums up the nature of her spiritual marriage by seeing herself as both the handmaiden and the bride of the Lord, and God as her Lord and her lover (D 1491: 'daz sie waere sin div v̄ sin brv̂t / er bediv ir herre v̄ ir trût'). With these revealing lines we find a parallel to what Rupert von Deutz had said of Mary, but more explicit in the reciprocity with which both partners in this heavenly marriage play a double role. Wernher uses *herre* (1492) in a double function, meaning not only 'Lord' in the religious sense (Mary as the handmaiden of the Lord, *ancilla Domini*), but also 'husband' (for she is his bride, *brût*). Even more pointedly than with Rupert this double role of each partner in a marriage informed by love anticipates what we shall find in *Erec* with Enite's view of the nature of her marriage (she regards Erec as both husband and lover, 6172f.). This suggests that what Chrétien and Hartmann were to advocate in their secular romances was already 'in the air', at least in religious circles interested in the features of spiritual marriage. In all this the importance of the Song of Songs is unmistakable (bridal symbolism applicable in the twelfth century to the individual soul as well as to Mary). It provides a model for an intense love relationship within the terms of marriage, and the active role of the bride in the Song grants the woman far more room for action than was possible in contemporary society.[24]

A further parallel between religious literature and romances about 1200 has been suggested by Bériou and d'Avray.[25] On the basis of some French sermons of the thirteenth century they discuss the image of the ideal husband, as presented in Christ in such a way that in the range of positive qualities attributed to Christ is meant to surpass any husband of this world. They show that these qualities correspond to those of an ideal husband sketched by Chrétien in some of his works (*Erec, Cligés, Yvain*). Christ therefore possesses all the qualities of a potential husband which in secular imaginative literature are attractive to a woman. D'Avray rightly avoids assuming that a preacher may have been influenced by Chrétien, suggesting instead that both probably reflect current social assumptions.[26] Religious and secular literature both draw on the same body of ideas circulating at the time. What is also interesting about this suggestion is the contrast it presents with works like *Hali Meiðhad, Seinte Margarete* and the *Speculum virginum*. In these works spiritual marriage is compared favourably with the entirely negative picture of earthly marriage, but in the sermons marriage to Christ

---

[24] Keller devotes her last chapter, pp. 231–62, to this in the emphatic form of what she calls 'the aggressive female lover' in devotional literature and images.
[25] Bériou and d'Avray, 'Image', pp. 31–69.   [26] D'Avray, *Marriage*, p. 63.

shares positive qualities with what is found in Chrétien's works. Both spiritual and imaginative literature project a view of the ideal husband, seen from the woman's position, which is conceived as a counter-model to the predominant reality of the day.

This devotional literature works with two models of marriage and husband, one spiritual and the other secular, set side-by-side and contrasted with each other. Of course, all the dice are loaded in favour of the spiritual model, but in doing this the authors, like the canonists and theologians, had no choice but to outline a picture of marriage incorporating qualities lacking in contemporary practice. Feminists may well stress negative aspects of this religious counter-model (the abandonment of the world it preached, the escapist nature of its solution), but for us it is more important to stress the positive features it incorporated: a conception of marriage based on the free choice of both partners and informed by affection and comradeship on both sides. The juxtaposition of these two models, one reflecting contemporary practice (however distorted for propaganda purposes) and the other undeniably utopian, opened the doors to a more intense debate on the nature of marriage, to be taken up for the benefit of laypeople in court literature. In considering this literature we shall have to see whether it, too, operates with a similar juxtaposition of two models, one passing implicit judgment on the other, and whether it also advocates the possibility of finding love within marriage, especially in the form of reciprocity and freedom of choice. Implicit in these questions, of course, is the view of women they suggest, the extent to which the antifeminism latent in secular and ecclesiastical society was continued, called into question or occasionally overcome.

Before we consider these vernacular romances in detail, however, it will pay to look at a Latin work of the eleventh century which has been described as incorporating a range of different attitudes towards love and marriage.[27] By that fact, by its early dating and its Latin form (suggesting clerical author and recipients) the epic *Ruodlieb* illustrates that these two themes were up for discussion a century before Chrétien extended it to embrace the vernacular. In what follows we shall be concerned with one episode alone, but a remarkably informative one, the marriage concluded by the protagonist's unnamed nephew (XIV 1–99).[28] However, we are not to expect a realistic depiction of the formalities of a contemporary wedding, for the author, making use of the unconventional views he attributes to the

[27] Cartlidge, *Marriage*, p. 33.
[28] See Braun, *Studien*, pp. 84f.; Gellinek, *SG* 12 (1967), 562–70; Dronke, *Individuality*, pp. 57–60; Knapp, *Ruodlieb*, pp. 211f.; Cartlidge, *Marriage*, pp. 33–8.

independent-minded bride, uses the occasion to propose ethical commitments for both partners, meant as a critical argument with the practices of his day. The author also diverges from any simple reflection of reality by juxtaposing in his account, for reasons of contrast and questioning, elements from two distinct forms of wedding practice used in the Middle Ages: the so-called *Muntehe* or ward-marriage (arranged between a man, usually the bride's father, who held legal authority over her and on her behalf, and the husband-to-be, to whom that authority was transferred) and the *Friedelehe* or marriage by mutual, freely given consent. The latter was a form of legitimate marriage in force before the canonists developed their doctrine of *consensus* and was adaptable to their ends, whilst the former corresponds more closely to what we have elsewhere referred to as feudal marriage practice with its man-to-man (or family-to-family) negotiation and patriarchal bypassing of the woman's wishes.

The most sustained exposition of a patriarchal attitude to marriage occurs not in the nephew's wedding episode, but in words attributed earlier to the figure of the Rex Maior (V 484–94). Here a number of the major concerns governing feudal marriages find expression: the wife is to be of aristocratic birth (484), the aim of marriage is the procreation of children (485), it should be concluded only on the advice of the man's mother (487), the man is to remain the master (489: 'illi tamen esto magister') and the woman is expected to agree with him in all things (493: 'in cunctis bene concordet tibi rebus'), for there is nothing worse than when the man, who should rule, is himself made subordinate (492: 'si subiecti sint, quis debent dominari'). To this frank statement of a man's view of marriage must be added Dronke's pertinent comment that the marriage that conforms to it ends in a fiasco, whilst the nephew's marriage flouts almost every one of these precepts and ends in happiness.[29] But that is not to say that the nephew is not (initially) tarred with the patriarchal brush, for he makes a short-lived attempt to exercise authority over his bride, even threatening her (with no corresponding obligation on himself) with death in case of her infidelity (67: 'sic tibi stringo fidem firmam vel perpetualem, / Hanc servare mihi debes aut decapitari' In this way I bind you to a firm, lasting faithfulness, which you must keep or be decapitated).[30] In accordance with such an approach to marriage it is no surprise that the nephew's mother gives her approval (XIV 59) in conformity with the Rex Maior's words and that it meets with express approval that both parties are of equal rank and wealth (XIV 60f.).

---

[29] Dronke, *Individuality*, p. 60.
[30] On the legal implications of this detail see Meyer, *ZfRG (GA)* 52 (1932), 276–93.

Into this picture of 'marriage as a guarantee of social, economic and dynastic cohesion'[31] (but also of male authority over the wife) the author has inserted clear pointers to marriage as something much more, as an emotional bond between two individuals. We are left in no doubt that the couple's joint wish for marriage (25: 'Lege maritali cupientes consociari') arises from their love for each other (24: 'Mutuo diligerent sese'), a fact expressly repeated just before the couple, each separately, affirm their willingness to marry (48: 'Hic quod et haec ferveret in alterutrius amorem' that he and she were glowing in love for each other). Although a gap of two lines in the manuscript fragment now follows, enough remains to show that the bride responds positively (and humorously) to the question whether she gives her *consensus* (50: 'Illum si vellet, rogitant' They ask whether she accepts him), whilst the one word ('Illam' her) surviving from the beginning of the preceding line suggests that the corresponding question was also asked of the nephew. Both parties are therefore shown to be in love, both wish to continue this love within marriage, and both express their willingness to conclude the marriage. This leaves the nephew's patriarchal gesture out of account in claiming the right, soon to be abandoned, to punish any infidelity on his wife's part, to exercise extreme authority over her in this way. The first suggestion of the bride's sense of independence comes in the humorous tone of her answer to the question about *consensus*, for she makes what for the bystanders must be the outrageous suggestion that, since she has defeated the nephew in a game of dice, she may insist on the terms of their agreement and that, contrary to his authoritarian gesture, it is up to him to serve her steadfastly day and night (55: 'Serviat obnixe, volo, quo mihi nocte dieque'). The idea of the woman making a stipulation (*volo* it is my wish) and the demand that he, contrary to patriarchal practice, serve her are what is outrageous about her answer, but she tones this down by implying that it is meant humorously. She smiles a little when saying this (51: 'parum quoque ridet') and her remark is received in the same spirit, for the bystanders laugh, too (57).

Humour is the bride's best defence against what is for her the one-sided gesture of the man's claim to punish her for any infidelity, for again she smiles as she concludes her counter-claim (85). She shows herself fully aware of the fact that the nephew has been sowing his wild oats (his kinsmen rejoice that marriage will rescue him from the clutches of a prostitute, 28f.) and is therefore justified in demanding equal justice for both parties (70: 'Iudicium parile decet ut patiatur uterque'). She asks rhetorically why

---

[31] Cartlidge, *Marriage*, p. 36.

she should be expected to show him any more fidelity than he her (71f.) and whether Adam was allowed two Eves (72–6). To this claim for equal rights within marriage, opposed to his initial assumption that only he had a right, the nephew gives way, acknowledging humorously that if he were to go against this agreement she should be entitled to inflict on him the punishment with which he had threatened her (84: 'Istius capitis abscidendique potens sis' let it be in your power to cut off my head). The infectious laughter that pervades this scene is meant to sugar the pill of what is being proposed here: that in a marriage concluded for reasons of reciprocal love and with the *consensus* of both parties there is no room for unequal rights. We can be confident that the humour is not meant to weaken or detract from the seriousness with which this is proposed, for at the beginning of the bride's counter-claim the narrator allies himself with what she is about to say by commenting that her words are both clever and fitting (69: 'Quae satis astute iuveni respondit et apte'). Fiction this may be, but the counter-model with which it confronts feudal marriage (as did the arguments of canonists and theologians) is a disturbing one for a patriarchal society, even more so when it is treated at greater length in the vernacular romances for lay consumption.

To conclude this introduction some words are called for on the way in which the argument of the following chapters is conducted. To consider love and marriage in selected works of court literature involves looking at how women are regarded in them. Are they afforded any measure of equal treatment, as Gratian called for (within limits) and as is suggested more radically in *Ruodlieb*? Are they granted freedom of choice of their marriage-partner, as the canonists and the authors of devotional virginity literature recommend? Even to pose such questions means confronting head on the antifeminine prejudices of feudal marriage policy and much clerical tradition, so that these questions cannot be separated from the wider problem of medieval misogyny.

In a monograph devoted to this problem Bloch proposes a definition of misogyny ('a speech act in which woman is the subject of the sentence and the predicate a more general term'), but to this he adds what is for him an important rider, namely that the predication can be negative or positive, deprecatory or laudatory.[32] This definition is unsatisfactory in that it goes both too far and not far enough. It goes too far by sweeping into its net statements of both kinds, negative and positive. We shall see that Hartmann and Gottfried, for example, employ positive generalisations, such as Bloch

---

[32] Bloch, *Misogyny*, p. 5.

has in mind, about men without any suggestion that they imply misandry, so that we are given no reason why, when applied to women, they should now acquire a negative, misogynous function. As it stands, Bloch's definition leaves little room for nuance and is of little use in analysing specific situations.[33] He seeks to rectify the position by appealing to a 'historic real imbalance of possessory power' between the sexes, without devoting attention to historical (as distinct from literary) factors. We do better to follow Baldwin's restrictive variation on Bloch by seeing misogyny expressed in a generalisation about women 'with the effect of devaluing them, comparing them unfavorably or subordinating them to men'.[34]

Conversely, however, Bloch's definition does not go far enough when he restricts misogyny (as distinct from its expression) to a speech act (and Baldwin is similarly restrictive in this detail).[35] Misogyny pervades not merely the literature, but also the male-dominated society of the Middle Ages, secular and ecclesiastic, leading to a widespread marginalisation of women in social and educational life, but especially in the institution of marriage with the revealing slippage, especially in clerical circles, between misogamy and misogyny. Accordingly, although negative generalisations about women will occupy a central role, they must be extended and qualified on two flanks, so that the argument in each of the following chapters falls into three parts. First, we consider indications of misogyny, the inferior situation or treatment of women, that are not confined to speech acts. Next, we turn to negative generalisations about women in speech (and observe how in many cases their validity can be called into question by the author). Lastly, we consider indications, in speech acts or not, that are explicitly directed against misogyny and thereby amount to a defence of women against this prejudice.

Since negative generalisations about women (portraying one particular situation not as an individual case, but universalising it and seeing it as typical of the whole sex) play a central, but not exclusive, part in what follows, we must ask what constitutes them and how we are to recognise them. One way of linking the particular with the general is to pass automatically from singular to plural, as when Abelard seeks to patch things up with Heloise's guardian by seeing her as representative of what men know to be true of women at large, casting into ruin even the most eminent men since the beginning of the human race (*Historia* 185, 12: 'quanta ruina summos quoque viros ab ipso statim humani generis exordio mulieres deiecerint').[36]

---

[33] Watson, *Exemplaria* 8 (1996), 30.   [34] Baldwin, *Life*, p. 123.
[35] *Ibid.* ('misogyny is used here restrictively to denote any speech act ...').
[36] Muckle, *MSt* 12 (1950), 185.

Since the individual Heloise has to be pluralised (*mulieres*), this universal-isation also embraces men other than Abelard (*viros*), even more so when this is held to be true of the whole human race since the beginning. This generalising of the particular, always in what is presented as a blameworthy situation, can also take the form of saying that this (the particular case) is what *all* women do or, conversely, what *no* women do, what women *always* do or *never* do. For other examples of this linguistic usage I can confine myself to Book III of the *De amore* of Andreas Capellanus, a treasure trove of antifeminine topoi. For him every woman ('mulier omnis') envies other women or is a liar ('non est femina vivens, quae … non' there is not a woman alive who … not), just as no woman is constant in affection ('nulla posset femina reperiri' no woman can be found, 'nulla reperitur femina' no woman is found).[37] Such blanket statements obviously involve the time-dimension: women never ('nunquam') give another a chance to speak, but always ('semper') seek to dominate the conversation.[38] The same effect is achieved when it is categorically added that there is no exception to what is stated as a general rule ('omni exceptione carere', 'sine omni exceptione', 'pro generali regula', 'generaliter').[39] Alternatively, the word 'woman' can be used in the singular, but meant collectively, as when Andreas maintains that a woman ('mulier') can be goaded by pride, but sees her in apposition to the whole of her sex ('muliebrem … sexum').[40] Best illustrated from modern linguistic usage is the use of a singular noun with the indefinite article in a generalising, collective sense, as when a man, feeling exasperated, exclaims 'That is just like a woman' or 'That is just what a woman would do'. In such cases the indefinite article performs a double function. On the one hand it particularises and points to one specific instance. But if that were all, the more likely phrasing would be 'That is just like you' or 'That is just what you would do'. The second function is to pass beyond this and generalise, going as far as any woman or every woman. These examples of the word for 'woman' in the singular illustrate the linkage of the particular with the general which is central to these antifeminine generalisations, but even when Andreas frequently employs the noun in the plural his sweeping observa-tions are meant to include every singular case, 'without any exception'.

So sweeping are these criticisms of women's behaviour and nature (and not merely with Andreas) that they run the whole gamut of human vices and failings (including the less likely ones of drunkenness and gluttony), even though some recur with noticeable frequency as perhaps particularly true of their sex. I confine myself here to a few cases which play a marked

---

[37] Trojel, pp. 340, 351, 339.   [38] *Ibid.*, p. 352.   [39] *Ibid.*, pp. 342, 348, 345.   [40] *Ibid.*, p. 349.

part in the romances we have to consider. Especially popular is the topos of woman's fickleness (already with Virgil: 'varium et mutabile semper femina', applicable to Dido, we are meant to believe, but more truly to Aeneas, who abandons her).[41] Andreas, of course, does not allow this point to escape him: no woman is so bound by affection and constancy ('tanta ... affectione ... vel tanta constantia') that she remains true to her love if tempted, and one of his statements of a general rule concerns precisely this ('Inconstans etiam mulier regulariter invenitur' it is a rule that woman is found to be inconstant).[42] Talkativeness or garrulity of women is another obvious target through the misogynous ages and also with Andreas: they are all free with their tongue ('Est et omnis femina virlingosa') and their tongue or breath never tires ('nec unquam posset sua lingua vel spiritus fatigari loquendo').[43] Andreas also sees women as true to their mother Eve in their inherent disobedience and rebelliousness against prohibitions ('inobediens et contra interdicta renitens'), all of them tainted by this vice ('Inobedientiae quoque vitio mulier quaelibet inquinatur') and struggling against what has been forbidden ('contra interdicta venire').[44] Another antifeminine topos which finds an echo with Andreas is woman's lustfulness ('Luxuriosa est etiam omnis femina mundi' Every woman in the world is lustful), so great that she is unable to resist the approach of any potential lover. As if the emphatic generalisations employed by Andreas ('omnis femina mundi' every woman in the world, 'nulla in hoc saeculo' no woman in this world) were not enough, he goes further in putting this forward as one of his general rules that do not mislead in the case of any woman ('Et haec quidem regula pro nulla reperitur femina fallax').[45]

The very frequency and emphasis with which Andreas, and others who argue similarly, claim the universality of their criticisms of women, admitting no exceptions whatsoever, suggest the possibility of a nagging doubt, not necessarily about their conviction that what they say is true, but about whether others may be persuaded of this truth. Such doubts, if they indeed held them, were justified, since there is a body of evidence calling into question the legitimacy of these negative generalisations about women and asking whether it is justifiable to proceed quite so easily from the particular to the general.

An early example comes from Ovid's *Ars amatoria*, well known in the Middle Ages. Despite his notorious antifeminism the Latin poet mounts at the start of Book III what is in reality a mock defence of women, opening

---

[41] *Aeneid* IV 569f.   [42] Trojel, pp. 339, 345.   [43] *Ibid.*, p. 352.
[44] *Ibid.*, pp. 340f., 348.   [45] *Ibid.*, pp. 353f.

with an explicit warning against generalising from the particular when criticising a woman. He recommends us not to pin the bad reputation of one or two on all women, but to judge each one by her own proper merits (III 9: 'Parcite paucarum diffundere crimen in omnes; / spectetur meritis quaeque puella suis'). Ovid tactically concedes some cases of evil women, but passes over quickly to exemplary ones and then inverts misogyny by adducing cases where it was men who were at fault (Jason abandoning Medea, Theseus betraying Ariadne).[46] Whether this defence was meant seriously or not, the misogynous Ovid is aware of the force of this argument, as are numerous medieval authors. Schnell has argued convincingly that scholarship on medieval views of women has wrongly presented them as uniformly misogynous because it was based on too narrow a range of evidence.[47] In taking other discourses into account Schnell differentiates the picture. One type of discourse where differentiations were made was the vernacular sermon addressed to laypeople, as an example of which (out of many) Schnell quotes the careful distinction made in this respect by the fifteenth-century preacher Geiler von Kaysersberg. He claims that what he has to say applies only to wicked and angry women, not to all women and certainly not to pious and honest ones ('... das wir hie nicht von allen Weibern reden oder lehren, dann es gehet solches die frommen vnnd ehrlichen nicht an, sonder wir sagen allein von bösen vnd zornigen Weibern').[48] We move closer in more than the chronological sense to the romances around 1200 with the thirteenth-century *Livres d'amours* of Drouart la Vache, who makes a comparable distinction (7533: 'Après ce que j'ai dit des dames / Vous devez des mauvaises fames / Entendre, qui sont diffamees; / Les autres, qui sont honorees / Bonnes dames et glorieuses ...' What I have said about ladies you are to understand concerning wicked women of ill repute; others who are respected, good ladies and renowned ...).[49] What is significant about this passage is that it comes from a vernacular translation of the *De amore* of Andreas, whose unqualified negative generalisations in Latin are here pointedly undone.

So far does the need to make distinctions rather than to generalise penetrate vernacular discourse on the sexes (which means above all, given the frequency of misogynous statements, discourse on women) that German uses the verb *scheiden* 'to separate, distinguish', above all with Walther von der Vogelweide, almost as a technical term. What is at issue here is the fact that in 'Minnesang' praise of woman is no longer unqualified, but can on occasions

---

[46] III 9f.   [47] See above, p. 7.   [48] Schnell, *Frauendiskurs*, p. 168.
[49] Schnell, *Andreas*, p. 167, fn. 583.

be withheld or even converted into criticism, a change of front that could call forth objections to Walther (58, 31: '... daz ich ir übel gedenke' that I think badly of them), just as it did to Wolfram whose criticism of one woman is taken by other women, operating a negative generalisation for their part, as a criticism of them all (*Parzival* 114, 15: 'mînen zorn gein einem wîbe' my anger with one woman and 19: 'dar um hânt mîn die andern haz' because of that the others hate me). With Walther the position is stated with greater systematic clarity,[50] for he claims to have bestowed unsurpassed praise on (German) women, with the proviso that he makes a distinction between the good and the bad (58, 35: 'wan daz ich scheide / die guoten von den boesen'). To the criticism which this calls forth Walther responds by asking rhetorically how things would look if he were to praise both indiscriminately (58, 37: 'lobt ich si beide / gelîche wol, wie stüende daz?').[51] By questioning positive generalisations as well as negative ones Walther shows that his target is not women, as their sex might think, but rather the undiscriminating practice of failing to make the necessary distinctions. So important is this concept of *scheiden* that it has been termed a new keyword in Walther's conception of 'Minne'.[52]

This concept finds an echo elsewhere. Ulrich von Lichtenstein, for example, in his *Frauenbuch* tackles the question the other way round by emphasising not the need to *scheiden*, but rather, in agreement with Walther's adverb *gelîche* (58, 38), the importance of not equating or identifying (*gelîchen*) where real differences are at stake. With Ulrich a woman defends her sex against the blanket accusation that they are prepared to offer their love and their body for material gain (671–4) by differentiating between the particular case and womankind in general (675: 'von swelchem wîbe man daz giht, / des sult ir uns zîhen niht' of whatever woman that may be said, it should not be attributed to us). In his translation Young adds 'allen' to 'uns', which goes beyond the text, but is in conformity to its meaning.[53] This is confirmed a few lines later when it is stated clearly that it is mistaken to equate all women together when in fact they differ in disposition (686: 'swer uns dan gelîchen wil / alle zesamen, der missetuot. / jâ hab wir alle niht einen muot' It is wrong to equate us all together. We are not all of the same frame of mind). As a matter of principle it is uncourtly behaviour for a man to consider women all alike in this way (699; 'ir sult uns niht gelîche hân, / ob ir waenet sîn ein hövescher man'), a view which the man in the dialogue is ready to accept, but applies it also to his own sex, saying that men too are not to be regarded as all alike (701–10). The core of the argument,

---

[50] Bumke, *Blutstropfen*, p. 119, fn. 22; Scholz, *Walther*, pp. 107–11. [51] Hahn, *Walther*, pp. 60–4. [52] *Ibid.*, p. 60. [53] Young, *Frauenbuch*, p. 91.

with either sex, is the illegitimacy of such blanket judgments critical of the other sex.

With examples from two other literatures we conclude this selection of the ways in which medieval texts, in addition to sweeping criticisms of the whole female sex, also bear testimony to explicit disagreement with this practice. In fourteenth-century France Jean le Fèvre argues at one point in his *Livre de Leesce* that it is unjustified to condemn all women because of the offence of one. He does this after recounting the traditional outrageous story of the widow of Ephesus (1414: 'Se male femme ou mauvais hom / Fait aucun mal particuler / On ne doit pas articuler / Qu'il soit pour tous a consequence' If a wicked woman or an evil man commits any one fault, it should not be maintained that it has a bearing on all.).[54] What is revealing here is not merely the telling contrast of the singular (*particuler*) with the plural (*tous*), but also the fact that men as well as women can be victims of this generalised criticism, so that we are dealing here with an extended, not a specifically antifeminine bias. Somewhat later the same kind of argument is employed by Christine de Pizan in her defence of women. In the *Livre de la Cité des Dames* she disagrees pointblank with those writers (inevitably of the male sex) who condemn the entire female sex for being sinful,[55] and devotes the rest of her book to discussing exceptions to this, so numerous that they easily disprove what Andreas Capellanus had termed the rule. With a more particular target in mind, she also attacks Jean de Meun for similar generalisations in his *Roman de la Rose*, a point which must have struck home, since her opponent in the debate about this work, Pierre Col, felt it tactically necessary to concede this ('Par Dieu! ce n'est pas blasmer tout le sexe femenin' By God, that does not amount to blaming the whole female sex).[56]

Finally, to conclude with an English example opposed to such generalising from the particular, we turn to the ending of Chaucer's *Troilus and Criseyde*. Because his story relates the unfaithfulness of Criseyde Chaucer feels called upon to apologise to women (V 1772–5), presumably on the grounds that, as was also the case with Wolfram's self-defence in *Parzival*, the fault of one woman might be attributed to all women as typical. Like Christine de Pizan, Chaucer then says that he could make this good with tales of exemplary women (Penelope, Alceste),[57] as he later does, with whatever qualifications, in his *Legend of Good Women*. But finally Chaucer inverts the misogyny which women might detect in his tale of a woman's

---

[54] Blumenfeld-Kosinski, *Speculum* 69 (1994), 718.   [55] Christine, *Book*, p. 18.
[56] Blumenfeld-Kosinski, *RR* 81 (1990), 283.   [57] V 1777f.

betrayal by warning them against being betrayed in their turn by men (V 1779: 'Ny sey nat this al oonly for thise men, / But moost for wommen that bitraised be / Thorugh fals folk'). By this inversion Chaucer, like Jean le Fèvre, brings men into his range and extends his criticism beyond anti-feminism to their sex as well.

In considering these generalisations one last step is called for, passing beyond the mere fact that they could be criticised as biased or illogical to some of the ways in which they could be effectively undermined in literary texts. We shall confine ourselves to three examples from French romances, all composed in the years before 1200 and illustrating some of the methods by which this persistent weapon of antifeminism could be rendered harmless.

Our first example illustrates what we have termed an extended negative generalisation, true not merely of women (as misogynists would have it), but also of men. If we may for the moment adopt an admittedly artificial procedure and look at a passage in the *Tristran* of Thomas of Britain in isolation we may read it as a conventional generalisation about women's fickleness and inconstancy. Thomas says of them that it is their custom to abandon what they possess for what takes their fancy, they try to arrive at what they set their hearts on (Sneyd¹ 287: 'Les dames faire le solent, / Laissent ço q'unt pur ço que volent / E asaient cum poent venir / A lur voleir, a lor desir'). That is conventional to the point of being a cliché, but Thomas gives it a novel twist in two ways. He goes beyond this in what follows by including men, for they, equally with women, are too fond of novelty, changeable in their inclinations and desires (292: 'Mais trop par aiment novelerie / Homes et femmes ensemble, / Car trop par changent lor talent / E lor desir et lor voleir'). But he also gives due warning that the generalisation embraces men as well by saying in advance that many a man (281–6: *maint, il*) has a change of heart and above all by the very context that calls forth these remarks, Tristran's inconstancy in abandoning one Ysolt for the other. Any knowing smile by men at women's weakness is wiped away here as much as when Chaucer in a similar context adds 'And so doon men' (*Franklin's Tale* 98).⁵⁸

A second example comes from Chrétien's *Yvain* where another hoary chestnut of the misogynist's repertoire is turned upside down, this time not by saying that it applies to men as well as women, but by showing that in this particular case it is even more true of the man than the woman. The passage concerns the readiness with which Laudine agrees to marry Yvain

⁵⁸ Mann, *Feminizing*, p. 89.

soon after he has killed her husband. Yvain expresses the hope that she may be persuaded with a typical comment on female fickleness (1436: 'Que fame a plus de mil corages. / Celui corage, qu'ele a ore, / Espoir changera ele ancore' For woman has more than a thousand moods. My hope is that she will yet change her present mood). As part of his 'case for women' in the Middle Ages Blamires emphasises the pile up of antifeminine topoi which inform Chrétien's presentation of this episode:[59] not merely this hope of Yvain's, but also the Ovidian misogyny that lurks behind it (funerals are a suitable occasion for looking around for a new husband),[60] the echo of the widow of Ephesus story illustrating the fickleness of widows, the narrator's apparent suggestion that Laudine, like other women, had an irrational streak (1640–4), and especially his clinching comment in conclusion that now Yvain is master, the dead man forgotten and his killer married and lying with his wife (2164: 'Mes ore est mon sire Yvain sire, / Et li morz est tot obliez. / Cil, qui l'ocist, est mariez / An sa fame, et ansanble gisent'). The effect of all this is to cast doubt on Laudine, and with her on her sex, by presenting her inconstancy as typically feminine. However, we do not need to apply what Mertens has argued in the case of Hartmann's *Iwein*[61] to his French model (that, given the precarious situation of an aristocratic widow in feudal society, Laudine was in urgent need of an alternative male protector) to see that *instabilitas*, a typical female failing in misogynists' eyes, more truly applies to Yvain in this work. It is he who is guilty of inconstancy and unreliability in thoughtlessly neglecting the deadline by which he had promised to return to his wife, and it is to his realisation and correction of this shortcoming that the rest of the work is devoted. Blamires describes the work as 'a text which pretends to accept, only to repudiate utterly, traditional gendering of changeability as feminine'.[62]

Our concluding example is provided by Chrétien's *Perceval* and illustrates a misogynous generalisation applied in an angry outburst by Orguelleus de la Lande to the damsel of the tent (Wolfram's Jeschute) whom he suspects of infidelity after discovering that Perceval had been with her in his absence. On learning that she had been kissed, Orguelleus launches into a tirade about what he claims to know about women. For him it is a well-known fact (and Ovid would have borne him out)[63] that even if a woman resists she wishes to win every battle except this one, that even if she puts up resistance she is eager for it, and that a woman who lets herself be kissed is ready to grant the rest (3863: 'Feme qui se bouche abandone / Le sorplus molt de legier done, / S'est

---

[59] Blamires, *Case*, pp. 159–62.   [60] *Ars amatoria* III 431f.   [61] Mertens, *Laudine*.
[62] Blamires, *Case*, p. 162.   [63] *Ars amatoria* I 663–70.

qui a certes i entende. / Et bien soit qu'ele se desfende, / Si set on bien sanz nul redout / Ke feme velt vaintre par tot / Fors qu'en ceste mellee soule … / Si volroit ele estre vencue. / Si se desfent et si li tarde, / Tant est de l'otroier coarde, / Si velt qu'an a force li face' A woman who lets herself be kissed easily grants the rest as long as the man has set his mind on it. There is no doubt about it that a woman wants to win every battle except this one, even if she puts up resistance … She would wish to be overcome. She puts up a fight, but longs for it, she is reluctant to grant it, and wants to be taken by force). But we have witnessed the previous encounter between Perceval and the damsel and are privy to a possibility unknown to Orguelleus and not even considered by him. We know in fact that the naive, inexperienced lad had done no more than clumsily kiss her (and take her ring), that his physical appetite had extended no further than some meat pies he found in the tent, and that in all this she had resisted strongly and genuinely, if in vain (693–763). For us the misogynous outburst of Orguelleus, wrongly accusing his lover and just as wrongly and misogynously seeing this as what is to be expected from any woman, has the ground cut from beneath it at the moment when he voices it.

After these introductory observations it is time to turn to three romance themes in French and German literature composed on either side of the year 1200, considering the ways in which they present their picture of woman, especially with regard to love and marriage. With the first theme, *Erec*, it is relatively straightforward to consider the French version of Chrétien alongside the German adaptation by Hartmann von Aue since only a few short fragments are missing from the latter. The position is not so satisfactory in this regard with the *Tristan* theme because both versions survive in incomplete form: that by Gottfried von Strassburg breaking off, with an overlap, shortly after the surviving fragments of Thomas of Britain begin. Our approach must therefore be to take both versions into account, even though they deal with different sections of the whole narrative, supplementing this, where relevant, by also considering the first German version by Eilhart von Oberg. (The other French version, by Béroul, yields little for our purposes.) The position with the third theme, *Parzival*, is rather better, but is still not perfect, since although the version of Wolfram von Eschenbach is complete, his source, the *Perceval* of Chrétien, was never completed. Any comparative treatment must perforce be partial.

CHAPTER 3

Erec

This work is important as the first Arthurian romance, the start of a new genre in France and Germany, but it is also frequently regarded as an early vernacular work combining love with knighthood, *amor et militia*.[1] This needs to be extended to include a third theme: love, marriage and knighthood. The first two themes bring women explicitly into the picture, but so does the third since, rarely in the romance genre, Enite accompanies Erec on his journey of knightly adventures and plays a crucial role in them. In all three respects a woman occupies an important place in the narrative, justifying a gendered discussion of the work. This discussion pays attention to both the French and German versions and is organised under three headings.[2]

PATRIARCHAL SOCIETY

The impact of patriarchal customs on a woman is revealed early in the French work in the form of feudal marriage practice when Erec gains Enide's hand from her father, a transaction in which she is not consulted and remains silent (684), so that it is less an exercise in courtship and more an exercise of male bargaining.[3] Chrétien makes it clear that Enide is an object of exchange in this: the father is to give Erec armour and his daughter (both are mentioned in the same breath: 659f.) so that he may enter the sparrowhawk contest, and in exchange he will marry her, thereby improving the material conditions of the impoverished family (662–5). The implications of this way of arranging marriage over the head of the woman are

---

[1] On this topos see Hanning, *Individual*, pp. 54–60.
[2] In references to the French and German versions I distinguish between them by referring respectively to Enide and Enite, Oringle and Oringles. Chrétien's Galoain is nameless with Hartmann, but for convenience I refer to him as Galoein. Since Erec's name is the same in both French and German the context should make it clear which version is at issue.
[3] See Pratt, 'Adapting', p. 71.

distorted to the point of caricature in the Oringle episode who, with Erec apparently dead, forces Enide into marriage with him against her will. True to the material considerations that informed feudal marriage policy Oringle holds out to Enide the prospect of high social standing and riches, an improvement of the position in which he found her (4794, 4799–4804: an echo of what Erec had dangled before her father). Furthermore, Oringle pays even less attention to Enide's wishes than had Erec and her father: he wants to marry her although she may not wish it (4722: 'Mes que bien li doie peser') and the wedding ceremony is made a mockery, quite apart from our knowledge that Erec is *not* dead, by the exercise of force against Enide's refusal (4769–73) – this at a time when canon law insisted, against lay aristocratic opposition, on the *consensus* of both parties to marriage. The compulsion to which Enide is subjected goes further when Oringle, not content with threats, strikes her in the face (4825f.) and silences the objections of his followers by saying that as her lord and master he may do with her as he will (4838f.). In forcing Enide into marriage (instead of 'merely' not consulting her) and in converting threats into actual violence, Oringle caricatures and invalidates Erec's behaviour. This sketch of contemporary practice, in which so far only the caricature presented by Oringle and the awkward suggestion that Erec may resemble him in attitude imply Chrétien's possibly critical view of what is narrated, is followed in essentials in Hartmann's version. With him, too, Erec negotiates marriage terms with the father without consulting Enite, promising social advancement for her (515–24) and, in exchange, for himself the means of restoring his honour after the encounter with Iders and his dwarf. Marriage to Enite is a means to this end. In all this, despite the distortion of the Oringles episode, a contemporary audience could recognise the outlines of its own attitude and practice, with one exception. It is certainly unrealistic that Erec, a king's son, should marry the daughter of an impoverished knight and that, as heir to the throne, he should do this without consulting father or court, but this detail has the advantage of stressing the freedom of Erec as a man by contrast with the woman's subordination to what men arrange for her.

What we have so far seen shows that both the father and the son-in-law act in a patriarchal manner, disposing of the woman as suits their own or their family's interests. How far a father's authority could extend is revealed in Chrétien's *Cligés* where Fenice says that when her father gives her to another man she dare not contradict him (3128f.), which makes a mockery of the need for her *consensus*. She adds that this man, as lord (*sire*) of her body, can do with it as he pleases against her wishes (3130f.), a marital right which Erec claims for himself and Oringle abuses even more brutally.

Chrétien makes clear the father's material considerations in *Erec* in the remark that he has been waiting for a king or count to take his daughter rather than others of lower rank who would gladly have had her (525–32) and in his agreement to Erec's offer, again suggesting that the decision is exclusively between two men. In giving his daughter to Erec the father equates her with the armour which he also hands over: both are objects confirming the bargain that has been struck. As with Chrétien, Hartmann has the father behave patriarchally towards his daughter in ordering her to act as a stable boy in looking after Erec's horse, a request to which she responds with due submissiveness (322: 'herre, daz tuon ich' Lord, I shall do so). Erec, disturbed by this, suggests in vain that he see to his horse himself – this emphasises how differently he later behaves after his marriage, when he has become Enite's lord and master, imposing far greater burdens on her in managing the horses he has captured in combat. It is an indication of the authority Erec has acquired as husband that when he imposes this task on Enite she replies with words that echo those to her father (3277: 'herre mîn, daz sol wesen' Lord, that will be done). This verbal echo shows that she has passed from the legal authority of her father to that of her husband, from one lord (*sire* or *herre*) to another.

This transfer of patriarchal authority shows that Erec, despite his initial wish to spare Enite the demeaning care of his horse, is tarred with the same brush as his father-in-law. After all, it takes two parties to make an arranged marriage and Erec is as willing to negotiate this as is Enite's father. After his victory in the sparrowhawk contest Chrétien's Erec is not slow to show, even before the wedding, that he intends to be the master. Again without a word to Enide, he rejects an offer to replace her ragged clothing with finer attire (1375–86), where the repetition of the verb *voloir* (1376, 1383, 1385; also 1406) indicates the strength of his assertive insistence, reaffirmed later to Queen Guinevere when the couple arrive at Arthur's court (1576–8). Others are shocked at the appearance Enide will present at court, but Erec brooks no interference with his plans, even concerning woman's clothing in which Enide might conceivably have her own preference. Erec's husbandly authority, deciding and speaking in place of his wife, is expressed linguistically, even before the wedding, by the term *seignor* or *sire*, used not as a term of polite address, but to convey the legal lordship that the husband exercises over his wife.[4]

Other aspects of Erec's patriarchy we can illustrate from the German version. After the crisis at Karnant and the departure of the couple on their

---

[4] 1313, 2481, 2594, 3464, 3468, 4634, 4818, 5022.

journey of adventure, Erec commands his wife to keep silent at all costs, a prohibition which she breaks whenever she sees danger in wait for him. The husband's repeated reaction is an outburst of anger at her disobedience and threats of dire punishment, including death. We may suspect that he will not go that far (not one of the threats is carried out), but Enite, to whose internal monologues we are privy, takes the threats seriously and is badly frightened on each occasion (3105: 'wan si vorhte sîne drô' for she was frightened by his threat). By having Erec threaten Enite with death (3094–3102) Hartmann accentuates the husband's authoritarianism with a detail absent from Chrétien (2768–75). The same is true of the threats later voiced by Erec (3404–12), for with Chrétien Erec's speech ends not with the prospect of death, but on a note of forgiveness on this occasion (3006). Coupled with these threats is the increasing burden Erec places on his wife as a punishment by forcing her to deal single-handedly with the horses captured from his defeated opponents. The contrast this represents with his concern for her being given a much simpler task by her father (again this has no parallel with Chrétien, 450–8) serves as an ironic self-condemnation. The irony may be clear only retrospectively, but that it was intended is clear from Hartmann's addition to Chrétien. In all this Erec forces his wife to play the part of a Griseldis, a literary figure to whom, as also to Enite, modern feminists react with scorn, anger and impatience with such female submissiveness. Hartmann goes beyond his source in emphasising this, as when Enite willingly accepts as just the servitude and subjection imposed upon her (3811–15), but the German poet exaggerates this not so as to present Enite as a model, but rather as a means of further highlighting Erec's deficiency. We do neither author justice (especially not Hartmann) if we read them as meaning naively or misogynously Enite's submissiveness as behaviour to be followed, and we do better to place them alongside other authors who question the Griseldis figure of whom Enite reminds us. For example, the author of the *Ménagier de Paris*, after recounting the story of Griseldis, says that he would not want so submissive a wife for himself since he is not worthy of her ('car je n'en suis digne') and in any case doubts whether a woman can be found who would put up with such treatment.[5] In Chaucer's version of the Griseldis story, *The Clerk's Tale*, the poet complains that there was no need to cause the woman such anguish and dread (462) and puts the blame squarely on the husband (621: 'O nedelees was she tempted to assay! / But wedded men ne knowe no mesure, / Whan that they

---

[5] I 125, 126; Schnell, *Frauendiskurs*, p. 232.

fynde a patient creature').[6] The unworthiness which the French author attributes to himself and the blame which the English author assigns to husbands also falls on Erec for his treatment of his wife.

A patriarchal society that treats women in such a manner especially in the context of marriage, stands close to being a society in which prejudice against women, far from being confined to domineering husbands, is found much more widely (as we have seen in the case of Oringle). It is typical of such an attitude that, when the crisis occurs at Karnant in Hartmann's version, Erec's court (which we must imagine in this context as male) is misogynously quick to lay the blame on the woman, not the man, seeing the cause in her seducing him rather than in his sensuality (2996–8). Behind this automatic reaction there lies not simply the antifeminine tradition of the medieval clergy (all evil stems from women, they are all daughters of Eve), but also resentment at the infringement of male bonding, as voiced by Gawein when he warns Iwein against repeating the error of Erec by neglecting his duty at tournaments (*Iwein* 2781–98). That the condemnation of Enite by the court of Karnant is mistaken is confirmed by the narrator's exculpation of her and attribution of blame to Erec instead.[7]

The antagonism to women in society at large has much more serious implications than merely blaming them when things go wrong. Chrétien, for example, makes this clear in the scene in which, in order to rescue Cadoc from his tormentors, Erec has to leave Enide temporarily alone in the wood while he deals with his opponents, but then hastens back to her, fearing the worst, namely that someone, finding the woman alone, might easily have abducted her. These adventures therefore take place in a setting where, once away from the immediate context of the court, the worst can easily befall a defenceless woman (4586–8). This is more than just a chance isolated detail, however, for the journey of adventure on which Erec sets out together with Enide rests on the same assumption. On departure Erec commands his wife, whom he had previously not hesitated to leave in her worst rags until they reached Arthur's court, now to put on her finest dress (2578–81) and mount her best palfrey, so that she acts very much as a decoy duck who, he hopes, will attract aggression from lustful knights whom he may forthwith defeat as a token that he has found his chivalry once again. This is precisely what happens, first with the robber-knights (2800–17, 2945f.), then in the episode with count Galoain. The journey of adventure thus takes place in terrain

---

[6] Mann, *Feminizing*, p. 117. Chaucer finishes *The Clerk's Tales* on a note similar to the *Ménagier*, stressing the impossibility of finding a Griseldis nowadays (1164f., 1180–2).
[7] See below, pp. 114f.

which harbours acute dangers of rape or abduction for a woman, a possibility which Erec had taken into account in dressing up his wife in her most attractive finery. In Chrétien's imaginary realm of King Arthur, the land of Logres, the dangers facing a woman in Enide's position are stated in all their unappetising crudity in his *Lancelot*.[8] In an explanation given to Lancelot the custom of Logres is described, starting off innocuously by maintaining respect for a solitary woman, for if a knight were to encounter one he would sooner slit his own throat than do her violence and bring dishonour on himself (1309: 's'il l'esforçast, a toz jorz / an fust honiz an totes corz' if he were to do her violence he would be forever dishonoured at all courts). However, this respect for women melts away if conditions change, for if the woman is led by another man then the knight who desires her may take up arms against the other and, if he defeats him, may do his will with the woman without incurring shame or blame (1311: 'Mes, se ele conduit eüst / uns autres, se tant li pleüst / qu'a celui bataille an feïst / et par armes la conqueïst, / sa volenté an poïst faire / sanz honte et sanz blasme retraire' But if she were accompanied by another and if he chose to do combat for her and won her by force of arms, he might do with her as he wished without earning shame or blame). This reveals a negative aspect of the realm of King Arthur: whereas the topos *amor et militia* would have it that a knight may gain a lady's love by doing combat on her behalf, the custom of Logres proclaims that violence, especially against defenceless women, is endemic in Arthurian society. If what is said of this custom in *Lancelot* also applies to Chrétien's *Erec* (and also to Hartmann's), this has two implications. First, that Erec would have been aware of it, but was nonetheless ready to expose his wife to this danger in order to establish his own knightly reputation, and secondly, that disrespect for women and violence against them are pervasive, going far beyond any individual cases.

Against this wider background we may turn to the individual cases of counts Galoein and Oringles (and also by implication Erec himself). Both these counts are presented as clearly negative figures, ready to use force and violence to have their way with Enite (and Galoein prepared to commit murder to achieve his end), but the disturbing suggestion is made that, in however distorted a form, they resemble aspects of Erec and differ from him in degree, but not in kind.

Hartmann's Galoein is meant to remind us of Erec in a number of respects, all to do with their relationship with Enite. In his readiness to use violence to take Enite away from her husband Galoein is shown clearly

[8] Gravdal, *Maidens*, pp. 66f.

to be in the wrong (3678: 'daz was doch wider dem rehte') and although he differs from Erec in this point the remaining parallels drawn between this shady character and the protagonist cast a dubious light on Erec by placing him in such company. The narrator makes it clear that Galoein's formerly upright character disintegrates in this episode (3685: 'wande wir haben vernomen / von dem grâven maere / daz er benamen waere / beide biderbe unde guot, / an sînen triuwen wol behuot / unz an die selben stunt' for we have heard of the count that he was indeed blameless and good, of upright disposition until that very moment). Exactly the same was earlier said by the narrator of Erec's decline after marriage at Karnant (2924: 'Erec was biderbe unde guot, / ritterlîche stuont sîn muot / ê er wîp genaeme' Erec was blameless and good, of chivalrous disposition before he took a wife), where the recurrence of the words *biderbe unde guot* drives this parallel home.[9] Another point is brought out by this parallel if we take account of Schnell's helpful distinction between two topoi commonly confused, between man as a 'Frauensklave' (enslaved to a woman, with antifeminine implications) and a 'Minnesklave' (enslaved to love, where the blame is diverted away from woman).[10] Whereas Erec's court (wrongly) puts the blame for Erec's decline on his wife (2996: 'si sprâchen alle: 'wê der stunt / daz uns mîn vrouwe ie wart kunt! / des verdirbet unser herre'' They all said: curse the hour when he met our lady, for because of her he goes to ruin), the narrator correctly attributes Galoein's degradation to the force of love itself (3691: 'dô tete im untriuwe kunt / diu kreftige minne / und benam im rehte sinne' the power of love then taught him deceitfulness and robbed him of his wits), a distinction which strengthens the exculpation of Enite visible elsewhere.[11]

In dangling before Enite the prospect of improving her material and social position upon marriage to him (3770–3; also 3858–62) Galoein shows himself to be as much wedded to the feudal conception of marriage as was Erec in striking his bargain with Enite's father, but whereas Erec had 'merely' made his arrangement over her head Galoein is prepared to go as far as murder. In this he shows as little regard for Enite's wishes as had Erec, for the count quite openly betrays that he will execute his plan even without her agreement (3830: 'welt ir niht güetlichen / mîner bete entwîchen, / sô geschiht ez under iuwern danc' if you are not prepared kindly to meet my wish it will come about without your agreement). Neither man pays heed to the woman's *consensus*: neither the husband in bargaining nor the count in

---

[9] Fisher, *Euphorion* 69 (1975), 165f.; Scholz, *Hartmann*, p. 780 (on 3684–90).
[10] Schnell, *Causa*, pp. 475–505.   [11] See below, pp. 114f.

plotting abduction. A final distorting parallel between these two men occurs when Galoein, realising belatedly that he has been hoodwinked by the loyal Enite, curses himself for not having acted earlier and for losing honour because of his indolence (4096: 'swer sîne sache / wendet gar ze gemache, / als ich hînaht hân getân, / dem sol êre abe gân' whoever settles for idleness, as I have done this night, must lose his honour). This generalisation by Galoein is also meant to pass judgment on Erec's indolence (*verligen*) at Karnant, but it distorts Erec's past position, for Galoein sees *gemach* as responsible for preventing attainment of a goal so brutal that it could never have brought him *êre* in the sense meant by the author and attained by Erec at the close of the work (10124).[12]

The second count, Oringles, whom we have briefly mentioned in Chrétien's work, may now be looked at in the German version, where the role he plays as a distorting mirror image of Erec is broadly comparable with Galoein's. Quite apart from the sexual attraction Enite exercises, he sees marriage to her in feudal-political terms, regarding her birth and status as adequate to a ruler of his rank, but takes care to consult his advisers and obtain their agreement, which is immediately forthcoming (6199–6212). Likewise in accord with feudal marriage politics are the attractions which he feels confident marriage to him can offer Enite, converting her present poverty (he judges her by the condition in which he finds her) into wealth as the wife of a count (6262: 'sich wandelt iuwer armuot / benamen hie in michel guot. / ich bin ein grâve genant' your poverty will be transformed into great wealth here. I have the title of a count). What he regards as an elevation in her status echoes what Erec was able to offer Enite's father and what the latter was quick to seize upon. So persuaded is Oringles that social improvement is a major feature of concluding a marriage that he refers to it again (6469–79), once more with echoes of what marriage to Erec was meant to offer the daughter of an impoverished family,[13] and is confident that he can replace Erec as husband (6390–4).

Like his predecessor Galoein, but not so explicitly on this second occasion, Oringles is shown lapsing from initial goodness to brutality under the force of his desire for Enite. On first encountering her lamenting over her presumably dead husband he consoles her and earns the narrator's approval for that (6213–5),[14] but this opening positive impression is soon

[12] On the irony of Galoein's statement: Green, *Viator* 6 (1975), 132f.; *Irony*, p. 327; Scholz, *Hartmann*, p. 787 (on 4087–4102).
[13] Green, 'Alieniloquium', pp. 125f.; *Irony*, pp. 162f.; Scholz, *Hartmann*, pp. 858f. (on 6471–94).
[14] Scholz, *Hartmann*, p. 851 (on 6185–6211 and 6213–6215).

dispelled by the emotions that overcome him, by his growing impatience with her continued grieving, and by the headlong decision for immediate marriage before the supposed corpse has even been buried. Oringles's fall from grace is far speedier and more concentrated than was Erec's, it therefore repeats it in exaggerated form. In yet another respect this count resembles, but goes far beyond the protagonist: in forcing marriage upon Enite without her agreement and against her opposition (6348: 'si wart im sunder danc gegeben. / ez enhalf ouch niht ir widerstreben' she was given to him as wife against her will. Her resistance was of no avail; 6427: 'er zôch si hin sunder danc' he pulled her away against her will). In being given to Erec by her father Enite may not have been consulted by either party, but there was no mention of her actual unwillingness, let alone opposition to the arrangement. Finally, the compulsion with which Oringles pushes through his marriage plan takes the extreme form of physical violence against Enite, as he angrily beats her until she bleeds (6518–23) and strikes her across the mouth (6578f.). On their journey Erec may more than once angrily threaten Enite with physical punishment, but nowhere does he carry these threats out in practice. The point of these distortions, showing Oringles like Galoein before him going beyond what Erec does, is not so much to depict Erec as less bad than these two counts, but rather to show that he is uncomfortably akin to them, likewise given, if not so extremely, to disrespect for Enite's qualities and her right to choose.

The disrespect for Enite as a woman which these three figures (Galoein, Oringles and above all Erec) show is undermined by context or narrative action. The defence of women (in the form of a defence of this one woman) is not a direct one, but implicit, embedded in a narrative world which reflects recognisable features of medieval patriarchy, shared by Erec and other male characters, but also identifiable to a contemporary audience. Against this background the case against misogyny is made by implication (and therefore more subversively) and put up for debate, appealing to women in the listening or reading audience, but also raising questions which men were to ponder. Hartmann, like Chrétien, approaches the problem indirectly, making his case by implication. We should appreciate that both authors are the first to make this sustained case in their respective vernacular literatures and that for them to have done so directly could have been counter-productive and called forth point-blank opposition from feudal listeners. Their technique is more subversive precisely by not being so obvious and its implications become clear only in details which we have yet to consider.

ANTIFEMININE ATTITUDES

By placing their story of Erec against a background of feudal marriage politics and a general lack of regard for women Chrétien and Hartmann have opened the door for generalised remarks about women which can be simply contemptuous or frankly antifeminine, but we must be careful how we interpret them. It will not do, for example, to complain that Hartmann's version is characterised by 'sweeping remarks about women', for that is itself a sweeping remark.[15] What we need to do instead is to differentiate these remarks by asking who makes them, for example the narrator or a character whose judgment we may have much less reason to trust.

Two examples illustrate that Hartmann may not be given to making straightforward negative generalisations against women in a misogynous sense. The first comes from a lyric poem by him, a 'Frauenlied' dealing with the unfaithfulness of men in their relationship to women (*MF* 212, 37).[16] Delivered in the female voice, the criticism is at first directed at one man in particular, accusing him of flattering deceitfulness, seen through by the woman as meaning that she will be the one to suffer. The third stanza, however, places this one offender in the context of all men (213, 19: 'alle man'), only to reject this generalisation as unjustified, for there are no grounds for criticising the whole male sex for the failings of one (213, 19: 'Begunde ich vêhen alle man, / daz taete ich durch sîn eines haz, / wie schuldic waeren si dar an?' If I were to hate all men because of one man, what guilt would they have incurred?). Indeed, there are many men who treat their lady better (213, 22: 'jâ lônet meniger sîner baz'). Despite her victim status the woman speaker is objective enough to see the flaw in any argument by generalising from one case, and it may well be that a woman, whose sex was exposed to such negative generalisations throughout the Middle Ages, was in a better position to realise this. But we are dealing here, of course, not with a woman, but with a woman's voice expressing sentiments given her by a man, Hartmann, whom it is therefore difficult to imagine arguing thus if he did not also mean it to apply conversely as a rejection of negative generalisations directed against women.

Our second example comes from Hartmann's *Erec* itself, from the episode in which Enite, confronted with Galoein's intention to kill Erec in order to gain possession of her in marriage, has to decide for herself how best to cope with this danger. She employs subterfuge, pretending that she had first believed him to be joking and not serious (3846f.). She justifies her

---

[15] Pratt, 'Adapting', p. 83.   [16] Kasten, *Frauenlieder*, pp. 68–70, 237f.

belief by a negative generalisation, this time critical of men, to the effect that men deceive women by lying promises which they have no intention of fulfilling (3848: 'wan ez ist iuwer manne site / daz ir uns armiu wîp dâ mite / vil gerne trieget / (ich entar gesprechen: lieget), / daz ir uns vil ze guote / geheizet wider iuwerm muote: / dâ von ich dicke hân gesehen / wîben michel leit geschehen' for that is the custom of you men with which you readily deceive us women (I dare not say that you lie to us), promising us much that is far from your minds. I have seen that much suffering falls to women from this). These lines incorporate the two typical features we are concerned with: the negative nature of what is criticised (deception and harm done), but also the extension of an individual case (Enite and Galoein) to a universal ('uns armiu wîp', 'wîben' and 'iuwer manne site'), both summed up in what men do to women ('ir uns'). We have no justification to interpret these lines, in which Enite accuses men of deceiving women at the moment when she is deceiving Galoein, as implying Hartmann's wish to point out 'that if men do lie, women are by no means exempt from that vice'.[17] Quite apart from the fact that that would still not be specifically antifeminine, but rather an extended generalisation involving both sexes, there are clear pointers that we are not meant to equate Enite with Galoein in this way, thereby reducing her in this detail to his level. On the one hand, the count is condemned point-blank by the narrator (3841: 'den vil unge-triuwen man' the dishonest man), but on the other Enite is described as faithful (3943: 'vrouwe Enîte was ein getriuwez wîp'), namely to her hus-band. But Hartmann goes further in defending Enite's use of deception on this occasion, saying expressly that she committed no sin in this (4026: 'diu hete den grâven betrogen / und âne sünde gelogen' she deceived the count but lied without sinning), and even praises her womanly subterfuge (3940: 'mit schoenen wîbes listen'), the means by which she protects both her own honour and her husband's life. 'In this context *list* involves the intention to deceive but is practised for a morally good purpose'.[18] Enite's remark therefore changes the conventional target of negative generalisations from women to men. The whole episode makes the issue of gender explicit.

Warned by these examples that Hartmann's apparently sweeping remarks about women need to be looked at closely and differentiatingly, we may now consider three further classes of evidence. We discuss first the ways in which the narrator correlates the particular with the universal (the central feature of any generalisation), then his employment of the crucial

[17] Blumstein, *Misogyny*, p. 137, criticised by Scholz, *Hartmann*, p. 782 (on 3848–55).
[18] Jones, 'Empathy', p. 293.

gender term *wîplîch* 'womanly' (what does it reveal of his attitude to women and feminine nature?), and lastly the occasions when characters in the work, as distinct from the narrator, indulge in pointedly antifeminine outbursts.

Hartmann's technique of correlating the particular with the general is a marked feature of his style, enabling him to set a detail against a norm of how things always are or against an ideal of how they ought to be.[19] By this means he serves his didactic purpose of depicting a secular ideal in positive terms, presenting individual events in universal terms or judging them in the light of a courtly ideal of timeless validity. This feature is well adapted to presenting a positive picture and, since it occurs with male as well as female characters in the work, it qualifies the relevance of Pratt's dissatisfaction with the author's 'sweeping remarks about women'. How this works in practice can be shown first from the range of generalising constructions applied to men. When Erec takes careful steps to conceal the nature of his departure from Karnant the narrator says of his preparations: 'er tete alsam der karge sol', he acted as the intelligent man does (3070), and when he attends Mass before combat with Mabonagrin this is commented similarly: 'er tete als die wîsen tuont', he acted as the wise do (8633). In neither case does the narrator say simply that Erec acted intelligently, but rather that he acted as intelligent men do or should do (the use of *sol* in the first example underlines the obligation to conform to such an ideal norm). The word *sol* is used similarly in describing how a knight is well equipped, applied to Erec by Guivreiz (4336: 'dar zuo sît ir gewâfent wol, / als ein guot ritter sol' Moreover, you are well equipped, as befits a good knight), and by the narrator (4155: 'dâ was er gewâfent gar, / als ein guot ritter sol' He was well equipped, as a good knight should be). In both these examples the first line would have sufficed to describe the individual situation, but the second line places it against the behaviour, expected of all knights, to which Erec conforms. The positive norm suggested by *sol* can be replaced by *gezemen* to suggest what should fittingly be done, as when Erec is the first to take part in a tournament (2566: 'Erec der êrste an si kam, / als einem ritter gezam' Erec was the first to reach them, as befitted a knight), but elsewhere conformity to a courtly ideal can be conveyed by the adjective *gelîch*, 'resembling, conforming to'. The first meeting between Erec and his future father-in-law illustrates this of both parties. Despite his impoverishment the old man's bearing is that of a lord and nobleman (288: 'sîn gebaerde was vil hêrlîch, / einem edeln manne gelîch' his bearing was lordly, resembling a nobleman), while Erec's gesture points to his breeding (298: 'sîn hende

---

[19] See Green, *Irony*, pp. 231f. (looked at from the point of view of ironic undercutting).

habete er vür sich, / einem wol gezogenen manne gelîch' his hands he held before him, as does a well-bred man). In these cases the force of the indefinite article *ein*, far from particularising, is to suggest the bearing of any or every nobleman, to convey the ideal of a nobleman at large.

Against these positive examples only two cases point in the opposite direction. The unhorsing of Keii by Erec casts a dubious light on the former's knighthood (4733: 'ungelîch einem guoten knehte' unlike a good knight), so that Keii fails to live up to the knightly ideal (which remains intact in the form of Erec's success). Conformity to a negative pattern of behaviour is demonstrated by Mabonagrin's surly approach to Erec on first seeing him (9025: 'und gruozte in ein teil vaste, / gelîch einem übelen man' and greeted him in a surly manner, like an evil man). The discrepancy between the positive examples and this one case of conformity to a negative generalisation underlines the didactic importance for Hartmann of sketching a positive ideal of chivalry.

This generalisation technique, so far applied exclusively to men, is used only twice of a woman, in both cases Enite while still in a state of youthful inexperience. When she takes tearful leave of her mother this is presented as typical behaviour to be expected from someone young (1457: 'als einem kinde wol gezam'). Enite's youthful shyness is manifest a little earlier (after Erec's defeat of Iders), when she is termed a young maiden (1318: 'daz kint vrouwe Enîte'), acting shyly as any maiden does (1321: 'einer megede gelîch'). That the indefinite article, as in the male examples, has generalising (not particularising) force is brought out by its replacement soon after by the plural (1323: 'ir aller site'; 1325: 'sam diu kint'). The passage 1320–33 suggests however the narrator's misogynous view that such female modesty is short-lived and always gives way to a sexuality that cannot be checked by blows and punishment.[20] If this seems to point forward ominously to the crisis at Karnant it would be wrong to see Enite's sexuality as the cause of this,[21] for she repays blows by fidelity at all costs (in contrast to 1332f.). Employing a technique also used by Wolfram,[22] Hartmann's narrator with his hint of pretended misogyny proves himself wrong in the subsequent narrative.[23]

Listing these examples reveals an imbalance in Hartmann's usage: nine examples applied to male characters, but only two to Enite. This is unlikely to be because the narrative focus is directed on the male protagonist, not on the female, because Hartmann's version, like Chrétien's, can be termed a

---

[20] Palmer, 'Vocabulary', p. 81.   [21] See below, pp. 114f.   [22] See below, pp. 204–8.
[23] Palmer, 'Vocabulary', p. 82.

roman à deux,[24] devoted to two protagonists. The second third of the work presents events essentially from Enite's point of view, so that there would have been ample opportunity to make greater use of this technique for her. Instead, this imbalance prompts the theoretical question whether a male author may have been perfectly ready to conceive of a positive behaviour pattern for men (and present it by predominantly positive generalisations), but not for women. To meet this suggestion of possible prejudice on the part of Hartmann we turn now to his employment of a word like *wîplîch* (womanly), looking at it in the general sense of any member of the female sex and asking what view of womankind it suggests as the background to the particular context in which it is employed. We shall consider this word under three possible connotations: neutral, positive and negative.

When *wîplîch* is used with a neutral connotation, neither praise nor criticism of typical womanly behaviour is made explicit, but even so some cases may imply praise from their context. Our first example comes when Enite learns of the discontent with Erec's behaviour at his court, but keeps her worry to herself, not daring to complain to him for fear of losing him. The phrase that concerns us is used of her keeping her anxiety to herself 'in a womanly way' (3009: 'si begunde dise swaere / harte wîplîchen tragen'). To register this as a neutral example reflects the divided views of present scholarship, with some condemning her fear of losing Erec as a selfish neglect of what she should have done, while others judge her motives as altruistic.[25] Similarly, although some take the preceding lines as an admission of guilt by Enite (3007: 'ouch geruochte si erkennen daz / daz ez ir schult waere' she also recognised that the guilt / cause lay with her), others point out that *schult* need not mean 'guilt', but simply 'cause, occasion', that the verb *geruochen* suggests a generosity of spirit in accepting responsibility and that this passage follows on the narrator's praise of Enite in calling her honest and good (3003: 'wan si was biderbe unde guot'). For want of scholarly consensus on this passage I include it under the neutral heading. A second example comes when, midway on their journey of adventure, Erec and Enite briefly rejoin Arthur's court. Enite is taken by Queen Guinevere into her private chamber, where the two women talk and ask questions of each other 'as women do' (5107: 'vil wîplîche'). It might be possible to take this as a jibe at women's love of gossip and chatter, but this is rendered unlikely by the narrator's remark about Guinevere's kindness in taking care of Enite (5100–6) and by the latter's understandable wish to talk after silence

---

[24] See below, pp. 120–4.
[25] 'Selfish': Quast, *ZfdA* 122 (1993), 162–80. 'Altruistic': Scholz, *Hartmann*, p. 744 (on 3011f.).

has been imposed on her by Erec.[26] With a third example, Enite's cursing of Death after Erec has supposedly died, it is difficult to understand how she did this 'in a womanly manner' (5913: 'vil wîplîchen si in dô schalt'). How are we to understand *wîplîchen* here? Presumably it could mean 'wifely' (as with 6380 below), suggesting Enite's grief and frustrated anger at the loss of her husband, but also 'womanly' (grief amounting to an irrational reaction). But the word also involves the narrator's compassion with Enite, and if he is imagined smiling at this, it must be because of her impotence (but would that not also be true of a man in such a situation?).[27] Lastly, when Oringles compels Enite to sit down with him at what he imagines to be a wedding feast, she refuses to eat, saying that to do so would be disloyal to her husband and an offence against womanly nature (6386: 'daz waere ein unwîplîch maz'). A norm of correct behaviour is invoked here, confirmed in the next line by the verb *zemen* ('to be seemly') which we saw used of a positive generalisation in the case of a man. However, it is not clear in this passage how far the stem *wîp* shades over from 'woman' to 'wife', because it is preceded by two lines referring to the couple as man and wife (6384f.), so that the norm which Enite follows is that of loyalty and love for a husband she believes she has lost. In any case, there can be no suggestion of criticism of her.

If some examples of even these neutral usages of *wîplîch* suggest the possibility of a positive interpretation, it is no surprise to find many more where the word is given an expressly laudatory meaning. When from the beginning of their journey Erec orders his wife to manage the horses he has captured, her inability to do this (3288–90) is put down to her womanly nature (3280: 'vil wîplîchen si dô leit / dise ungelernet arbeit' being a woman, she suffered from this unaccustomed trial), but what is criticised here is not Enite (3278: 'diu vil guote' the good woman), but Erec, especially by contrast with his earlier consideration for her on being ordered by her father to see to his horse (342–6). With the words chosen to describe Enite's successful hoodwinking of Galoein (3940: 'mit schoenen wîbes listen') we come teasingly close to an antifeminine topos (the deceitfulness of a beautiful woman) which is precisely what is not meant here, because the adjective describes not the woman, but her subterfuge, showing it to be employed to a good end, saving Erec's life, but also qualifying her as a faithful wife (3943: 'ein getriuwez wîp').[28] Another example takes us back to

[26] McConeghy, *PMLA* 102 (1987), 774.
[27] Scholz, *Hartmann*, p. 841 (on 5913), with reference to Kuttner, *Erzählen*, p. 82.
[28] See above, p. 94.

Enite lamenting the apparent death of her husband, for she tears her hair and strikes herself 'as women do' (5702: 'nâch wîplîchem site'), for they have no other way of coping with such a crisis (5765: 'dâ wider entuont die guoten niht' the good women do not know how to deal with it). That comment has been called 'patronisingly masculine'[29] and may lie behind Pratt's discontent with Hartmann, but there are two other points to be made here. First, this comment is followed by an emphatic, highly personal attack by the narrator on those men who impose hardship on women, thereby undermining their own manly nature and virtue (5770–3). Secondly, this general condemnation of such men also has a particular application, for it points critically to the hardships imposed on his wife by Erec.[30] The condescension towards women is revealed as a means of criticising men.

When Oringles first comes across Enite bent over Erec's body his spontaneous reaction is one of sympathy (6213–5) and understanding for the grief she displays as a woman or wife (6223: 'ich muoz iu des von schulden jehen / daz ir wîplîchen tuot, / und dunket mich von herzen guot / daz ir klaget iuwern man, / wan dâ schînet iuwer triuwe an' I must admit that you behave like a woman/wife and I regard it as praiseworthy for you to mourn over your husband, for that demonstrates your faithfulness). We have no reason to doubt the truth of this judgment, made by the count before falling victim to the power of *minne* and undergoing his moral decline. His words in this passage act as a condemnation of the change in his behaviour which rapidly follows. Two other examples, placed close together in the same context, refer to what is a common object of anti-feminine criticism, the propensity of women for talk, but as with Enite and Guinevere this is interpreted positively and depicted as a sign of sympathy and kindness. These examples concern Enite and the mistress of Mabonagrin, disconsolate after her lover's defeat. Enite's reaction is the same as Guinevere's had been, she seeks to distract the other woman by conversation (9707: 'wechselmaere'), but is driven to do this by her own womanly disposition and kindness and is awarded the laudatory epithet *süeze* for this by the narrator (9701: 'nû begunde si dô bescheinen / ein wîplîch gemüete. / ir vil grôziu güete / betwanc et die süezen' then she gave proof of a womanly heart. Her great goodness drove the sweet one to do that). A few lines later we are told that as a result the two women came closer together in companionship, 'as women do' (9710: 'und geselleten sich dâ mite / nâch wîplîchem site').[31] It would be difficult to detect in this episode

---

[29] See Fisher, *Mediaevistik* 14 (2001), 90.   [30] *Ibid.*   [31] McConeghy, *PMLA* 102 (1987), 774.

any trace of the criticism which normally informs this topos of women's talk.[32] Our last example of *wîplîch* employed positively comes when the eighty widows, restored to courtly life by the fairytale ending of Erec's victory, are brought before King Arthur, all described not just in identical clothing, but as possessing the same qualities. This rhetorically emphasised description (9932–9) reaches its climax in the impression it makes on Arthur, that they were 'womanly and good' (9940: 'diz dûhte in wîplîch und guot'), an explicit equation of feminine nature with virtues which is confirmed by some of the qualities attributed to all these women, embracing not merely courtly features such as beauty and youth, but also constancy and loyalty (9935), breeding and virtue (9937).

Of the seven examples of *wîplîch* as a positive epithet we have considered it is worth recording that three divert any possible criticism of women and direct it instead on men (Erec and Oringles) and two convert an antifeminine topos (women's talk) into a positive demonstration of sympathy and readiness to help. In view of this tendency and the fact that all are positive examples, it is not surprising that, when turning to the use of *wîplîch* as a negative generalisation we find only two examples, both of which again divert their critical implications away from women.

In the description of the last stages of the combat between Erec and Iders it is said that the two knights have by now exhausted themselves and can do no more, so that their blows now fall as if delivered by a woman (894: 'ir slege wîplîchen sigen'), so weakly that they both agree that it is a disgrace to continue a fight in which they can no longer act as men (904: 'unser slege engânt niht manlîchen' our blows are no longer delivered in a manly way). For the men's exhaustion to be compared to the weakness of women does not amount to a criticism of women, but rather of the men at this stage of the encounter, of their insistence (soon to be abandoned) on continuing so that they do no honour to their manhood. With an admittedly far cry we can compare this with Hildegard von Bingen's view of her age as a feminine one (*muliebre tempus*).[33] This has been taken as suggesting that Hildegard may have internalised the negative view of women as weak (in every sense of the word, not just the physical) and thus regarded an age of decline as womanish. Against this, however, it can be argued that Hildegard's criticism was aimed at men (clerics who had lethargically neglected their pastoral duties), so that the tasks which rightly should have fallen to men now had to be taken over by women. In Hartmann's combat, however, the men pull

---

[32] On Enite's speech (and silence) see below, pp. 111–14.
[33] On this concept see Newman, *Sister*, pp. 238–40.

themselves back from being womanish by agreeing on a pause for rest in which to regain strength and manhood. But the critical force of these lines is to reveal the danger of decline which they faced. Admittedly, the cliché of women's weakness remains intact in both cases, but more decisively its critical force is directed away from them towards men.

The remaining negative example involves not the adjective *wîplîch*, but the noun *wîp* (woman), used in the plural in application to Enite alone, so as to bring out the generalising force of this passage. It occurs in the Oringles episode after Enite's emphatic rejection of the count's tactless and overhasty suggestion of marriage. Oringles feels confident that he can win Enite over to his plan (or force her to it) and bases this on his 'knowledge' of women and conviction of their inherent inconstancy, as he makes clear to his followers (6303: 'diu wîp suln reden alsô, / dâ von man irz niht wîzen sol: / si bekêret sich wol / von ir unmuote' women are said to speak like this, so that she is not to be criticised for it. She will get over her grief). The inconstancy of women had long played a part in the repertoire of antifeminism, and the generalising of the particular instance which we are following through is represented in the first two lines of the last passage with the transition from generalising plural ('diu wîp') to singular instance ('ir[z]'). But we are shown more than Oringles, a prisoner of his prejudice, can realise, for we have already been given ample evidence of her constancy and faithfulness (even after what she assumes to be Erec's death) and this is confirmed by ensuing events. Once again an antifeminine topos is trailed before us only to be shot down as totally invalid, and the importance which Hartmann attached to this demonstration is shown by the fact that it is his own work, for it has no counterpart with Chrétien.

With this last example we have moved from the employment of *wîplîch* to consider the disproving of an expressly antifeminine sentiment. To this prejudiced topos of Oringles two other cases can be added, misogynous outbursts by two men, one in the French work and the other in the German. In Chrétien's version the role of misogynist is now played by the first count, for when Galoain's suggestion to abduct Enide from Erec is rebuffed by her, he bursts out in a diatribe of thwarted lust and injured pride, correlating the particular case of Enide with what he regards as the pride of women in general. Since praising and begging Enide has brought him nowhere, he puts this down to the ways of women, contemptuous of men who praise or beg them, but amenable to those who shame or mistreat them, as he himself proposes to do (3349: 'Ne feriiez rien que je vuelle? / Bien est voirs que fame s'orguelle, / Quant l'an plus la prie et losange: / Mes qui la honist et leidange, / Cil la trueve mellor sovant' Would you do nothing that I wish? It is indeed the case that the more one requests and praises a woman the more she grows proud, but the man who shames and ill-treats her often finds her better disposed). We already know enough of Enide to see that the pride with which Galoain reproaches her (3347, 'fiere'; 3350: 's'orguelle') is wide of the mark with this humbly patient Griseldis figure,[34] and Galoain himself later comes to see how mistaken his judgment was (3640–3). The events which he brings about thereby disprove his own antifeminine diatribe. What at first might surprise us, given the comparable technique used by Hartmann to subvert misogyny, is the absence of this outburst in the corresponding scene in the German version (3826–37), the failure to place one misogynous count alongside the other, as Chrétien had done, and to show them both up as wrongheaded.

We find an explanation for this in turning to the second misogynous outburst, this time with Hartmann. It occurs at the close of the encounter with the robber-knights, successfully disposed of by Erec after his wife, disobedient to his command to keep silent, had warned him of the danger. He turns angrily on her, castigating her for going against his order, but then typically moves from the singular in which he addresses her (3238: 'wie nû, ir wunderlîchez wîp?' how now, strange woman?) to a plural generalisation about the whole sex (3242: 'daz ich von wîben hân vernomen' what I have heard about women). The generalising tirade into which he now launches combines several traditional antifeminine topoi: women's disobedience, their tongue-wagging, and their waywardness in being tempted to do precisely what has been forbidden them (3239–58). As was the case with Chrétien's Galoain, we are shown how mistaken is Erec's judgment of Enite (she disobeys him by speaking in order to save his life, and her waywardness is really the constancy of her faithfulness and love for him) and, again as with Galoain, the misogynist Erec later comes to see his misjudgment (6788: '... daz er an ir haete / triuwe unde staete / unde daz si waere / ein wîp unwandelbaere' that he found faithfulness and constancy in her and that she was a faultless wife). In the case of Hartmann's Erec, too, events disprove his misogynous diatribe. This is the point of Erec's sweeping remark about women (to use Pratt's words, who quotes this passage as an example): it does not represent Hartmann's point of view, but is attributed to Erec who later sees his error. Important in this respect is the fact that Erec's outburst has no parallel in the French text (2916–24), which underlines the independent way in which the German author works here: he drops the diatribe by Galoain and introduces instead one by Erec himself.

[34] On Enide and Griseldis see above, p. 87.

This has important consequences for how we are meant to assess Erec in the German work: the patriarchal attitude which we have detected in him extends as far as outright misogyny, awaiting an occasion when anger will allow it to come to the surface. In addition, by transferring this outburst from Galoain to Erec, who is thereby also thrust into association with Oringles and his misogyny, Hartmann does even more to present his protagonist in such unsavoury company.

In both versions of the *Erec* romance a picture of a patriarchal, even misogynous society is presented, focused on a woman's subordinate position between two men (father and husband), but extending beyond this to the Arthurian realm at large. Against this background Hartmann (on whom we have concentrated in this section) attempts by indirection to question, or at least raise for debate, the attitude to women which informs this society. He does this by subverting the negative generalisations about women with which misogyny operates and by illustrating how mistaken was an antifeminine outburst by his protagonist. But just as medieval misogyny extended far beyond its verbal expression, so too did the defence of women go beyond what we have seen in this section. To this extension of the case for women we turn in what follows.

QUESTIONS AND REVISIONS

In this section we consider several features of the *Erec* romance which, although treated in scholarship, have not been adequately viewed explicitly as part of what concerns us, the relationship between man and woman, especially in the bond of marriage. We start with one feature whose novelty has certainly been seen, but not placed in its wider context: the reconcilability of love with marriage, as expressed in both versions in a categorical formula. To deal with this problem means focusing on two of three themes that make up this work: not on the correct relationship between love and society or between marriage and society, but between love and marriage.[35]

To Schnell we owe a debt for his long-standing efforts to show that even under the conditions of feudal marriage policy it was not inconceivable that, as a result of living together and gaining mutual respect and affection, a couple whose marriage had been arranged could come to feel love for one another.[36] In this he stands against the view of Lewis who from his conception of courtly love argued that any 'idealization of sexual love, in a society where marriage is purely utilitarian, must begin by being an

---

[35] Schnell, *Sexualität*, p. 425. [36] Schnell, *Causa*, pp. 115–26; *Sexualität*, pp. 421–70.

idealization of adultery'.[37] Schnell marshals an impressive range of arguments against this, but to the extreme view that love could not be found in feudal marriage he does not oppose the equally extreme contention that such marriages would naturally or even normally bring about love between the partners. Feudal marriages were contracted for pragmatic, impersonal and non-emotional purposes in which love played a part neither as a motive nor as an anticipated (but perhaps hoped for) result. If love did not always feature in contemporary discussions of marriage, this may be because love was not regarded as relevant to a definition of marriage (which is not the same as claiming that love was not possible within marriage).

Two Latin sources underline this discrepancy between marriage and love in all clarity. In her correspondence with Abelard Heloise rejects the idea of marriage to him for a number of reasons, amongst them the contrast between the compulsion imposed by marriage and love freely bestowed ('ut me ei sola gratia conservaret, non vis aliqua vinculi nuptialis constringeret' that I should be kept for him by affection alone, not compelled by any force of the marital bond).[38] She goes so far as to declare that she would prefer to be known as his lover (*amica*) than his wife (*uxor*) in order to preserve the element of freedom in love jeopardised by the marriage bond. This is paralleled, against an utterly different background, by the statement attributed by Andreas Capellanus to Marie de Champagne, who argues likewise that love is as incompatible with marriage as a freely granted favour is with necessity ('Nam amantes sibi invicem gratis omnia largiunter nullius necessitatis ratione cogente' For lovers grant each other everything as favours without the compulsion of any necessity).[39] These statements of principle, made in Latin, suggest the difficulties Chrétien and Hartmann faced in arguing the opposite case in the vernacular, the language of laymen, the people affected by the whole issue. These difficulties were accentuated by the discriminating aspects of feudal marriage policy and by the reflection of the discrepancy between love and marriage in other vernacular texts. In Marie de France's *Eliduc* the roles of lover and wife are admittedly combined in one person, but shared between two men (Guilliadun and Guildeluëc) and the same is true of Guinevere (between Lancelot and Arthur) and in the *Tristan* story of Isolde (between Tristan and Marke).

The treatment of this question by Chrétien and Hartmann is also concentrated on a heavily weighted statement of principle, rightly termed the central problem of *Erec*, which makes it disappointing when Scholz, in his otherwise detailed and informative commentary, has no more to say

---

[37] Lewis, *Allegory*, p. 13.   [38] Abelard, *Historia calamitatum*, p. 189.   [39] *De amore*, p. 153.

about the relevant passage than to refer us to Nellmann who, commenting on a parallel in Wolfram's *Parzival*, says that it reveals a conception of marriage unusual in the high Middle Ages.[40] This must be taken further.

The passage in question, in which the romance pleads that love and marriage are indeed reconcilable,[41] occurs in the episode when Oringles comes across Enite grieving over Erec whom both take to be dead and asks after her relationship with him. With Chrétien the count asks whether Enide was Erec's wife or lover (4688: 'S'ele estoit sa fame ou s'amie'), to which she replies that she was both (4689: "L'un et l'autre', fet ele'). With Hartmann the import of this brief exchange is the same, but it is presented to us from a different point of view. Oringles now asks not about *her* relationship with Erec, but whether *he* was her lover or her husband (6172: 'was er iuwer âmîs oder iuwer man?'), to which her reply is the same as with Chrétien (6173: 'beide, herre'). Common to both versions is the striking contrast of Enite's reply to the count's assumption that she must be *either* wife *or* lover, but also, to judge by how he continues to act, his complete incomprehension of what she may mean. But how do these passages tie up with the rest of the narrative and what follows from the change of perspective between the two versions?

With Chrétien the conjunction of *fame* and *amie* in our passage points back to a verbal forerunner in the critical scene after the married couple's return to Carnant, where Erec neglects his chivalry and gives himself over to excessive love of his wife, described as caressing her and making her his lover (2438: 'A sa fame aloit donoiier:/De li fist s'amie et sa drue' He went to caress his wife and made of her his sweetheart and his beloved), linking *fame* with *amie* within two lines and emphasising the latter by adding *drue* ('beloved'). (That this combination was fundamental for Chrétien's Enide is shown by her scotching the treachery of count Galoain in persuading him that she would be his lover and his wife, 3482: 's'amie et sa fame'.) Hartmann, of course, has retained the crucial scene in which Erec is the lover of his wife (2924–53), but nowhere does he employ the verbal combination used by the French author. From this difference between the two versions it follows that Hartmann has dispensed with what Chrétien had illustrated: that the combination of love and marriage affirmed for herself by Enide to Oringle was complemented by Erec towards her at Carnant. In other words, Hartmann, unlike Chrétien, affords this fundamental insight to the woman, but withholds it from the man. This exclusion of the

[40] Schulze, *PBB* 105 (1983), 14 (subtitle). Scholz, *Hartmann*, p. 851 (on 6172f.).
[41] Schmid, 'Spekulationen', p. 115.

German Erec from what is illustrated with his wife is confirmed by a detail
in the Galoein episode. In both versions Erec and the count are engaged in
conversation with each other before the latter turns his attention towards
Enite. In this conversation (with no parallel in Chrétien, 3283–303), Galoein
asks Erec whether Enite is his wife (3738: 'ist disiu vrouwe iuwer wîp?'), thus
providing him the opportunity to reply in terms similar to those used by
Enite to Oringles. In his answer, however, Erec does not take up this
question. The decisive, categorical answer is given us only later by the
woman, who lives in accordance with it through all the sufferings imposed
upon her.

In both versions the answer given by Enite to Oringles, and the view of
marriage which it incorporates, amounts to the same, but the German
author has taken care to present the woman advocating it. Indeed, as
Schmid has pointed out, the trials of the journey of adventure illustrate
how marriage, once love has been withdrawn from it, amounts physically
and emotionally to a miserable existence for the woman in particular.[42]
This has ramifications beyond the particular instance of this work because,
given the largely utilitarian and impersonal nature of feudal marriage
practice, women had more to gain from the inclusion of love and affection
in marriage. Their inclusion added emotional intimacy and support to a
marital relationship otherwise characterised for women by subordination,
drudgery and continuous exhausting and dangerous childbearing. Mutual
affection promised a reciprocal relationship in marriage as an amelioration
of the man's legal and social lordship over his wife, but also the hope for
protection against marital violence, the right for which was again conceded
legally to the husband.[43]

Mutual affection within marriage was best guaranteed when the relationship was freely entered into by both parties, when *consensus* was readily
given by the woman as well as the man, as ecclesiastical law was seeking to
put into practice during the course of the twelfth century. This explains the
emphasis placed in *Erec* on mutual *consensus* as the basis of marriage,
however much this may have conflicted with feudal marriage practice. It
is represented with Erec and Enite before their actual marriage, first in the
form of their erotic longing for each other, which Hartmann depicts in two
passages (1484–97, 1861–75) replete with pointers to their shared feelings
('wehselten … blicke', 'beide ein ander', 'einz daz ander', 'in beiden', 'ir
beider gedanc'). This anticipates the *coitus* which in twelfth-century ecclesiastical debate about marriage played a part for some as constituting

---

[42] *Ibid.*, p. 113.   [43] His, *Strafrecht* II 101f.

marriage by mutual agreement.[44] But Hartmann does not stop at that, for he strengthens his case by having the couple together express consent more formally. Just before their wedding he says of them (2122): 'wan si wârens beidiu vrô', but this means much more than simply their shared gladness at the prospect. The adjective *vrô* can convey the idea of one's pleasure or wish, as when Erec abruptly answers Galoein's question why Enite sits apart (3751: 'ich bins vrô' that is what I want). The statement about the couple being *vrô*, declaring their readiness, comes immediately before their formal union by the bishop (sic!) of Canterbury (2123–5), so that it amounts to a joint declaration of freely given assent.[45]

The importance of this for Hartmann's depiction of marriage can be confirmed by two contrasting details. When Enite decides that the way to ward off the danger from Galoein is to persuade him that she will fall in with his plan of marriage, she expresses her agreement with him (3895: 'sô bin ich iuwer bete bereit' I am ready to agree to your request) and confirms this with a formal oath (3900–5), which the count takes as sealing their marriage.[46] This union is of course quite invalid and the narrator calls the oath a dubious surety (3904: 'ein ungewissez phant'), for Enite's husband is still alive and Galoein has extracted agreement by threatening violence. Threats are converted into actual deeds in the other contrasting example, Oringles's marriage to Enite against her opposition. The count's disregard for her wishes is already clear with Chrétien, with whom he says that he wishes to marry her although Enide may not wish it (4722: 'Mes que bien li doie peser'), but Hartmann gives this much greater weight (6346: 'swiez der vrouwen waere / widermüete und swaere, / si wart im sunder danc gegeben. / ez enhalf ouch niht ir widerstreben' Although it was repugnant and grievous for the lady she was given to him in marriage against her will. Her resistance was of no avail.). This second count's marriage is invalid for the same reasons as the first, but goes beyond it in distorting what a true marriage should be by its complete disregard for the woman's *consensus*. How grotesquely any trace of reciprocity has been cast aside in this episode can be seen from the reaction of Oringles when his followers protest at this brutal treatment of Enite. He pays glib lip-service to a reciprocal relationship in marriage, saying that Enite is his and he is hers, but then discloses what he means by this: nobody has a right to intervene and stop him doing to her what he pleases (6548: 'ich entuo ir swaz mir gevalle!').[47]

---

[44] Brundage, *Law*, p. 188.   [45] Smits, 'Enite', p. 15.   [46] Schmid, 'Spekulationen', p. 121.
[47] Scholz, *Hartmann*, pp. 860f. (on 6525–38).

The ramifications beyond the single case of *Erec* concerning a woman's miserable fate in a loveless marriage are also to be observed with regard to the combination of *amîs* and *man* (or their female counterparts *amie* and *wîp*), for the problem is taken up in many other works after this first Arthurian romance. We find this combination of terms (and therefore the argument that love and marriage should be reconcilable) in Latin with Andreas Capellanus, contradicting the view which he attributes to Marie de Champagne, when a noblewoman ('femina nobilis') argues that the man she chooses for her embraces (she therefore claims the right for *consensus* for herself) occupies for her the position of a husband and a lover ('qui mecum valeat mariti et amantis vice potiri' who for me may be able to occupy the position of a husband and a lover).[48] In the vernacular a wife can be presented as the lover (*amie*) of her husband by Benoît de Sainte-Maure in his *Roman de Troie*,[49] but apart from that the initiative seems to have lain at about the same time with Chrétien (and through him with Hartmann), not merely in the former's *Erec*. At the close of his *Cligés* Chrétien states his case at greater explanatory (and argumentative?) length when the two lovers, Cligés and Fenice, are eventually married. He makes the point that in their new status their love suffers no diminution, that the wife plays the double role of *amie* and *fame* (or *dame*) and that their relationship is essentially reciprocal (6631: 'Et s'amie a fame li donent, / Endeus ansanble les coronent. / De s'amie a feite sa dame, / Car il l'apele amie et dame, / Et por ce ne pert ele mie / Que il ne l'aint come s'amie, / Et ele lui tot autresi / Con l'on doit amer son ami. / Et chascun jor lor amors crut' And they give him his beloved to be his wife and crown them both together. He has made his beloved his wife, for he calls her beloved and lady, and she loses nothing thereby, for he loves her as his beloved, and she him likewise, as one should love one's lover. Each day their love grew). In the need to explain his position at greater length and also in the fact that Enide's explanation to Oringle meets with the latter's incomprehension (and also that of the male members of the audience?) a polemical note has been detected in Chrétien,[50] or at the least the attempt to persuade doubters, reflecting a difference of opinion which may also be seen in the two opposing views on love in marriage reported by Andreas Capellanus.

This polemical note, possibly audible in Hartmann's version too, is lost when we turn to authors, in France as in Germany, who follow Chrétien's

---

[48] *De amore*, p. 145. See Schnell, *Sexualität*, p. 468.
[49] Benoît de Sainte-Maure, *Roman de Troie* 1433–36.   [50] Schumacher, *Auffassung*, p. 108.

lead, since with them the combination of titles has become conventional-ised, no longer needing to be established either verbally or by the course of the narrative. Two German authors may exemplify this, both acquainted with his work. In his *Tristan* Gottfried, talking of the queen of Ireland, refers to her husband as 'ir friunt', thereby using a term which he elsewhere applies to lovers[51] and implying a relationship of love within marriage which, with one crying exception, he presents elsewhere.[52] But nowhere does he feel it necessary to comment on, let alone explain the nature of this relationship between Gurmun and his wife. The same holds true of Wolfram's *Parzival*, where both marriage partners can be referred to, very much in passing, in their double function. Thus Parzival is acclaimed by Condwiramurs and her subjects alike as her *herre* and her *âmîs* (200, 5–7), just as conversely Parzival addressing his wife in an internal monologue uses a term of courtly love (302, 7: 'vrouwe und wîp' lady and wife). Nor does Wolfram restrict this feature to his protagonist couple. In Book VII Obilot anticipates the marriage between her sister and Meljanz which soon takes place (397, 6f.) by describing Obie as his *âmîe* (396, 14) within marriage, while Meljanz is declared 'zeinem herren und zeinem âmîs' lord and lover (396, 16). This double relationship is also true of Orilus and Jeschute. They are man and wife (Jeschute refers to him as 'mîn man', 132, 12, and the narrator calls her 'sîn wîp', 133, 4), but when the man suspects an affair with someone else he refers to this rival as another lover (133, 10: 'ein ander âmîs, cf. 264, 10), thereby revealing that he regards himself as her lover, within marriage. (Especially in view of Orilus's subsequent treatment of his wife there is more to be said of this couple, to whom we shall return in Chapter V.) What these German examples suggest is that Chrétien's (and Hartmann's) conception was rapidly adopted, even conventionalised, in literature, not needing to be argued, perhaps because it met a need already felt and therefore found a ready response.

In France, too, we find echoes of Chrétien's innovation. In the Occitan romance *Jaufre* the protagonist's beloved promises him her love within marriage (7902: 'Aissi. us tenrai ieu per amic et per seinor' Thus I shall regard you as lover and as lord).[53] An Anglo-Norman treatise, *Un art d'aimer*, makes marriage more palatable by holding out the prospect that

---

[51] When Blanscheflur addresses Riwalin as 'friunt unde hêrre' (1548, 1555) she is taking his proposal to take her back with him to Parmenie as an offer of marriage. Other examples of *vriunt* as 'lover': 4187, 11982, 13072 (synonymous with *gelieben*, 15053). *Friuntschaft* (5406f.) can also denote an illicit love affair outside the bonds of marriage, which illustrates by contrast how far Gottfried can link the word with marriage without feeling any necessity for explanation.
[52] Schnell, *ZfdPh* 101 (1982), 334–69.   [53] Schnell, *Sexualität*, p. 461.

the partners will still be lovers (680: 'amys et amie'), while a fourteenth-century treatise, *Puissance d'amours*, advises the Duke of Brabant that whoever wishes to gain a wife must persuade the woman that he will treat her as his *amie* after their marriage.[54] A passage in the *Roman de la Rose* sees the relationship between love and marriage more in terms of hierarchy, rejecting both the woman's role as mistress in love and the man's function as lord in marriage in favour of a bond of equal companionship on both sides (9395: '... sa fame, / qui ne redoit pas estre dame, / mes sa pareille et sa compaigne, / si con la loi les acompaigne, / et il redoit ses compainz estre / sans soi fere seigneur ne mestre' ... his wife, who for her part must not be his lady, but his equal and his companion, as the law makes companions of them both, and he in his turn must be her companion without making himself lord or master).[55]

What first found vernacular expression with a French author was carried not merely to Germany, but also to England (perhaps assisted by the fact that Chrétien may well have composed his *Erec* for the English court).[56] The debate poem *The Owl and the Nightingale* discusses marriage at length, and says at one point that the unmarried woman who has chosen a partner in a secret illicit affair may make this good in the eyes of the Church by marrying him, having him as her lover ('leofmon') within the bonds of the Church (1425–30), adding however, in a manner reminiscent of Wolfram's point in his dawnsong *Der helnden minne*, that she can now go to him by daylight and not in the dead of night (1431f.).[57] The same idea found earlier expression in a group of religious texts in the vernacular meant for anchoresses who were of aristocratic birth and, while still secular, acquainted with court literature. One work in this group, the *Wohunge of ure lauerd*, has the recluse address Christ as one who has fought on her behalf and rescued her from her foes (one thinks of Parzival rescuing Condwiramurs from the clutches of Clamide), so that she now enjoys Christ's embraces as his lover and his spouse, *leofmon and spus* (568–77), just as Parzival and Condwiramurs were lovers and married.[58] In another work belonging to the English group, *Seinte Margarete*, the saint's persecutor, the pagan Olibrius, like Chrétien's Galoain towards Enide, promises Margaret authority and power, but also that she will be his lover and his wedded wife (50, 26–8: 'mi leofmon ant min iweddede wif').[59] As was the case in the French work, the

---

[54] *Ibid.*, pp. 463, 424, fn. 15.   [55] Payen, 'Mise', pp. 231f.
[56] Schmolke-Hasselmann, *Versroman*, pp. 190–210.
[57] Cartlidge, *Marriage*, p. 185. Wolfram: Wapnewski, *Lyrik*, pp. 146–69.
[58] Cartlidge, *Marriage*, p. 136.   [59] *Margarete* 50, 26–8. Cartlidge, *Marriage*, pp. 137f.

offer of Olibrius is shown to be invalid by his threat of violence opposing Margaret's will, but the point of this passage, as with the *Wohunge*, is that, if not in the secular sphere, the combination of love with marriage is to be found with the virgin's spiritual marriage with Christ.

As might be expected, we find a more clear-cut expression of this position in secular literature. Chaucer depicts this, as part of what has been called the 'Marriage Group' of his *Canterbury Tales*, in the *Franklin's Tale* more in terms of dominance and subservience, as in the *Roman de la Rose*, than expressly as love in marriage, as with Chrétien and Hartmann. Chaucer has the Franklin describe the marital relationship between Arveragus and Dorigen in terms of an interplay between love and marriage, a doubling of roles for each partner, expressed from the woman's point of view, seeing her husband as lord in marriage, but as subservient in love ('Thus hath she take hir servant and hir lord – / Servant in love, and lord in marriage. / Thanne was he bothe in lordshipe and servage. / Servage? nay, but in lordshipe above, / Sith he has bothe his lady and his love; / His lady, certes, and his wyf also').[60] However, what we have seen of other vernacular evidence on this question should make us doubtful about Spearing's sceptical judgment of the Franklin's view. For Spearing the 'normal' medieval view of the 'natural' relationship in a marriage was one in which the husband was dominant.[61] That may well have been true in practice, but the views expressed by some theologians and found in vernacular literature from the twelfth century on should teach us that companionship and love within marriage came to call the 'normal' and the 'natural' more into doubt. The *Erec* romance is the first occasion for this to be argued in the vernacular for the laymen whom it concerned.

The second feature of *Erec* to be considered, Enite's speech and silence, concerns the misogynous topos of women's propensity to talk, questioned here by subversion, much as Chrétien undermined the view of female inconstancy in *Yvain*.[62] The topos of women's talk throughout the Middle Ages derived support from the Pauline injunction that women were not to speak in public, but to learn in silence at home from their husbands.[63] Hartmann was acquainted with male exasperation with women's talk. When Iwein comes across women working together in a sweat-shop he recognises their breeding from the fact that they do not chatter, as might

---

[60] *Franklin's Tale* 120–5. Mann, *Feminizing*, pp. 90f.; Blamires, 'Pulpit', p. 149.
[61] Spearing, *Franklin's Prologue and Tale*, pp. 30f. Spearing bases his view on Bartholomeus Anglicus (man is the head of woman), but Blamires, 'Paradox', pp. 13–29, has shown that this 'normal' view was not uncontested.
[62] See above, pp. 81f.   [63] I Cor. 14, 34f.; I Tim. 2, 11f.

otherwise be expected (6293–6), and in *Gregorius* the young protagonist knows all about female gossip (1427–31).[64] Whatever the position in these works, we now have to ask how Hartmann poses the question in *Erec*.

From the beginning Enite is presented as a woman of few words, showing in that her submissiveness to patriarchal father and husband. Her first brief utterance is one of obedience to her father (322: 'herre, daz tuon ich' Lord, I shall do so), not even present in Chrétien and echoed in the first words we are shown her addressing to Erec (3277: 'herre mîn, daz sol wesen' Lord, that will be done).[65] Before this second utterance she speaks the fatal words about the court's criticism of Erec (3026–32), but says these to herself, thinking that he is asleep. Up to this point Enite is presented as a patriarch would have a woman be, silent until spoken to, and it is this which the ensuing narrative questions.

Hartmann does this by stressing the desirability and need for woman's speech, both at Karnant and on the journey of adventure. He may not follow Chrétien, with whom Erec quickly admits that Enide and the court are in the right (2576f.), but the Limors episode shows Erec's belated awareness that his wife's words revealed the truth to him, taking him away from his *verligen*. This is brought out in both versions by parallels in situation and in words between two turning points: Karnant (where the crisis breaks out) and Limors (where it is resolved). With Chrétien, on the first occasion Erec lies in shallow sleep in the bed in which he spends so much of his time in *recréantise*, but is wakened by Enide speaking to herself (2510: 'Si l'a tresoï en dormant. / De la parole s'esvella' While sleeping he half heard her and awoke at her words). This is taken up again at Limors, when Erec, lying in what is presumed to be the sleep of death, regains consciousness as if he were waking up (4854: 'Revint Erec de pasmeisons / aussi con li hon qui s'esvoille' Erec recovered consciousness, like someone who wakes up) on hearing Enite's voice (4859: 'Quant la voiz sa fame antandi') as she cries out at the violence done her by Oringle. With Hartmann these verbal echoes are lacking, but the parallel in the situation is clear enough: with him, too, Erec is brought back to life on hearing Enite's cries of distress.[66] But Erec does more than hear her voice (for the narrator twice uses the verb *erkennen*, 6609, 6614), recognising not simply her voice, but also the situation in which she finds herself (6609–11). In both works and on both occasions Erec awakes in a double sense: at Karnant from physical sleep to a confrontation with the reality of his present position

[64] McConeghy, *PMLA* 102 (1987), 773, 774.
[65] Scholz, *Hartmann*, pp. 635 (on 322), 768 (on 3277–90).   [66] Fisher, *DVjs* 60 (1986), 369.

(even if he is still resistant to accepting it), at Limors from the sleep of near-death to a new life with Enite (their reconciliation follows immediately after this episode). In both scenes it is the voice of the woman, condemned to silence by patriarchal convention or an express order, that eventually brings the man back to reality.

On the journey itself Enite's disobedience in speaking as she sees danger ahead is repeatedly instrumental in saving the life of her husband, warned by her and therefore dependent on her speech (3186: 'dir sint ritter nâhen bî / die dir schadent, mugen sî' knights are approaching who will harm you if they can; also 3419f.; 4135f.). Moreover, the internal monologues of Enite before she plucks up courage to speak out reveal her positive motivation to us, more emphatically with Hartmann than with Chrétien. The latter has Enide reproach herself with cowardice if she were not to give warning (2840–3), but in the German version we are told that it was the woman's faithfulness and love (*triuwe*) which led her, despite what had been threatened to her, to go against Erec's reiterated commands. In these monologues Enite debates with herself (as the listeners are meant to with themselves) which is to have priority: the conventional patriarchal view of a woman's submissiveness and silence or disobedience to a husband, expressive of love for him and a means of protecting him. She thereby overrides one conventional view (the requirement of a woman's silence) by another (disobedience). She does this through her persistent quality of *triuwe*, exemplified first in each of the two encounters with the robber-knights (3184, 3367f.), then twice in the Galoein episode, once when she alerts Erec to the count's murderous plan (3993) and once when she realises that they are being pursued (4145), and finally at the approach of combat with Guivreiz (4319).[67] These attestations of the purity of Enite's motives in speaking are carefully accentuated: in the first three it is she who is speaking or thinking, in the fourth confirmation comes from the narrator, and in the last Erec himself recognises this quality of hers (4319: 'dô wart im aber ir triuwe erkant' Once more he recognised her faithfulness). From the crisis at Karnant on we are meant to see, contrary to the initial patriarchal depiction of a demurely silent woman, the positive value of woman's speech, first on what is also a symbolic level in restoring the man's link with society by showing him how his court regards him, then by alerting him to dangers in a more concrete sense.

Despite what we have so far seen, there are some who seek to justify in some measure Erec's treatment of his wife by arguing that some fault lies

---

[67] Ruberg, *Schweigen*, pp. 190–92; McConeghy, *PMLA* 102 (1987), 775.

with Enite, either as the cause of her husband's sexual indulgence or precisely through not alerting him earlier to what the court was saying about him. McConeghy, for example, maintains that Enite's error at Karnant lies in her silence rather than in her speech and that, aware as she was of the court's dissatisfaction (whereas Erec was ignorant of it), she should have informed him of it sooner than she did.[68] Her failure to do this for fear of losing him would therefore have to be accounted selfish, so much so that for Quast she is guilty of not upholding the reciprocity of marriage and thereby of a breach of marriage ('Ehebruch').[69]

Against such a line of argument others, now in the majority and massively reinforced by Scholz's commentary,[70] stress the indications that exculpate Enite. A verbal contrast at the point of crisis is revealing here, for on the one hand it is said, with narratorial omniscience, that until his marriage and neglect of chivalry Erec was worthy and good (2924: 'Êrec was biderbe unde guot, / ritterlîche stuont sîn muot / ê er wîp genaeme' Erec was blameless and good, of chivalrous disposition before he took a wife), whereas Enite is so little involved in this fall that shortly afterwards she is described in the terms no longer applicable to him (3003: 'wan si was biderbe unde guot' for she was blameless and good).[71] This contrast (where the exculpation of the woman amounts to emphasising the man's fault) also affects the nature of Erec's fall, described at the critical point as a change for the worse (2934: 'sîn site er wandeln began' he began to change his habits). This highlights the point that, at the moment of the couple's reconciliation, Erec at length realises what we have seen all along in terms of Enite's *triuwe*, that no such decline had affected her (6788: 'daz er an ir haete / triuwe unde staete / unde daz si waere / ein wîp unwandelbaere' that he found faithfulness and constancy in her and that she was a faultless wife). Scholz rightly emphasises the irony of the fact that Enite proves that she is *unwandelbaere* precisely by disobeying her husband's command and breaking her promise to obey him.[72] She proves that she possesses *triuwe unde staete* by doing just the opposite of what a conventionally patriarchal husband would expect from his wife.

The ambiguous evidence for Erec's punishment of Enite (is it merited or not?) prompts a debate about the respective rights and wrongs of both partners in the marriage, and it is possible that the debate in modern

---

[68] McConeghy, *PMLA* 102 (1987), 779.   [69] Quast, *ZfdA* 122 (1993), 162–80.
[70] Scholz, *Hartmann*, especially pp. 871–3 (on 6771–77).
[71] Fisher, *Euphorion* 69 (1975), 164; Scholz, *Hartmann*, p. 742 (on 3003).
[72] Scholz, *Hartmann*, pp. 877f. (on 6783–91).

scholarship reflects a twelfth-century debate by the audience, or at least one which the two authors hoped to stimulate. This debate concerns more the position of the woman than that of the man, since the ambiguity attaches essentially to Enite (was she at fault or not?), whereas the failure of Erec, as the argument on behalf of his wife has already hinted, is more obviously clear-cut. In modern scholarship Erec has a bad press because of a variety of faults that have been attributed to him. These go beyond what concerns us, his attitude towards his wife and his treatment of her. His shortcomings are shown up in the course of the journey of adventure (where his patriarchal behaviour places him in the dubious company of Galoein and Oringles), but also already at Karnant. Hartmann makes this clear, at greater length and more pointedly than in Chrétien's corresponding passage (2438–49), in the lines describing the *verligen* itself (2929–53). In both versions we have a string, not of plural verbs, as we might expect, describing the couple's absorption in each other, but of singular verbs with Erec as the subject. The action, or from the point of view of the court the inactivity, proceeds from Erec alone, things are depicted from his point of view, not Enite's.[73] On only one occasion does Hartmann switch briefly to plural verbs, with man and woman as joint subjects, but then precisely to render the interval when they leave their bed to go to Mass in the chapel (2940–45). This switch is not meant to suggest that Enite is not emotionally and physically one with Erec in their bedchamber, but rather that the decline and *wandelunge* which this scene registers are his, not hers. He is the active party and the blame attaches to him.

In one sense, the question of allotting blame to one party or the other may be sidestepped since, from the point of view of misogyny, the problem of Enite's fault or otherwise is irrelevant, so that we are entitled to cut the Gordian knot. On the one hand, if Enite is innocent of any fault, there can be no antifeminine criticism of her. On the other hand, if fault were to be found with her, this is also the case with Erec, and even more so, so that we would be dealing with an extended criticism of both man and woman, not with a misogynous focus on the woman alone.

In different ways, therefore, the misogynous topoi to be found or presupposed in *Erec* are called into question and subverted.[74] The silence which a patriarchal husband imposes upon Enite is shown to be irrelevant, precisely what is not called for, either at Karnant or on the couple's journey. The woman's speech, outwardly the token of her disobedience, arises instead from her *triuwe*, meaning much more than the faithfulness expected

---

[73] *Ibid.*, p. 732 (on 2924–27). [74] On Chrétien, see also Pérennec, 'Fautes', pp. 79f.

of a wife and implying love and devotion rising above any mere acceptance of what has been ordered from without. Erec's punishment of his wife for the criticism she had voiced at Karnant in the German version, far from the (admittedly short-lived) acknowledgment of his own fault with Chrétien (2576f.), amounts rather to a suppression of such criticism by projecting it onto her. With that the readiness to place the blame on women is shown up as a threadbare evasion.

This criticism of Erec by comparison with his wife appears to be contradicted by a passage, present in both versions, in which superlative praise is lavished on him. Some time ago I discussed these passages in terms of irony,[75] but this was before Schnell made a valuable contribution in distinguishing between two topoi, men as the slaves of women and as the slaves of love, bringing out the antifeminine implications of the former, but not the latter.[76] These two passages must now be looked at in this light.

Each passage is strategically placed immediately after Erec's outstanding performance at his wedding tournament, but on the brink of the crisis which breaks out at Karnant, barely 100 lines later. In each he is praised in general terms (Chrétien 2263–5, Hartmann 2811f.) which are then specified by his comparison with four traditional *exempla*: the wisdom of Solomon, the beauty of Absalom, the strength of Samson, the generosity of Alexander.[77] Erec therefore not merely equals each of these worthies in their respective attributes, he is meant to surpass them by combining all these virtues in his person. However, as Schnell has shown, these four figures (with or without others) also play a traditional part with regard to the relationship between man and woman, the theme brought to the fore at Karnant.

This relationship can be seen in two ways. When meant negatively, with man deceived, seduced and enslaved by woman, we are dealing with the antifeminine topos, popular with clerical misogynists, of man as the slave of woman ('Frauensklave'). According to this view Adam (not present in our vernacular passages) was not deceived by the Devil, but by Eve, Solomon was led by pagan women to worship false gods, and Samson was obviously the victim of Delilah's guile.[78] The position is well summed up by a line in the *Speculum humanae salvationis*, quoted by Schnell, holding out little hope if such figures, and so many, were brought low by women's guile ('Si tales et tantos decepit ars mulieris').[79] The use of Adam as a prototypical

---

[75] Green, 'Alieniloquium', pp. 147f.; *Viator* 6 (1975), 151f.; *MLR* 70 (1975), 798–804; *Irony*, pp. 38–40.
[76] See above, fn. 10.   [77] Chrétien 2266–70; Hartmann 2813–21.   [78] Schnell, *Causa*, pp. 476, 478.
[79] *Speculum* I 57; Schnell, *Causa*, p. 477.

victim, together with other biblical figures, points to the clerical origins (already from the third century on) of this misogynous tradition in which the Fall of Man is seen in sexual terms as the defeat of reason (of the man) by the flesh (incorporated in woman).[80] Accordingly, this tradition is especially at home in Latin and finds its way only later into vernacular literature,[81] in works of clerically educated authors. It is a hallmark of this tradition, whether Latin or vernacular, that the action, involving the deception or capture of the man, should be seen as proceeding from the woman. We have seen this with the cunning deception (*ars*) practised by women in the *Speculum humanae salvationis*, and the same is true of a didactic saying, asking what man can be safe in view of woman deceiving ('Femina decepit') a range of biblical men.[82] Such men are not merely beguiled, they are made captive to the power of women: in the *Priesterleben* of Heinrich von Melk Solomon was forced into idolatry by women (159: 'daz in diu wip des noeten' women forced him to do that) and Marbod of Rennes warns to the same effect ('Mulier pretiosam viri animam capit. Cave ergo ne te captivet' Woman captures the precious soul of a man. Take care therefore that she does not make a captive of you).[83]

The position is quite different whenever the same figures (to whom non-biblical ones such as Alexander or Virgil can be added) are presented as overcome not by women, but by the power of love ('Minnesklave'). These *exempla*, above all at home in court literature preoccupied with the theme of love, no longer serve as warnings so much as provide a measure of consolation to courtly lovers,[84] but more important in our context is the fact that, by now depicting the action proceeding from the power of love, they ensure that any blame no longer falls on woman. Seen in this light, Solomon is now subject to the power of love, as with a lyric by Veldeke, who sees little hope in avoiding this if it overcame one so wise (*MF* 66, 16: 'Diu minne betwanc Salomône' love overcame Solomon), in striking contrast with the *Speculum*. The same is true of a secular figure such as Alexander who, for all his power as conqueror, was himself conquered by love according to Ulrich von Gutenburg (*MF* 73, 5: 'Alexander der betwanc / diu lant von grôzer krefte: / doch muoste er sunder sînen danc / der minne meisterschefte / sîn undertân' Alexander conquered lands with great power, yet against his will he was forced to be subjected to the domination of love).[85]

---

[80] Schnell, *Causa*, p. 478. [81] *Ibid.*, p. 490. [82] *Ibid.*, p. 481 (quoting Wattenbach).
[83] Heinrich von Melk: Maurer, *Dichtungen* III 267; Marbod, ep. 6, *PL* 171, 1481f. Cf. Schnell, *Causa*, pp. 477, 480, fn. 573.
[84] Schnell, *Causa*, p. 490. [85] *Ibid.*, pp. 493f.

This distinction between two topoi, established by Schnell, is relevant to the invocation of the four worthies in *Erec*[86] on the brink of the crisis at Karnant. In both versions, as we saw in the description of the *verligen*, the action does not proceed from the power of love in place of the woman (which would have been enough to absolve Enite),[87] but rather from the man, who is the subject throughout (Chrétien 2434–49, Hartmann 2929–53). If at one point in the German passage the subject is plural when the couple go to Mass (2940–4), this 'reduction' of Enite's role to merely accompanying Erec serves the positive purpose of absolving her from his fault in the rest of the passage. This avoidance of blaming Enite goes beyond the description of this scene, however. With Chrétien there is still to be found a trace of antifeminine sentiment in the way in which the court, as is seen by Enide, blames her for having made Erec her captive (2563: 'Que si vos ai lacié et pris' That I have so bound and captured you). The court therefore regards Erec as enslaved by her ('Frauensklave'). However much with Hartmann the court may regret Enite's arrival (2997f.), the German author has expunged this particular trace of antifeminism and taken care to emphasise Erec's responsibility for what happens.[88]

We bridge the gap between criticism and hyperbolic praise of Erec if, as I argued long ago, we can accept that irony may be involved here, that a negative *exemplum* lurks behind the praise of Erec, illustrating the dangers of a faulty relationship between man and woman. By that I mean that the four worthies listed as *exempla* all traditionally share one feature in common, namely their enslavement to a woman and that Erec, in the eyes of his misogynous court (if not for the author himself) is also such a victim.[89] To demonstrate this Hartmann uses what was from the beginning an antifeminine topos, but diverts criticism from the woman and displays instead the man's shortcoming.

In his commentary Scholz has discussed the German passage and expressed doubts whether in fact irony is at stake here, so that account must now be taken of his objections.[90] Let me start by conceding two points where he is right, for he correctly points out that, contrary to what I earlier said, two of the qualities for which Erec is praised (his wisdom and his generosity) have already been demonstrated by him, so that there are

---

[86] In the light of Schnell's distinction I must now correct what I said in *MLR* 70 (1975), 801, about these figures: Absalom belongs to the slaves not of love, but of women, and the four figures were not enslaved by love and by a woman, but by a woman alone.
[87] Here I differ from Reinitzer, *DVjs* 50 (1976), 610, 611f.
[88] See above, p. 115.   [89] Green, *MLR* 70 (1975), 801f.
[90] Scholz, *Hartmann*, pp. 725–28 (on 2811–21).

no grounds for doubting the truth of the praise of him on this score.[91] However, when Scholz suggests that for me Hartmann's passage constitutes no more than pretended or sham praise ('Scheinlob') he goes further than is justified.[92] I refer to the author's words as 'ironic praise, not so much untrue as irrelevantly true' and say that the 'force of Hartmann's comparison goes much further than we at first suspect ... behind this praise, behind the comparison with such worthy figures there lurks Erec's failure, soon to be revealed to us'.[93] Nor would it do to dismiss irony in these lines by basing oneself on an extreme view of irony as saying the opposite of what is true,[94] for this passage does speak the truth (if not the whole truth) about Erec. Such an extreme view may cover some cases of irony, but is deficient,[95] since irony can also speak with a discrepancy of meanings[96] or say less than the truth (as with litotes, falling short of what is to be reconstructed as the author's intention).[97] This possibility is applicable here, not at the moment when praise is voiced, but in recital-time very soon afterwards, when Erec is shown to share a further (but negative) quality with the figures he has been compared with positively. The difficulty for Scholz appears to lie in interpreting this passage in the light of what is told us not merely later, but almost immediately afterwards.[98] For him this passage is quite distinct from other laudatory statements whose irony is more obvious because they come after Erec's failure has been made clear, as when he is 'praised' by the ironic narrator for the 'virtue' of at least allowing his followers (if not himself) to attend tournaments,[99] or when, as his followers desert him in disgust, this is described as the 'praiseworthy reputation' he has won.[100] The presence of irony in these cases (after the crisis) prompts the question whether it may also be considered immediately before.

There are indeed cases in medieval literature where a statement, not in itself ironic, is shown retrospectively to have ironic implications, and I have elsewhere discussed these under what I term 'structural irony'.[101] One such long-term example occurs in the German *Erec*, when Erec's disquiet at seeing Enite commanded by her father to see to his horse is in marked contrast to the far heavier task with horses which Erec later imposes on her

---

[91] *Ibid.*, p. 725.   [92] *Ibid.*   [93] Green, *Irony*, pp. 38, 39.
[94] Discussed as the 'Irony of inversion': Green, *Irony*, pp. 199–208.   [95] *Ibid.*, p. 4.
[96] *Ibid.*, pp. 208–12 (the 'irony of divergence').   [97] *Ibid.*, pp. 189–94.
[98] Scholz, *Hartmann*, p. 728.
[99] *Erec* 2954–65, especially 2956 ('der tugende er dannoch wielt') and 2965 ('ich lobe an im den selben site'). See Scholz, *Hartmann*, p. 737, on these lines.
[100] *Erec* 2974–83, especially 2983 ('den lop hete er erworben'). Scholz, *Hartmann*, pp. 739f., accepts the irony of this line.
[101] Green, *Irony*, pp. 326–58.

as punishment. The irony of this contrast, revealed only much later, has been pointed out by Fisher, whose assessment of it as such has been apparently accepted by Scholz, with no sign of difficulty.[102] One wonders why a retrospectively revealed irony (operating in this case over an interval of hundreds of lines) should not also be entertained with an interval of merely 100 lines. Scholz suggests that an ironic reading of the passage praising Erec on the brink of his crisis destroys the overwhelming impact of the fall when it comes,[103] but, on the contrary, praise so placed heightens the shock effect of the crisis. In denying this Scholz fails to see how structural irony works, 'informing the relationship between ... two scenes' and presenting a scene 'as seemingly complete and meaningful in itself, but ... then revealed as having a very different aspect, containing implications other than what we first expected'.[104] Only by looking back (or receiving the work on a second occasion) can irony be recognised, amounting to a criticism of Erec in addition to his praise. But whether we accept the ironic implications of the placing of this passage or not, two points stand out: first, that after this passage the praise of Erec is shortlived, and secondly that both authors make use of an originally antifeminine topos to divert blame from the woman to the man.

What throughout this chapter we have seen of the marital crisis between Erec and Enite and of their joint journey of adventure must make us hesitant to accept, certainly in this particular case, the blanket assessment of the romance by some feminists as a genre primarily concerned with a male hero and hence the marginalisation of women, 'seemingly at the center of the courtly dilemma', but 'marginalized from the action'.[105] As far as *Erec* is concerned, Pratt agrees with Kellermann that Chrétien's intention was to write the romance of a couple ('Doppelroman'), whereas Hartmann focused on the figure of Erec, although elsewhere she qualifies this by terming Chrétien's version 'androcentric'.[106] As against these views, Smits has stressed that the central problem of Hartmann's work, as we have seen, is the marital relationship, the partnership of man and wife.[107]

Chrétien states in his prologue that he is to tell the tale of Erec, son of Lac (19: 'D'Erec, le fil Lac, est li contes'), but this apparent exclusion of the woman is made good in his prologue to *Cligés*, where he refers to his earlier work with a double title (1: 'Cil qui fist d'Erec et d'Enide' He who wrote of Erec and Enide), uniquely so in all his works and not to be dismissed as

---

[102] Fisher, *Euphorion* 69 (1975), 170; Scholz, *Hartmann*, p. 638 (on 342–6).
[103] Scholz, *Hartmann*, p. 728.   [104] Green, *Irony*, p. 348.   [105] Krueger, *Readers*, p. 34.
[106] Kellermann, 'L'adaptation', pp. 513f.; Pratt, 'Adapting', pp. 81, 70.   [107] 'Enite', p. 13.

simply providing an easy rhyme with *Ovide* in the next line. This finds explicit expression when Chrétien underlines the equality of their partnership (1504: 'Mout estoient igal et per' They were equally and evenly matched), insinuating that this is the story of a couple.[108] Hartmann works differently, but in the same direction. Although the fragmentary beginning of his work lacks a prologue, what survives soon makes it clear that Erec is presented as the protagonist (4: 'durch den diu rede erhaben ist' who is the hero of the story), but, as with Chrétien, this is later qualified. The German author does this emphatically at the close of his work, showing that he has related the story of a couple, by saying that they *both* lived long and happily (10115: 'ze wunsche wurden si beide alt'), after which God rewarded them *both* with eternal life (10128: ' … im und sînem wîbe,/mit dem êwigen lîbe'). In one small detail Hartmann even goes a step further than Chrétien in emphasising the individuality of the woman. In the French version she is named for us as late as the day of her marriage (2025–31) on the grounds that unless a woman is called by her proper name she is not married. Her naming is thus a function of her marriage, of her being joined to a man, whereas with Hartmann she is given her name from the beginning, when we also learn the names of her parents (428–31). It is of course true that the German author's practice is to name his characters earlier than Chrétien, who has a liking for initial anonymity and later naming,[109] but it is significant (and cannot have escaped Hartmann's notice) that on this occasion he was granting Enite a measure of individuality not dependent on her relationship with Erec.

Giving Enite this degree of individuality means that Hartmann is well placed to highlight the interaction between man and wife. Although this interaction begins only at Karnant, it grants Enite a marked role in the establishment of Erec's identity,[110] but this role is by no means simply subordinate to his. In one important sense he is actually dependent on her, for on their journey it is she who is aware of dangers and can warn him, while Erec, physically, but also symbolically encumbered by his armour,[111] is unable to see or hear. With this ironic reversal of the knight's conventional role of protecting the weak, it is in fact the woman who repeatedly rescues the man. When in the German text Erec is early appointed *rex designatus* by his father Lac (2919–23), the inclusion of Enite in this appointment is

[108] Pérennec, *Recherches* I 129.
[109] Green, 'Namedropping', pp. 89–101.   [110] Sosna, *Identität*, p. 68.
[111] Scholz, *Hartmann*, p. 788 (on 4150–65), calls this passage an apparently realistic explanation of Erec's incapacity because, despite his armour, he is later (after the couple's reconciliation) fully aware of approaching danger (6872–80).

strikingly out of the ordinary[112] and has no parallel in Chrétien, who brings no more than their actual coronation at the close of his work (6859, 6893). This early inclusion of Enite is taken up at the end of the German text (10119–23) where, contrary to any patriarchal control of wife by husband, the 'king's duty to act honourably upon his wife's promptings does not detract from her counsel as a valid component of the exercise of kingship'.[113] Enite's involvement in Erec's kingship I have elsewhere referred to by comparison with *Parzival*.[114] Parzival resembles Erec in forfeiting his royal title *in absentia* because of his prolonged knightly quest and it is restored to him, too, only towards the end of the work. Just as Parzival acquires his royal title again when he rejoins his wife, so does Erec regain his title *künec* when he is reunited with Enite.

The couple's royal status also plays a part in the carefully chosen terms used to plot the progress not merely of Erec, but also of Enite in Hartmann's work. The distribution of these terms is in three stages, the first of which covers their youthful immaturity and inexperience. At this stage Erec's youth is expressed by the adjective *jung* 'young' (18, 145, sometimes underlined by the remark that this was his first chivalric exploit, 1264–9, 2252–5), but also by *juncherre* 'young lord' (150) and *jungelinc* 'youth' (708, 757). *Kint* 'child' and *kintlîch* 'childish' are also used of him (765, 711). Correspondingly, at this stage Enite is also called a child, *kint* (309, 1318), but in addition a maiden, *maget* (310, 323, 804) or *magedîn* (1542). Enite can also be termed *juncvrouwe* (344, 352) at this stage and *vrouwe*, but as a term of polite address applicable to a young noblewoman, as is clear from its conjunction with *kint* (1318) and with *maget* (804, 1530).

New terms come into play when we enter the second stage, dealing with the couple's adult experience. At this stage, the terms used of Erec indicate two aspects of his maturity: as a knight and as a married man. His newly acquired knighthood is expressed by various terms: *ritter*, especially when he is victorious (898, 1266), *ritterlîch* for chivalric behaviour (1807, 2489), but also *man* (961, 1288, 1307), *manlîch* (2534) and *manheit* (2685, 2830). Other terms include *guoter kneht* (3112), *degen* (4330, 5498) and *herre*, especially after victorious combat (1369, 2572). Two of these terms for a man's maturity also serve to express his new status as a married man: *man* (3138, 3942) and *herre* (6100). At this second stage, however, Enite's position is different for, as a woman in patriarchal society, she has no function in society at large, but only in terms of her relationship to her husband. In the

[112] *Ibid.*, p. 730 (on 2918–23).   [113] *Ibid.*, p. 998 (on 10119–23). Quotation: Jillings, 'Ideal', p. 122.
[114] Green, 'King', pp. 175–83.

sense of 'wife' *wîp* is therefore now used of her, above all repeatedly in the critical scene at Karnant (2925–67), but this word also designates her as a member of the female sex (3169, 3371), even as no more than a sex object in the eyes of predatory males (3213, 3333).

Up to this point, a feminist objection is easily imagined: in all this Enite's progress is not independent or woman-centred, but geared to a man, at the first stage to her father, then to her husband. After what we saw two paragraphs earlier it is no surprise that the position is rectified when we come to the third stage, the couple's eventual royal status.[115] This does not start promisingly, for when Erec is first declared *rex designatus* (2921), this is followed in the next line by the equivalent for Enite: the woman is termed *künegîn* only because the man is *künec*, she is a function of him. After this scene, however, these royal terms are withheld from both of them for a long stretch of the narrative and are restored to them, some time before their concluding coronation, in symbolic terms once they have established their merit. The decisive feature about this, however, is that the title *künegîn* is restored to Enite (6507: 'diu edel künegîn') at the moment when she resists Oringles's attempt to persuade her to join him in a wedding banquet, well before it is at length conferred on Erec again (6763) as the couple ride from Limors in new-found reconciliation. These two passages come a long way before their eventual formal coronation, they incorporate a metaphorical or symbolic concept of kingship (see much later 9891: 'der êren krône' the crown of honour), to which Enite gains access independently of her husband and earlier than he. She may ascend to this point in parallel with him, but her progress is not slavishly geared to his.

This suggestion that we are dealing with a 'Doppelroman' in which the progress of two individuals is sketched and in which the woman is no mere functional appendage to the man can be confirmed by a feature of narrative structure of the work. What Lacy has observed of Chrétien's version (that he operates with a shifting centre of consciousness) is also applicable to the German adaptation.[116] Lacy sees this reflected in the three parts of the romance. Up to the Carnant episode and then again after the second encounter with Guivret (immediately following the couple's departure from Limors) events are narrated from Erec's point of view, with an eye to his thoughts and with scant attention to Enide's. In between, however, during the journey of adventure the reverse is the case: we are made privy to Enide's internal monologues, to her fears and doubts, but now Erec's inner

---

[115] On this see Pérennec, *EG* 28 (1973), 295f.; *Recherches* I 102, 104, 131.
[116] Lacy, *Craft*, p. 40; Jones, 'Empathy', pp. 300–3.

life is largely withheld from us. What started and (with qualifications) finishes by being a story of Erec (as both authors early said it would be) has become, over this long middle stretch, a story of Enide. In both key episodes (Galoain and Oringle) Erec's role depends on Enide's, these episodes are hers, rather than his.[117] On a lower, numerical level of analysis Huby has strengthened the view that Hartmann, like Chrétien, composed a *roman à deux*, and for Quast the German version is a work with two protagonists.[118] It would be going too far to equate Chrétien's first Arthurian romance in this respect with his Grail romance, with the two protagonists Perceval and Gauvain, but it would be as wrong to regard Erec's wife as marginalised as it was for modern scholarship to marginalise Gauvain in the Grail romance for so long by neglect.

In both versions of this romance, especially in their advocacy of love within marriage and what it can offer women, there is an undeniably strong utopian element. That is clear early on, admittedly with regard to the man rather than the woman, in Erec's unrealistically free choice of partner in marriage: as the son of a king he marries, if not for love, at least for personal reasons without the need for consultation with father and court, thereby flying in the face of contemporary feudal marriage policy.[119] If that measure of freedom is granted the man, but not the woman, that represents the position against which partnership and reciprocity in marriage are advocated, values that could be realised, with good luck, in arranged marriages, but whose presentation as an ideal (*amîs* and *man*) is undeniably utopian. As Tomasek has shown in the case of Gottfried's *Tristan*, the presentation of a utopian ideal cannot ignore the reality which it implicitly criticises and against which it pits itself. In Tomasek's monograph this criticism concerned feudal society at large,[120] but for us it is directed more specifically at the marriage policies of that society and the place of women in it. But a shrewd awareness of the difficulties involved goes further than that, more so with Chrétien (more realistic or conscious of the obstacles as the first vernacular advocate?) than with Hartmann. Chrétien may present Erec, after his marriage, making his wife his lover (2439: 'De li fist s'amie et sa drue'), but this happy achievement of the author's ideal is rendered precarious by the ensuing crisis and by the cruelty of his treatment of Enide.[121] Hartmann's Erec may decline likewise, but not from a provisional attainment of this ideal, absent from the German text at this point. Moreover,

---

[117] Blosen, *OL* 31 (1976), 96f.   [118] Huby, *RG* 6 (1976), 3–5. Quast, *ZfdA* 122 (1993), 180.
[119] Schulze, *PBB* 105 (1983), 28 ('utopischer Entwurf'); Mertens, 'Enide', p. 72.
[120] Tomasek, *Utopie*, pp. 41–123.   [121] Sargent-Baur, *RPh* 33 (1980), 384.

Chrétien suggests that even the final reconciliation of the couple may contain difficulties by leading us to wonder how thorough Erec's abandonment of patriarchal behaviour may be, even in the act of now placing himself at the service of his wife (4926: 'Tot a vostre comandemant / Vuel estre des or an avant' Now I wish to be henceforth entirely at your command), for to this he adds the words 'as I was before' (4928: 'Aussi con j'estoie devant'). When indeed did he act in that way? This unsettling detail is again absent in the German text. Finally, in the same context the French Erec condescendingly forgives Enide her words at Carnant (4929: 'Et se vos rien m'avez mesdite, / Jel vos pardoing tot et claim quite / Del forfet et de la parole' If you have in any way offended me, I pardon and forgive you what you may have done or said), whereas in the German version he shows more insight into his own failings and seeks forgiveness (6796: '... daz si wolde vergeben / als ungeselleclîchez leben / unde manege arbeit / die si ûf der verte leit' that she might forgive him the loveless life and the tribulations she had undergone on the journey). Whilst the French version, in having Erec say that he will place himself at his wife's service 'as before', leaves it open whether his future behaviour will be any better, Hartmann has him expressly promise that it will be (6800: 'bezzerunge er ir gehiez, / die er benamen wâr liez' he promised her an improvement which he also carried out). In all these passages the German author has modified his source in the direction of a greater idealisation that has long been seen as a feature of him, removing some of the qualifications and doubts which Chrétien has more realistically allowed to be visible.

Not all the authors who make use of the *amie* and *fame* formula simplify the difficulties in achieving it, as Hartmann had in some measure done. The precarious nature of this combination which Chrétien had illustrated by applying it to Erec at Carnant just before his lapse into patriarchalism on the couple's departure can also be found in Wolfram's *Parzival*. Here the relationship between Orilus and Jeschute has been modelled on Erec and Enide, as has long been recognised,[122] but the fact that Orilus regards himself as her *amîs* (just as Erec had regarded his wife as his *amie*) does nothing to protect her against his brutality. In both intertextual episodes the presentation of love in marriage is shown to be precarious, which suggests that at this point Wolfram was more indebted to Chrétien than to Hartmann. Nor should we expect an author like Chaucer to be any less shrewdly aware of the impact of human shortcomings on the idea of love in marriage, as illustrated in his *Franklin's Tale*. Reverting to the passage

[122] Wand, *Wolfram*, pp. 20f.; Draesner, *Wege*, pp. 200–17.

quoted above, presenting the husband as servant in love and lord in marriage,[123] we must now focus on a linguistic detail. In summing this up, Chaucer leaves the fact of lordship intact, but raises a doubt about the other pole ('Servage? nay, but in lordshipe above'), a doubt resembling that suggested by Chrétien regarding Erec at the *comandemant* of his wife. Mann has questioned whether the marriage sketched in these terms by Chaucer can truly be called one of equality,[124] but to this observation must be added the disparity between the two poles, for whereas the man's lordship was a legal fact of medieval marriage his 'servage' was based on nothing more than a literary fiction. However, that does nothing to diminish the historical importance of this fiction, for Chrétien and Hartmann, standing at the beginning of a vernacular tradition, present for discussion by laymen the possibility of reconciling love with marriage.

How this possibility was received by men and women in the audience can only be surmised. Men may have recognised the outlines of their own patriarchal behaviour in Erec, seeing him as a role model, but they may also have reacted like the court at Karnant and regarded him as a warning against subjection to women ('Frauensklave'). They may have been worried by the indications of Erec's moral inferiority to his wife or by the fact that even as a knight he was dependent on her vision, both in reporting the court's reaction to him and in warning him of dangers on their journey. As regards the central question of *amie* and *fame*, they could have been put at ease by its fictional nature or disturbed by the introduction of potential reciprocity, even equality into vernacular discussion of marriage.

Our assessment of women's possible reaction must be equally hypothetical. Did they recognise, with whatever degree of resignation or dissatisfaction, the picture of contemporary feudal patriarchalism presented in the romance as an unchanging fact of medieval life and did they show particular interest in the by no means marginalised role played by a woman in this narrative? Were they particularly attracted by the pointers to Enite's moral superiority, even indispensability to her husband? Did they regard the question of *amie* and *fame* as so much wishful thinking, remote from the experience of many women, or did they welcome the introduction of this idea into contemporary discussion?

As against such questions, to which we have no certain answers, two points stand out from the course of our argument. First, it is by no means justified to describe this work, in either version, as a male-oriented text[125] or to suggest that Hartmann's text was not meant, as Chrétien's was, to

[123] See above, p. 111.   [124] Mann, *Feminizing*, pp. 90f.   [125] Cartlidge, *Marriage*, p. 157.

provoke debate.[126] There may be a difference of degree between them, but not of kind. Secondly, we cannot agree with the assessment of *Erec* made by C. S. Lewis, very much in passing and from the standpoint of a now questionable view of courtly love, when he judges the work on the basis of the scene in which Erec and Enide's father negotiate marriage terms. He says: 'The whole scene, however true it may be to the marriage practices of the time, is strangely archaic compared with the new ideals of love'.[127] It is impermissible to proceed from this one scene to a judgment of the whole work, in which contemporary marriage practices are scrutinised critically, while to suggest that the work, like this scene, is archaic entirely misses the novelty of what Chrétien (and with him Hartmann) is suggesting in the vernacular. If the term archaic must be used at all, it refers not to work or author, but to Erec himself.

---

[126] Pratt, 'Adapting', pp. 68, 84.   [127] Lewis, *Allegory*, p. 26.

CHAPTER 4

Tristan

The same three themes we considered in *Erec* (love, marriage, knighthood) also recur in the Tristan story,[1] but under very different auspices. Love and marriage are present here, too, but divided between three people, not incorporated in one couple. Here the narrative is concerned with the position of Isolde between lover and husband and also, after the lovers' separation, with Tristan's position between lover and wife. As regards love and knighthood, Schausten rightly objects to judging Eilhart by reference to the later author, Gottfried, and to emphasising his depiction of Tristrant more as a warrior than as a lover by contrast with Gottfried's priorities.[2] Eilhart's original audience, however, would have judged his work by reference to those of heroic tradition known to them, summed up programmatically in the prologues to the *Annolied* and later to the *Nibelungenlied* as essentially warlike.[3] Seen in this light, Eilhart presents something new, a work treating not simply heroic exploits, but also love (52: 'von manheit und von minnen'). His novelty in literary history lies in treating the subject of love (and, with it, marriage) in a combination of themes. With Gottfried the theme of knighthood is still present, if reduced in scope and less central (mainly in the narrative before the potion scene and after the lovers' separation). With him, although all three themes are treated, the focus is more on love and marriage. In both these earliest German versions of the Tristan story ample scope is found for the important role of women.

PATRIARCHAL SOCIETY

Early on in Gottfried's version we are reminded of the authority wielded by men over women in feudal society. When the pregnant Blanscheflur thinks

---

[1] In this chapter the names of the lovers are distinguished according to the different versions: Tristrant and Isalde with Eilhart, Tristran and Ysolt with Thomas, Tristan and Isolde with Gottfried. To avoid confusion I refer to Isolde's mother (also called Isolde) as the Irish queen, and to Isolde of the White Hands as the second Isolde.

[2] Schausten, *Erzählwelten*, pp. 52f.   [3] *Annolied* 1, 1–6; *Nibelungenlied* 1, 1–4.

that she is to be deserted by Riwalin she fears the worst from her brother Marke (their father having presumably died), anticipating at least disinheritance and at the worst even death (1468–84). Whereas a feudal marriage was normally negotiated between the woman's father and her future husband, here Blanscheflur stands in a similar gender-disadvantaged position between her brother (to whom she refers as her lord, 1468: *hêrre*) and the lover who she thinks is about to leave her. Even Rual, Riwalin's loyal marshal in Parmenie, whose marriage is sketched as harmonious, is given a patriarchal touch in giving an order (4242: 'gebôt') for his wife to carry out rather than a request. That in such a society women were not merely subject to male authority, but also exposed to violence is shown in the episode in Eilhart's version where count Riole of Nantes asks his ruler Havelin for his daughter, is rebuffed by Havelin on grounds of a mésalliance (5546f., 5560f.), but then wages war against his lord to gain his daughter by force. A similar, but successful abduction of a woman by force is found in the version of Thomas of Britain (Douce 939–46): the knight Tristran le Nain (no relation of the protagonist) complains that his lover (*amie*) was abducted by force by Estult li Orgillus, who now holds her captive in his castle.

Against such a background it is no surprise that women can be handed over very much as exchange objects from one man to another. In Eilhart's version, in which the effects of the love potion wear off after a time, Tristrant expresses his willingness to hand back Isalde to Marke (4915–8), an action which is then carried out by the two men without any mention of the woman's role (4974–81). Gottfried develops his criticism of such an attitude most emphatically in the episode concerning the Irish baron Gandin, a would-be lover of Isolde who tricks her away from Marke by exploiting the latter's rash promise to give him any reward of his choosing for playing on the rote. Underlying this episode is the degradation of a woman to an object of exchange or reward by two men, her husband and would-be lover (not Tristan).[4] Gandin, whose role as an admirer of Isolde is made clear from the beginning (13131: *amîs*), is criticised as a deceiver (13206: *trügenaere*, see also 13419, 13421), but above all for instituting the degradation by regarding Isolde as his reward (13208: *miete*). Suitable judgment is passed on him in the shame with which, after Tristan has in turn outwitted him, Gandin returns to Ireland (13430–3). However telling this criticism of Gandin may be, it is outdone by the scorn heaped on Marke, the ruler who makes a rash promise and the husband who, in handing over his wife as a reward, is complicit in treating her as an object. Tellingly this biting

---

[4] Tomasek, *Utopie*, pp. 66f.

criticism of Marke is voiced by Tristan when he returns to the court with Isolde, reproaching him with lightly giving his wife away and making common property of her for the sake of a performance (13442–52). Confident in his superiority Tristan the lover can impudently recommend the husband to keep better guard of his wife in future (13453f.). Gottfried's treatment of this episode differs from what we have just seen of Eilhart, however, not merely in his criticism of commodifying women, but also in the way in which the woman's reaction to such humiliating treatment is not neglected, which we shall see is also true of the scene with the Irish steward at the court of Dublin. When Gandin takes her away with him from Marke Isolde is shown weeping passionately and showing great distress (13267: 'vil inneclîche weinende / und manege klage erscheinende') and is still in tears when Tristan catches up with them (13294f.). With Gottfried Isolde may still be the passive victim of men's behaviour in this episode, but we are at least confronted with the emotional cost of her victim status.

In a love-romance in which knighthood plays a part, one specific way in which a woman can be handed over from man to man is to treat her as the victor's prize. With his stress on *manheit* as well as *minne* this is true of Eilhart's work. The Irish king promises his daughter Isalde in marriage to whoever may slay the dragon infesting his land (1603–7, 1738–47), and when the Irish steward's claim as victor is unmasked as false even he is forced to acknowledge that Isalde should justly be Tristrant's (2210: 'ez solde habin Tristrant / die vrauwin billîche'). Here again the matter is adjudicated by the men involved (king, Tristrant, steward), while the woman is left out of account. A similar situation occurs between Tristrant and the second Isalde, whose brother Kehenis suggests to Tristrant, after the latter's victory in battle, that he ask his father to give him his daughter in marriage, both as a suitable prize for the victor and also because Tristrant, unlike count Riole, would be a fitting match for a king's daughter (6116–19, 6225). As far as Gottfried's version is concerned, we shall soon turn to his treatment of the rival claims of Tristan and the Irish steward as dragon-slayer, but for the moment may observe that the protagonist, as the true victor and as one negotiating on behalf of the marriage plans of the Cornish court with that of Ireland, can rightly claim Isolde as his reward (11283: 'nu weset der triuwen gemant: / iuwer tohter stât in mîner hant' Remember your promise: your daughter is mine). Gottfried does not leave it at that, but up to this point he presents a recognisably patriarchal view of things.

A patriarchal society in which women are marginalised and subordinated to male authority and in which men make the important decisions amongst themselves can produce not only rivalry between men (Eilhart's Riole and

Tristrant) or opposition between them (Tristan and the Irish steward in both German versions), but also a close, even intimate sense of male bonding and companionship. Eilhart depicts this unmistakably in the case of Marke and his nephew Tristrant (756f.: *vrûntlîche* friendly, *libe* affection; 768: *minneglîche* lovingly; 779: 'der koning in dô kuste / und druckte in zu sîner bruste' the king then kissed him and pressed him to his breast), where the key terms correspond to those used later of the love between Tristrant and Isalde (3255: '… he kuste / und dwang sie zu sînen brusten / gar minneglîche' he kissed and pressed her to his breast lovingly). Similar terminology is used of Tristrant's relationship with other male friends: with Tinas (4082f., 4090–2) and with Kehenis (6106–13, 6202). How central this male bonding between Marke and Tristrant is to the whole narrative is seen in the fact that for the king this at first overrode any idea of marriage (and hence of any son as heir) and that from this stemmed the envy of other courtiers and the subsequent action in Ireland (1337–48). Thomas, too, suggests a similarly close friendship between Tristran and Kaherdin, involving fellowship, love and friendship (Douce 1094f., 1111–21), even deserving the key term from courtly love, *fine amur* (1120f.). Gottfried's depiction of the intimacy between Marke and Tristan has been discussed at length by Krohn.[5] Although he concedes that Gottfried proceeds most discreetly here, Krohn concludes that what is suggested is a homosexual inclination of Marke for his young nephew, and that this is meant to incriminate Marke and thereby transpose to him some of the guilt later attaching to the adulterous lovers. Quite apart from the fact that this leaves unexplained the other cases mentioned here, the most telling objection has been voiced by Jaeger who, basing himself on the distinction between 'homosexual' and 'homosocial' (describing a non-sexual male friend-ship), argues that the terminology of love could be used of homosocial relationships in many medieval contexts, including that of ruler and courtier.[6] We do not have to accept the thesis of Jaeger's *Ennobling love* to see that the friendship and love of a ruler (*amicitia*, *dilectio*) could mean 'entry into the narrow circle of the king's advisers'[7] (precisely what called forth the envy of others at Marke's court) and need not suggest any homosexual inclination. Whether we accept this or not, whether we read this particular relationship as homosocial or homosexual, this does not alter the fact that in either case a male relationship was meant at first by Marke to exclude marriage.

We cannot remain content with this, however, for a story of heterosexual adulterous love cannot by definition avoid presenting a view on love,

[5] Krohn, 'Erotik', pp. 362–76.   [6] Jaeger, 'Mark', pp. 183–97; *Love*, pp. 15, 17.
[7] Jaeger, 'Mark', p. 189.

marriage and women. Here Schnell has done pioneering work in criticising
the view that Gottfried set up the love of Tristan and Isolde as an ideal
relationship opposed to what is found within the confines of marriage.[8]
To show that Gottfried did not regard love and marriage as irreconcilable
and that the contrast he depicted was between love and a loveless marriage
Schnell considers three cases in Gottfried's work where love is indeed to
be found in marriage. His first case is Tristan's parents, Riwalin and
Blanscheflur, whose loving union with each other is depicted well before
their legal marriage, so that they take a freely chosen mutual love into their
marital relationship.[9] Moreover, Riwalin's marshal Rual recommends him
to marry Blanscheflur on the grounds that since she has been kind to him
she should now reap the benefit (by avoiding the disgrace that would
otherwise have befallen her). In other words, so far from being forced into
an arranged marriage the woman's interests are here taken into account and,
to judge by the implications of the disgrace if she were to have her child out
of wedlock (1493: *kebeslîche*), this marriage is precisely what she wants.[10]
Schnell's second example is the picture of a pretended marriage which
Tantris (alias Tristan) fabricates in order to convince the Irish queen that
he must return to his wife.[11] The terms with which he depicts his marriage
are revealing: it is a fully legal union (8193: *êlich wîp* wedded wife), he loves
his wife as much as he does himself (8194: 'die minne ich als mîn selbes lîp')
and the word he uses to describe his heartfelt love for her (8192: *herzeliebe*) is
one used elsewhere of Riwalin and Blanscheflur before their marriage (1430)
and of Tristan and Isolde (13760, 16522). Tantris's picture of his marriage
may be made up, but it has the advantage of plausibility, as is shown by the
queen's immediate acceptance of its truth (8205–9), so that the presence of
love in marriage cannot have been quite so rare as is implied by Gislebert of
Mons in the case of Baldwin of Hainaut.[12] Finally, Schnell considers what is
revealed to us of the marriage of Isolde's parents or rather what is said of
Gurmun's attitude to his wife.[13] He respects her for her intrinsic qualities of
beauty and wisdom (9725), but this respect for her is coupled repeatedly with
love and affection (9719: 'sîn liebez wîp' his dear wife, cf. 9724, 9727). This
explains why he can be called the lover of his wife (9730: *friunt*), a conjunction
of roles whose programmatic importance we considered in *Erec*.

Not discussed by Schnell, but put forward by Chinca,[14] is an argument *ex
negativo*. Both Thomas and Gottfried make use of the language of canon

[8] Schnell, *ZfdPh* 101 (1982), 334–69.   [9] *Ibid.*, pp. 340–4.   [10] *Ibid.*, pp. 341, 344.
[11] *Ibid.*, pp. 344–9.   [12] See above, p. 25.   [13] *ZfdPh* 101 (1982), 349f.
[14] Chinca, *Gottfried*, pp. 26–32.

law on marriage in their depiction of the lovers' adulterous relationship. Three features are employed in this vindication of illicit love. The love of Tristan and Isolde is presented as indissoluble (despite Tristan's later backsliding), as the Church held marriage to be. The lovers' bond is symbolised by the ring given by Isolde to Tristan at their parting, as the wedding-ring was a ring of fidelity (*anulus fidei*). The lovers' relationship is founded on mutual *consensus*, which is as important for Thomas and Gottfried in love as it was for the canonists in marriage. The purpose of these parallels is to justify adulterous love, but their force can also be turned round to suggest that ideally marriage should be like this, based on mutual love and *consensus*.

Schnell's argument is important in qualifying the opinion that in *Tristan* Gottfried depicted the necessary contradiction between love and marriage in his day, but in its turn this argument needs to be qualified itself.[15] In the first place, the examples he adduces must be termed marginal to the work, by no means central. The nearest a case of love in marriage comes to what Tristan and Isolde exemplify outside marriage is Riwalin and Blanscheflur. The genesis and strength of their mutual love are depicted at length in the prehistory, but the phenomenon that concerns us is not love, but love in marriage, and this aspect of their relationship is given markedly short narrative space, for their marriage is followed very soon after by the death of both of them, Riwalin in battle, Blanscheflur in childbirth. Moreover, Rual's recommendation that Riwalin should allow Blanscheflur to reap the benefit of her kindness is coupled with the shrewd recognition that his lord's standing is likely to benefit from marriage to the sister of a renowned ruler (1610–17), so that an element of feudal marriage policy is present even here. This strongest example of love in marriage neither belongs to the main story nor is granted much narrative scope. The other two cases are even more marginal and episodic, while Tantris's story of his pretended marriage, however plausible, remains a fabrication, and is not presented as a narrative fact.

We must go beyond this, however, for Schnell's survey of marriages in *Tristan* leaves out of account one marriage from which love is indeed absent, moreover a marriage which is neither marginal nor episodic, but instead fundamental to the whole work, namely that of Marke and Isolde. Here there can be no doubt that love, as Gottfried meant it to be understood, is not to be found: Isolde's love belongs entirely and exclusively to Tristan, while Gottfried makes it unmistakably clear that what Marke feels for his wife is not love, but lust (17771: *geluste unde gelange*). This central marriage is

---

[15] See Schausten, *Erzählwelten*, pp. 176f.

represented in addition to the possibilities of love-marriage we have looked at, it is a foil to the picture of ideal love incorporated in the lovers. Their love is therefore contrasted not with marriage as such, but with a loveless marriage characteristic of much (if not all) marriage practice of the time. But what are the features of the marriage of Marke and Isolde that remind us of feudal marriage practice?[16]

In the first place, the idea that Marke should marry comes not from him, but is a suggestion made to him by the Cornish barons for political reasons which they know will carry weight, even though their motive may be jealousy and a wish to oust Tristan from his position as Marke's favourite. They argue that the king needs to ensure an heir to the throne (8359–61), meaning of course that for them anyone would be preferable to Tristan. They also bring into play the possibility that marriage might have the political advantage of peace between Cornwall and Ireland (8494–8501) and dangle before Marke the enticing prospect that, since Isolde is the only child of the Irish royal couple, Ireland might one day be his (8503–8). These are reasons of state which a ruler is meant to take into account, they leave little room for personal inclination, let alone love as a motive for marriage. Such considerations are matched by a similar attitude at the Irish court, whose predisposition to such a policy is set by Gurmun's public offer to give his daughter to whoever would rid him of the scourge of the dragon, provided only that he be of noble birth (8913–17). When informed of Gurmun's agreement to the Cornish proposal the Irish barons accept it, as the Cornish ones had suggested, as a guarantee of peace (11386–90) and see political advantage in having Isolde as queen of Cornwall and England (11395–401). What Gottfried omits in all this is any express mention of Isolde's *consensus* to this marriage. It must have been given for the marriage to be legally valid,[17] but the narrator's silence on this score is significant. Instead, what we are shown, as we shall see with the Irish steward, is something of Isolde's reactions to these negotiations over her future, but also, on the voyage to Cornwall, her sense of having been commodified in this deal between two kings (11594: 'i'ne weiz, wie ich verkoufet bin' I do not know what I have been sold into), accentuated by the way in which she is not married to the man who slew the dragon, but is to be passed on by him to someone else.[18]

What stands out in these political and dynastic features of marriage policy is their complete exclusion of personal feelings (hinted to us only in the case of the woman victim), above all with Marke himself, both with his initial

[16] On this see Combridge, *Recht*, pp. 48–79.   [17] *Ibid.*, p. 59, fn. 91.   [18] *Ibid.*, p. 61.

disinclination for marriage and in his passivity in all that ensues. His impersonal feelings about this marriage are presented drastically to us on his wedding night, when Brangaene acts as a virginal substitute for Isolde, for Marke is condemned for his failure to tell the difference between Brangaene and Isolde as little as with brass and gold. The damning verdict is passed on him that he could not see the difference between one woman and the other (12670: 'in dûhte wîp alse wîp' for him one woman was like another; 12673: 'ime was ein als ander' for him there was no difference between them). What Marke brings to his marriage is therefore not only his lack of personal feeling for the individual woman Isolde, but also lust rather than love. Against this particular loveless marriage, concluded for reasons of feudal marriage policy, the extramarital love of Tristan and Isolde is set up as a counter-model.

Central though this loveless marriage may be to Gottfried's purpose, it is not the only example he presents, for in the figure of the Irish steward, falsely claiming Isolde as his prize for supposedly disposing of the dragon, we are also confronted with the same implications, if only as a hypothetical prospect, not an achieved fact. This episode has been interpreted as a satire on the topos of a knight serving his lady in combat. The steward is introduced in this guise as the would-be lover of Isolde, but without her approval (8954: 'der was ouch unde wolte sîn / der jungen küniginne amîs / wider ir willen alle wîs' he wanted to be the young princess's lover, in every way against her will), so that from the beginning we are made privy to her reaction. To complete the picture he is described as wanting to be her lover and knight (9099: 'friunt unde ritter') and as boasting of what he has undergone for the sake of a woman (9228–30, 9249f.). His claims are deflated for us when, declaiming his service of Isolde in fashionable French (9169f.), he charges on horseback against the dragon whom we and he know to be already dead, despatched earlier by Tristan. The most pointed criticism of him, however, comes from Isolde's mother who dismisses this lady's knight (9909: 'vrouwen ritter') as effeminate, too versed in the secrets of the boudoir (9910: 'du weist der frouwen art ze wol: / du bist dar în ze verre komen, / ez hât dir der mannes art benomen' You know women's ways too well, you have come too far in them and they have deprived you of your manhood) to be truly a man. How skin-deep the steward's service of a lady really is becomes clear in his venomous attack, when thwarted, on womankind at large (9870–96), accusing them all of contrary and bewildering waywardness in loving what hates them and hating what loves them.[19]

---

[19] On this negative generalisation see below, p. 146.

There is however another side to the picture, for what the steward is after is not just Isolde's love, but marriage to her as the daughter of the otherwise heirless royal couple, so that the Irish court is the scene of one marriage plan pitched against another. Gurmun had patriarchally created this opportunity by promising his daughter to whoever should rid him of the dragon and the steward sees this as a means of self-advancement (9804–10). What lies behind his façade of love service are the prospects of a profitable marriage. In this light Gurmun's offer of his daughter to the dragon-slayer is matched by the steward who maintains his wish for Isolde against her wishes (8956: 'wider ir willen alle wîs'). Her lack of *consensus* to this putative arranged marriage is expressed by her contemplating suicide rather than succumbing to his will (9292: 'ê sîn wille an mir ergê') and by her mother's emphatic contrast between his wishes and her daughter's (9930: 'du wellest Îsôte, / und si enwelle dîn niht' you want Isolde and she wants nothing to do with you). What had been arranged by Gurmun over his daughter's head runs up against her wishes, a situation arising from feudal marriage policy which Gottfried highlights by depicting the woman's point of view. The focus of Gottfried's narrative at this point can best be seen by its contrast with Eilhart, with whom Isalde's reaction is simply one of disbelief, a conviction that the steward could not possibly have dealt with the dragon (1749: 'vatir, des geloube mir. / hê hât nicht rechte gesaget dir. / her begîng doch nî vromigheit. / wâ nam he nû die manheit, / daz her in torste bestân?' Father, believe me, he did not tell you the truth. He accomplished no brave exploit, where did he find the manhood to dare to face it?). With Gottfried, however, Isolde's reaction is internalised more emotionally into repugnance and despair rather than incredulity. The prospect facing her causes Isolde's heart to die within her (9274) and she faces a living death (9596). Underlying this reaction is her revulsion at being treated as a bargaining object, a reward held out by her father and claimed by whoever kills the dragon (9809: *ze solde* as payment; 9842: *lôn* reward). She sees herself as little more than an object put up for sale (9859: 'enwil ich niemer veile sîn' I shall never be up for sale). What is conventionally depicted as a marriage arranged between men is here shown up negatively from the woman's point of view.

Isolde's objection to being commodified in this way also finds expression in her complaint on the voyage from Ireland at not knowing what she has been sold into (11594: *verkoufet*), so that her view of the matter (11603–8) emerges by contrast with what Tristan, still acting as Marke's representative in an arranged marriage, describes as the material advantages of such a union (11596–602). Schnell discusses this scene and questions whether it reflects the utilitarian considerations of feudal marriage policy.[20] He argues on negative grounds, objecting first that Isolde had voiced no objection to being put up as *solt* by her father in the first place. But what say did any woman have in such a situation? Does Enite have any say in her marriage to Erec as the victor in the sparrowhawk adventure? Secondly, Schnell points out that Isolde likewise raised no objection to being an object of exchange in the debate with the Irish steward. Instead, though, we are more convincingly shown her inwardly voiced emotional repugnance, while the debate is most effectively conducted, if not by her, then at least by another woman, her mother. Schnell would have it that Isolde restricts her argument against the steward to the falseness of his claim, so that the paltry hardship he has undergone (9858: 'alsô maezlîche nôt') or the trifles mentioned by the mother (9856: 'alse kleiner geschiht') are meant to refer to no more than his carrying away the dragon's head from the scene of Tristan's combat. But the inward objections of Isolde, together with the repeated stress on *lôn*, *solt*, *veile* and *verkoufet*, suggest that what is in fact paltry or a trifle is the claim to win a woman as a prize in combat. Although Tristan, still acting in an official capacity, attempts to show her that marriage to Marke represents an escape from the steward's claim (11615–22), Isolde has as little choice in being married to Marke as she would have had to the steward. The irony of Gottfried's employment of the *amor et militia* topos at Dublin lies in this: as with Erec and Enite before their marriage at Arthur's court or with Parzival and Condwiramurs before their marriage, love also comes into play in *Tristan* to make the knight's claim for the woman somewhat more acceptable. But in *Tristan* this love, incorporated in the potion, is between the woman and the victor, Tristan, not her husband, Marke.

In describing in some detail two disastrous loveless unions, one an accomplished fact and the other only narrowly avoided, Gottfried employs many features of contemporary reality against which to set up his utopian vision of love. We may conclude this section by turning to two other German versions of the Tristan story, one before Gottfried and the other after him, which may fail to present a utopian view, but which nonetheless also reflect something of reality with all its deficiencies.

The earlier example comes from Eilhart, from his episode dealing with the unhappy marriage of Gariole and her obsessively jealous husband Nampetenis, whose pathological suspicions reach the point that whenever he is absent he has his wife locked inside the castle.[21] This does not fail to act

---

[20] *ZfdPh* 101 (1982), 363f.   [21] 7924–31. See also 9128–31.

as a challenge to her lover Kehenis (to whom she had promised herself even before her marriage, 7945–9) and his companion Tristrant when they procure a wax impression from which a duplicate key is made, so that we have here a triangular relationship reminiscent of that between Marke, Isolde and Tristan. Nampetenis reflects Marke in details which underline the former's pathological folly. He imposes surveillance on his wife: the term *hûte* (7874, 7879, 7940) is used of this, just as we shall see that it is in Gottfried's criticism of Marke's surveillance of Isolde in the excursus on women. Moreover, Gottfried's attack on husbands' surveillance of wives is paralleled by Eilhart's narrator denouncing its folly, too (7878–86). He does this effectively by means of a negative generalisation against husbands who behave in this way (no criticism is directed at Gariole), standing out by its timeless present (7878, 'mich wundert wes he denkit …' I am amazed at what he is thinking of)[22] from the surrounding narrative past (7874: 'hûte' watched over, 7887: 'daz wart an desin dingen schîn' this became clear). The position sketched by Eilhart in this episode is reminiscent of that in some of the lais of Marie de France, with whom a major theme is the lot of the *mal mariée*, trapped in an unhappy marriage imposed upon her against her wishes.[23] As with Eilhart, women are kept under watch (as with him, not always successfully), imprisoned either literally in a castle or by close surveillance, both symbolising what marriage without love was felt to mean from the woman's point of view.[24] The particular appeal of these lais (and perhaps of the Tristan theme) to women may explain why Denis Piramus in his *Vie de seint Edmund*, when talking of the popularity of Marie's lais at court, makes specific mention of the pleasure they give women (46: 'Les lais solent as dames pleire, / De joie les oient e de gré' The lais please the ladies who hear them gladly and with pleasure).

Our last example is provided by the *Tristan* continuation of Ulrich von Türheim. Early on the author has to deal with the situation where Gottfried's text broke off, with the triangular position of Tristan and the two Isoldes, accentuated by his decision, after separation from the first, to marry the second. By its nature, this is a loveless marriage since, although Isolde has fallen in love with her husband, Tristan is still emotionally tied to the first Isolde and fails to consummate the marriage. In the course of the wedding ceremony the bride is asked whether she is ready to marry Tristan, but her reply is couched in terms that fall short of a positive assent. She says

[22] In this line I take *he* as the equivalent of *swer*.   [23] Green, *Women*, pp. 240f.
[24] Bloch, *Marie*, pp. 52, 56f., 58–60.

that if she were to say No, that would anger her father, so that she had better refrain from that and instead do as her parents wish (200: 'spraeche ich nû, herre, "nein ich", / daz waere mîme vater zorn, / des ist ez bezzer verborn: / swaz wil mîn vater, daz wil ich. / vater und muoter des vröuten sich' If I were to say 'No, my lord' that would anger my father and is therefore better avoided. What my father wants is what I want. Father and mother were glad of that). How far from truly voluntary *consensus* this obedience to parental wishes could be is shown in Chrétien's *Cligés* (3128f.): here too Fenice says that she dare not contradict her father if he wishes to give her to another man.[25] This scene with Ulrich has every appearance of an arranged marriage, but this is crossed by the question asking for the woman's *consensus*, even though, to judge by the hesitancy of the bride's reply, this seems to be no more than a formality. As such it could reflect one of the ways in which feudal families could subvert the requirement of *consensus* by emotional pressure on the woman. More telling, however, is the fact that the question is addressed to the bride by Tristan and the way in which he does it. He seems to be asking her point blank (199: 'juncvrouwe, welt ir nemen mich?' Young lady, are you ready to accept me?), but this is twice undercut, first by the way in which it is explicitly said that he put his question jokingly (197: 'Tristan schimphlîchen sprach') and secondly by the laughter of bystanders (198: 'dâ von ze lachene in geschach'). This laughter conveys the impression that the question cannot be meant seriously (which would confirm the negative tone of the bride's reply), that the very idea of asking the woman is a joke, even ludicrous. A parallel suggests itself to this scene, too, if we recall the humorous tone pervading the marriage scene of the protagonist's nephew in *Ruodlieb*,[26] particularly the smile with which the bride accompanies her stipulation of equal treatment for wife as well as husband, and the laughter with which this is greeted by the bystanders. Her suggestion cannot apparently be taken all that seriously, either. In both works something still not usual or palatable has been given passing expression: with *Ruodlieb* equality of both partners in marriage, with Ulrich's *Tristan* the very idea of asking a woman for her *consensus*. Both works presuppose feudal conventions on marriage, but with both the curtain is lifted briefly to give us a glimpse of other possibilities. That this should be done so tentatively by Ulrich and that Gottfried's suggestions of love in marriage are marginal or episodic demonstrates that in the Tristan tradition these two phenomena could still be regarded as distinct, if not as actually opposed.

[25] See above, p. 85.   [26] See above, pp. 73f.

ANTIFEMININE ATTITUDES

In Hartmann's *Erec* we saw that the adjective *wîplîch*, used in a general sense to describe the nature of any member of the female sex, could shed light on how women were regarded in that work. With Gottfried's *Tristan* it is the substantive *wîp*, used in the same general sense and applied to a particular instance, which is more informative, telling us how women, their actions, thoughts and feelings were judged by the speaker in question, whether the narrator or a character in the work. We consider this substantive under two headings, positive and negative.

A laudatory connotation of *wîp* is suggested early with regard to Blanscheflur when it is said that whoever beheld her could not fail as a result to love woman (in the general sense) and virtuous qualities all the more (637: '... ern minnete dâ nâch iemer mê / wîp unde tugende baz dan ê'). When Isolde, having discovered Tristan's identity as the killer of her uncle, threatens him with his sword, the narrator asks in alarm how one whose womanly heart had never known bitter rancour (10242: 'diu siure an wîbes muote / noch herzegallen nie gewan') could strike a blow. She is prevented from doing this not so much by her own disposition as by sweet womanliness in the abstract (10259: 'diu süeze wîpheit lag ir an / unde zucte sie dâ van'; cf. 10269, 10281) in combat with an equally abstract Anger (10264). Gottfried's narrator clearly has a special liking for Floraete, the wife of Riwalin's marshal Rual, although here we must be careful how we interpret *wîp*, either in the general sense of someone of the female sex or more specifically as (Rual's) wife. Both senses are present when Floraete is praised for taking care of Blanscheflur and later her son Tristan (1647: 'Sîn selbes [Rual's] wîp, / ein wîp, diu muot unde lîp / mit wîplîcher staete / der werlt gewirdet haete' His own wife who with womanly constancy had brought honour to courtly society with mind and body). In these lines *wîp* refers to Floraete as a wife, but *wîplîch* denotes not her wifely, but her womanly virtue. In other cases where *wîp* is used the meaning is 'wife' (in 1799, 1892f. the marshal and his wife are mentioned together), but a little later it is her womanly honour and true virtue that are praised (1905: '... diu wîbes êre ein spiegelglas / und rehter güete ein gimme was' ... who was a mirror of womanly honour and a jewel of true goodness).

Still in this general sense, *wîp* can also be used with a negative connotation, but the implicit criticism is significantly not directed against women. As part of his criticism of conditions in Cornwall Gottfried tells us that no man dared stand up to the challenge of Morolt any more than would a woman (5979: 'dehein man / ... getorste wâgen den lîp / iht mêre danne ein wîp') and this criticism is focused more sharply on Marke when his fears about Tristan's forthcoming combat with Morolt are likened to those of a timid woman afraid for her man (6525: 'Der guote künic Marke / dem gie der kampf sô starke / mit herzeleide an sînen lîp, / daz nie kein herzelôsez wîp / die nôt umb' einen man gewan' The good king Marke was so deeply distressed by this combat that no frightened woman ever suffered such pain for a man). In these two passages women may be equated with lack of bravery (yet only in a military context), but the object of criticism is not women, but men who fail to live up to their manhood, much as the criticism of her age by Hildegard von Bingen (*muliebre tempus*) was aimed at the failings of men, clerics who neglected their responsibilities.[27]

However, there are other cases where Gottfried faced a problem: on occasions when Isolde is presented actively deceiving her husband how could he avoid any implicit criticism of her behaviour being seen as a typical feature of the whole female sex? (This potential extension from the particular to the general was a risk run, as we shall see, by Wolfram in his 'Selbstverteidigung' and by Chaucer in this depiction of one woman's inconstancy in *Troilus and Criseyde*.)[28] One way for Gottfried to avoid this was to replace *wîp*, used hitherto, by *frouwe*, thereby dispensing with a word for an individual woman which also meant any member of her sex. We find this, for example, when Isolde hoodwinks Marke by switching on her tears at will, a ruse on which the narrator comments by saying that ladies (*frouwen*) show no greater guile than an ability to weep when it suits them (13899–906). Gottfried may say 'all ladies' (13899), but this socially restrictive term falls well short of incriminating all womankind, as *wîp* would have done. Nor can we say that the addition 'as we hear them say' (13901: 'alsô man ûz ir munde giht') is meant to question this ('That is what they say, but we know otherwise'), for this more probably refers, as Okken's commentary suggests, to the stress laid on this by misogynous tradition with which Gottfried is playing here without committing himself to it.[29] Irony is however exploited a little later when Isolde defends herself against the common accusation that ladies (*frouwen*) hate their husbands' friends (13991: 'man sprichet von den frouwen, daz / si tragen ir manne friunden haz'), referring in this case to Tristan. Unlike Marke, we do not need to be convinced that this is not true in Isolde's case, for in the other attested sense

[27] On *muliebre tempus* see Newman, *Sister*, pp. 238–40; Green, *Women*, p. 230.
[28] Wolfram: see below, pp. 198f.; Chaucer, *Troilus* V 1772–8.
[29] Okken, *Kommentar* I 495f. See also Krohn, *Tristan* III 139.

of *friunt* ('lover', and even more pointedly in an illicit relationship)[30] she bears Tristan anything but hatred. This misogynous topos is therefore undermined on the level of speech which we share with Isolde, but also by its restriction to *frouwen* rather than *wîp*. A last example of exculpation in this manner occurs in Gottfried's casuistical defence of Isolde against the charge of deceiving Marke. In the first place, he brings Tristan into the picture as well (17763: 'weder si entroug in noch Tristan' neither she nor Tristan deceived him), so that we pass beyond any specifically antifeminine charge. However, the gist of Gottfried's more general argument is that ladies (*frouwen*) cannot rightly be accused of deceiving their husbands when the latter can see with their own eyes and are blinded only by their lust (17787–804). Emphasising how unfounded the charge is (17789f.: 'deheine schulde' no guilt, 'unschuldic' guiltless), the narrator can afford to see Isolde's situation in more general terms (she is included in a defence of ladies in the plural) without going as far as to invoke all her sex. If the word *wîp* makes a belated entry by the backdoor (17794), this is significantly in the sense of 'wife', not more generally as a member of the female sex.

Already in the examples we have discussed the singular case can often be related to the plural, the particular to the general, so that we may pass now to consider generalisations used by Gottfried about women, positive, negative or neutral, as we did with Hartmann's *Erec*. Here, too, a preliminary glance at generalisations about men may help us with those about women.

Generalisations can be used neutrally about men, as when the young Tristan's weeping, when cast ashore by the Norwegian merchants who had kidnapped him, is correlated with what children in general do in such a situation (2482: 'dâ saz er unde weinde alsô / wan kint enkunnen anders niht / wan weinen, alse in iht geschiht' there he sat and wept, for children can do nothing but weep when anything happens to them) or when Rual's weather-beaten appearance after searching for Tristan for years is compared with all who are exposed to the elements (4008: 'dar zuo was er sô wetervar, / als alle die von rehte sint ...' Moreover he was so weather-beaten as everyone rightly is ...). As with Hartmann, Gottfried employs positive generalisations much more frequently, again like his predecessor often with a *sol* construction to denote what should be done or expected. Tristan's reunion with Rual is as affectionate as any son's should be towards his father (3942: '... und kuste den getriuwen man, / als ein kint sînen vater sol' and kissed the loyal man, as a child should his father), Rual's behaviour towards his own children is presented similarly

---

[30] See 4187, 11982, 13072, but also 5406–13.

(4129: 'und gan den guotes also wol, / als dehein man sînen kinden sol' and wishes them well as any man should his children), Morgan greets strangers as a courteous man should (5367: 'Morgan enpfie die geste / ... als man die geste enpfâhen sol') and Morolt's charge on horseback is judged against an ideal of what any brave warrior does in combat (6848: 'der tete, reht als si alle tuont, / die ûf rehte manheit / alle ir sinne hânt geleit' he acted as all those act whose concern is with true manhood). Lastly, Gottfried very much avoids expressly negative generalisations about men (with Hartmann, too, they were rare), so that they may be illustrated by an example from Eilhart, namely the folly of Nampetenis in imposing surveillance on his wife, where the particular narrative situation is presented in the past tense, but the generalising commentary, passing judgment on him and his like, in the present (7874–87).

Generalisations about women must first be illustrated briefly with two examples from Thomas, one of them decisively negative. A narrator's comment in his text is occasioned by the scene in which the second Ysolt's anger is roused on overhearing Tristran's conversation with her brother and learning of her husband's love for the other Ysolt, an anger which leads to the tragic climax of Tristran's death. The commentary (Douce 1323–35) proceeds from this particular situation to a general condemnation of women's proneness to anger. It applies to Ysolt (1336), whose anger occasions it (1340: *irrur*), but is phrased in general terms: *femme* (1323) is a collective singular, followed by a string of plural possessive pronouns (*lur*) and verbs (*sevent, sunt*), and the effect of this anger concerns all men (1324: *chaschuns*). The narrator makes no bones about an antifeminine generalisation, caused by the negative role played by Ysolt at this point, destructive of any sympathy with her by him, for he knows that love turned to hate will lead to her treachery in eventually causing Tristran's death.

This is, however, not the whole story about negative generalisations used by Thomas, since we have already considered an earlier passage (Sneyd[1] 287–90) whose antifeminine bias is invalidated by being framed by other passages (281–6, 291–6) including men in the same criticism, so that we are dealing with an extended generalisation, not one directed exclusively at women.[31] It is difficult to know how to assess the contrast between these two generalising commentaries by Thomas, one of which is aimed at men as well as women and is occasioned by the failing of a man, Tristran, but the other is exclusively antifeminine. Is it the case that, like the misogynous outburst of Hartmann's Erec against Enite, Thomas's anger with Ysolt (a reflection of her anger with Tristran) here brings antifeminine prejudice to the

---

[31] See above, p. 81.

surface, overcoming the earlier, more 'balanced' view that such human shortcomings are common to both sexes? Or are the two generalisations, one exculpating women as the sole offenders and the other inculpating them alone, left as statements to be compared and pondered over, inviting further thought on the matter by Thomas's audience? In either case, these two passages should warn us against any attempt to impose a unity devoid of contradictions on medieval authors dealing with a theme which occasioned so much debate throughout the Middle Ages.

As was the case with men, Gottfried has a few neutral generalisations about women. On learning of Riwalin's wounding in battle against Marke's foes Blanscheflur seeks out her nurse and pours out her fears to her as women in her position have always done and still do (1205: 'als si ie tâten und noch tuont, / den ir dinc stât, als ez ir stuont' as they always did and still do, whose situation is as hers was). When Morolt's corpse is brought back to Ireland the queen and her daughter Isolde lament over it in the heart-rending way in which women behave who are deeply afflicted (7173: '... si quelten manege wîs ir lîp, / als ir wol wizzet, daz diu wîp / vil nâhe gênde klage hânt, / dâ in diu leit ze herzen gânt' they punished their bodies in many ways, as you know how heart-rendingly women behave when they are sorely afflicted). This is a case in which it is unjustified to find a trace of male condescension which has been read into a comparable situation in Hartmann's *Erec*,[32] for the pain that afflicts these women is also meant to rend our hearts (*nâhe gênde*) in compassion with the women, no matter what we may think of Morolt.

More common with Gottfried, as with Hartmann, are expressly positive generalisations about womanly nature. Blanscheflur's growing affection for Riwalin is seen not just in terms of herself, but as behaviour as a living person should act and as a lover does (1348: '... und tete, reht' alse der lebende sol / und alse der minnende tuot'), where the masculine serves as a common gender, embracing male and female in the generalisation. Brangaene does not simply ask for her greetings to be conveyed to Isolde, but sees this against the norm of what a young lady's behaviour should be towards her mistress (12845: 'grüezet si von mir alsô wol, / als ein juncfrouwe ir frouwen sol'), where the indefinite article *ein* has generalising force and *sol* sets up the norm of behaviour. But it is with Floraete in particular that such generalisations are frequent, thus confirming what we saw of Gottfried's manifest liking for her. When on her husband Rual's instructions she takes the orphan Tristan into her care she displays her good qualities, praised as

---

[32] See above, p. 99.

such by the narrator (5256), in the manner best available to any woman (5259: 'daz bewaerte s' alse wol, / als ein wîp allerbeste sol'). Here, as in the last example, *ein* is meant generally and *sol* suggests the ideal to which she conforms. On Tristan's eventual departure from Parmenie and return to Cornwall the marshal's wife, whose virtues are once more expressly summed up (5865: *triuwe und êre* faithfulness and honour), not merely subjects herself to torments, but does this as a woman (5868: *wîp*) rightly does on whom God has bestowed a worthy life in womanly honour (5867: 'diu leite marter an ir lîp, / alsô mit allem rehte ein wîp, / der got ein gehêrtez leben / an wîbes êren hât gegeben'). The author's readiness to use *wîp* in a generalising context of praise stands in marked contrast to his avoidance of this word in favour of *frouwe* whenever the situation is more dubious.

Alongside these generalisations, neutral and positive, may be set one example of an extended generalisation. It comes when Isolde, musing about Tristan after the dragon-fight and idly contemplating his equipment, is depicted (in a manner which at first glance could indeed be seen as male condescension) giving way to her whims and fancies as she does so and as young ladies and children are given to doing (10070: '... daz si daz swert ze handen nam, / als juncfrouwen unde kint / gelustic unde gelangic sint'). That seems the derogatory tone of a superior male, but this impression is immediately destroyed by the addition that, as God knows, that is also true of many a man (10073: 'und weizgot ouch genuoge man'). With this line what appeared as a condescending view of young ladies (specifically Isolde on the brink of her tragic love affair) by equating them with children is converted into an extended generalisation applicable to both sexes and therefore not explicitly antifeminine. This undermining of what could have been a misogynous generalisation reminds us of Chaucer, who, when talking in the *The Franklin's Tale* of women's desire for liberty, achieves the same end by likewise including men (98: 'And so doon men').[33] It also reminds us of a parallel closer to Gottfried, of Thomas's framing of a misogynous generalisation (Sneyd¹ 287–90) by two passages explicitly including men (and Tristran specifically) in this failing, although Gottfried's example is more effective by reason of its very pithiness. Can it be said, however, that Gottfried also made use of explicitly negative generalisations critical of women, as Thomas did with the second Ysolt?

To answer this question we must consider two statements, one by a character in Gottfried's work (whose view is therefore not necessarily Gottfried's own) and one by the narrator, where the position is much

---

[33] Mann, *Feminizing*, p. 89.

more complex. In the first example the character in question is the Irish steward who, as we saw, when thwarted in his claim for Isolde bursts into a vicious attack on womankind at large (9870–96), thereby showing, as with Thomas's narrator, that anger often brings latent or concealed anti-feminism to the fore. Already before his tirade we are alerted to the steward's patriarchal attitude towards women in his attempt to exclude the Irish queen from the debate, possibly and rightly fearing her rhetorical skill, on the grounds that Gurmun, rather than a woman, should speak on this matter (9830: 'frouw', ir tuot übel, wie redet ir sô? / mîn hêrre, der ez enden sol, / der kan doch selbe sprechen wol: / der spreche unde antwürte mir' My lady, you act wrongly, why do you speak thus? My lord, who has to settle the matter, can speak for himself. Let him speak and answer me). This attempt to deny a woman public speech fails when Gurmun asks his wife to speak on behalf of all (9834f.). When the young Isolde expresses her refusal, the steward addresses her in particular (9860) and has her in mind in what he says, but then immediately slips into a generalisation and sees her as representative of all women (9871: 'ir tuot vil rehte als elliu wîp' You act just like any woman; 9872: 'ir … alle'; 9876: 'iu allen' all of you). But the acceptability of his criticism of her and all women (their contrary wayward-ness, hating what loves them, loving what hates them) is undermined for us by the negative and ridiculous qualities of the suspect figure making a false claim and whose annoyance at being thwarted is all too obvious, as well as by the counter-attack soon launched by the Irish queen.

In his tirade the steward acts from uncomprehending vexation that a woman should not be prepared to fall in with the convention that the 'brave' deserve the fair, that she should not automatically be ready to accept his service as her knight or agree to him as husband after his presumed victory. However, he is ill-advised to argue on the grounds he chooses, namely women's contrariness in hating what loves them and loving what hates them, for that opens the door to the counter-attack by Isolde's mother, criticising him for effeminacy on the basis of his own definition of woman's nature, for he, too, loves Isolde who has no love for him (9939: 'ich selbe enwart dir ouch nie holt. / ich weiz wol, alsam tuot Isolt' I never had any liking for you. I know the same is true of Isolde). This confirms Isolde's own words, 9868: 'i'ne wart iu nie getriu noch holt' I never had any liking for you. Significantly, this controversy takes place between the steward and the two women, Isolde and more decisively her mother, since Gurmun, having initiated the difficulty by his patriarchal promise of his daughter to the dragon-slayer, now stands aloof from the consequences, leaving the matter in his wife's hands. Informing this controversy is the one-sidedness of the steward's wishes, unquestioned by him, but countered by the mother's argument that Isolde would cheapen herself if she were prepared to accept any man who laid a claim to her (9944: 'si waere ze gemeine, / ob si iegelîchen solte / wellen, der si wolte'). Her recommendation to him is to seek someone who would want him (9926: 'und minne, daz dich minne; / welle, daz dich welle' love that which loves you, want that which wants you). The conditions for Isolde's marriage rashly put forward by her father and which the steward claims to have met are here rejected by mother and daughter, not only because the steward's claim is false, but also on the principle of having regard for the woman's wishes, the need to take her agreement into account. The skill with which the mother conducts her argument against the steward, accusing him of possessing the very qualities for which he criticised womankind, is the final invalidation of his misogynous generalisation, for he has shown himself to be as much inculpated as any woman in what is thereby revealed as an extended generalisation.

The second passage in Gottfried's *Tristan*, spoken this time in the voice of the narrator, concerns a lengthy digression which was once called an excursus on love ('Minneexkurs'), but for which the title 'excursus on women' ('Frauenexkurs') has been proposed by Schnell as more fitting.[34] For that reason the generalisations about women which it includes qualify it for inclusion in this section. The passage which Schnell analyses in detail forms part of a longer excursus on surveillance of lovers (and of women in particular), itself occasioned by the watch placed on the lovers by Marke once his suspicions are roused. The focus which Schnell has directed on his chosen passage must be narrowed further in what follows, for in place of Schnell's discussion of the whole of this excursus we are concerned only with what Gottfried has to say specifically about women. How easily the transition from the theme of surveillance to women could be made can be seen in a comparable, but much shorter passage in Eilhart's work, concerning the jealous husband Nampetenis and his wife Gariole. We have already seen that this situation called forth a negative generalisation against the husband, correlating his behaviour with the stupidity of such men at large (7874–79), but this is followed by a generalisation concerning the woman. It is stated in general terms that surveillance in such a case is pointless against a woman's wishes, for without her agreement she will unfailingly find a lover (7880: 'wen stât ir ir gemüte / nicht williglîchen dar, / sô mag he nimmer sie bewarn / mit allen sînen sinnen. / wen, wil sie einen minnen, / sie tût ez âne sînen dang' If her mind is not willingly so disposed he can by no manner of

---

[34] Schnell, *ZfdPh* 103 (1984), 1–26.

means prevent her. For if she wishes to love someone she will do it without his agreement). This generalisation about the woman is tied up with the particular narrative situation (7887: 'daz wart an desin dingen schîn' That was shown in this case), a line which refers to the generalisation about women as much as to that about men. Like Eilhart, Gottfried has more to say about women than men in this kind of position – this is where the slant of his interest lies. Like Eilhart, he also employs the antifeminine topos, already found with Ovid, but also in the clerical tradition, that there is no point in watching over a virtuous woman, while others will outwit their guardians.[35] This is, however, not the only topos used by Gottfried and converted to new ends. Three of these themes must now be considered, omitting other points in what is a richly allusive argument by the author, who adopts a procedure described by Jackson as taking up antifeminine arguments and turning them to his own advantage.[36]

The first theme is surveillance itself, from which the whole of the excursus on women flows. The antifeminine implications of the clerical argument that an unchaste woman will always find ways and means of fulfilling her desires need not surprise us in the least (their wantonness and disobedience are sufficient explanation), but Gottfried himself argues in similar terms. He maintains that a good woman does not need to be watched over, but an evil one cannot be successfully guarded (17876: 'huot' ist verlorn an wîbe, / dar umbe daz dehein man / der übelen niht gehüeten kan. / der guoten darf man hüeten niht, / si hüetet selbe, alsô man giht' Surveillance is wasted on women since no man can keep watch over a wicked woman and there is no need with a good one, she is said to keep watch over herself). To the extent that disobedience is involved in this the later reference to women as the daughters of Eve (17965: 'Sus sint si alle Êven kint') points in the same direction, whilst the reference to what is commonly said ('alsô man giht') may be a reference to the tradition, Ovidian and clerical, to which Gottfried appears to conform. The mention of appearance here is called for, since the author questions this antifeminine topos by what he says before and after his excursus, stressing first that not just Isolde alone, but both Tristan and she were straining to overcome the obstacle of surveillance (17836: 'alsam tet Îsôt und Tristan' Isolde and Tristan acted likewise) and later that both of them were suffering from Marke's surveillance and his prohibition (18121: 'Îsôte und Tristande / den was diu huote ande, / verbot daz tet in alse wê'). The effect of these remarks is to produce a framing of what might otherwise be seen as a misogynous

---

[35] *Ibid.*, pp. 6f. for examples of this tradition.   [36] Jackson, *Anatomy*, p. 243.

condemnation of women which is comparable with what we saw with Thomas. With both authors, if the man is involved as well (with Thomas admittedly more so) the hint of criticism cannot be aimed at the woman alone. Moreover, there are reasons for focusing on women in particular in the context of surveillance quite distinct from any suspicion of them, for in a patriarchal society it is women or more specifically their chastity that was the valuable object to be guarded, both before and during marriage. In addition, Schnell points out that whereas the poets of courtly love see surveillance as a threat to their love, Gottfried sees it from the woman's point of view, as a threat to her reputation (17866–74), thereby stressing the woman's position and her reaction to it,[37] much as he had in the controversy with the Irish steward. Finally, in differentiating between good and evil women (17878f.), as admittedly his clerical predecessors did on this point, Gottfried makes it difficult to argue that we are dealing with a negative generalisation applicable to all women (as the Irish steward rashly generalised). As he later says, Eve's heritage may live on in women,[38] but he also suggests that praise is due to those who break free from it.

The mention of Eve brings us to a second theme in the excursus with antifeminine potential. The weakness of humans (in more than just the physical sense) and their susceptibility to seduction are exemplified in traditional exegesis on the Fall primarily in the person of Eve, rather than Adam.[39] For patristic and medieval exegesis the Fall represents the capitulation of reason (*ratio*, incorporated in Adam) to the flesh (*caro, sensualitas*, represented by Eve), particularly in the context of sexual temptation, with an obvious potential relevance to the Tristan story. This is reflected in Gottfried's mention of the susceptibility of Eve at the Fall, and therewith of all women since (17936: '… weiz got der ist in an geborn: / die frouwen, die der arte sint, / die sint ir muoter Even kint; / diu brach daz êrste verbot' God knows, this is inborn in them. Women of this kind are the children of their mother Eve who went against the first prohibition). As a consequence, the Fall is presented in terms of Eve's actions, with no mention of Adam (17954: 'ir êrste werc, daz sî begie, / dar an sô bûwete sî ir art / und tete, daz ir verboten wart' In the first thing she did she proved true to her nature and did what had been forbidden) or even of the Devil as tempting her. Gottfried not only shows his acquaintance with biblical exegesis, he even refers pointedly to what clerics say on the matter (17947: 'die pfaffen sagent uns maere'), more explicitly than with what people say (17880) about the vain surveillance of women. But for Gottfried to make use of clerical

---

[37] Schnell, *ZfdPh* 103 (1984), 8.   [38] 17937f., 17965f.   [39] Schnell, *ZfdPh* 103 (1984), 10f.

arguments does not mean that he accepts them. In the first place, although he cannot go as far as exculpating Eve he does at least relieve her of a measure of responsibility by saying that she would never have acted thus if it had not been expressly forbidden her (17952: 'Êve enhaete ez nie getân, / und enwaere ez ir verboten nie'), thereby teasingly implying a parallel between the patriarchal God of the Old Testament and the patriarchal husband who imposes surveillance on his wife.[40] Furthermore, in support of the exegetical equation of Adam or man with *ratio* and of Eve or woman with *sensualitas* Schnell quotes a passage from the commentary of Bruno (founder of the Carthusian order) on a Pauline epistle.[41] This commentator makes the conventional equations, but adds that he cannot deny that both qualities are to be found in each sex, so that the male attribute of reason may be found in a woman and female sensuality in a man ('... non tamen negamus quin utrumque sit in utroque, et ratio in muliere vir dicitur, et sensualitas in viro mulier appellatur'). That may be added very much as a last-minute concession, but that destroys none of its validity as a far-reaching extended generalisation confirming, in its application to the *Tristan* excursus, what Gottfried tells us both before and after his digression, that Tristan's sensuality was involved in this as well as Isolde's.

Finally, just as the excursus with its use of topoi implying criticism of women is concluded with a eulogy of them (18055–118), so too does Gottfried complement his references to the Fall with allusions to paradise regained, in both of which a crucial role is played by a woman. Behind this lies the theological relationship between Eve, who deprived us of paradise, and Mary, who restored it to us.[42] With Gottfried Eve is explicitly introduced into the context of paradise lost, but Mary has to be referred to indirectly, first by the suggestion that the ideal woman praised in the concluding eulogy is capable of granting her lover a living paradise (18070: 'der hât daz lebende paradîs / in sînem herzen begraben' he has the living paradise within his heart),[43] and secondly, only a few lines later, when it is said that a man so blessed will not be pricked by the thorn when he plucks the rose (18074: '... daz in der dorn iht steche, / sô er die rôsen breche'), a clear reference to the standing epithet of Mary as a rose without thorn.[44] Theologically there is an asymmetry between Eve and Mary, in that the negative quality of the former was held to be passed on to all women, her daughters, while the

---

[40] Jackson, *Anatomy*, p. 244; Huber, *Gottfried*, p. 113.

[41] *PL* 153, 182; Schnell, *ZfdPh* 103 (1984), 11. See also Schnell, *FMS* 32 (1998), 313–16.

[42] Schnell *ZfdPh* 103 (1984), 16, fn. 53, and 25, fn. 79 (quoting Jerome: 'Mors per Evam, vita per Mariam').

[43] Tomasek, *Utopie*, p. 197.   [44] Salzer, *Sinnbilder*, pp. 541–5 (Mary as *rosa sine spina*).

positive function of the latter is unique, for Mary is alone of all her sex, as expressed in an early hymn ('Sola in sexu femina').[45] However, this imbalance is made good to the extent that the woman praised by Gottfried in mariological terms for restoring paradise to her lover is to be seen as Isolde herself, for Gottfried concludes with the confident assertion that such Isoldes are still to be found in his day (18115: 'der suochte, als er solde, / ez lebeten noch Îsolde'), if only one looked for them.

A last topos exploited by Gottfried concerns the manner in which he defines the nature of this ideal woman. He states that if a woman grows in virtue, retains her reputation and to do this lays aside her womanly nature, this makes of her a woman only in name, but in her mind a man (17975: 'wan swelh wîp tugendet wider ir art, / diu gerne wider ir art bewart / ir lop, ir êre unde ir lîp, / diu ist niwan mit namen ein wîp / und ist ein man mit muote' If a woman acquires virtue against her inborn nature and keeps intact her reputation, honour and person, she is a woman only in name, but a man by disposition). To make a concession by praising women as if they were truly men at heart is very much a backhanded compliment to their sex and, as with the other topoi used, has an established clerical origin in the concept of the *femina virilis*, at home above all in hagiographic tradition.[46] Christian women (martyrs, saints, abbesses) who conform to this ideal are said to have a male breast within a woman's body, to withstand temptations like men although they belong to the weaker sex (a view expressed, for example, by Otloh von St Emmeram).[47] How far Gottfried stands from embracing an opinion such as Otloh's he makes clear at a later point in his narrative, after the separation of the lovers, in Tristan succumbing to the name and charms of the second Isolde, whilst the first remains free from such backsliding.[48] Here the man, far from representing the norm to which the virtuous woman conforms, is shown very much as her inferior. It is hardly surprising that Gottfried, in referring to the topos of the *femina virilis*, should refrain from endorsing the clerical, even ascetic view of woman it conveys. Almost immediately after mentioning the topos he passes over to delineating his own quite different picture of the ideal woman (17990–18118). Such a woman is not concerned to renounce her sensual nature, but strives rather to reconcile the needs of her body with the demands of her honour (17992: '... sô daz si wider ir lîbe / mit ir êren

---

[45] Kesting, *Maria–Frouwe*, p. 16.
[46] Schnell, *ZfdPh* 103 (1984), 16–21. See Newman, *Woman*, p. 4, on Jerome ('As long as a woman is for birth and children, she is different from man as body is from soul. But when she wishes to serve Christ more than the world, then she will cease to be a woman, and will be called man').
[47] *PL* 146, 233, 234; Schnell, *ZfdPh* 103 (1984), 18.   [48] See below, pp. 159f., 166f.

vehte / nâch ietweders rehte / des lîbes unde der êren! / si sol den kampf sô kêren, / daz sî den beiden rehte tuo' … so that, together with her honour, she fights with her body for the rightful claims of body as well as honour. She must wage the fight so as to do justice to them both). The predicate of purity which in the clerical tradition of the *femina virilis* belongs to the woman who successfully battles against her physical nature is granted instead by Gottfried (17991: *reines*) to the woman who does not forgo the claims of her body (18029–32), but instead struggles to do justice both to them and to her honour. Gottfried may well quote the hagiographic ideal (with its subordination of woman to a male norm), but only to show that he does not share it.[49]

Amongst the authors who deal with the Tristan theme it is with Gottfried that we find the most concerted attempt to defend women against misogynous prejudice. Lexically, he employs the term *wîp* predominantly in a positive context and takes care to undercut any critical implications. Similarly, his generalisations about women, based on particular instances, may be neutral, positive or extended, whilst the only clear example of a negative generalisation is called into question by what we know of the Irish steward, the character who voices it. Of Gottfried's technique at large it can be said that, in addition to this damning of a view by association, he more than once converts what appears to be an antifeminine opinion into one which, affecting men as well, is no longer gender specific and that he takes steps to undermine the force of a number of traditional antifeminine topoi. That he goes even further and emphasises the superiority of a woman, Isolde, to a man, Tristan, we shall consider in the following section.

QUESTIONS AND REVISIONS

In the corresponding section in Chapter 3 we looked at a number of features in *Erec* which called into question the conventional view of the time about the relationship between man and woman in love and in marriage. This can now be done for the Tristan story under three headings which illustrate that greater attention could be paid to the role of women, if not in actual society, then at least in the literature meant for that society.

Peculiar to this story is the importance of love as incorporated in the love potion drunk inadvertently by Tristan and Isolde, where it is immaterial for us whether the potion was meant to be seen as causing or symbolising love. The potion is drunk after Tristan has slain the dragon and in terms of

---

[49] Schnell, *ZfdPh* 103 (1984), 20.

narrative convention won the right for Isolde (as with Erec and Enite or Parzival and Condwiramurs).[50] To introduce the birth of love between the two people involved serves to humanise the position somewhat for the woman, but in *Tristan* her situation is made even worse for although the couple fall in love Tristan has acted on behalf of Marke, to whom Isolde is duly handed over. Against this background the drinking of the potion represents a drastic irruption of something new and unexpected, as is exemplified already by Eilhart in Isalde's reaction, presented to us in a lengthy internal monologue. This is something new in literary historical terms (I leave on one side the chronological relationship of this passage with Lavinia's internal monologue in Veldeke's *Eneasroman*), but also in the course of Eilhart's narrative hitherto.[51] An internal monologue, spoken by a woman on the experience of love and occupying 200 lines, stands out as an erratic block and is meant to draw our attention. Isalde registers her love symptoms in the physical terms deriving from classical literature, above all Ovid: she can neither eat nor drink (2407), she suffers from a fever (2497–9) and regards her condition as a mortal sickness (2408f.), all of which robs her of her wits (2491). She has her explanation of how all this has arisen for, in addition to the magical power of the potion which we know she has drunk, she invokes the classical deities of love, Venus (2404: *frauwe Amûr*, also further medievalised as *frawe Minne*, 2505) and Cupid (2467). The combined power of this assault is seen by her as the power of love (2533) which has made her a captive (2494). Yet the subjection to this assault does not deprive Isalde of all personal reactions: she sees her own heart and mind as the seat of her new-found feelings for Tristrant (2442: *herze unde mûd*) and she dwells on his personal qualities that attract her to him (2422–31). More telling is her fear that Tristrant has no regard for her (2552–5) and her admission to herself that her father should have given her in marriage to him (2556: 'dô mîn vatir solde / mich im zu wîbe habin gegebin'). This admission of her personal preference throws light on the change in Isalde's position. Although she now stands passively between two men (Tristrant and Marke, to whom she is about to be married), as she had previously as the prize for the victor (Tristrant and the Irish steward), the irruption of love has disturbed the balance drastically, for now she stands between the compulsion of love (potion, deities) and the compulsion of a feudal marriage arranged over her head. The future course of Eilhart's narrative shows unmistakably how the former, once introduced, wreaks havoc with the latter. By comparison Gottfried's presentation of the power of love may be

---

[50] On this narrative convention see below, pp. 216–25.   [51] Keck, *Liebeskonzeption*, p. 97.

much more sophisticated and internalised, but the effect is the same: with him, too, it sweeps aside the material, impersonal calculations of a feudal marriage[52] which we considered in the first section of this chapter.

For a second feature we turn to a question which also concerned us in the *Erec* romance: what narrative space does *Tristan* afford to women, specifically to Isolde, and can it in any sense be described as the romance of a couple, rather than one of a single (male) protagonist? Our starting point is therefore the feminist complaint about the romance as a genre, that it only appears to place women at the centre of the action, but in reality marginalises them as much as in the actual society of their day.[53]

This complaint appears to be borne out by the narrator's indication that he regards the figure of Tristan as the focus of his story. In his prologue Eilhart summarises the events of the story on which he is embarking by first mentioning the birth of Tristrant (36f.), then his death and exploits (38–41). Only after this is Isalde mentioned by name, and then simply as the object of Tristrant's wooing expedition ('Brautwerbung') on behalf of Marke (42f.).[54] Nowhere in this summary is the love of this couple actually mentioned as a theme, although it could be implied in the reference to each of them eventually dying because of the other (45: 'he dorch sie und sie dorch in' he because of her, she because of him) and by the subsequent description of the work's theme (52: 'von manheit und von minnen' manly deeds and love). This opening focus on the man, in which the woman is no more than the object of an exploit of his, is confirmed by a corresponding summary of the narrative in the epilogue, where again it is the birth, life and death of Tristrant that are mentioned, with no talk of Isalde (9449: 'wie [der kûne] Tristrant irstarp / und wie he geborn wart / und wie ez umme sîn lîp quam').[55] For Eilhart the man is the sole protagonist.

At first, the position appears to be little different with Gottfried's version, for he too, when he mentions the child of Riwalin and Blanscheflur after the latter's death, refers to him as the orphan from whom his tale arises (1862: 'von dem diu maere erhaben sint'). He uses the same kind of construction when referring to Tristan as the 'child' of Floraete (5252: 'daz kint, des disiu maere sint' the child of whom this story tells), in each case introducing a child as the protagonist of his story in much the same way as Hartmann first referred to the youthful Erec in the fragmentary start of his romance (4: 'durch den diu rede erhaben ist') and as we shall see is also the case

[52] Tomasek, *Utopie*, pp. 148f.   [53] Krueger, *Women*, p. 34.
[54] Keck, *Liebeskonzeption*, pp. 80f. See however Schausten, *Erzählwelten*, pp. 54f.
[55] Keck, *Liebeskonzeption*, p. 77.

with Wolfram's *Parzival*.[56] In a manner similar to Eilhart's summary of his tale as a biography of Tristrant, Gottfried also provides an early forecast of the young Tristan's life and death (2007–15) as the theme of his story (2006: 'diz maere') without any mention of a woman in that story. This exclusion (or at the least marginalisation) of Isolde seems also to be confirmed if we take account of her position in the narrative. In purely quantitative terms: in a work which in its uncompleted state amounts to nearly 20,000 lines, the love potion scene, and therewith the start of Isolde's role alongside Tristan, comes after more than 11,000 lines given over to the story of Tristan's parents and to his youth, including exploits such as his knightly combats with Morgan, Morolt and the dragon.[57] All of these would have fitted in well with what Eilhart had stressed as his hero's *manheit*, but it is only after the last of these that Isolde first enters the narrative in any active sense. In just about half the work as we have it she plays no direct part.

These appearances deceive, certainly in the case of Gottfried. In the first place, corresponding to his early mention of Tristan as his protagonist Gottfried also suggests the same in Isolde's case. He does this in his account of Tristan's early exploits when, in the guise of Tantris, he is given the task of the young Isolde's education (her role is therefore still passive and receptive) and it is said that this story is about her (7723: 'und von der disiu maere sint'). Already some time before the potion scene we are meant to see tentatively that this tale deals with a couple, not with a single hero. Even in terms of the quantitative argument mentioned in the last paragraph Isolde can be said to begin to play some active role before the potion scene. It may be the case that her mother plays a more active part than her still inexperienced daughter at the Irish court after the slaying of the dragon (although it still needs to be said that it is a woman who takes matters in hand away from her husband), but her prominent part does not exclude an important role for her daughter. As Ranke pointed out long ago, she is significantly active on three telling occasions: it is she who, when the three women seek for him, discovers the dragon-slayer; it is she who recognises him as the minstrel Tantris; it is she who identifies Tantris with Tristan.[58] These occasions come before the experience of love liberates Isolde from passivity and allows her to take the initiative as a mature person.[59] Gottfried sketches this growth from youth to maturity, admittedly in shorter compass than with Tristan, but still as a separate process in which she gradually moves towards partnership with him. Later, as we shall see, she is even

---

[56] See below, p. 214.   [57] Wagner, *Euphorion* 67 (1973), 52f.
[58] Ranke, *Tristan*, pp. 200–3; Wagner, *Euphorion* 67 (1973), 53f.   [59] Wagner, *Euphorion* 67 (1973), 57.

presented as ethically and emotionally superior to her lover, no longer merely a function of him.

We are not helped in our inquiry by asking how medieval readers considered Gottfried's story. Rudolf von Ems may regard it as one dealing with Tristan alone (*Alexander* 3195), as did those who wrote the rubrics of various manuscript versions, giving 'Tristan' as the work's title. Against this, however, we may set Gottfried's two continuators. In the prologue to his version Ulrich von Türheim mentions the two lovers together (40–3), as he does also at the close of the work (3718f.). Heinrich von Freiberg refers to neither lover in his prologue, but begins his narrative *in medias res* at the point where Tristan comes to Arundel and he therefore mentions him alone at first (85–7), but finishes with the burial of the two lovers side-by-side (6818–21). Whether for need of an abbreviated reference, or in order to show that the story tells of a couple, different readers of Gottfried read his work in different ways.

We must go a step further, however, for Gottfried does not allow us to wait far into the narrative to see that his work is indeed a *roman à deux*. He shows us this discreetly in his wording of the prologue, at the point where Eilhart had not permitted Isalde to come to the fore as a second protagonist. Gottfried tells us what he is about to undertake, a tale of noble lovers who gave proof of perfect love (128: 'ein senedaere, ein senedaerin, / ein man, ein wîp, ein wîp, ein man, / Tristan, Îsot; Îsot, Tristan' a lover, a beloved; a man, a woman, a woman, a man; Tristan, Isolde; Isolde, Tristan). Of these lines it has been said: 'Gradually logical and syntactical relations break down and Gottfried … can do nothing other than place them and their names in incantatory fashion nakedly side by side',[60] to which one might add: 'and in chiastic embrace'. A little later in the prologue when Gottfried expands on the nature of his tale he emphasises its joint nature, telling of two lovers (211: 'von den diz senemaere seit' of whom this love story tells), of *their* name and history (215: 'ir name und ir geschiht'), continuing this with a string of plural, in reality dual pronouns (220–32).

The chiastic embrace of the lovers which we saw in 129f. also finds visual expression in the form of an acrostic, starting in the prologue and continuing at intervals throughout the work, which likewise is made up of the names of the lovers entwined together (TIIT, RSSR, IOOI, SLLS, and presumably through the rest of the incomplete work).[61] This device for showing the lovers as a pair embracing is essentially visual, accessible only to readers alerted by the capital letters that make up the acrostic,[62] but a

---

[60] Johnson, 'Gottfried', p. 215.   [61] Schirok, *ZfdA* 113 (1984), 210–13.   [62] Green, *Listening*, pp. 131f.

chiasmus such as 129f., especially with its incantatory force, would have been equally borne in on listeners. Both types of recipient, readers as well as listeners, were meant to see that this is a work with two protagonists: a man and a woman.

What importance Gottfried attached to the symbolic force of the chiasmus can be shown from some of its later occurrences and their placing in the narrative. After the potion has been drunk the last lines of Brangaene's address to the lovers, telling them of its nature, and the first lines of what the narrator then adds contain a chiasmus of their names (11709: 'ouwê Tristan unde Îsôt, / diz tranc ist iuwer beider tôt! / Nu daz diu maget unde der man, / Îsôt unde Tristan …' Alas, Tristan and Isolde, this potion is the death of both of you! Now that the maiden and the man, Isolde and Tristan …). Here the chiastic embrace is somewhat 'distant' (the names are separated from one another by two lines), because at this stage the two have not yet confessed, let alone consummated their love. As the lovers begin to recognise what has happened and draw nearer to each other in the scene where they confess their feelings this gap between them is removed from the chiasmus (12040: '… der man die maget, diu maget den man' the man the maiden, the maiden the man) and the same is true of them much later in the love grotto (16908: 'dâ was doch man bî wîbe, / sô was ouch wîp bî manne' There man was with woman and woman with man). So closely does love bring the two together and make one of them (11720: 'si wurden ein und einvalt, / die zwei und zwivalt wâren ê' they became one and onefold who had earlier been two and twofold) that in one sense Gottfried could be said to undo the force of my present argument by his claim to write the story of one person, but only in the sense of two united in love.

If the long stretch of Gottfried's narrative dealing with Tristan's youth excludes any role for Isolde, the pre-history dealing with Tristan's parents can still find alternative space for a woman alongside a man, for Blanscheflur as well as Riwalin. This pre-history can therefore be said to amount to a *roman à deux* on a miniature scale in which the reciprocal symmetry of their relationship is presented in much the same way a generation later with Tristan and Isolde. When the two earlier lovers exchange the kingdoms of their hearts with each other even before either is aware of the other's feelings, this is expressed chiastically (813: 'die teilten wol gelîche / ir herzen künicrîche: / daz ir wart Riwalîne, / dâ wider wart ir daz sîne' They shared equally their hearts' kingdoms: Riwalin's became hers, in exchange hers became his). The same construction is used of Blanscheflur undergoing the torments that have been described of Riwalin (957: 'diu was ouch mit dem selben schaden / durch in, als er durch sî, beladen' she was oppressed by the same torment on his account as he was on her account), but this differs markedly from the apparently similar wording of Eilhart (45: 'her durch sie und sie durch in' he because of her and she because of him), for the earlier author's chiasmus describes the joint death of Tristrant and Isalde, with no reference to their shared love. Chiasmus constructions are also used of Riwalin and Blanscheflur when each realises that their feelings are recip-rocated (1101: 'daz er si meinde als si in' that he loved her as she did him) and most fittingly of all after they have just consummated their love (1356: 'sus was er sî, und sî was er, / er was ir, und sî was sîn; / dâ Blanscheflûr, dâ Riwalîn, / dâ Riwalîn, dâ Blanscheflûr' Thus he was she and she was he, he was hers and she was his; there Blanscheflur, there Riwalin, there Riwalin, there Blanscheflur). With this verbal embrace these lovers of the earlier generation attain the unity claimed for Tristan and Isolde in the prologue. What lies behind their embrace is their emotional symmetry, each wishing for whatever the other wishes (1542: 'wan swaz ir wellet, daz wil ich' for whatever you wish, I wish), a shared *consensus* of two lovers to be carried over into their subsequent short-lived marriage.

This same joint affirmation of agreement to what the other wishes, but now a *consensus* in love which has nothing at all to do with marriage, is found with Tristan and Isolde as yet another token that the former cannot be conceived as protagonist without the latter. Despite or even as a result of the potion as a symbol of love they possess enough individual will to make such an affirmation. From the beginning, as they make their confession to each other, it is clear that their *wille*, which I take as meaning not only desire, but a readiness to accede to the other's wishes, is a joint one, shared by both (12033: 'Dô die gelieben under in / beide erkanten einen sin, / ein herze und einen willen ...' When both the lovers recognised that between them they had one mind, one heart and one will ...), which paves the way for the two chiasmus constructions that follow (12040, 12042). As a result, when *wille* recurs later it can be seen not as a harmony of the wills of two separate people, but as one will in the singular shared by them (12366: 'dô sî begriffen daz zil / gemeines willen under in' when they reached the goal of shared desire between them; 16447: 'mit dem gemeinen willen' their shared will; see also 16574: 'des herzen sô gemeine' so one at heart). When after their confession and on their approach to Cornwall it is said that the lovers freely had their will together many times (12413: 'wan sî ir willen under in zwein / frîlîche haeten enein / dick' und ze manegem mâle') the adverb 'freely', used in conjunction with *wille*, suggests that however much actual power may be attributed to the potion, it was not enough to rob the lovers of the privilege of consciously and willingly affirming their physical and emotional unity. This affirmation, significantly voiced by Isolde and not by Tristan, reaches a climax in the words she addresses to him on his departure, proclaiming that despite their coming separation they will remain one and undivided (18356: 'Tristan und Îsôt, ir und ich, / wir zwei sîn iemer beide / ein ding ân' underscheide' Tristan and Isolde, you and I, we shall forever be one and undivided). Here, on the brink of separation and as a means of overcoming it, we proceed from the names of two separate individuals and two distinct personal pronouns to a dual construction (*wir zwei*) which finally dissolves into one (*ein ding*). With that we reach the anomalous position previously mentioned in passing. Gottfried demonstrates that his romance is not devoted to one (male) protagonist, but to two, Tristan and Isolde, most convincingly when he makes of these two but one entity.

The importance of this reciprocal relationship between the lovers can be tested with two counter-examples illustrating the catastrophic results whenever this is not the case. The first counter-example is provided by the loveless marriage of Marke and Isolde in which by definition there can be no reciprocity in the sense meant by the author, for Marke's feelings are dominated by lust and Isolde's are directed elsewhere. Just before the excursus on women Gottfried turns his critical comments on Marke, thereby diverting any possible accusation away from Isolde. He does this by accusing the husband of wilful blindness, of closing his eyes to what is quite obvious (so that, casuistically, there can be no talk of deception by Isolde) because his feelings are dominated by lust even though he is aware that she bears him no love (17764: 'er sach ez doch mit ougen an / und weste ez ungesehen genuoc, / daz sî im deheine liebe truoc / und was si'm doch liep über daz. / "war umbe, hêrre, und umbe waz / truog er ir inneclîchen muot?" / dar umbe ez hiute maneger tuot: / geluste unde gelange …' He saw it with his eyes and knew well enough without seeing that she felt no love for him, yet she was dear to him despite that. But, tell me, why did he feel affection for her? For the same reason that many do to-day: lust and desire …). With these last two lines, Gottfried, whose argument is continued in what follows (17774ff.), extends the narrative position of Marke and Isolde into his own present, thereby demonstrating the deficiencies of many loveless marriages by contrast with what his two protagonists achieve outside, even in conflict with, marriage.

The other counter-example concerns another marriage destined for failure, that between Tristan and the second Isolde, which cannot be termed loveless in the same sense, for she certainly falls in love with Tristan. What is absent in this marriage, however, is reciprocal love for, despite feeling attracted by the second Isolde, Tristan still yearns after the first and is torn between the two. Despite appearances to the contrary (both the second Isolde and her family are taken in by them) Gottfried makes it emphatically clear that there is no reciprocity here, these two are not one. Both Tristan and Isolde suffer anguish (and we know from the prologue that suffering is an integral part of love),[63] but in different ways, so that their grief is not truly shared. The source of Tristan's suffering is another Isolde, whilst the present Isolde desires no other Tristan (19300: 'Sus triben si zwei die stunde hin / mit ungemeinem leide. / si seneten sich beide / und haeten jâmer under in zwein; / und gie der ungelîche enein. / ir minne unde ir meine / die wâren ungemeine: / sine giengen dô niht in dem trite / gemeiner liebe ein ander mite, / weder Tristan noch diu maget Îsôt. / Tristan der wolte z'einer nôt / ein ander Îsolde, / und Îsôt diu enwolde / keinen andern Tristanden' Thus these two passed their time with unshared suffering. They both felt longing and grief, but their grief did not converge. Their love and affection were unshared, they did not keep pace with each other in mutual love. For his sole suffering Tristan longed for another Isolde, while Isolde desired none other than Tristan.). These decisive lines make it clear just how radically the marriage that ensues is devoid of reciprocated love. The chiasmus of names in the last lines of this quotation, weakened in any case by being spread over four lines, is more apparent than real, for the name Isolde refers to two different women. The feelings of Tristan and the first Isolde are towards each other, but here feelings are directed away from one another, they are anything but shared (*ungemeine* is used twice, *gemeine* occurs in a negative clause; cf. also *ungelîch*). Here indeed we have in small scale a *roman à deux*, but hardly in the sense Gottfried may have intended. How far reciprocity, as expressed by chiasmus, is foreign to this relationship is suggested at a point which signals Tristan's greatest betrayal of the first Isolde, for the reciprocity of their love is now applied to this new situation (19123: 'er meinde sî, si meinde in'). Hatto translates these lines by 'she was in his thoughts, as he was in hers',[64] but we should rather be more explicit and talk of 'loving thoughts'. (That is not just an interpretation of *meinen* in this context, for this verb is often attested elsewhere with the meaning 'to love'.)[65] This is clearly the indication of the similar phrase used of Riwalin and Blanscheflur (1101) and in the longer passage we have just considered the nouns and verbs *minne(n)* and *meine(n)* occur together twice (19305, 19315). In thinking that he is reciprocating this Isolde's love for him Tristan betrays his true Isolde, which in his wavering emotions he soon comes to realise in accusing himself of unfaithfulness (19146, 19158). Negatively in such examples, but also

---

[63] *Tristan* 108–18. [64] Hatto, *Gottfried*, p. 292. [65] BMZ II 107f.

positively in many more, Gottfried's lovers are so interwoven and entwined in their life (18508f.: *enein geweben* and *verstricket under in*) that together they make up a romance with two protagonists.

Seen from a medieval patriarchal point of view it must have seemed bad enough to grant women narrative space, but things must have reached a pretty pass if, as a result of allowing women characters in a work to act alongside men, they could be implicitly compared with men and shown in some respects to be superior to them. This we have seen in Chapter 3 with Enite and Erec, and something similar is true of Isolde and Tristan. We must be careful, however, how we assess Isolde's character, for Gottfried knows human beings, and women in particular, well enough not to ascribe perfection to them. That is certainly the case with Isolde in his work. She not merely deceives her husband in her adulterous affair (so much so that attention has to be diverted from this by presenting Marke negatively and the lovers' enemies at court in the blackest colours), she also has no compunction in requesting Brangaene to take her place as a substitute virgin in Marke's marriage bed and later attempting to remove this potentially incriminating witness by murder. Our concern, like Gottfried's, is certainly not to argue for any idealisation of her behaviour at large. The author's presentation of the lovers derives much of its strength from its close focus. He illustrates, for example, their loyalty or faithfulness (*triuwe*) not towards the world (Tristan's towards Marke as his uncle and feudal lord, Isolde's towards Marke as her husband), but rather in their relationship with each other as lovers. It is in this closer, but intense context that we are invited to consider the lovers and in which Isolde can be said to be free of faults that Tristan shows in the concluding stages of Gottfried's incomplete work and in the fragments of Thomas's story.

If Tristan's shortcomings are brought to light particularly in the closing stages of the German text after the lovers' separation, it is important to register two points before this, one an episode in itself and the other no more than three brief remarks that alert us to this possibility, even though their true significance may emerge only retrospectively.

The episode in question concerns the wonderful dog, Petitcriu, the heart's delight of Tristan's close friend Duke Gilan.[66] The animal is not merely supremely beautiful to behold, but is equipped with a magical bell whose tinkling has the property of banishing sadness. This is what attracts Tristan's attention and he resolves on a ruse to win the dog from Gilan and to present it as a gift to Isolde from whom Tristan, at this stage only

---

[66] Gnädinger, *Hiudan*, pp. 18–48; Wessel, *Probleme*, pp. 444–53; Tomasek, *Utopie*, pp. 61–3.

temporarily, is separated. Criticism of the way in which Tristan tricks this dog away from his friend can certainly be made, for it resembles the ruse by which Gandin managed deceitfully to win Isolde from Marke after the latter's rash promise. If Gandin's behaviour towards Marke earns him the epithet of a trickster (13206: *trügenaere*), the same could equally be said of Tristan's towards Gilan. But that is not the point in the present context, for we are not invited to pass judgment on Tristan in any context other than his relationship with Isolde. Seen in this light, Tristan's action could seemingly be judged positively, for he intends all along to present the dog as a gift to Isolde, a means to assuage the longing from which he rightly knows she must be suffering (15903: '... oder mit welhen sinnen / er möhte gewinnen / sîner frouwen der künigîn / Petitcriu daz hündelîn, / durch daz ir senede swaere / al deste minner waere' ... or by what means he might obtain the little dog Petitcriu for his lady the queen so that her love pains might be assuaged). But is this how Isolde judges the gift and how we are meant to assess it?

Isolde's reaction on receiving what Tristan had thought to be a generous gift is revealing: she breaks off the bell from the chain around the dog's neck and thereby destroys its property of magically banishing grief (16392–7). She knows why she does this and we are left in no doubt about her motives. Just as Tristan knew that she would be suffering in his absence, so she knows the same about him, but – and here she differs radically from him – she refuses to accept the possibility of joy, alone and not shared with him, that he was ready to thrust upon her. For this gesture she earns the epithet 'faithful' from the narrator (16403: 'sine wolte doch niht frô sîn: / diu getriuwe staete senedaerîn, / diu haete ir fröude unde ir leben / sene unde Tristande ergeben' she did not wish to be happy. The faithful, constant lover had given over her joy and her life to love and to Tristan). Having recognised that the bell has the property of banishing grief, Isolde is alerted to the danger it represents, as Tristan had not been, of granting relief to one party, but not to the other, thereby destroying their unity (16374: 'war umbe wirde ich iemer frô / deheine stunde und keine frist, / die wîle er durch mich trûric ist' Why should I ever be happy for any time at all when he is sad because of me?). Isolde incorporates the truth, as Tristan does not, which had been voiced programmatically in the prologue, that true love involves both joy and sorrow and that this is the essence of the love story about to be recounted (201–17). To that extent in this episode Tristan, but not Isolde, falls short of what the author understands as love. Tristan's failure to grasp what the gift of Petitcriu really means also has implications for the future, for his far greater offence against love after the separation from Isolde when, as we shall see, his need to relieve himself of suffering and to find joy is meant to excuse his turning to the second Isolde. In this way the Petitcriu episode prepares us for Tristan's failure to come.

What might be expected of her lover also finds expression in three remarks by Isolde in her words to him at their leave-taking: three times in quick succession she warns him against turning to any other woman while they are separated. First, he is to see to it that no other woman is to come between the two of them (18304: 'nu sehet, daz mich kein ander wîp / iemer von iu gescheide' Now see to it that no other woman ever separates me from you). Secondly, the ring she gives him on parting is to act as a concrete reminder that he should love no one else (18314: '… op ir deheine sinne / iemer dar zuo gewinnet, / daz ir ân' mich iht minnet' if you should ever take it into your mind to love anything but me). Thirdly, he is to let no one come closer to his heart than Isolde (18324: 'und enlât iu niemen nâher gân / dan Îsold', iuwer friundîn!' and let no one be nearer to your heart than Isolde, your lover). Every one of these remarks has a bearing on the situation between Tristan and the second Isolde. The first, with its emphasis on no one coming between them (*gescheide*) points forward to the realisation of Isolde's fears (19481f.: *gescheiden*).[67] The second, with the ring as a token, anticipates the scene on Tristan's wedding night when he draws back from consummating his union with his wife on catching sight of the ring Isolde had given him. Although Gottfried's text breaks off before this scene, it occurs in the continuation by Thomas (Sneyd[1] 395–400), so that we may assume that Thomas's text lay before Gottfried when he composed his leave-taking address by Isolde and that he consciously built in this antici-patory reference. Lastly, Isolde's third remark, that Tristan should love no one other than Isolde, is laden with an irony which becomes clear only later, for the other woman against whom this warning is formulated is also called Isolde. In composing this address by Isolde Gottfried was aware of the future course of events, but Isolde could have no knowledge of them, so that we must ask what may have prompted her warning, expressed with some degree of urgency fully three times. The answer must lie, I think, in the Petitcriu episode for, although neither the narrator nor Isolde herself expresses any criticism of Tristan, behind his generosity in presenting the dog as a gift to console Isolde there lies a disturbing discrepancy between the two lovers' attitudes, the first indication that any prolonged separation will impose strains on him which he may not always be able to withstand. If

[67] See below, p. 167.

Isolde saw this at the time she would find it all the more necessary to speak as she did when it came to their leave-taking.

These last two points, the Petitcriu episode and Isolde's remarks to Tristan on his departure, point forward and prepare us for the episode in which Tristan, on encountering the second Isolde, undergoes his most marked decline, to which we now turn in conclusion. This last stage of Gottfried's unfinished work is pervaded by Ovidian echoes. In an age which has been described as Ovidian that is not in the least surprising and was already true of the depiction of love in the first romance to give prominence to this theme, Veldeke's *Eneasroman*.[68] In addition to betraying a detailed acquaintance with Ovid's love poetry, however, Gottfried leaves us in no doubt about his critical attitude towards the Latin poet's view of love, an attitude which has a bearing on his presentation of Tristan's decline, for the author attributes qualities to him which are Ovidian in origin and which he elsewhere rejects as false.[69]

Gottfried's argument with Ovid is not confined to the last stage of his work, it is already present in the prologue, winning us for the German poet's conception of love and preparing us to regard Tristan finally as critically as he does. Three central points in the prologue are relevant here. As its title implies, Ovid composed his *Remedia amoris* as a literary antidote to the sickness and suffering of love, advising his patients how they may best free themselves from what could otherwise prove mortal, how to regain health by escaping from the tyranny of love (21: 'Qui, nisi desierit, misero periturus amore est, / Desinat' Let him abandon it who, if he does not, will die miserably of love). With Gottfried, however, the advice is rather to embrace such suffering as the hallmark of true love (108: 'swer innecliche liebe hât, / doch ez im wê von herzen tuo, / daz herze stêt doch ie dar zuo' Whoever loves deeply, although it causes pain to his heart, still stands firm). Secondly, Ovid warned against leisure (*otium*) as the fomenter of obsessive thinking about love, recommending all kinds of physical activity (hunting, husbandry) as a distraction, so that by being busy one can escape the toils of love (143: 'Tam Venus otia amat; qui finem quaeris amoris, / Cedit amor rebus: res age, tutus eris' So much does Venus approve of leisure: you who seek to put an end to love (love gives way to activity), seek activity and you will be safe). Gottfried, however, turns this upside down, stating categorically that no pursuit is to be followed which ill becomes true love (93: 'und gerâte ich niemer doch dar an, / daz iemer liebe gernder man / deheine solhe unmuoze

---

[68] Kistler, *Heinrich*, passim.
[69] Meissburger, *Tristan*, pp. 7–13; Hahn, *Raum*, pp. 111–18; Wisbey, 'Living', pp. 268f.

im neme, / diu reiner liebe missezeme' and I would never advise a man seeking love to engage in any activity that ill becomes pure love). Finally, against his own best interests as an author Ovid recommended avoidance of love poetry because of its inflammatory effects on the love-sick (757: 'Eloquar invitus: teneres ne tange poetas!' I speak unwillingly: do not touch the love poets), but once more the German author reverses this, recommending the lover to pass his time with love tales (97: 'ein senelîchez maere / daz trîbe ein senedaere / mit herzen und mit munde / und senfte sô die stunde' let a lover spend his time with a love story with his heart and his lips). These reversals of Ovidian precepts inform the whole of Gottfried's work, but it is the first two that are especially relevant to the period of Tristan's relationship with the second Isolde. Gottfried quotes Ovid not merely to disagree with him, but also to express criticism of Tristan for acting in conformity with Ovid at this stage. Two aspects of Tristan's activity come under critical scrutiny.

The first is the theme of knightly warfare. Amongst the distractions from obsessive love prescribed by Ovid as a remedy warfare played a notable part (154: 'Vel tu sanguinei iuvenalia munera Martis / suspice' Or undertake the vigorous duties of bloody Mars) and he quoted the example of Aegisthus, an adulterer only because he had time on his hands while others were fighting at Troy (161–7). This has a bearing on Tristan's arrival at the duchy of Arundel after banishment from Marke's court, for the ruler there, Duke Jovelin, is engaged in warfare in which Tristan promises his assistance. Together with Kaedin and the troops he has summoned from his homeland Parmenie, Tristan succeeds in defeating the foe. To others, to Jovelin and Kaedin, Tristan presents a positive picture as a knightly saviour, but in the only context which counts for the author, Tristan's relationship with Isolde, we are granted a different view of Tristan's motivation. When he first hears of warfare at Arundel and is accordingly drawn there, he does this in the hope of forgetting some of the pain of separation (18722: 'er gedâhte sîner swaere / aber ein teil vergezzen dâ'). This explanation of his reason for fighting at Arundel merely continues the series of military adventures he sought out in various regions immediately on leaving Cornwall (18447–62). Behind this feverish search for military action lies a similar reason, the need to recover from the agony of separation (18442: 'nu gedâhte er, solte im disiu nôt / iemer ûf der erden / sô tragebaere werden, / daz er ir möhte genesen, / daz müese an ritterschefte wesen' he thought that if this pain were ever to be endurable, so that he might survive, it would have to be through knightly deeds). The suggestion of recovery (*genesen*) implies that Tristan regards warfare as an Ovidian remedy against the pains of love, precisely the concept of the Latin poet which Gottfried criticises because of his conviction that suffering in love has to be affirmed as well as joy.

The second respect in which Tristan falls disastrously short of the author's view is his encounter with the second Isolde at Arundel, for here too the Latin *magister amoris* teaches him the wrong lesson. Ovid had recommended having two mistresses (or more) at the same time as a means of lessening the force of any one affair (441: 'Hortor et, ut pariter binas habeatis amicas / ... Alterius vires subtrahit alter amor' I recommend that you have two lovers at the same time ... One love affair weakens the power of the other). Tristan proves an all too ready pupil in this respect, seeing in the second Isolde a means of reducing the pains of love for the absent one (19064: '... ze ir liebe ûf den gedingen, / ob ime sîn senebürde / mit ir iht ringer würde'... to love for her in the hope that his lover's burden might be eased). How closely Tristan follows Ovid's teaching is brought out by two details. First, in arguing that a new love may help to diminish the pain of the old he uses the images of reducing the force of the Rhine's current by drawing it off into a number of channels (19439–46) and of fighting a conflagration by distributing it into single, weaker fires (19447–51). These images were also used by Ovid to illustrate his recommendation of two mistresses (445f.). When Tristan uses these images as an excuse for himself he refers discreetly to a written authority on which he bases himself (19436: ich hân doch dicke daz gelesen / und weiz wol, daz ein trûtschaft / benimet der anderen ir kraft' I have often read and know it well that one love can diminish the power of another), an obvious rendering of *Remedia* 444 ('Alterius vires subtrahit alter amor'). But the reason why Tristan is prepared to listen to such advice is also made clear, it is his need to assuage one love through another (19433: 'sol mir daz ûf der erden / iemer gesenftet werden, / daz muoz mit fremedem liebe wesen' if I am to find any relief anywhere it will have to be with another love affair). Following Ovid's advice and using it as a specious justification means breaking away from his exclusive attachment to the first Isolde.

By breaking away from Isolde in this way Tristan's physical separation from her becomes an emotional one as well. This is clear towards the end when he convinces himself that whereas he is in a wretched state Isolde must be happy, that whereas he is pining for her, the converse cannot be true (19488–92). In imagining this discrepancy between them and recriminating Isolde for it Tristan is yet again in agreement with Ovid who had said that the lover could find relief by dwelling in his mind on his mistress's faults (315: 'Profuit adsidue vitiis insistere amicae, / Idque mihi factum saepe salubre fuit' It helped to dwell repeatedly on my lover's faults. Doing that often brought relief). With the German as with the Latin author the issue here is what the man persuades himself the woman is doing, not what we are actually told of her actions or thoughts, so that the distancing between Tristan and Isolde proceeds from him, not from her. That such a distancing takes place here is evident to Tristan himself, for he is aware that things are not what they were when they shared one joy and one woe together (19483: 'ez enstât nu niht als wîlen ê, / dô wir ein wol, dô wir ein wê / eine liebe und eine leide / gemeine truogen beide'). The present loss of shared experience (*gemeine* is put firmly into the past) is in marked contrast with the earlier use of the same word used of the lovers' joint experience (12367, 16447, 16574)[70] and is further strengthened by Tristan's preceding admission that the life they shared has now been separated (19481: 'diz leben ist under uns beiden / alze sêre gescheiden'). From what we have been shown we realise that this separation is more than just geographical and that the distancing has proceeded from Tristan, which is precisely the danger expressed by Isolde in the first of her warning remarks to Tristan, using the same verb *gescheiden* (18305).

If in gaining the dog Petitcriu Tristan could be seen as a trickster comparable with Gandin who indeed was explicitly termed a deceiver (*trügenaere*), the same epithet can be applied even more justifiably to Tristan at Arundel. In addition to what we have seen of his Ovidian betrayal of the first Isolde, we are told unmistakably of his deception (19407: *trügeheite*) of the second by his dishonest courtship of her (19401: 'daz was des schult, si was betrogen. / Tristan haet' ir sô vil gelogen / mit disen zwein handelungen / der ougen unde der zungen' this was his fault, she was deceived. Tristan had lied so much to her in two ways, with his eyes and his tongue). But Tristan's betrayal lies deeper, for it amounts to self-betrayal when, still following Ovid, he tries to become a Tristan free of woe (19468: 'ein triurelôser Tristan') and thereby to cast off his essential self, as expressed in the meaning of his own name (2001–15). That, too, comes from taking Ovid's lessons to heart.

With Thomas, to whom we turn briefly to show that he presents Tristran's position between two women in much the same way, the protagonist sees that he, too, cannot avoid deceiving one or other of the women or rather that he must break faith with both of them (Sneyd[I] 461: 'Ne sai a la quele mentir, / Car l'une me covient traïr / E decevre e enginnier, / U anduis, ço crei, trichier' I do not know to whom to lie, for I must betray, deceive and hoodwink one or, so I believe, trick both of them). In the same Ovidian manner as Gottfried Thomas underlines Tristan's imagined contrast between his own loss of joy and Ysolt's amorous delight (Sneyd[1] 9: 'Jo perc pur vos joie e deduit, / E vos l'avez e jur e nuit; / Jo main ma vie en grant dolur, / E vos vostre en delit d'amur' On your behalf I am deprived of joy and pleasure, while you have it both day and night. I lead my life in great suffering, while you spend yours in love's delight). In saying that since he cannot have his first love he will have to take what he can (Sneyd[1] 35f.) Tristran comes dangerously close to the position of Marke in Gottfried's version, seeing no difference on his wedding night between Isolde and Brangaene. The same is true when Tristran wishes to test whether, despite his love (for the first Ysolt), he may have pleasure with his wife (Sneyd[1] 207: '[Coment] se puisse delitier / [Enc]ontre amur od sa moillier'). Tristran takes this so far that in longing for his pleasure with the second Ysolt he hates his yearning for the first, but for whom he could satisfy his lust (Sneyd[1] 610–12), a detail which suggests that in imputing sexual pleasure with Marc to Ysolt Tristran is doing no more than accusing her of his own weakness.

How unfounded Tristran's suspicions are is made clear by a switch in the narrative from his erotic turmoil back to Ysolt in Cornwall, where she is presented in her chamber, sighing for Tristran on whom, and on no one else, her desire is focused (Sneyd[1] 649: 'Ysolt en sa chambre suspire / Pur Tristran que tant desire, / Ne puet en sun cuer el penser / Fors ço sulment: Tristan amer; / Ele nen ad altre voleir / Ne altre amur, ne altre espeir, / En lui est trestuit sun desir' In her chamber Ysolt sighs for Tristran, for whom she longs so much, she cannot think of anything else in her heart but this alone: loving Tristran. She has no other wish, no other love, no other hope. In him is all her longing). The addition of 'nothing else' underlines the difference between her and Tristran and the lack of any grounds for his imputation.

The difference between them is also brought out in the German version with a switch back to Isolde in Cornwall. She declares that her sorrow is shared and that she does not suffer alone for she is convinced that, however great her suffering may be, Tristan's must be greater (18559: 'mîn leit ist doch gemeine, / i'ne trage ez niht al eine: / ez ist sîn alse vil sô mîn, / und waene ez ist noch mêre sîn' my suffering is shared, I do not bear it alone: it is as much his as mine, and I think even more his). The difference between this statement and Tristan's could not be greater. Whereas Tristan was so tied up with himself that he could not conceive that Isolde was suffering likewise and sought to justify his wavering by accusing her of enjoying her pleasure with Marke, she is still so imbued with a sense of unity that she does not question Tristan's pain and is even ready to see it as surpassing hers. Her conviction of their unity and shared suffering is so firm that she uses for it the word *gemeine*, true of their love from the beginning, but now abandoned by Tristan in Arundel. At one stage, however, in his emotional wavering Tristan acquires enough clarity, however short-lived, to see that he has fallen far behind Isolde, acknowledging his faithlessness in loving two women while his other self, Isolde, loves only one Tristan (19158: 'ich triuwelôser Tristan! / ich minne zwô Îsolde / und hân die beide holde, / und ist mîn ander leben, Îsolt, / niwan einem Tristande holt' Faithless Tristan! I love two Isoldes and have them both dear, while my other self, Isolde, has only one Tristan dear). However, that flash of insight gives way immediately to the renewed danger of his courting the other Isolde. Whether Tristan in Gottfried's text was ever to win through to lasting self-knowledge we cannot of course tell, but at the point where the work breaks off it is obvious that in the author's eyes he has sunk low, whereas Isolde has not.

Against this background we may revert to the previous point at which we considered Gottfried's work as a *roman à deux*. Despite the prologue's presentation of the involvement of both lovers, despite the chiastic emphasis on their mutual love, and despite the depiction of Riwalin and Blanscheflur as a couple, one fact remains unaffected. In purely quantitative terms a long stretch of the narrative is still devoted to Tristan before the love story even begins (his youth, abduction, knighthood, involvement with Marke and the barons). It is as if the story of this man had developed an interest all of its own, which is changed radically when he encounters Isolde, but notably late in the whole narrative. An answer to this problem might lie in correlating this focus on Tristan in the first part of the work with the role played by Isolde in what follows. Not merely is she as active and resourceful as Tristan in coping with the dangers at court, but more importantly, as we have seen in the recent pages, she comes to take control of the story in that she remains true to Gottfried's ideal of love, whereas Tristan does not (just as in *Erec* it is Enite who is the spokeswoman for the idea of love in marriage). Tristan may dominate the narrative action in the first part, but Isolde comes to the fore at the close in a more important sense. In these different ways both Tristan and Isolde are the subjects of this work.

At the close of Chapter III I attempted to surmise how *Erec* may have been received by men and women in the contemporary audience, and the same attempt with *Tristan* must be equally hypothetical. Men may have been more interested in Eilhart's version in what has been shown of its closeness to heroic epic tradition[71] (especially in the depiction of the lengthy

[71] Keck, *Liebeskonzeption*, pp. 85–7.

battle fought by Tristrant and Kehenis against Riole) and Tristrant's standing as a warrior. Nor is this feature absent from Gottfried's version before the love potion scene, but also to some extent afterwards, although men of such traditional literary taste may have been somewhat put off by the author's cursory dismissal of Tristan's knightly adventures after leaving Cornwall (18461–70). The traces of male bonding detectable may also have appealed to male interest, and also the more prominent suggestions of patriarchal marriage policy, disposing of women between men and for the benefit of men.

About the possible reaction of women to the Tristan story we can also only hypothesise. None of the Tristan versions we have discussed, unlike Wolfram's *Parzival*, gives any indication of being meant for women recipients in particular, and the idea that women sponsored them may be possible, but is not certain. With Thomas it is indeed probable that he wrote for the court of Henry II of England, but his theme may well have appealed more to Eleanor than to her husband.[72] Eilhart's association with the court of Henry the Lion at Braunschweig is also likely, as is the involvement of Henry's wife, Mathilde, Eleanor's daughter, in the production of *Tristrant*, as with the *Rolandslied*.[73] The position is much more hypothetical with Gottfried. His clerical education is generally accepted. If he was connected with the cathedral at Strassburg and if what is known of concubinage amongst cathedral canons elsewhere in northern Europe was also true of Strassburg, then in such an educated milieu, as we know with Heloise at Paris, women of intellectual standing could be found capable (as recipients, if not as sponsors) of appreciating a work such as Gottfried's.[74] Apart from this, the place of Isolde at the centre of the action probably appealed more to women than an exclusively male-populated work, but also, given their disadvantaged position as the main victims of arranged marriages in the Middle Ages, the stress on love in this work, especially in overturning the utilitarian and impersonal calculations of dynastic marriage policy. Is it too much to think that they may well have applauded Gariole's

---

[72] Lejeune, *CN* 14 (1954), 33–5; Bezzola, *Origines* III 302; Wind, *Fragments*, p. 13; Hatto, *Gottfried*, pp. 355–8.

[73] Bumke, *Mäzene*, pp. 109–13, especially 111; Mertens, *Literatur*, pp. 207–9. Mertens has doubts whether Henry the Lion's literary tastes would have been attracted by the Tristan theme, but ignores the fact that sponsorship by a ruling couple can embrace divergent tastes between them, as we know with Mathilde's mother and with her half-sister and their respective husbands. See Schirmer and Broich, *Studien*, pp. 195f., 198f., 202f.; Green, *Women* pp. 215f.; and also Benton, *Speculum* 36 (1961), 585f., 587f.

[74] On non-celibate canons and the position of Heloise see Brooke, *Idea*, pp. 78–92. I thank Mark Chinca for this suggestion.

successful hoodwinking of her jealous husband Nampetenis, and indeed the long series of scenes in which Isolde turns the tables on Marke? This surmise might be supported by what we learn from Denis Piramus about Marie de France: that women at court found particular pleasure in her lais, in which the outwitting of unloved husbands is a notable feature.[75]

---

[75] Piramus, *Vie*, 46–8; Bloch, *Marie*, pp. 58–65.

CHAPTER 5

Parzival

The three themes around which we have organised our discussion of *Erec* and *Tristan* (knighthood, love, marriage) are also combined in *Parzival*. Knighthood in Wolfram's work has long preoccupied scholarship in the form of knightly homicide, but also, with an eye to its effects on the other sex, in the grief of women over the death of knights.[1] Gahmuret gives priority to knighthood in deserting Belakane for the sake of adventure and then leaving Herzeloyde for warfare in the Middle East, with fatal results.[2] True to their father, both Parzival and Feirefiz devote their careers to knightly combat and keep it present throughout the work. Revealingly, Parzival can be reintroduced into the narrative in terms of the combats on which he has been engaged while temporarily lost to view (734, 17f.),[3] Feirefiz is brought onto the stage in terms of his fighting capacity (734, 30) and both are allowed to give an exotic list of their many encounters and victories (769, 29–770, 30 and 771, 24–772, 23).

Although Gahmuret may give priority to knighthood he sees this essentially in combination with the second theme, seeking both combat and love (35, 25: 'strît und minne was sîn ger'). In this he personifies one of the work's major concerns, *amor et militia* (the 'chivalry topos') or the reward of love for knightly service rendered to a lady.[4] Contrary to Gahmuret's priorities, love is in fact the dominant theme in the work, informing all its constituents.[5] In purely numerical terms this is reflected in the fourteen couples (married or lovers) discussed by Christoph and the thirty-seven couples, separated by death, listed by Karg.[6] The importance of love and relations with a woman may seem to be drastically qualified by the protagonist's absence from his wife Condwiramurs over most of the narrative, but of the

[1] Green, 'Homicide', pp. 11–82; Sieverding, *Kampf,* pp. 166–9; Brackert, 'Parzival', pp. 143–63; Neudeck, *IASL* 19 (1994), 52–75.
[2] Emmerling, *Geschlechterbeziehungen*, p. 258.   [3] See also 434, 10–16.
[4] Hanning, *Individual,* pp. 54–60.   [5] Bumke, *Wolfram,* p. 113.
[6] Christoph, *Couples*; Karg, *Erzählen,* pp. 17–31.

strength of his feelings for her there is no doubt and it underlies his qualification for ultimate Grail-kingship. Moreover, this position is more than made good by the work's second 'protagonist', Gawan, revealingly described as yearning for love (512, 19: 'der minne gernde man'), for in the many books devoted to him to the almost total exclusion of Parzival love and the relationship with three different women are the dominant theme.[7] As we shall see, for Wolfram love is essential to the work's third theme, marriage, for although Chrétien may have argued for their reconciliation in *Erec* and *Cligés*, many of his couples in *Perceval* are not presented as married. Wolfram takes care to rectify this, for example with Parzival and Condwiramurs or Orilus and Jeschute by contrast with their French counterparts. By adding the many marriages depicted in the German work to his source Wolfram lays the groundwork for the discussion of love and marriage, together with their problematic relationship with knightly violence, that informs his romance.[8] Schultz gives a gendered reading of *Parzival* from the point of view of masculinity,[9] whereas in this chapter as in its two predecessors we are concerned more with women's position. Between the two approaches there is of course common ground, but whilst Schultz pays due attention to love service he gives much shorter measure to marriage.

This combination of themes opens up a narrative space for women in *Parzival*, which raises the question of the roles allotted to them in the action, what attitudes are adopted to them, and in particular what reflections of the antifeminine currents of his day are to be found in Wolfram's work. Certainly, his French predecessor has not escaped criticism, not always justified, on this last score. In the case of two misogynous tirades we shall later consider (by Orguelleus against the damsel of the tent and by a *vavasseur* against the sister of the king of Escavalon) the necessary distinction is not always made between what the author thinks and what his characters say when their antifeminism is imputed to Chrétien.[10] With regard to the particular theme of rape it has even been suggested that Chrétien, in agreement with the character he has created, thinks that women really take pleasure in being violated and that the representation of rape is central to the value system of his works.[11] Such critical fire has also been aimed at the German work, as when, for example, a traditional clerical antifeminism inculpating Eve and her daughters alone for the Fall is taken

---

[7] Zimmermann, *Kommentar*, pp. 2f.; Emmerling, *Geschlechterbeziehungen*, p. 7.
[8] Wiegand, *Studien*, p. 48.   [9] Schultz, *ZfdPh* 121 (2002), 342–64.
[10] Lefay-Toury, *CCM* 15 (1972), 291 (but see Pérennec, *Recherches* II 158).
[11] Buschinger, 'Viol', p. 374; Gravdal, *Signs* 17 (1991/2), 563.

out of context and considered to be the view of the author.[12] With Scheuble
the position is even more extreme. He questions whether the court romance
at large presents a counter-model to patriarchal reality rather than a dis-
guised affirmation of its values (although what we have seen in *Erec* and
Tristan must raise doubts).[13] From this Scheuble proceeds to the suggestion
that Wolfram's romance emphatically reproduces the misogynous attitude
to women of his day, and he affirms that Wolfram takes the side of men and
does not regard violence against women as a deplorable state of affairs
needing to be rectified.[14] These are views which, even though I have already
suggested my reservations about them, will have to be taken into account in
this chapter which for reasons of clarity I divide into the same three sections
as with the last two chapters.

PATRIARCHAL SOCIETY

We start with women's position in feudal society, as depicted in *Parzival*,
corresponding recognisably to the conventional role granted them in
Wolfram's day. As we saw in *Erec* and *Tristan*, a young woman before
marriage was subject to her father's authority, a situation reflected in
Parzival with Liaze and Bene. The part played by the former, the daughter
of the old knight Gurnemanz who has lost his three sons in battle, in
her father's plans for her, his family and his lands is made clear to us from
the start.[15] Left without any male heirs, he uses Liaze as a bait to attract the
young Parzival as a son-in-law to replace his losses (177, 13–16). In all this the
young woman's role is entirely passive: her wishes are not consulted, her
passivity is expressed by her silence in the whole episode and she obeys
without question what her father tells her to do (175, 24–7; 176, 24f.), an
unquestioning compliance reminiscent of Enite's obedience to her father.
Gurnemanz may regret Parzival's departure, who recalls Liaze fondly, but
her feelings are dismissed without comment. Even more drastic is what the
knight Plippalinot expects of his daughter Bene, whom he offers for the
night to his guest Gawan.[16] To some extent Plippalinot's motives resemble
Gurnemanz's: it is suggested that as an impoverished knight he may need
generous support from Gawan and with this in view he tells Bene to do
all that their guest may desire (550, 20), adding that he gives his consent

---

[12] Lähnemann, 'Tristan', p. 230.   [13] Scheuble, *Sozialisation*, pp. 16, 148.   [14] *Ibid.*, pp. 149, 349.
[15] Christoph, *Couples*, pp. 203–7; Emmerling, *Geschlechterbeziehungen*, pp. 311f.
[16] Christoph, *Couples*, pp. 207–12; Emmerling, *Geschlechterbeziehungen*, p. 93, fn. 59; Scheuble,
Sozialisation, pp. 184–6.

(of hers no mention is made).[17] When a little later Bene confesses to Gawan her readiness to do all that he may command (554, 17f.), this is not so much a declaration of inclination towards Gawan as obedience to her father. Gawan may decline to profit from this liberal hospitality, but this does not weaken the crux of this encounter: that Plippalinot was prepared to use his daughter to this end and she was unquestioningly ready to accept her role.

The patience and passivity of these two figures (qualities which patriarchy valued in women) are shared by other female characters in Wolfram's narrative world. The earliest (and leading) example of this is Jeschute, the long-suffering victim of undeserved punishment from a violent husband, Orilus.[18] In conformity to the patriarchal ideal she acknowledges his legal authority over her (136, 13f.), makes no complaint about her fate, and regrets only what befalls her husband, not herself (137, 23–6), thereby resembling Hartmann's Enite, whose suffering at the hands of Erec is taken up by Wolfram in Jeschute and Orilus not merely thematically, but also by kinship (by an ironic reversal Jeschute is Erec's sister).[19] Other examples of uncomplaining suffering by women at the hands of men include Cunneware (she voices no word of complaint about the physical brutality of Keie in beating her), Condwiramurs (on being rejoined by Parzival towards the end of the work after his prolonged absence her only complaint is to reject the anger she could rightly feel: 801, 9) and the unnamed messenger of Arthur raped by Urjans (after lodging her accusation she lapses into complete silence).

The marginalisation of women in patriarchal society, imposing on them roles of passivity and patience, severely restricts their choice of action in the work. A noblewoman who loses her husband (or husband-to-be), especially if she inherits rulership over land, has little choice but to marry again (the literary precedent for this is Hartmann's Laudine who is followed in *Parzival* by Herzeloyde and Amphlise) or to withdraw from society at large (Herzeloyde at a later stage and Sigune, in very different ways) or to die after their loss (Belakane and Sigune, whose withdrawal is one long death).[20] These are leading women characters at key positions in the narrative action and, in agreement with feudal society in his day, the world sketched by Wolfram affords them limited scope for action. By far the most extreme case of a woman reduced to mere passivity and restricted scope, even when her

---

[17] Coxon, *Wolfram-Studien* 17 (2002), 124, fn. 34, calls this patriarchal demand 'peremptory' (*barsch*).
[18] Christoph, *Couples*, pp. 71–82; Emmerling, *Geschlechterbeziehungen*, pp. 269–71; Scheuble, *Sozialisation*, pp. 291–9.
[19] Yeandle, *Commentary*, p. 361.   [20] Scheuble, *Sozialisation*, p. 153.

husband is still very much alive, is Condwiramurs, abandoned for many years. Her position is such that her sole activity lies in keeping her womanly heart pure until she is rewarded (734, 10–14), but it is Parzival who brings that about (734, 15: 'Parzivâl daz wirbet').

All this, however, is far from being the whole story, it provides a recognisable backcloth against which a counter-model can be set. In contrast to the passive role allotted to Parzival's wife, the position with Gawan is quite different: in each of the narrative segments concerned with him a female character (Obilot, Antikonie, Orgeluse) plays an important part, is not confined to the background, can even take charge of the action, and is not reduced to being a function of Gawan at whatever stage in his knightly career.[21] Nor is Condwiramurs (or other women such as Liaze and Sigune) the only character to be allotted a role which presents her as little more than a function of Parzival, for the same is true of men such as Gurnemanz and Trevrizent, so that the technique cannot be characterised as gender specific.[22] Furthermore, against the admittedly extreme example of Condwiramurs must be set an equally extreme counter-example. When he observes that women figures enjoy minimal scope for action Bumke adds that Orgeluse goes against such a generalisation, for she preserves ample freedom of action for herself in a variety of ways.[23]

As Bumke remarks, Orgeluse successfully retains rulership over her territory (514, 28: 'diu was frouwe überz lant') by herself, but that is only the initial aspect of her independence.[24] Here she stands out against other women figures like Belakane, Herzeloyde and Condwiramurs who cannot cope with the difficulties, especially military, this entails and are forced to rely on male assistance for protection. Orgeluse's importance lies in showing that this dependent role was not always unavoidable. Where Orgeluse has no choice but to seek knightly assistance it is not to safeguard her realm, but to gain vengeance on Gramoflanz. As an efficient independent ruler she assumes what was regarded as a male role, even to the extent of using counter-violence to achieve her ends, waging a long campaign against Gramoflanz,[25] from whose imprisonment after abduction she had shown initiative in escaping. She shows initiative in other ways, too. In her quest for someone who could avenge her on Gramoflanz it is she who makes the approach to the man in question, first in choosing Amfortas for this role (617, 2: 'den ich … erkôs'), with disastrous results, then in setting her cap at

---

[21] Emmerling, *Geschlechterbeziehungen*, p. 177.   [22] *Ibid.*, pp. 293f.   [23] Bumke, *Wolfram*, p. 116.
[24] Dimpel, *ZfdPh* 120 (2001), 40, 45–7; Emmerling, *Geschlechterbeziehungen*, p. 142.
[25] Lienert, 'Diskursivität', p. 226.

Parzival with the same intention, only to meet with a rebuff, but in each case it is she who adopts the role conventionally reserved for the man. These apparently minor details have important ramifications for the whole work, granting Orgeluse a central position in its structure, for the wound Amfortas received in knightly service of Orgeluse disqualified him from Grail-kingship, which triggered off the whole narrative action, whereas Parzival's rejection of her approach to him confirms that the error will not be repeated.[26] Behind Orgeluse's quest for vengeance may lie the offence committed by a man, Gramoflanz, as the ultimate cause, but the disqualification of one Grail-king and the qualification of another are demonstrated as reactions to her activity. She also shows independence and initiative in two other respects, both of which we shall consider later. First, she is independent enough to warn Gawan from the beginning against assuming that there is any automatic link between knightly service and the reward of love, thereby putting under strain the convention of *amor et militia* which Wolfram calls into question elsewhere, especially from the woman's point of view. Secondly, it is she who, as a woman and as a result of her experience of being abducted by Gramoflanz, takes the initiative in arranging for due punishment of the rapist Urjans, by contrast with the leniency shown him by Gawan and the Round Table. All these details contribute to a picture of an independent-minded woman far removed from Condwiramurs after her marriage to Parzival and bring it home to us how distorted a picture emerges if we concentrate, as scholarship for so long did, on the Parzival action alone.

Orgeluse may be outstanding, but she is not the only exception. Especially in the Gawan story, as Emmerling has shown, Wolfram depicts a number of women (Obie, Antikonie and Orgeluse above all) who know what they want in matters of love, take active steps to achieve it and cannot be reduced to mere functions of men.[27] Significantly, however, this quite unconventional picture of women's place in society is not restricted to the Gawan story and can even be found in Condwiramurs before her marriage to Parzival, in contrast to her later submissiveness (which I see as an unavoidable result of her being pushed into the narrative background on Parzival's departure). This more active side of Condwiramurs we see from the beginning in her spirited rejection of Clamide's attempt to win her hand and land by force of arms (177, 30f.), and in the lead she takes in coming by night to Parzival's bedside to plead her cause (192, 1–4). With such an initiative she crosses the border of conventional gender stereotyping, a fact underlined by the comparison of her

---

[26] Emmerling, *Geschlechterbeziehungen*, p. 154.   [27] *Ibid.*, pp. 159, 168, 330.

silk nightdress with battledress (192, 14–17) in an encounter in which this woman, too, assumes a role normally granted only to men. Her independent spirit is also shown not merely in expressing *consensus* to marriage with Parzival, but also in taking the lead in doing this, and in public (199, 26–8). In this she resembles Orgeluse rather more than her later role, forced upon her by circumstances, might allow us to think.

Other women likewise take the lead. Belakane does this in almost wooing Gahmuret herself rather than waiting for his move.[28] Over the outcome of the tournament at Kanvoleis both Herzeloyde (who has arranged the contest and laid down its terms) and Amphlise (the Queen of France whom Gahmuret had served as a knight, but who is now recently widowed) claim their man, Gahmuret, for themselves. (The unreality of this emphasises how important it was for the author to depict women, not the man, in charge of the action.) Where the usual romance convention was for the man to seek to gain the woman and her land, here it is these two women who offer themselves and their lands to him.[29] Towards the end of the work, when at Joflanze a disastrous combat is averted at the last minute, it may be Arthur who acts officially as peacemaker, but only because women (Bene and Itonje) have actively been at work urging him in this direction.[30] One is reminded of the Polish proverb: 'Man may be the head, but woman is the neck that swivels it'. Finally, as Emmerling has shown in detail that cannot be repeated here, the three women who play such an important part in the Gawan story all have in common, in different ways and to a varying extent, their rebellion against what patriarchal expectations might demand of them.[31] In this they go against the conventional code of behaviour to which women were meant to conform. Although Gottfried is more indebted to Ovid, even in opposition to him, than Wolfram, it is not far-fetched to describe the latter in terms used of Ovid in his *Heroides*, moving away from a single-hero focus and allowing 'some of his woman characters to emerge as prominent figures in the narrative and as powerful advocates of their cause'.[32]

Against this background of a number of women characters taking matters to some extent into their own hands we may now question whether the ethical qualities attributed by Wolfram to women in his work always correspond to patriarchal views about their place in feudal society. The author follows convention in his prologue (he would be ill-advised to go against it quite so soon) in listing the essential qualities desired of women (with whom

---

[28] *Ibid.*, pp. 226f.   [29] 60, 15–17; 77, 1–4.   [30] Emmerling, *Geschlechterbeziehungen*, pp. 172f.
[31] *Ibid.*, pp. 13 (Obie), 45 (Antikonie), 139–45 (Orgeluse).   [32] Gillespie, 'Study', p. 193.

he is concerned as much as with men: 2, 23–5). The qualities he mentions in quick succession (3, 2–6) include *kiusche*, *triuwe*, *mâze* and *scham*. Scheuble has no doubt that these qualities were meant to incorporate a patriarchal view of woman's ideal qualities, onesided in their application to her sex above all and confining her to an inferior, passive position in society, granting her no more than a functional role in relation to men.[33] Although Scheuble does not expand on this passage, it is not difficult to see what desirable qualities these key terms convey to patriarchal listeners. In their view *kiusche* would mean above all a woman's chastity (a key value to be safeguarded for the father before his daughter's marriage and for the husband after), *triuwe* would connote faithfulness, especially to her husband, *mâze* stands for moderation (a woman should know her place in a male-dominated society) and *scham* signifies modesty (no forwardness in a woman).

With regard to what Scheuble sees as the onesidedness of these terms it has often been said that in *Parzival* the word *kiusche* (the first to be listed and on which most work happens to have been done) is used more often of women than of men. That may be numerically true, but the figures (thirty-five times for women, twenty-six times for men) hardly suggest a onesided usage.[34] It might be possible to rescue the position by recalling the use of *wîplîcher kiusche* of Sigune (260, 8), suggesting that *kiusche* is an essentially feminine virtue, but against that may be set the description of Isenhart, Belakane's lover killed in battle, as exceeding women in this quality: *noch kiuscher denne ein wîp* (26, 15). That may still imply that women are essentially *kiusche*, but more important is the fact that men can be, too, and in this particular case can even surpass women in this. Possession of this quality does not make a man effeminate, but imbues him with a feminine feature alongside his masculine ones. Thus, the description of Isenhart just quoted is followed by a line praising his daring and bravery (26, 16: 'vrecheit und ellen truoc sîn lîp'), there are other cases where *kiusche* is combined with other warrior terms regarded as masculine (*manlîch*, *vrävel*, *vrecheit*)[35] and Pérennec has stressed that Parzival is granted the female attributes of beauty and *kiusche* without any weakening of his knightly virtues.[36] Schultz goes beyond this in stressing that Wolfram couples other courtly attributes with manliness: *manlîch und wol gemuot* (172, 7), *manlîch zuht* (188, 15), *manlîch höfsch* (430, 20), *manheit bî zuht* (745, 10).[37] However, Schultz then suggests that the 'anxiety' with which Wolfram repeats this so often implies

---

[33] Scheuble, *Sozialisation*, pp. 151, 158, 351.
[34] I take these figures from Kinzel, *ZfdPh* 18 (1886), 447–58.   [35] E.g., 823, 24; 437, 12; 737, 20f.
[36] Pérennec, *Recherches* II 247f.   [37] Schultz, *ZfdPh* 121 (2002), 349.

either that courtliness may not be as manly as all that or that those who regard courtliness as effeminate need to be challenged. The latter alternative seems to be much more convincing. What is true of *kiusche* also applies to the other terms. *Triuwe* is far from being gender specific, and is applied to Parzival, but is also the overriding attribute of God. *Mâze* can be used of Gahmuret as well as Parzival; the same is true of *scham*, which is also recommended as a key virtue by Gurnemanz, to be cherished by Parzival, but also by anyone of either sex.[38]

What must also be emphasised about these terms is their semantic range, extending beyond the patriarchal understanding of them suggested above. Here again I confine myself to what can be more briefly demonstrated with *kiusche*. It certainly does occur in the restricted sexual meaning 'chastity' of its modern German equivalent and as such is applied both to men (Trevrizent, Amfortas, the Grail-knights) and to a woman (the messenger raped by Urjans, who thereby loses her 'chaste virginity').[39] But to restrict the medieval term to the reduced function of the modern one, in the case of either sex in Wolfram's work, does little justice to its semantic elasticity, as has been seen by commentators or translators. Already in the nineteenth century Kinzel saw in it such different qualities as moderation, austerity, abstinence, purity of heart, humility and self-control.[40] Hatto translates it in different passages as courtesy, modesty, austerity, a pure life, sobriety, self-control and gentleness,[41] whilst in his discussion of the term Pérennec suggests shame, self-control, humility, asceticism and moral integrity.[42] A key witness against seeing *kiusche* as no more than 'chaste' is Antikonie, praised by the narrator for a range of widely different qualities, including *kiusche* (427, 5–15), even though she is not exactly slow to respond to the speed of Gawan's erotic advances. We cannot single out this one quality alone as meant ironically by the narrator in this instance, but do better to read it straightforwardly, with Buettner and Emmerling, as meaning 'personal integrity',[43] as Antikonie amply demonstrates towards Gawan in the ensuing action. Antikonie is one of the women in *Parzival* from whom conformity to a patriarchal view of a woman's place in society can least be expected. She and the others demonstrate that *kiusche* and the other 'womanly' virtues listed in the prologue are not to be read conventionally and patriarchally.[44]

---

[38] E.g., *triuwe* (477, 29; 462, 18f.); *mâze* (33, 19; 202, 2 and 19); *scham* (170, 16f.; 319, 6f.).
[39] 458, 8f.; 472, 29f.; 493, 24; 526, 5.   [40] Kinzel, *ZfdPh* 18 (1886), 447–58.
[41] Hatto, *Parzival*.   [42] Pérennec, *Recherches* II 246–55.
[43] Emmerling, *Geschlechterbeziehungen*, p. 46; Buettner, *Gawan*, pp. 88, 89, 90, 91, 103.
[44] Emmerling, *Geschlechterbeziehungen*, pp. 231, 241.

Although Antikonie and other women like her carve out a narrative space for themselves, they (and even more so their less assertive sisters) are still exposed to the various forms of violence against women which were endemic in medieval society and which we shall consider in the rest of this section. The danger of physical violence existed already in the domestic, marital context, as is made clear in Orilus's declaration of punishment for his wife Jeschute when he adds (so briefly that it must be taken as an everyday expectation) that many men beat their wives for lesser offences (135, 27). Wolfram has located this remark within the domestic sphere by making of this couple man and wife (here he differs from Chrétien) and suggested the frequency of such violence not merely by the reference to many men, but also by his intertextual parallel between this couple and Hartmann's Erec and Enite. Dangers of violence exist more pronouncedly for women in society at large. Chrétien refers in passing to widows, deprived of property and lands and forced to seek refuge elsewhere,[45] whilst with Wolfram Clinschor seized and imprisoned women for many years (784, 17–20). The literary precedent (to which Wolfram makes intertextual references) for the dangers that beset women is Hartmann's *Iwein*, whose protagonist's rehabilitation largely consists in bringing assistance to women in various forms of distress (besieged by a count, threatened by a giant, falsely accused, threatened with loss of inheritance, held captive). Wolfram's intertextual technique shows that this is the same society, infested with violence, which is present in his own work. This is brought out by a parallel with what we have seen in Chrétien's *Erec*. When Orilus recognises that some of the blame for what had befallen Jeschute when Parzival came across her may lie in his own neglect of the duty to protect her (262, 4f.) by leaving her thus exposed to danger, the risk this conjures up is reminiscent of Erec's position when, answering a call of distress from a woman by freeing her mate from gross ill-treatment, he hastens back to where he had left Enide in the wood, fearing that someone might have abducted her in the meantime.[46]

That violence is endemic in this society, inflicted on women as its weakest and least protected members, is clear from another feature we came across in considering *Erec*, namely the reference in Chrétien's *Lancelot*, but implicit in his picture of the Arthurian world at large, to the custom of Logres.[47] This custom theoretically affords safety to a woman travelling alone (but only theoretically, as the fate of Urjans's victim demonstrates), but not to one accompanied by a knight, whose defeat

---

[45] *Perceval* 7574–8.   [46] See above, p. 88.   [47] See above, p. 89.

exposes her to becoming the victor's prey, to do with as he will. We find an echo of this custom in Wolfram's work (it is established that he knew Chrétien's *Lancelot*) in the fate that befell Orgeluse, whose husband Cidegast was killed by Gramoflanz and who was then abducted by him. In this respect it is significant that Orgeluse is Duchess of Logroys, the region in which this custom holds sway.[48] In this case, as in the others, both the victim and the perpetrator belong to the aristocratic class – a clear indication that violence against women was at home in the highest ranks of feudal society.[49]

In looking at Wolfram's presentation of violence against women in *Parzival* we must bear in mind that his literary reflection of a feudal world recognisable by his audience as their own need not imply the author's agreement with that practice, a distinction not always made by those who see in him an antifeminine bias. Knightly violence was a perennial social problem in the Middle Ages. Looked at with regard to the men involved, as it generally was before the rise of feminine studies brought about a shift of attention and posed new questions, it is present in the Parzival story in the dominant form of knightly homicide, whether in pitched battle, in a tournament or in the quest for adventure by a solitary knight.[50] In Chrétien's work Pérennec has distinguished three groups who incorporate for the protagonist the effects of knighthood: the women whose loss plays a dissuasive role; men from the ranks of knighthood such as Gornemanz, who disappears relatively early in Perceval's career (but whose sons in the German version illustrate the tragic consequences of knighthood); men such as the Roi Pêcheur and the *ermite* who have renounced knighthood and thus reinforce the dissuasive lesson.[51] In Wolfram's version I have earlier discussed the treatment of knightly homicide and its organisation of the structure of the whole work. However, the problem of violence must also be looked at from another perspective, that of the women affected. First indirectly, as victims they mourn the loss of husband, lover or son, a pervasive theme discussed by Sieverding and Brackert.[52] Secondly, however, knightly or male violence exercised directly against women, which is our concern here and plays a central role in both the French and German texts.

Two figures, encountered early in his career by Parzival, illustrate the difference between these two perspectives, but also their possible combination in one person. Clamide (together with his henchman Kingrun) lays siege to Condwiramurs's castle in the hope of forcing her into marriage with

---

[48] 606, 6–8; Scheuble, *Sozialisation*, p. 327, fn. 408.   [49] *Ibid.*, pp. 341f.
[50] Green, 'Homicide', pp. 11–82.   [51] Pérennec, *Recherches* II 128.   [52] See above, fn. 1.

him (behind this lies the prospect of gaining control of her lands). During the course of this siege and the pitched battles that accompany it we are left in no doubt about the number of knightly victims the campaign claimed (195, 1–6 and 16f.; 198, 6f. and 21f.), nor about the grief which all this caused Condwiramurs, driving her to contemplate suicide (194, 27–195, 1). The double effect of male violence, on opponents in battle and on a woman, is also illustrated in the figure of Orilus, at once one who plays a malign part together with his brother Lähelin as a killer-knight and also a husband who exercises prolonged violence against his wife Jeschute.

That Wolfram as an author was concerned with women as the victims of violence emerges from the conclusion of Book VI. His words are explicitly directed at women, both as potential readers of his work (337, 1–3) and because he hopes above all for approval from them or at least from one of them (337, 27–30). He recommends himself for women's approval by reminding them of the various women victims whose suffering he has so far depicted with compassion and names them as Belakane, besieged at Zazamanc; Herzeloyde, learning of Gahmuret's death in battle; Guinevere, mourning the killing of Ither; Jeschute, brutally punished by her husband; Cunneware, equally brutally mistreated by Keie.[53] This self-recommendation draws its persuasive power from the frequency, to be continued over the remaining ten Books, with which the author finds space in which to depict woman's victim status and his attitude to it.

In what follows we shall be concerned with four categories of violence against women. The first is military violence (as with Clamide laying siege to Condwiramurs), the second is disciplinary violence (as with Orilus's treatment of Jeschute) and the third is sexual violence (consisting of abduction or rape). A fourth category, verbal violence, we shall consider in the next section.

Military violence against women usually takes the form of a conventional literary motif in the romance: a single woman ruler, unmarried or widowed, either is actually besieged or fears the prospect of such an attack. The precedent for Wolfram was Hartmann's Laudine, widowed and in need of a new protector. This literary motif derives its force as an adaptation of the argument repeatedly advocated by the Church on the social obligations (and justification) of Christian knighthood: to defend widows, orphans and the Church (for example, 'defensio … ecclesiarum, viduarum, orphanorum').[54] In the romance utilisation of this motif the Church is generally

---

[53] 337, 5–20.   [54] Erdmann, *Entstehung*, p. 330 (*Defensio ensis noviter succincti*).

ignored, orphans are preferably female[55] so that, together with widows, they are in a position to provide *lîp unde lant* to any knight who may rescue them from their attackers. A woman in such a situation is in urgent need of protection, which explains and justifies Laudine's need for re-marriage as soon as possible,[56] but which also heightens Iwein's offence in leaving her unprotected later, as it does also Parzival's absence from Condwiramurs.[57] (Both authors leave conveniently unmentioned any dangers that may have confronted these two women during this period.) That the subjects of a woman in such a position recognise the danger it entails for the land as a whole is clear from what we are told of the counts of Brabant (before Loherangrin arrives to rectify the situation), angrily urging the princess to marry (824, 14–18).

A brief list of women in *Parzival* who are exposed, or expected to be exposed, to this danger may indicate that Wolfram was fully aware of this type of violence to them. To a much less extent this is already true of Chrétien's version, where a damsel is besieged at Montesclaire, with Gauvain ready to rescue her.[58] In the German version Belakane may not be attacked for possession of herself and her lands, but rather for vengeance for the death of Isenhart, for which she is held responsible, although this still need not exclude an eye for her *lîp unde lant*. If we disregard the motivation, the situation in which she finds herself, with Gahmuret as her rescuer, is no different from that of other women in distress (16, 11–18; 26, 4f.; 28, 21f.). Herzeloyde is twice depicted in the position of a widow. After the loss of her first husband, Castis, she organises a tournament with the aim of marrying the victor as a man strong enough to take over the role of protector.[59] How justified her need to find a protector was is shown when she is eventually widowed again on Gahmuret's death, since she later makes it clear that Lähelin seized her lands from her princes (128, 3–7; 141, 7). If this seizure took place before her retirement to Soltane with her son, her situation would match that of the widows in Chrétien's version, forced to seek refuge because they had been deprived of lands and property.[60] Our next example is a prospective one, for Liaze's father Gurnemanz wishes not merely to safeguard the position of his lands by acquiring Parzival as a son-in-law, but also to protect his daughter against what he knows too well might happen to her on his death, left in sole charge in a violent world.[61] Condwiramurs

[55] See Chrétien, *Perceval* 6467: 'Ou veve dame ou orfenine'.
[56] Mertens, *Laudine*, pp. 14–33. More generally: Brackert, 'Parzival', p. 143; Bumke, *Wolfram*, pp. 115f.
[57] Schu, *Erzählen*, p. 419.   [58] *Perceval* 4706–10.
[59] *Parzival* 60, 15–17; Hartmann, *Gahmuret*, p. 28; Schu, *Abenteuer*, p. 100.   [60] *Perceval* 7574–8.
[61] Brackert, 'Parzival', p. 143; Karg, *Erzählen*, p. 34.

occupies two positions in the pattern of events we are following. Her initial position, because of the death of her father Tampenteire, is that of an orphan with responsibility for his lands (194, 18–20). This unfailingly attracts the attention of Clamide who, together with Kingrun, has laid waste all the realm except the castle Pelrapeire, which he now besieges with the hope of legitimising his position by forcing marriage upon her (194, 14–17). That Clamide has an eye as much on her lands as her person is made clear by his own use of the double formula *lîp unde lant* (204, 6f.) and by his inability to see that Parzival may have different priorities (213, 27f.). Like Clamide, Gramoflanz seeks to force Orgeluse into marriage with him, not by means of a siege, but by holding her prisoner to weaken her resistance.

Our second category of violence against women takes the form of disciplinary punishment which medieval law allowed to men, especially husbands dealing with their wives.[62] We have to consider two examples in *Parzival*, the first of which is Orilus's punishment of Jeschute for what he regards as her unfaithfulness in her encounter with the young Parzival as he sets out on departing from his mother. In this episode Orilus claims his legal right to punish his wife, whereas in the French version no such right exists since the couple are not married and the woman anticipates ill-treatment from her lover.[63] Orilus regards himself as more justified since many a husband has punished his wife with blows for far less (135, 25–7), whereas he will impose 'no more than' an extreme form of separation from bed and board, enough to cause her much suffering. It is a measure of his self-centredness that he sees what happened between Jeschute and Parzival not as violence done to his wife, but as dishonour done to him (266, 13f.). The fact that, as his wife's legal lord (264, 4: *rehter vogt*), he has failed to protect her means that he regards her fate as an offence to his authority. What makes matters worse is that he refuses to listen to her defence, cutting her short by accusing her of being too proud and uppity (136, 24), whereas, conscious that Jeschute has married beneath her, he compensates for this by his own exaggerated pride, boasting at length of his knightly victories over others, including his wife's brother Erec (134, 1–19; 134, 23–135, 24), a long catalogue of 'achievements' in which, in another field of violence, he condemns himself as the ruthless killer knight he is. The length of this catalogue and the headlong search for repeated combats it betrays register the psychological need of Orilus to raise himself in his own esteem and in that of his wife. In all this Wolfram paints Orilus in blacker colours than had Chrétien Orguelleus de la Lande and highlights this by describing Jeschute's

---

[62] *HRG* I 836–9.   [63] *Perceval* 730f., 775–7.

submissive patience. (As with Hartmann's Enite this is not meant as a patriarchal model of how a woman should rightly behave, but as a foil to her husband's negative qualities.) In agreement with this the narrator takes care to emphasise to us Jeschute's complete innocence in the matter, saying that Orilus passed judgment on her without any guilt on her part (264, 12–15), that what she suffered at his hands was undeserved (257, 27) and that she was a guiltless victim of his anger (272, 23f.). Such repetitiveness shows that the narrator attached importance to this, as does also the fact that he invites our sympathy for Jeschute by expressing his own grief for her and inviting his listeners to lament with him (137, 27–30). When Lienert argues that this sympathy for Jeschute depends upon her maintaining her role of passive patience[64] this ignores the fact that the Griseldis picture of this woman, like that of Enite, is meant to heighten criticism of the husband. This emphasis on the victim's suffering and innocence, together with the sympathy they evoke, means that in this episode things are presented from her point of view as well as Orilus's, so that we are given two perspectives on events. Whereas Orilus self-centredly puts forward his view of the matter at some length, Jeschute's is largely shown us through the words of the narrator, which heightens the impression of sympathy with her.

The presentation of this episode from two different angles (husband and wife) recurs on a different level when we pay attention to the legal aspect of the couple's relationship. These have already been suggested: first by Orilus insisting on his legal position as the lord (*vogt*) of his wife, by his earlier refusal to listen to her defence (136, 15: *gerihte*) and the repeated denial of any guilt (*schulde*) on the woman's part. The narrator takes the matter a decisive step further when he intervenes, saying in full accordance with medieval law that Orilus as husband had every right to withhold his favour from his wife and that, since husbands have legal authority over their wives, no one should prevent that (264, 16–19).[65] A few lines later, however, the situation is made a little more even when the narrator claims that both Orilus and Parzival are in the right (264, 25: 'mich dunket si hân bêde reht'): Orilus in the legal sense of a husband's authority and right to punish, but Parzival in the more general sense of upholding what he knows to be right, in accordance with the truth, namely Jeschute's innocence. By confronting *reht* in one sense with *reht* in another, by suggesting that the husband's authority can conflict with the truth Wolfram may be unable to contest medieval marital law, but can at least show up its deficiency. That insistence on the husband's *reht* can amount to injustice being done to the woman is

[64] Lienert, 'Diskursivität', pp. 230f.   [65] Emmerling, *Geschlechterbeziehungen*, p. 269.

suggested by the narrator's comment (139, 22: 'unrehte geschach dem wîbe').

With our second example of disciplinary violence, Keie's punishment of Cunneware at Arthur's court for acknowledging that, against all appearances when the inexperienced young Parzival arrives there, she recognises his exemplary status, we leave the sphere of domestic violence for the public discipline at court which Keie as seneschal is meant to uphold. We are left in no doubt about the extreme brutality Keie exercises in his treatment of the woman, seizing her by the hair and beating her on the back with a stick through clothes and skin (151, 21–30). It may be Keie's duty as seneschal to uphold patriarchal order at Arthur's court, but against this extreme way of carrying out his task not a trace of protest is made by any member of the Round Table. From this silence it is difficult to tell whether this is meant to demonstrate the patriarchal nature of the court, unconcerned about such treatment of a woman, or whether it is meant to reflect Arthur as a weak ruler.[66] In either case, the impression created is a disturbing one: whereas in *Erec* violence threatened women only once they had left the civilised safety of the court, here they are exposed to it at the court of King Arthur himself. Wolfram cannot leave it to the possibly patriarchal members of his audience to be at all put out by such behaviour, so that he builds in a number of hints calling it into question. First and foremost is the fact that, as with Orilus's punishment of Jeschute, Keie's treatment of Cunneware is based on a false premise, for Parzival is in fact an exemplary figure and the listeners will at this point have followed him long enough to realise that he is indeed the protagonist and therefore, according to romance convention, exemplary. The mistake underlying Keie's action is expressed when he utters the words accompanying his blows, for the narrator describes him as unwise (152, 1: 'dô sprach der unwîse'), depriving his action of its justification. This criticism is taken further and given legal backing when it is said that no royal court would have given Keie the right to punish the woman in such a manner (152, 14f.). If a few lines later the information is given that Cunneware was by birth a princess (152, 19) this is a fact which the royal court would have taken into account in deciding on the case, it is not enough to suggest that what is being condemned here is not violence against a woman as such, but against one of high birth.[67] We know what such a court could not know: that Parzival is an exemplary hero, that Cunneware was right in recognising this and Keie wrong in his reaction. A little later, when stating his reaction to this scene, Parzival refers to the great insult done to him (158, 22) in that a

---

[66] *Ibid.*, p. 276.   [67] As suggested by Scheuble, *Sozialisation*, p. 315.

woman was so mistreated on his account, and to Keie forgetting himself with Parzival in doing this (158, 24–6). However, he adds immediately that he is still touched to the heart by her cries of pain (158, 27–30), words of compassion that recall his involuntary reaction on seeing the violent blows (153, 17). Lienert seeks to play down this (male) sympathy with a woman's suffering by claiming that what is more deserving of condemnation here is the insult felt by the hero, not the suffering inflicted on the woman.[68] She gives no reason why one motive should outweigh the other or why both should not come into play, and we shall soon come across a similar bias against giving a man an honourable reaction to women's pain. Unlike some of his modern interpreters, Wolfram is not an author to favour monocausal explanations.

With sexual violence against women, our third category, we come to what is the most common offence against them depicted in the romance. It takes two forms, both expressed by the Latin term *raptus* and not always distinguishable in our literary texts, namely abduction of a woman and enforced sexual intercourse (what we understand by rape).[69] If abduction took place with the woman's consent it amounted to elopement, if without it came close to rape or indeed led to it. As a crime it was regarded not merely as an offence against the woman, but also against the man (father or husband) who had authority over her. *Raptus* in either sense plays a prominent part in the French romance (as it also did in feudal society and in the highest ranks) and it occurs in one form or another in all of Chrétien's romances.[70]

Central to this phenomenon, as we shall see it also is to Wolfram's view of marriage, is the woman's agreement, *consensus*, or lack of it.[71] In the case of abduction her *consensus* makes of abduction an elopement which can issue in marriage, while her refusal can make it the equivalent of rape. On the other hand, rape can only be invoked when it takes place without the woman's *consensus*, a fact underlined whenever (but not always) this is expressly added (for example: 'mit gewalte und ân iren danc', forcibly and against her will, or 'genôtzogt ân irn danc', violated against her will).[72] The

---

[68] Lienert, 'Diskursivität', p. 235.

[69] *HRG* I 944f., 1210–14; Brundage, *Law*, pp. 47f. (on Roman law); Paterson, *World*, p. 240 (medieval law); Saunders, 'Matter', p. 106.

[70] French romance: Rieger, *CCM* 31 (1988), 241–67; Baldwin, *Language*, p. 202. Chrétien: Owen, *FMLS* 21 (1985), 376–86; Gravdal, *Maidens*, pp. 42–71; *Signs* 17 (1991/2), 558–85. Historical examples from feudal society: Rieger, *CCM* 31 (1988), 243–6; Buschinger, 'Viol', pp. 369–73.

[71] Discussed with regard to the Middle English romance by Saunders, 'Matter', pp. 105–24.

[72] Ottokar von Steiermark, *Österreichische Reimchronik* 63485, 71514, quoted by Rieger, *CCM* 31 (1988), 243, fns 13 and 14.

central importance of *consensus* by the woman plays a part in assessing the author's attitude towards the abductions and rapes he depicts, for if Wolfram grants it such an essential function in his view of what marriage should ideally be he is hardly likely to change his stance when it comes to rape, as Lienert and Scheuble suggest, and indulge in rape-phantasies or present a trivialisation of rape.[73]

Two examples of abduction occupy us in *Parzival.* The first case, concerning Clinschor and Uterpandragun's wife, is referred to early in the work, but finds its resolution only towards the end. Although we are first told that Clinschor absconded with the woman (66, 4: 'ein phaffe … mit dem diu frouwe ist hin gewant'), so that it may be a case of elopement with the woman's agreement, the express mention of Clinschor's command of magic (66, 4: 'der wol zouber las') could imply the use of magic to compel her against her will.[74] Later developments confirm this suspicion when it emerges that the woman in question, Arnive, and other close women members of her family and a whole battery of other women are all still held prisoners many years later at Schastel Marveile.[75] We are told this at the end of Book VI (334, 1–7), so that their captivity must have lasted nearly twenty-five years. Since Clinschor has cast a magic spell over the castle we may assume that it was by the same means that he was able to abduct his victims and not with their agreement. In Chrétien's version the women seek refuge in a castle after having been deprived of their lands (7574–8): they too are victims of violence, but of a different kind.[76] A further suggestion that with Wolfram we are dealing with an involuntary captivity of these women comes when it is made clear to Gawan that it falls to him to free them (564, 6–8), confirmed after the event when Arnive greets him as a liberator (660, 29–661, 2). The suffering endured by these women is reported at considerable length by Arnive (656, 3–661, 2), giving us a woman's perspective on things. This amounts to a clarification of events for Gawan and for us, but again as seen by the woman victims. Although Scheuble concedes that all this is Wolfram's innovation on his French source, he seeks to play this down by arguing that the long lapse of time between abduction and final liberation means that, although early attempts to track down the women were made, neither Uterpandragun and after him Arthur nor Lot and Gawan were in effect concerned with the fate of these women over the years.[77] That is a shaky argument *ex silentio*, resting on the assumption that

---

[73] Lienert, 'Diskursivität', p. 239; Scheuble, *Sozialisation*, pp. 278f., 288.
[74] Scheuble, *Sozialisation*, p. 265 and fn. 298.   [75] Emmerling, *Geschlechterbeziehungen*, p. 112.
[76] *Ibid.*, p. 111.   [77] Scheuble, *Sozialisation*, pp. 271–4.

what is not narrated did not happen, and it improbably expects of a medieval author an explicit, even pedantic mention of every detail of interest to modern scholarship. It also ignores a characteristic feature of Wolfram's narrative technique: the gradual and eventually still partial disclosure of information.[78]

Although the second example of abduction, by Gramoflanz of Orgeluse, indirectly plays a central part in the narrative we can treat it more briefly at this point. In the French text we are told that Guiromelanz killed the lover of Orguelleuse, abducted her, but that she refused his love (and thus still had an element of choice?) and escaped.[79] With Wolfram these details are reported by Gramoflanz to Gawan with not a speck of remorse (606, 6–13). In accordance with his wish to introduce marriage as much as possible Wolfram makes of Orgeluse's former partner, Cidegast, her husband, but otherwise, doubtless to the frustration of those who expect all details to be recounted, a number of details are left unclear. Where did Gramoflanz hold Orgeluse in abduction for a year? Why should he, the killer of her husband, not go further than 'merely' abducting her? How did she effect her escape? Leaving these questions on one side, we may see in the imprisonment of Orgeluse an attempt to demoralise her and break her will, thereby bringing about an enforced *consensus* by her, presumably to marriage, since Gramoflanz offers her his crown and his land (606, 9). In this Orgeluse has been reduced to an object of exchange (enforced by killing) between two men. This is also brought about by what we have already touched upon, the implication that behind the encounter between Gramoflanz and Cidegast there lies a hint of Chrétien's custom of Logres.[80] This allowed Gramoflanz, after dispatching Cidegast, to do as he wanted with Orgeluse, but if he did not rape her he certainly enforced his will on her by abducting and imprisoning her.

We now go further than did Gramoflanz by turning to rape, dealing with three cases. The first of these occurs before Parzival leaves his mother's retreat in Soltane and is his first encounter with knighthood: Karnahkarnanz rides in pursuit of another knight, called Meljakanz, who had seized a woman Imane in the former's land and taken her away (121, 13–27). Because of the ambiguity of the words *nôtnunft* and *roup* (122, 18 and 20) we have no certainty at this stage which form of violence, abduction or rape, is involved here. In either case we realise that violence of some kind is at issue because we are made aware of the woman's suffering (121, 22; 125, 8 and 14). By naming the abductor Meljakanz Wolfram has set intertextual alarm-bells ringing, for

---

[78] Green, *Art*, pp. 11–14.   [79] *Perceval* 8561–75.
[80] See above, pp. 181f.; Gravdal, *Signs* 17 (1991), 582; Scheuble, *Sozialisation*, pp. 326f.

his listeners will know of him in that capacity already, if not from Chrétien's *Yvain* and *Lancelot*, then at least from Hartmann's *Iwein*, in which by means of a cunning word-trick he has won for himself and taken off Guinevere, rather like Gandin and Isolde in Gottfried's *Tristan*.[81] This reinforces the impression of a woman subjected to male violence, but still tells us nothing about abduction or rape. This issue is settled only much later at the start of Book VII when a page describes Meljakanz as one to whom no woman ever gave her love, but who always took it by force (343, 24–9).[82] That is enough to brand him a rapist, who therefore deserves capital punishment (343, 30), as medieval law demanded for this crime.

Several features of this episode suggest that Wolfram is working independently to raise the question of violence done to a woman. It is he, not Chrétien, who specifies the fact of abduction or rape and subsequently makes the latter clear.[83] It is he, not Chrétien, who reports the later rescue of the woman by Karnahkarnanz (125, 12f.). It is he, not Chrétien, who has this knight pronounce the damning verdict on his opponent's breach of the knightly code (122, 16f. and 19). Scheuble mentions these features, but still maintains that Wolfram wished to present Meljakanz as responsible for no more than a petty offence ('Kavaliersdelikt') to be settled between men, thereby marginalising the offence done to a woman.[84] In reply to this we may ask why Wolfram introduced these details into what he found in Chrétien. With an argument resembling that used by Lienert on the Cunneware episode Scheuble also suggests that Karnahkarnanz was less concerned with Imane's suffering than with the disgrace falling to him by her abduction from his land.[85] This leaves unexplained why one factor should outweigh the other (again: why not both?), ignores the priority given by Karnahkarnanz to the woman's pain when he asks his question of Herzeloyde's peasants (125, 1–3) and does not consider the possibility that the disgrace (121, 20: *schande*) might be as much to the knightly code which he soon invokes (122, 17) as to himself. For Wolfram, aware of Imane's suffering, it is enough to finish the episode with a mention of her rescue (125, 12f.), but Scheuble argues that since no punishment of Meljakanz is referred to none took place and the offender was let off scot-free.[86] However,

---

[81] Hartmann, *Iwein* 4585–7. That Wolfram, if not his audience, was acquainted with Chrétien's *Lancelot* is clear from *Parzival* 387, 1–8.

[82] Scheuble, *Sozialisation*, p. 281, makes an unconvincing, strained attempt to play this down by suggesting that the page is an unreliable source.

[83] By contrast with *Perceval* 184f., 209–11, 255f., 279f., 291–3.   [84] Scheuble, *Sozialisation*, pp. 278f.

[85] 121, 18–22; Scheuble, *Sozialisation*, pp. 274f.   [86] *Ibid.*, p. 280.

this supposed trivialising of his offence against a woman once more rests on a dubious argument *ex silentio*.

Our next example brings us back to a second case of Jeschute as a victim, this time subjected to the inexperienced force exerted by the young Parzival when he encounters her alone in the tent. This is at first suspected by her as an attempted rape, but her jealous husband assumes otherwise, accuses her of having an affair and punishes her for that. In this episode we are dealing therefore with an apparent rape. The narrator certainly allows his listeners to think that this is what he is about to offer them, for in contrast to Chrétien he describes in some detail the sexual charms of Jeschute, as she lies asleep with her bedclothes flung back (130, 3–25), so persuasively that he feels tempted himself.[87] The young Parzival, misunderstanding his mother's advice, uses force to seize a kiss and her ring from Jeschute, force which is expressed by a variety of terms (*twingen, ringen, drucken, brechen, roup*),[88] all of which confirms Jeschute's fear that she faces rape. Her first thought is that she is being dishonoured (131, 8: *entêret*), she calls out aloud in alarm (131, 11), the *gerüefte* on which medieval law insisted if rape was to be established, and she struggles in resistance (131, 19 and 21), thereby showing, as with Chrétien, her lack of *consensus*.

When the word *roup* is used of what Parzival seizes by force from the woman (132, 25) this refers to the ring and brooch he has taken, not to the sexual violence anticipated by Jeschute and recently intended by Meljakanz in abducting Imane (122, 20). So far is this from being the case that Jeschute's erotic attraction leaves the young boy cold. In contrast to the narrator's description (we see Jeschute through his eyes) Parzival, following his mother's instructions, has eyes only for the woman's ring and it is this rather than Jeschute herself that drives him to her bed (130, 26–8), where the verb *ringen* describes not the love play which we and Jeschute expect, but the struggle to obtain the trophy on which his gaze is fixed. The switch from what the narrator sees to what Parzival sees (130, 26) comes just when we expect the narrator's detailed description to reach the upper part of Jeschute's body, uncovered by bedclothes, but the shift to what really attracts Parzival's attention shows that there is to be no rape.[89] Even when, after securing the ring, Parzival clumsily kisses and embraces Jeschute, this is no act of instinctive intimacy, but a rather mechanical following of his mother's advice.[90]

---

[87] 130, 14–16. See below, p. 209.   [88] 130, 27 and 131, 13; 130, 28 and 131, 21; 131, 15; 131, 18; 132, 25.
[89] Emmerling, *Geschlechterbeziehungen*, p. 266.   [90] *Ibid.*

If we were to assume a 'male gaze' in the description of Jeschute (its enthusiastic details, the narrator's erotic phantasies, the expectation he arouses in his listeners), the author's purpose here is to subvert, to leave us in the lurch before the climax and to show just how different Parzival is, whose inexperience or *tumpheit* (which it may be tempting to ridicule at this point) is the reverse side of the coin of purity demanded of the protagonist as future Grail-king and in which Amfortas had signally failed.[91] By presenting himself as all too human and by enticing his listeners into complicity with him on this the narrator elevates by contrast the status of his protagonist even at this early stage. The same end is achieved when the narrator, looking back later on the encounter with Jeschute, observes with a sense of humour which is so often apparently out of place that if Parzival had resembled his father Gahmuret he would have behaved very differently and made use of the opportunity provided by coming across Jeschute (139, 15–19). Rather than argue that the reference to Gahmuret makes a victim of Jeschute for a second time,[92] we may see in this alignment of father, narrator and complicit listeners a combined function of throwing into relief how different Parzival is from others. The appearance of rape with which this episode began (Jeschute's charms, Parzival's violence, the woman's fears and resistance) is therefore undercut twice: once by Parzival's youthful innocence and then by Orilus's jealous assumption that his wife is conducting an affair with a lover (133, 10: *ein ander âmîs*).[93]

In this connection we may mention in passing one other example of apparent rape, concerning Gawan and Antikonie. Wolfram has omitted what he found in the French text, a misogynous outburst against women voiced by a *vavasseur* who came across the two in intimate circumstances. In Wolfram's version the knight who comes across the couple assumes rape by Gawan, in addition to the murder of which he has already been (wrongly) accused (407, 16–19). We know however that the accusation of rape is likewise unfounded since the scene before this interruption makes clear the couple's shared readiness, hence the woman's *consensus* and the lack of any violence on Gawan's part (407, 3–9).

For an episode in which rape is certainly committed we turn finally to the evil figure Urjans. Wolfram presumably attached importance to him because he expands on his French source by giving details of the offender's trial (and adding Gawan's report of it to Orgeluse). By signalling Urjans's knightly, even princely rank (522, 11; 545, 30) he confirms what we learn

[91] On the wide spread of functions of this term see Haas, *Tumpheit*.
[92] Scheuble, *Sozialisation*, pp. 163, 290.   [93] Emmerling, *Geschlechterbeziehungen*, p. 269.

from historical sources, namely that this form of violence against women was endemic in feudal society. Chrétien makes it clear that his corresponding figure (Greoreas) is not merely an abductor, but also a rapist, offending against the woman, but also against King Arthur's authority in safeguarding the protection of woman according to the custom of Logres.[94] Both these details are present in the German version, but Wolfram brings Orgeluse more closely into this episode by making of her, after the death of Cidegast, ruler of Logroys. That Urjans in fact raped the unnamed woman who was Arthur's messenger and under his protection is made clear beyond doubt. As was the case with Parzival's encounter with Jeschute, the verb *ringen* is used of Urjans's violence, enforcing his will on the woman without her agreement (525, 20–2), depriving her of her virginity (526, 3–5), where *roup* (527, 9–11) is used in the context of rape, thereby constituting what was a capital offence in medieval law. As with Jeschute, the woman cries out in distress (525, 23).

When the matter comes before the royal court of justice after Gawan captured Urjans and brought him to trial, the fact that Gawan had spared the offender in combat by granting him surety (*sicherheit*) is used by the latter to suggest that any death penalty would tell against Gawan's word of honour (527, 26). The quandary in which Gawan now stands does not show him in the best light, for he sets the possible loss of his own knightly honour above the woman victim's appeal on behalf of her maidenly honour (526, 29). To rescue himself Gawan makes an appeal to the woman for mitigation of the death penalty, which is then granted by the court. However, Gawan's argument (527, 28–528, 10) contains a string of antifeminine sentiments:[95] womanly goodness (528, 1: *wibes güete*) is turned against her to cajole her into clemency; the rape committed against her is cynically equated with love felt for her (528, 3: *ir minne*),[96] which in turn was brought about by her beauty (528, 5), so that she herself is meant to be ultimately responsible for what befell her.[97] (The hair-raising equation of Urjans's behaviour with 'service' of the woman, 528, 6f., we shall consider later.) Not on the only occasion in his work Wolfram presents Gawan in a negative light, giving priority to his own interests over the victim's, whom he treats with antifeminine prejudice.

---

[94] *Perceval* 7118–31.   [95] Scheuble, *Sozialisation*, pp. 333f.
[96] See the use of *minnen* to denote rape in Heinrich der Glichezare, *Reinhart Fuchs* 1192.
[97] We saw above (p. 18) that in clerical misogynous tradition woman, the object of temptation, could be seen as its cause.

These details about the trial of Urjans are presented to us indirectly in what Gawan later reports to Orgeluse, whose angry reaction to such male justice, making light of what had been done to the woman, is significant.[98] It takes a woman, moreover one who had suffered the humiliation of being abducted by Gramoflanz, to stand up for another woman victim and procure the punishment which Urjans deserved.[99] In a manner typical of Wolfram this punishment is meant to be read from what is implicit in the later narrative, carried out behind the scenes by Lischoys Gwelljus on orders from Orgeluse and bringing the rapist to the death which he had escaped at Arthur's court. The fact that Wolfram, presenting it in what Mohr has called his 'epische Hintergründe', leaves it to his listeners to read this conclusion out of a later detail[100] does not allow us to assume with Scheuble that he voices no criticism of the faulty justice advocated by Gawan and agreed to by Arthur.[101] It was after all the German author who expanded this episode to include Orgeluse, her reaction to Gawan's account and the subsequent punishment of Urjans. If he found nothing with which to disagree in Gawan's address to the violated woman what purpose did it serve to introduce Orgeluse in this way and, using her as a mouthpiece, voice doubt about Gawan's position? Orgeluse is convinced that the reduced punishment inflicted on Urjans by Arthur is no true punishment at all (529, 7: 'sît ez der künec dort niht rach'), but this statement from a woman's point of view casts a light on what Gawan has just reported on the outcome of the trial and punishment falling far short of death for the rapist. For him (and for those complicit with him at court) enough has been done: in this way the woman has been avenged (528, 30: 'sus wart diu frouwe gerochen') and in this way the offender has been purified (528, 25: 'sus wart sîn lîp gereinet'). Scheuble reads the passage in which these two lines occur literally as wiping out the offence and not calling for any critical comment by the narrator.[102] This ignores the reaction by Orgeluse and the contradiction it presents to what Gawan and the court think is adequate, and it also fails to consider another reading. Gawan's passage (528, 25–30) emphasises the word *sus* by using it twice in the stressed position at the beginning of each line, inviting us to consider in exactly what manner amends may be said to have been made. One of the conventional signals for irony is the use of a demonstrative part of speech (including

---

[98] 529, 2–16.   [99] Emmerling, *Geschlechterbeziehungen*, p. 102 and fn. 87.
[100] Mohr, 'Hintergründen', pp. 177f.; Lienert, 'Diskursivität', p. 238.
[101] Scheuble, *Sozialisation*, pp. 337f.   [102] *Ibid.*, pp. 335, 337.

MHG *sus, sus getân, solh* or the definite article when metrically stressed).[103]
We have come across an example with the definite article in the narrator's
ironic praise of Erec, but Gottfried and Wolfram also use *sus* in this function.[104] The purpose of these demonstratives is to insinuate a comparison
and ultimately an incongruity between what is said and what is meant.
This incongruity we find in the Urjans episode between what Gawan maintains and Orgeluse contests. It is from her position, as a woman and herself a
victim of violence, that we are invited to judge this episode and the men
involved in it.

ANTIFEMININE ATTITUDES

In a society such as that depicted by Wolfram in *Parzival*, in which the
widespread attempt is made to subordinate and marginalise women and in
which they are exposed to various types of male violence, it is only to be
expected that antifeminine attitudes will also find verbal expression in the
work. As with *Erec* and *Tristan*, negative generalisations play a central role in
this but, as in the last section, we must ask how far, if at all, such statements
can be regarded as reflecting the author's own opinion.

We start with two remarks by leading male figures in the narrative who
expressly refuse to extend any criticism of one particular woman to the
whole of her sex. The first example concerns an encounter, not narrated but
reported in retrospect, between Parzival and Orgeluse. It is preceded by a
conventional expression by Parzival of respect for women, invoking God's
blessing on them (696, 1f.), which prepares us for what comes, namely
Orgeluse's embarrassment at having to greet him, since, in search of a
knight capable of gaining vengeance for her on Gramoflanz, she had once
offered Parzival her love and her lands, but had been rejected (696, 8–14).
We know enough of Parzival's love for Condwiramurs to see why he acts
thus, but Orgeluse, like other victims of misogyny, assumes that in rejecting
one woman – herself – he must be railing at all women (697, 16: 'welt ir
bevelhen mir/den der frouwen spotten kan?' do you intend to recommend
to me a man who rails at women?). This restores something of her wounded
self-esteem, but also suggests how ready she is, as a woman in a patriarchal
society, to assume a negative generalisation. Parzival leaves her in no doubt
that she is wrong, stating in principle (as we know already from 696, 1f.) that
he does not mock all women (697, 21–24). In assuming misogyny Orgeluse

[103] Green, 'Recognising', pp. 30–5; *Irony*, pp. 24–6.
[104] *Erec* 2983: see above, p. 119, fn. 100. Gottfried, *Tristan* 7132–4. Wolfram, *Parzival* 537, 30–538, 3; 567, 19.

had proceeded from the singular (her individual case) to the plural (697, 17: *frouwen*), whilst in his rebuttal Parzival denies the relevance of the plural (697, 24: 'der mîdet spottes elliu wîp' refrains from mocking the female sex). Parzival's mention of *all* women (*elliu wîp*) suggests that Orgeluse's reference to railing at women in the plural was meant as a generalisation, which he denies.

The second example forms a close parallel to the first: it concerns Amfortas in relationship to Orgeluse once again. Earlier in her quest for vengeance she had approached Amfortas, successfully this time, who contrary to what was prescribed for a Grail-king had sought knightly adventures in her secular service. The punishment for this was the wound which brought him long and excruciating suffering, the paralysis that lay over Munsalvaesche and his forfeiture of Grail-kingship. Amfortas therefore had every reason to curse his service of Orgeluse and also her for tempting him into it, but further, as we have seen in other cases, to slide from anger with one woman into misogyny at large. This is, however, one temptation which he resists. After Parzival has succeeded him as Grail-king Amfortas, now healed, abandons knightly service of a woman, but at the same time refuses to bear a grudge against all womankind (819, 30: 'ein wîp gab mir herzesêr. / Idoch ist iemmer al mîn haz / gein wîben volleclîche laz' one woman caused me heart's pain, but I am totally without hatred towards women). Like Parzival he refuses to make the step from singular to general.

The connection between these two details is clear: they both concern the same woman and illustrate the disqualification of one Grail-king alongside the qualification of his successor. If Orgeluse can be said to occupy a central position in initiating the whole narrative action through the wounding and incapacity of Amfortas,[105] then these two passages also share that central position. In other words, these statements by Parzival and Amfortas cannot be brushed aside as chance remarks, but instead, together with the argument they share (a rejection of antifeminine generalisations) they establish a principle of some importance for the author. This observation is subject to one qualification, however. Each of these remarks is made not by the narrator, but by a character in his work. If it is impermissible to accuse Chrétien himself, for example, of misogyny because of a misogynous remark by one of his characters, is it any more justifiable to regard the attitude revealed by Parzival and Amfortas as shared by Wolfram or his narrator? Light may be shed on this by looking at what Wolfram's narrator has to say on this subject.

---

[105] See above, p. 177.

It has long been recognised that Wolfram is no friend of black-and-white judgments of human beings of either sex. At the start of Book VII he argues against the idealisation of his protagonist (338, 8–10) and advocates *lop mit wârheit* (338, 12), a combination of praise with criticism where this is due. Amongst his male characters Gahmuret has his faults (as his son Feirefiz knows, 750, 20–6), of Gawan it has been said that he has stains on his waistcoat,[106] and with regard to Parzival his wife, if so inclined, could certainly have reacted like Laudine and criticised his neglect of her (801, 9). The same is true of female characters. Wolfram feels it necessary to defend both Obie and Orgeluse against faults that could be found in them, and Herzeloyde has been shown to have her shortcomings.[107] This psychological realism comes close to Walther's argument for the need to *scheiden* – to differentiate between positive and negative features in each individual and in the sex to which he or she belongs.[108] Each must be judged individually, not by reference to an unreal norm supposedly representative of their respective sex at large.

Wolfram makes his position clear in the prologue. He sees men as divided into good and bad, but more commonly a mixture of both (1, 1–14), and he likewise sees two types of woman, good and bad (3, 3–10). At the beginning of Book III the narrator also distinguishes between two classes of woman (116, 8f.), lamenting that all bear the same name of woman (116, 5f.). He may qualify the bad as 'many' and the good as only 'some', but more important is the differentiation on which he insists, making any generalisation, positive or negative, impossible.[109] (How relevant this is has been shown by Schnell: precisely Wolfram's distinction between two types of woman distinguishes him from the misogynous statements found in Ovid and Chrétien, whose Orguelleus quotes Ovid closely.)[110] Wolfram's narrator carries out these statements of principle in practice by building objections to negative generalisations into his work, voiced either by women or applied to them. The first possibility is suggested in the 'Selbstverteidigung' where the narrator feels exposed to women's criticism at large because they are affected by his criticism of one particular woman (114, 14–20).[111] In other words, these women, sensitised to misogynous insinuations in a patriarchal society, have operated a negative generalisation in reverse, wrongly inferring from his

---

[106] Gahmuret: Noltze, *Orientfahrt*, pp. 195–8; Hartmann, *Gahmuret*, pp. 226f. Gawan: Emmerling, *Geschlechterbeziehungen*, p. 100.

[107] Obie: 365, 24–366, 2. Orgeluse: 516, 3–14. Herzeloyde: Endres, 'Minderwertigkeit', pp. 382–4; Yeandle, *Euphorion* 75 (1981), 11, 13f.

[108] See above, pp. 78f.   [109] Schu, *Abenteuer*, p. 157.   [110] Schnell, *Euphorion* 69 (1975), 156f.

[111] Zimmermann, *Kommentar*, p. 25; Schu, *Abenteuer*, pp. 146–8.

attitude to one of their sex a view of them all. This is taken up again at the end of Book VI when the narrator, recommending himself to the women in his audience, reminds them that his strained relationship with one woman was no obstacle to his speaking well of many others (337, 5), whom he then lists.[112] These women in the audience, suspiciously expecting the worst and needing to be convinced of the contrary, resemble Orgeluse who likewise expected Parzival to generalise from the particular. This suggests that Parzival, like Amfortas, was speaking with the narrator's voice.

More frequent are the cases where the generalisation to be contradicted is made not *by* women, but *of* them. When complaining that both types bear the name of woman (116, 5f.) the narrator adds that there are two sides to the question (116, 10: 'sus teilent sich diu maere'), where *teilen* has the same discriminatory force as Walther's *scheiden*. When a few lines later Herzeloyde's faithfulness (*triuwe*) is contrasted with the many unlike her nowadays (116, 19–25), this sails close to a negative generalisation, but is converted into an extended one when men are included in this sweeping judgment (116, 26: 'man und wîp mir sint al ein: / die mitenz algelîche' men and women are the same in my eyes; without exception they would all avoid it). The narrator also plays teasingly with an antifeminine generalisation when comparing Sigune, loyally grieving over her dead lover, with Hartmann's Laudine who followed Lunete's advice in re-marrying quickly by referring to fickle women (253, 10–18). This is no true generalisation: not 'women are fickle', but 'those who are fickle' ('wîp die man bî wanke siht'). Moreover, the remark has a particular application, namely literary polemics against the specific case of Hartmann's work, and Laudine is made use of as a foil to Sigune whose praise is at issue here, not any criticism of the female sex.[113] Very similar is a passage stressing Parzival's beauty, so captivating that it would induce constancy even in a fickle woman (311, 20–6). As with the Sigune passage, the reference is not to fickle women as a generalisation, but to those women who are fickle, and here, too, the purpose is not condemnation of the female sex, but to present a foil to the protagonist's manly beauty. In both these cases the topos of woman's fickleness is alluded to, but made to serve a different purpose. Finally, we might mention in this connection the two passages where the narrator warns against premature judgment of two women characters whose behaviour may well have given offence to patriarchally minded listeners: first, Obie (365, 20–366, 2) and

---

[112] A similar point is made 313, 26–8 (the negative description of Cundrie has no bearing on other women).

[113] Backes, *Munsalvaesche*, pp. 35f.

then Orgeluse (516, 3–14). Far from launching into a negative generalisation, which would have been all too easy, the narrator conveys to us the possibility of a defence of each woman.

All these remarks advocating the need to differentiate and avoid blanket generalisations critical of women are made by the narrator, but how far can he be identified with the author? Are these also Wolfram's views? At this point we must emphasise the relative, but revealing, frequency of these remarks. This suggests that an author harbouring antifeminine sentiments would have been hardly likely to give his narrator such ample opportunity to express contradictory views with no hint of disagreement. Nor is it likely that Wolfram would have arranged for his narrator to confirm the views expressed by such important characters as Parzival and Amfortas if he had little sympathy with their opinions.

On the face of it, it may come as a shock if we now turn to the undeniable presence of negative generalisations against women in the Parzival story, but the shock can be lessened first by our looking at such statements by characters in the work (with whose opinions the author is not necessarily to be identified) and secondly by the fact that of the three passages in question two occur in the French text and only one in Wolfram's.

The first example with Chrétien is the deeply misogynous tirade of Orguelleus de la Lande against the damsel of the tent which we looked at in the Introduction to Part II.[114] The generalisation informing this outburst against this particular woman is clear from the transition from the singular (3846: 'ceste demoiselle') to the general statement of proverbial truth in misogynous tradition (3860: 'Qui baise feme' Whoever kisses a woman; 3863: 'Feme qui' Any woman who). Parallel with this is the direction of the man's thinking: at first he is prepared to entertain the possibility that the woman was assaulted against her will (3855: 'Et s'il le baisa mal gré suen'), but this gives way to the view that what happened was with her agreement, since any woman who lets herself be kissed easily gives the rest (3863f.) and wants to be taken by force (3875). Orguelleus therefore assumes misogynously with Ovid that all took place with the woman's consent.[115]

In the corresponding scene with Wolfram we have no such diatribe by Orilus: he keeps to the particular case and does not slip into any generalisation. He accepts as fact that Jeschute was subjected to violence (264, 3 expresses this as a fact in the indicative: 'was genôtzogt' was violated), but he also comes to suspect her of unfaithfulness (wrongly, as expressed by *wânde*

---

[114] See above, pp. 82f.
[115] Ovid, *Ars amatoria* I 664–76. See also Schnell, *Euphorion* 69 (1975), 147, 156f.

and the subjunctive, 264, 6f.) with another lover (264, 10). Orilus accepts his wife's innocence on the one hand because he had left her unprotected in the tent, but suspects her of unfaithfulness because her comment on Parzival's beauty (133, 17f.) led him to assume the worst (133, 21f.; 271, 4f.).[116] In both the German and the French version the man's criticism of the woman, whether generalised or not, rests on a mistake (as will also be the case with our next example), so that the misogyny of Orguelleus lacks justification. His antifeminine tirade has been dropped by Wolfram, in whose version there remains a more closely focused picture of the relationship between one man and one woman, with no hint of a generalisation criticising women.

The other example from Chrétien has to do with the approach to lovemaking between Gauvain and the sister of the king of Ascalon, thwarted by the untimely arrival of a *vavasseur* on the scene. This intruder immediately recognises Gauvain as one accused of killing his lord, the young woman's father, but directs his torrent of abuse at the woman for letting herself be caressed by such a man. Here again we witness the typical movement of misogynous thought, starting in the singular as the *vavasseur* addresses one particular woman in one particular situation (5840: 'Feme, honie soies tu!' Shame on you, woman!), making love with the murderer of her father, but quickly passing over to generalities against womankind. These start with the misogynous question of whether a woman can do anything right (5855), equating the whole sex with hatred of the good, but then associate the particular with the general in seeing the lord's daughter as a typical woman (5861: 'Mais tu iez feme, bien le voi' But I can see that you are a [true] woman). In concentrating on the woman and heaping all his blame on her, even though he recognises Gauvain as guilty of a greater offence, the *vavasseur* speaks in full accord with the tradition of clerical misogyny, accusing woman of sacrificing every consideration to physical pleasure (5864f.).[117]

Wolfram changes this picture radically. With him the old knight who comes upon the couple also recognises Gawan as one whom he takes to be the killer of his lord and, more naturally than with Chrétien, regards him as guilty of the further offence of using violence against the lord's daughter (407, 19: 'irn nôtzogt och sîn tohter hie' you are also violating his daughter here). Wolfram has taken care in advance to let us know that Gawan was in fact not guilty of murder,[118] but we have seen enough of the couple's

---

[116] Backes, *Munsalvaesche*, p. 95.   [117] Emmerling, *Geschlechterbeziehungen*, pp. 33, 35.
[118] 398, 13 and (later) 413, 13f.

love-play together before they are interrupted to see that no sexual violence was exercised on Antikonie. Her *consensus* is made obvious by the readiness with which she responds to Gawan's approaches and by the care with which the narrator stresses that love overcame both the man and the woman (407, 5f.) and that both were intent on the same thing (407, 9). All this makes clear to us what escapes the intruder, that violence or *nôtzuht* does not come into question here and that Gawan is innocent of both the charges for which the alarm is raised by the intruder (which is perhaps why his judgment is questioned by the reference to *übel ougen*, 407, 8). One result of Wolfram's concentration on Gawan here stands out clearly: by contrast with Chrétien's account Antikonie steps very much into the background in this passage, no accusation is made against her, and the lengthy negative generalisation of the French text has been dropped entirely.

Both these episodes in Chrétien's work incorporating an antifeminine generalisation rest on a mistaken assumption. Orguelleus jumped to the faulty conclusion that his lover gave her consent to Perceval's approaches, whilst the intruder in the second example failed to entertain the possibility that it was freely given.[119] In each case the mistaken assessment arises from misogynous assumptions: Orguelleus is convinced that no woman can resist a sexual approach, whilst the *vavasseur*, despite having every reason to attack Gauvain, automatically focuses on the woman. Chrétien leaves it to his audience to perceive that the mistaken assessments of two misogynous characters of his are not necessarily shared by him, but Wolfram goes further. By omitting these generalisations altogether Wolfram leaves no shadow of doubt about Jeschute's innocence and likewise leaves Antikonie untouched by any criticism within the narrative, just as he raises her in our esteem in other respects, too.[120]

Against these two examples from Chrétien, rejected in the German text, must be set one from Wolfram, based on clerical exegesis and affecting the narrative action only in the widest sense, not so immediately as with the French examples. It concerns the passage in Trevrizent's religious instruction to Parzival in which he treats the Genesis theme of the creation and the Fall (463, 19–22). It is not surprising that the hermit, living in penance and with religious reading-matter to hand, should follow clerical tradition in seeing Eve created from Adam's body (the second version of Genesis) and as alone responsible for the Fall (Adam's involvement, even secondarily, is not mentioned). Strictly speaking, this is no generalisation such as the two examples from Chrétien, but an antifeminine interpretation of the Fall

---

[119] Schu, *Abenteuer*, p. 333.   [120] Emmerling, *Geschlechterbeziehungen*, pp. 41–50.

with a general application because of its malign effects throughout history. In reconciling this isolated theological antifeminism with what we have so far seen of Wolfram's attitude to women we have no need to invoke what has come to be perceived as Trevrizent's occasional unreliability,[121] but do better to place the hermit's remark in the wider context of his religious discourse.

Trevrizent disposes of Eve's creation from Adam in one line and of her responsibility for the Fall in three, but then goes on to discuss Cain's killing of Abel at much greater length (463, 23–464, 22), a shift of emphasis which casts a different light on the matter. Cain's violence is seen in two respects, in the first of which it is directed at his brother Abel (464, 16f.). In his discussion of Parzival's knightly guilt Mohr emphasised this particularly, seeing a connection between this primal sin of violence and Parzival's killing of Ither, his kinsman, but also his brother in the Christian sense.[122] With this shift of emphasis Trevrizent has geared his summary of Genesis to the spiritual needs of the knight he is counselling, recognising him as professionally exposed to repeating Cain's offence. To the remark made by Mohr that Wolfram establishes a connection between Trevrizent's account of Cain's deed and Parzival's killing of Ither Nellmann has added a persuasive rider. He points out that the observation that Cain killed Abel for a trifling possession (464, 17: 'umb krankez guot') is unknown to the Bible and exegetical tradition, but could allude to Parzival's acquisition of knighthood by killing Ither and robbing the corpse of its armour.[123] But Trevrizent also sees Cain's violence in a second sense, arguing, in an exegetical manner which the hermit sees needs further explanation, that Cain's same act of violence had another victim, for the drops of blood which fell to the ground violated the virginity of Adam's mother, the earth (464, 13 and 18f.).[124] Cain's primal sin of violence thus has lasting consequences throughout history (464, 21f.) and in *Parzival*, too, which rival those flowing from Eve's first disobedience (463, 22). By giving greater weight to Cain than to Eve, Trevrizent by no means denies Eve's offence, but also draws our attention towards the offence committed by a man, just as some of the commentaries on Genesis apportion a share of the blame to another man, Adam.[125] In depicting Cain's offence as a double one, violence against another man and also against a femininely conceived earth whose virginity is violated,

---

[121] Schu, *Abenteuer*, pp. 307–21. [122] Mohr, 'Schuld', pp. 201, 203, 205.
[123] Nellmann, *Wolfram* II 675 (on 464, 17).
[124] On this exegetical tradition see Köhler, *Germania* 7 (1862), 476–80.
[125] Blamires, *Case*, pp. 114, 116.

Wolfram has incorporated in these lines the two problematic aspects of male violence that preoccupy him in *Parzival*.

From the three cases we have discussed (two from Chrétien, one from Wolfram) the antifeminine sting could be drawn by remarking that all three statements are made by a character in the work in question whom we have no automatic right to regard as the author's spokesman. This defence falls away, however, when we now turn to passages where it is the narrator himself who makes a negative generalisation or indulges in what could be termed verbal aggression against women, especially when we recall that these are all additions to the German text.

Of the five apparently antifeminine generalisations made by the narrator the first refers to the attractive young daughters of the pilgrim family which directs Parzival on his way to Trevrizent's nearby hermitage. We are given a description of their erotic charms (449, 28: their lips are red, full and hot), reminiscent of our first view of Jeschute, but to this the narrator adds the generalising comment that this is how women always are (450, 5: 'wîp sint et immer wîp'), capable of bringing even a warlike man down, as they have done repeatedly. Behind this smiling indulgence towards women there lurks, according to Pérennec, a fundamental misogyny[126] – but is the passage itself meant misogynously? Although the two daughters' seductive charms are made clear in terms that show that the narrator is himself aware of their female attractiveness, we are invited to inquire more closely into the act of seduction. We are shown the women from Parzival's position, we see what he sees (449, 26: 'Parzivâl an in ersach') and this is reinforced by the narrator's excitement, regretting that he himself has no opportunity to kiss such lips (450, 1–4). If anybody offends against the serious requirements of a Good Friday (449, 30) it is the narrator for introducing such thoughts. This point of view technique reminds us that Erec's court at Karnant misogynously (and wrongly) placed the blame for the crisis there on Enite, that antifeminine tradition was apt to explain a seduction by the woman's seductiveness rather than the man's sensuality, and that Gawan outrageously sought to defend Urjans by putting the rape down to the woman's physical beauty.[127]

Just as Hartmann took care to diminish Enite's responsibility at Karnant, so does Wolfram present these two daughters in a positive light. He makes clear their own religious motivation (*kiusches herzen rât*) in the pilgrimage they make with their parents (446, 17–21), their father approves the offer of hospitality they extend to Parzival (449, 13) and the narrator likewise praises

---

[126] Pérennec, *Recherches* II 244f.   [127] See above, pp. 18 and 194.

their good intentions and sincerity (449, 21–5). Although the warmth in a cold season of the year these women offer in their humane invitation (448, 27–449, 1) is mentioned immediately after their father had indicated the track leading to the hermit Trevrizent, their gesture should not be seen as potentially leading a sinner away from the spiritual advice he needs. Hardly fortuitously, warmth is the first thing Trevrizent offers Parzival when he reaches him (456, 15), which we may take symbolically as warming and softening the frozen heart of a sinner.[128] In that sense the two daughters potentially share in the same process of symbolic warming.

This short encounter, beginning the spiritual warming-up process carried through by Trevrizent, rests on the discrepancy between the erotic thoughts introduced by the narrator and the serious disposition adequate to pilgrims on Good Friday. The question whether, against all the other indications, these women are to be blamed for this discrepancy because of their attractiveness arises from the line immediately following the description of their lips (449, 29: 'die stuonden niht senlîche'). The difficulty lies with the word *senlîche*, which can denote pain or sorrow, a reading followed by Hatto in saying that their lips were out of keeping with the sorrows of that holy day.[129] But this word was also used to connote the pain of love-longing ('mit schmerzlichem liebesverlangen'),[130] in which case these women's lips, however attractive, need not have been meant seductively and were therefore in full keeping with the holy day.[131] Erotic ideas come into this scene not from the women, but from a man, the narrator, who apparently puts the blame on women. But by underlining their humane sympathy and the sincerity of their motives Wolfram shows that they are free of what is imputed to their sex. The function of the discrepancy in this scene is to enable us to see through the antifeminine generalisation as inapplicable.

For a second example we turn to Wolfram's explanation of the misshapen appearance of Malcreatiure, the brother of the equally deformed Cundrie. The author follows the tradition of clerical anthropology in this (with parallels in the *Wiener Genesis* and *Lucidarius*), attributing misshapen beings to the disobedience of Adam's daughters to his warning to avoid certain gynaecologically dangerous herbs (518, 9–24).[132] The daughters pay no heed

---

[128] Mersmann, *Besitzwechsel*, p. 133.
[129] Hatto, *Parzival*, p. 230, with whom Young, 'Construction', p. 260, agrees in seeing the discrepancy as symbolising 'the negative potential of women'.
[130] BMZ II 2, 249.
[131] This is the sense in which Kühn (in Nellmann, *Wolfram* I 745) translates 449, 29f.: 'Doch standen sie [die Lippen] nicht sinnlich offen, / und dies entsprach dem Feiertag'.
[132] For a full discussion see Wisbey, 'Wunder', pp. 180–214.

to this (with the inevitable result), but the narrator introduces this by saying that these women did precisely what women do (518, 25: 'diu wîp tâten et als wîp'). Within this clerical tradition an antifeminine reference to Eve's daughters acting as women do is fully at home. Wolfram draws on this tradition for an explanation of Malcreatiure's appearance, but could have done this without this misogynous remark, reinforced by the reference to women's weakness (518, 26) and the contrast with Adam's firmness (519, 1). These details are superfluous to accounting for Malcreatiure, but the author's purpose in employing them may have been to build in a reference to an antifeminine tradition against which he sets his own counter-model. These women are the first daughters of Eve in this tradition, so that it was fitting to begin with them. Criticism of women in Genesis put forward in this passage is a counterpart to what Trevrizent had to say about Eve, where criticism of women was re-directed against man. Taken together, these two passages consider events in Genesis from a point of view which is not gender specific.

With our next example we jump forward in the story to the scene in Book XIV in which, as part of the all-round reconciliation brought about as the work approaches its close, Orgeluse is persuaded, very much against her will, to kiss Gramoflanz, the killer of her husband Cidegast. She does kiss him, but is urged to weep as she does so in memory of Cidegast and compelled by womanly anguish (729, 18–24). It must be stressed that she does not weep simply for her anguish, but out of the anguish of any woman, so that with *wîplîchiu nôt* (22) we are dealing with a generalisation beyond Orgeluse's specific case. Nothing so far implies that this generalisation is meant negatively, but the following line (729, 24: 'welt ir, des jeht für triuwe') has been translated by Hatto as 'Set it down to fidelity if you like',[133] where the conditional clause insinuates an element of doubt whether this kiss of reconciliation really demonstrated fidelity to the dead husband. Scheuble goes further in maintaining that these words make Orgeluse's *wîplîchiu nôt* look ridiculous and illustrate what Wolfram really thinks about female fidelity.[134] Such an interpretation, criticising Orgeluse, but also womankind at large, ignores what Nellmann has shown of the contact between Wolfram's narrator and his audience, more particularly the way in which he involves them, or pretends to involve them, in the process of narration.[135] Wolfram can create the impression that he tells his story in taking account of his listeners' wishes, leaving them to decide on a particular

---

[133] Hatto, *Parzival*, p. 363.   [134] Scheuble, *Sozialisation*, p. 195.
[135] Nellmann, *Erzähltechnik*, pp. 40–3.

point, yet in the very act of appearing to depend on them he directs the course of his narrative himself. One of the formulas he uses for this purpose is *welt ir* or *ob ir welt*.[136] In view of this it makes better sense to see the narrator in charge of events here, too, so that the words could be rendered, exclusive of any doubt, by 'That is what I think and I invite you to agree with me'. This reading harmonises much better with what Wolfram shows us of the importance of Orgeluse's fidelity, a *triuwe* that informed her life after the loss of her husband,[137] leading her to seek vengeance on Gramoflanz by turning to knight after knight for that purpose without deserving to have it called into question at the very end.

Our last two examples come right at the close of the work and concern Parzival's son Loherangrin. The first deals with the marriage of Loherangrin, sent out from Munsalvaesche to marry the princess of Brabant, under the strict condition that she never asks who he might be. We are told that she gave a woman's pledge (*wibes sicherheit*) to obey his command, but that she later broke this pledge, although the addition that she did this out of affection provides a measure of excuse for her (825, 25–30). As things stand, this could be taken as another typical antifeminine cliché, seeing the woman in terms of the inconstancy and disobedience of her sex, shown already in Eve and all Eve's daughters.

However, it is not completely certain that this is necessarily so. The uncertainty is provided by the word *wîp* which, as we saw with *Erec*, could mean either 'woman' or 'wife'.[138] Both Hatto and Kühn accept the former meaning,[139] but the latter is also possible. This distinction is important in judging whether antifeminism is involved here or not. 'Wife' would refer to this one individual, a princess of Brabant about to be married to Loherangrin, but 'woman' would signify this one person, but also all the members of her sex. Only the latter meaning would imply a negative generalisation, whereas the former would connote the failure of this one individual, with no further application. There are indeed suggestions that the princess makes her pledge as one about to be made a wife. The pledge is made on the brink of marriage as a condition to be met (825, 16–18); Loherangrin's command to her (825, 27: *gebote*) which she is never to disobey (825, 28) reflects the duties of a wife towards her husband in a patriarchal marriage (Hatto uses 'husband's bidding' at this point); finally, the marriage duly ensues (826, 1–3). Volfing reads *wîp* as meaning 'wife', referring to 'wifely liebe' (825, 26), adding however that

[136] 327, 26; 349, 28; 353, 1; 403, 10; 502, 30; 639, 2; 815, 21.
[137] Emmerling, *Geschlechterbeziehungen*, pp. 148–50.   [138] See above, p. 98.
[139] Hatto, *Parzival*, p. 409; Kühn in Nellmann, *Wolfram* II 405.

this 'does not exculpate her, but only highlights the potentially self-indulgent nature of her affect'.[140] That may indeed be the case, but still does not amount to an inculpation of the whole of her sex.

Following this and no more than thirty lines from the conclusion of the whole work comes a brief comparison between Loherangrin's position (after his wife has broken her promise and asked the forbidden question) and Erec's. The narrator says that Erec would have something to say here and that he knew how to rebuke a woman going against his command (826, 29f: *hie solte Ereck nu sprechen:/der kund mit rede sich rechen*). The force of this intertextual reference is to suggest that the position of Erec and Enite is repeated with Loherangrin and his wife, such is the nature of any woman, so that we are dealing implicitly with a negative generalisation. Hartmann had questioned the justification of Erec's behaviour towards his wife, and Wolfram's pattern of the relationship between Erec and Enite reflected in Orilus and Jeschute suggests that he shares these doubts about Erec.

Nellmann proposes three possible interpretations of these two lines.[141] First, they could imply criticism of a woman for her inquisitiveness, disobedience or inconstancy (but how likely is that at the conclusion of a work throughout which antifeminine clichés are called into question in one way or another?). Secondly, the object of criticism could be Erec's stubborn behaviour or, thirdly, Loherangrin's rigorism. One of these interpretations inculpates a woman, the others a man (and more tellingly by giving an antifeminine topos a barb directed at the other sex). If Wolfram's audience were meant to consider these different possibilities (as well as the meaning of *wîp* used of the princess of Brabant), might this not suggest an invitation to them to weigh one against the others and to debate the issue after the conclusion of a work in which other issues are left open for the same purpose?[142]

We conclude the argument of this section by considering examples of what could be termed the narrator's verbal violence against women, significant because of the frequency with which the narrator's humour involves women and because these examples are all Wolfram's innovation. I place them here, rather than together with other forms of violence against women (military, disciplinary, sexual), because the present section deals with what is conveyed by words, not by physical deeds. The author faced a problem throughout his work: how to praise some of his characters without going against his proclaimed principle of *lop mit wârheit*. He can insinuate such praise indirectly, using humour to do his work for him and manipulating his

[140] Volfing, *PBB* 126 (2004), 74, fn. 26.   [141] Nellmann, *Wolfram* II 788f.
[142] Bumke, *DVjs* 65 (1991), 236–64.

male listeners into a position where they are to recognise that their patriarchal prejudices make them inferior to characters, male or female, in the story. To achieve this the narrator can show himself apparently close to such listeners in order the better to spring his trap on them.

Jeschute is a special object of the narrator's humour, being exposed to it three times. After describing the charms of the sleeping woman when we together with Parzival first come across her, subjecting her to the male gaze of the men in the audience, the narrator draws close to them, becomes complicit with them by expressing his own wishes in such a situation.[143] In a manner reminiscent of his attitude to the daughters of the pilgrim family he regrets that no one will accustom him to kissing so beautiful a mouth, for such things never fall to his lot (130, 14–16). This identification of the narrator with the male listeners amounts to their joint distancing from Parzival, for although he is in a position to see what they see he is still so tied to his mother's instructions that he has eyes only for Jeschute's ring (130, 26f.).[144] The narrator's erotic imagination (misplaced when the woman is soon to suffer dire consequences) is meant to contrast with Parzival's naiveté, inexperience and ultimately purity. The object of the narrator's humour here is not any further victimisation of the woman, subjecting her to a visual rape arranged for the audience by a like-minded narrator, but to show, against all expectation, how far Parzival surpasses them.

The same effect is achieved by more drastic means a little later when it is said of Parzival, with regard to the same encounter, that if he had learned his father's ways (and had his experience in love) he would have seized the opportunity for sexual aggression (139, 15–19). The image used in these lines, the knight's lance aimed directly at the boss of the opponent's shield, is used commonly to denote sexual intercourse[145] and the line in question (139, 12) is rendered by Hatto with 'the tilting would have been more on the mark'. In this passage Gahmuret joins the male listeners (or viewers) in the earlier passage, as well as the narrator who has repeated his sexual humour, in shared male knowingness. The complicity in this case, too, is not meant to victimise Jeschute still further, as Lienert and Scheuble would have it,[146] but to highlight the distance between these men and Parzival. Nellmann comments that this amounts to an exoneration of the inexperienced protagonist, bought at the price of casting a shadow on his father[147] who, although not

---

[143] Schu, *Abenteuer*, p. 330.   [144] *Ibid.*, pp. 330f.
[145] Examples are given by Eichholz, *Kommentar*, p. 28, fn. 2.
[146] Lienert, 'Diskursivität', p. 233; Scheuble, *Sozialisation*, pp. 163, 290.
[147] Nellmann, *Erzählkunst*, p. 141.

guilty of violence against women, certainly cannot be classed as beyond reproach in his behaviour towards them.

When the protagonist and Jeschute encounter each other for the second time, her abject condition brought about by Orilus's prolonged harshness towards her is presented to us above all in her ragged, torn clothing. Her near-nakedness is the occasion of an untranslatable pun (257, 21–5),[148] but also of sexual humour. As with the earlier allusion to Gahmuret, a possible sexual encounter is seen in terms of a knightly one (where each attempts to get close to the other's bare side, unprotected by a shield). Of Jeschute's tattered state it is therefore said that from whatever angle one might get to grips with her it would have been on the bare side.[149] A few lines later the narrator brings this home again, saying that he would sooner take someone like her with little clothing than many a well-dressed woman (257, 31f.). None of this humour can be said to be at the woman's expense[150] for whom the narrator had earlier expressed his compassion (137, 29f.) and on behalf of whom he appeals to the courtesy (257, 26: *zuht*) of listeners to arouse sympathy, inviting them to react against his own inappropriate sexual innuendo, which he suspects they share. As with the first encounter, Parzival is shown to be immune to the woman's near-nakedness, even though this time he does see it, for he considerately offers his coverlet for her to conceal herself (in Chrétien it is the woman who covers herself: 3742f.).[151] Unlike the narrator, Parzival does not subject the humiliated and embarrassed woman to his male gaze, but his superior position has been brought into focus by the narrator deliberately presenting himself in such a negative light.

Not even Condwiramurs is spared the narrator's humour in the scene where, desperate to find help against the attacks of Clamide, she comes at night to the bedside of her guest Parzival to plead her cause. The ever suggestive narrator does not waste this opportunity, captured best in Hatto's words: 'She wore formidable armour: a white silken shift! What could be more challenging than a woman bearing down on a man in this fashion!' (192, 14–17).[152] Once more we are dealing with a *double entendre* (love play presented as battle play), as already with the invocation of Gahmuret in the Jeschute scene: Condwiramurs's silk nightdress is presented as battledress (*werlîchiu wât*) and her approach is as if for combat

---

[148] *Vilân* ('low born peasant') could be read as *vil an* ('much on'), so that Jeschute could not be called a peasant, because she did not have much on.
[149] Backes, *Munsalvaesche*, p. 64.   [150] As suggested by Scheuble, *Sozialisation*, p. 170.
[151] Schu, *Abenteuer*, p. 331.   [152] Hatto, *Parzival*, p. 106.

(*kampflîcher*). True to form, Scheuble regards this as humour at the woman's expense, seeing in it derision of her defencelessness and making fun of her despair, even catching an echo of the Ovidian cynicism (voiced by Chrétien's Orguelleus) that women desire to win every battle except the one alluded to here.[153] The antifeminism which this imputes to Wolfram's depiction of this scene is weakened in advance by the narrator's assertion that this chaste woman committed no breach of feminine decorum (192, 2–13), but also by the way in which, unlike what we have been led to expect, her silk nightdress is covered up by a long mantle (192, 18f.), contrary to the calculated seductiveness of Chrétien's Blancheflor.[154] The erotic implications of Condwiramurs's readiness for combat are finally cancelled by her insistence that Parzival is not to struggle with her (193, 29–194, 2: *ringen*). What is made fun of here is not the desperate weakness of this woman, but the sexual, at bottom antifeminine, knowingness of listeners stimulated by Wolfram's suggestive imagery and disappointed in their expectations.

Wolfram also appears to direct his humour at Antikonie when he describes her slender shape, fit for love, by the grotesque comparison of her waist with a hare on the spit and with an ant (409, 23–410, 4). That humour is present in the forced nature of these comparisons may be acceptable, but Scheuble goes further, seeing the humour at Antikonie's expense, because the purely physical description of her feminine attributes (409, 25 and 28f.) reduces her to the physical, even animal level, making her an object of desire (409, 30f.).[155] However, it is not simply the case that the narrator describes Antikonie in this way, since he presents his picture as Gawan sees her (409, 24: *ersach*). He also suggests that this is how his listeners may see her, too (409, 27: *gesâht ir*). The male members of Wolfram's audience thereby join Gawan in fixing their male gaze on Antikonie, an attitude which is shown as deficient, because it is misogynously reductive and blind to the courage and faithfulness to Gawan demonstrated by Antikonie and by the terms of praise heaped on her by the narrator (404, 24–30). It takes a woman like Orgeluse to put Gawan, and other men, in their place because of their male gaze (509, 30–510, 8).[156]

When Bene, obedient to her father's command that she place herself at their guest's disposal in all he may desire, comes to Gawan's bedroom while he is asleep,[157] the narrator adopts once more his inferior, deficient role, complaining in effect: 'Erotic adventures like this never come my way'

[153] Scheuble, *Sozialisation*, p. 164.
[154] Groos, *Romancing*, pp. 105f.; Hafner, *Maskulinität*, pp. 161f.; *Perceval* 2038–46, 2128–37.
[155] See also Scheuble, *Sozialisation*, pp. 179f.   [156] Schu, *Abenteuer*, pp. 348f.
[157] On this episode see Coxon, *Wolfram-Studien* 17 (2002), 114–35.

(554, 4–6). The humour of this remark is directed by the narrator at himself, not at Bene, who acts obediently in accordance with her father's patriarchal request. The narrator puts himself in his place in yet another way. We are led to imagine that, like Gahmuret whom he invoked in a Jeschute episode, the narrator would have made full use of the opportunity which a woman like Bene might present, yet Gawan declines the offer tacitly made to him.[158] Plippalinot, Bene's father, resembles Gahmuret (as invoked by the narrator) in (wrongly) assuming that Gawan has taken this opportunity (555, 19–30), even if force had had to be used (*betwungen, gerungen*). If the narrator's guise of one who always misses the best chance implies that, by contrast, the male listeners would have taken such a chance, this presents us with a group of males (narrator, listeners, Plippalinot[159] – and Gahmuret), all of whom differ from Gawan and fall short of him (he remains faithful to Orgeluse). In this episode we therefore have no humour at the expense of a woman, but as in the other cases humour employed as a means of elevating the protagonist by contrast with others.

Our last example concerns Gawan and Orgeluse. The task she set him was to pluck a wreath from a tree in Gramoflanz's possession, but Gawan asks where he may pluck the wreath that will give him so much pleasure (601, 15f.), using the phrase in the figurative sense of *deflorare*.[160] Angry and impatient with Gawan's submissiveness, the narrator now intervenes with a coarse jocular antifeminine suggestion to Gawan to fling this woman to the ground, as has happened to many a fine lady (601, 17–19).[161] This outburst, prompted by the narrator's anger, reminds us of the similar outburst in Thomas's *Tristran*, likewise prompted by anger (with the second Ysolt).[162] Wolfram's narrator suggests here that it is time for Gawan to assert his manliness and put this woman in her place, but by generalising his suggestion (601, 18f.) he implies the readiness of other men to agree with him. This amounts to an attempt at male bonding (narrator, listeners, Gawan) against Orgeluse (and other women). But the attempt fails, Gawan breaks loose from this bonding by refusing to act as recommended, by continuing to act in patient service of Orgeluse until a later consummation, with her *consensus*. The point of the narrator's antifeminine suggestion is that no such

---

[158] Scheuble, *Sozialisation*, p. 185.
[159] This grouping is also suggested by Coxon, *Wolfram-Studien* 17 (2002), 123.
[160] Nellmann, *Wolfram* II 730 (on 601, 15–19).
[161] The narrator thereby recommends what a frustrated lover does in practice in the *Commens d'Amours*, possibly by Richard de Fournival. See also Rieger, *CCM* 31 (1988), 260.
[162] See above, p. 143.

thing happens: Gawan does not take Orgeluse by force, he abides by his earlier conviction (511, 12–16) that reward comes only after service.[163] This discrepancy between the narrator and Gawan shows that the former's attitude is inadequate, even wrong. By deliberately putting himself and those who might rashly agree with him in the wrong the narrator elevates Gawan's standing, as his use of humour does with Parzival.

A number of points emerge from this section which throw light on the attitude to women incorporated in *Parzival*. Two major characters in the work, Parzival and Amfortas, state expressly their refusal to expand from a singular case to a generalisation critical of women. The narrator likewise adheres to the need for differentiation (*scheiden*) between any particular woman and the whole of her sex. Two passages in Chrétien's *Perceval* where different characters make use of a negative generalisation are suppressed by Wolfram. Wherever the narrator himself makes use of such a generalisation its force is undermined in one way or another. What we have also seen of his verbal violence against women suggests that its purpose is not misogynous, but rather to elevate a protagonist (Parzival, Gawan). If, as this book has argued throughout, negative generalisations form a necessary, but not sufficient constituent of misogyny, at least in its verbal expression, then this prejudice cannot be said to play an important part in *Parzival*. The apparently antifeminine remarks to be found in this work, together with the men's jokes of a sexual nature we have considered, give the impression of aligning the narrator with the men in his audience. From this position of male solidarity he is able more effectively to subvert conventional antifeminism than would have been possible by means of a head-on attack, inviting opposition or outright rejection. What Newman has said in a much wider context applies to the particular case of Wolfram's work: in the patriarchal society of the Middle Ages authoritative teachings could not be contested point blank, so that more oblique gender strategies needed to be devised.[164] Failure to recognise this has exposed Wolfram in some modern scholarship to being accused of the antifeminism which he is in effect calling into question.

QUESTIONS AND REVISIONS

The description of *Erec* and *Tristan* as *romans à deux* (works in which a second character, a woman, plays a lesser, but still important role) cannot be applied to *Parzival* in anything like the same sense, for with Wolfram this

---

[163] Buettner, *Gawan*, p. 224.   [164] Newman, *Woman*, p. 3.

second role is played by another man, Gawan. As in the other two romances, Wolfram leaves us in no doubt who is the protagonist. At the beginning, the unnamed and as yet unborn Parzival is referred to as the man of whom the tale is to be told (4, 24f.) and at the time of his birth he is described as the one to whom the story is devoted (112, 11f.) and as its hero (17: *diss maeres sachewalte*).[165] When at length Parzival's name is confirmed for us[166] he is called the lord of this story (140, 13), as he also is when the tale moves for some time from him to Gawan (338, 7), just as, when it returns to Parzival, it is said to come back to its true stem (678, 30).

Unlike *Tristan*, where a similar phrase could also be used of Isolde, no such remark is made of Condwiramurs, who fades into the background from the end of Book IV. Nor is Gawan privileged by any such description, placing him alongside the protagonist, although this could be expected from the rough and ready numerical equation of seven Books allotted to each of these figures or the manner in which the narrative, when it first turns to Gawan's adventures, takes note of him beside or beyond the hero (338, 6: 'derneben oder für in baz'). If we take this into account *Parzival* could indeed be regarded as a *roman à deux*, but devoted to two men.

To qualify this, however, it is also made clear from the start that this is a work concerned with women as well as men. The distinctions made in the prologue do not all refer to men, but are also meant for women (2, 23–5), the narrator passes judgment on both men and women (3, 25f.), and the story he is about to begin tells of true womanhood as well as manly virtues (4, 9–12). How closely involved Wolfram expected women in his audience to be with a work devoted to them, too, is clear from the various poetological passages to be found in his work. With only two exceptions (the 'Bogengleichnis' and the prologue to Book VII) these digressions on how the work and the attitude to women expressed in it are to be understood in their deepest implications are all expressly concerned with, or addressed to, women (the prologue, the 'Selbstverteidigung', the beginning of Book III, the close of Book VI, and the epilogue, in which the last word in the work is left to a woman, 827, 30). In this connection Volfing makes the interesting suggestion that despite his criticism of love poetry as a genre the narrator's presentation of his work as 'Minnedienst' transplants to it conventions of love poetry, 'notably, the convention that the man speaks and that the lady listens and reacts to what she hears. As a result, the entire implicit audience

---

[165] Hartmann, *Gahmuret*, pp. 349f. (*sachewalte*, originally a legal term for the chief person at a trial, plaintiff or defendant, extended here to connote the main figure in the story).
[166] On the process of gradually revealing Parzival's name see Green, *Art*, pp. 17f., 65, 72f., 78–80.

of "Parzival" is effectively gendered as "female", to the extent that it is defined by its listening stance'.[167] The fact that Wolfram's narrator repeatedly addresses women in his audience, and on such issues as the reception of his work, is a distinct novelty,[168] but it is not the case that these women are participants in a gender discourse in which woman does no more than reflect man.[169] As Brackert has shown, the reflection of men's knightly adventures in the grievous loss they inflict on women and the presentation of combat from the woman's perspective are meant as implicit judgment on male activity.[170]

The biggest obstacle to recognising the presence of narrative space granted to women in *Parzival* is of course Condwiramurs who, despite repeated reminders that her husband sends defeated foes to pay tribute to her or that his goal constantly remains the Grail and his wife's love, takes no further part in the narrative action after his departure from her. How passive her role is by contrast with Parzival's is brought out towards the close when we are told that it fell to her to maintain her chaste womanly disposition (734, 10–13), but that the reward was won by Parzival's achievement (15: 'Parzivâl daz wirbet'). That is only part of the picture, however. Not merely does Condwiramurs play a distinctly more active role when first introduced into the narrative, so that passivity is no inborn quality of hers, but we are also shown with Orgeluse and other women how decisively they can take the initiative,[171] even, as we shall see, in contracting marriage (in clear contrast with contemporary practice in feudal society).

At this juncture the particular variation of the *roman à deux* which Wolfram's work represents (a tale of two men, rather than a man and a woman) assumes a new significance. It may be the case that Parzival's quest for the Grail and the knightly encounters in which this involves him, coupled with his unflagging loyalty to his wife, keeps him largely away from women (apart from the recluse Sigune and Orgeluse whose offer of love he declines), so that the narrative devoted to the protagonist from the end of Book IV has no possibility of becoming a *roman à deux* in the sense of *Erec* and *Tristan*. There is a compensation for this, however, for the narrative dealing with Gawan depicts him in close association with a number of women (Obilot, Antikonie, Orgeluse), with each of whom a separate *roman à deux* is unfolded. The theme of love (in various guises) and relationship with women, excluded from the protagonist's action, comes into its own in the Gawan story, more emphatically than with Chrétien and suggesting that interest in

---

[167] Volfing, *PBB* 126 (2004), 82.   [168] Nellmann, *Wolfram* II 450 (on 2, 23–3, 24).
[169] Schnyder, *DVjs* 72 (1998), 4.   [170] Brackert, 'Parzival', pp. 143–63.   [171] See above, pp. 176–8.

this theme, unrealisable with Parzival, may well have been the reason why Wolfram was ready to grant so much space to Gawan's adventures.[172] In each of his *romans à deux* Gawan is called on to restore order to disrupted society, but already Books VII and VIII illustrate that he does not do this alone, but side-by-side with a woman equally actively engaged, so much so that Gawan occupies a more passive position in Book VIII and is largely dependent on Antikonie's advice and control of events.[173] It is with Orgeluse, however, that we confront a woman who not merely exercises emotional authority over Gawan (and other men), but also, going far beyond this individual relationship, occupies a central position in the whole narrative, explaining the need for Parzival to prove himself a fit successor to the disqualified Amfortas.

Although Wolfram composed no *roman à deux* in the sense made conventional by Hartmann and Gottfried, he can be said to have made narrative space available to women as well as men. By doing this he made it possible to introduce two leading themes to which we now turn. These are, first, the so-called chivalry topos or *amor et militia*, knightly service of a woman for the reward of love (thereby treating the relationship between man and woman alongside the male theme of combat) and, secondly, marriage, or more especially, the role played in it by women.

The chivalry topos seeks to reconcile knightly activity with love by making each dependent on the other.[174] Its theory is that love of a woman encourages a knight to perform brave exploits, whilst the knowledge that this is done on her behalf encourages her to love. An early example of this symmetrical combination of aggression with eroticism occurs in the *Historia regum Britannie* of Geoffrey of Monmouth where in the festivities at court held in a period of peace during Arthur's campaigns of conquest it is said that the ladies granted their love only to those who proved themselves worthy in combat. With a good dose of wishful thinking the comment is made that as a result the women were more chaste and the men braver ('Efficiebantur ergo caste et meliores et milites pro amore illarum probiores').[175] This clear statement of the topos finds its way into the vernacular in Wace's version of Geoffrey's work, the *Roman de Brut* (from which it could be adopted by the authors of romance literature). In his debate with the warlike Cador Walwein (Gauvain) praises peace as a time for love affairs (10770: *drueries*), but adds that knights perform knightly deeds for the sake of love and their lovers (10771: 'Pur amistié e pur amies/Funt chevaliers

[172] Zimmermann, *Kommentar*, p. 3.   [173] Emmerling, *Geschlechterbeziehungen*, pp. 52–4, 56.
[174] Hanning, *Individual*, pp. 54–63.   [175] *Historia* [157], p. 112.

chevaleries').[176] Wace may not mention the ladies' chastity, but says enough to make it clear that he has adopted Geoffrey's topos.

The two other romances considered in this book also make use of the topos. In the early stages of Hartmann's *Erec* the protagonist, seeking to restore his honour in the sparrowhawk contest with Iders, is in need of a woman whose beauty he can confirm by gaining the prize of victory.[177] On promising marriage to Enite he receives her from her father, gains her as the prize of his knightly victory, but the mercantile nature of this exchange (from which Enite's father also stands to gain) is mitigated by the solution of having the couple duly fall in love. No criticism of this arrangement (as it affects the woman, handed over from man to man) is expressed, it is at the most implicit, but more readily visible to the women in Hartmann's audience. In *Tristan* the topos is treated, as we have seen, in the context of the dragon-slaying in Ireland, for Isolde's father has promised his daughter's hand to the man who kills the dragon.[178] Two men therefore claim Isolde as the prize for this exploit: the Irish steward falsely and Tristan as the true victor. Criticism of this arrangement is voiced from a woman's perspective (above all Isolde herself, but also her mother), not merely contesting the steward's false claim, but also objecting to this commodification of a woman.

The problematic nature of knightly exploits on behalf of a woman, implicit in *Erec*, but brought forward for closer scrutiny in *Tristan*, is revealed in the flaws of the system which are brought out in Wolfram's work.[179] Three questions are at issue here. First, the author highlights the deficiency of the topos by exaggeration when Belakane and Sigune go too far, as both come to recognise too late, in deferring the reward of their love until their lovers perform yet more exploits, in which both Isenhart and Schionatulander meet their end.[180] These are not the only examples of *amor et militia* going disastrously wrong, leaving the woman to grieve over the loss of the man or to die after him,[181] but in either case to reproach herself for not having granted him his reward in time. We are given fuller background information in the cases of Belakane and Sigune, since other examples are mentioned more in passing or have to be reconstructed out of more oblique allusions, but their very frequency shows that, seen particularly from the woman's position, this was a problem which preoccupied the author.

---

[176] Wace, *Brut* 10767–72.   [177] See above, p. 85.   [178] See above, p. 130.
[179] Riemer and Egert, *ABäG* 35 (1992), 65–86.
[180] Karg, *Erzählen*, p. 170; Emmerling, *Geschlechterbeziehungen*, pp. 248, 284.
[181] Brackert, 'Parzival', pp. 143–63.

A second feature which Wolfram shares with Gottfried is the commodification of a woman who is treated as a prize or reward, to be handed over by one man to another or to be fought over between two men. In questioning the implications of this practice, as we shall see at various places in his work, Wolfram goes against the patriarchal attitude towards women it betrays, exemplified in its complete failure to question itself, above all in the earlier example of one of the Latin poems in the *Cambridge Songs*. The story of Lantfrid and Cobbo does not deal with combat on behalf of a woman, but rather with a test of friendship between two men in which one friend meets the request of the other and hands over to him his wife, who is eventually returned untouched.[182] In this poem the woman serves as the man's property, exchanged with another man as a sign of the husband's love for his friend. This patriarchal treatment of a woman as chattel is what Gottfried criticised in the episode at the Irish court and is one of the rare issues where Wolfram agrees with his literary rival.

Thirdly, Wolfram can imply criticism of knightly service rendered to a woman by the ease with which it can be distorted and lend itself to abuse.[183] Of the negative role of Orilus as a killer knight in *Parzival* we are left in no doubt,[184] either in what the narrative reveals of the suffering he causes or in his boasting of his exploits to his wife. This murderous activity is conceived by Orilus, however, as being undertaken on behalf of Jeschute and in her service (134, 18f.; 135, 12).[185] The idea of serving a woman is even more grotesquely perverted in the rape committed by Urjans when Gawan seeks to defend him by putting it down to the woman's beauty and even invoking the suggestion of a man's heart suffering pain in the service of a woman (528, 6: 'unt ob ie man von wîbe / mit dienst koeme in herzenôt').[186] Equally out of place, with Chrétien as with Wolfram, is the implication of a service rendered to Orgeluse by Gramoflanz. He killed her husband, abducted her and held her prisoner, yet complains that his service was unable to win her love (606, 10: 'swaz ir diens bôt mîn hant, / dâ kêrt si gegen ir herzen vâr' whatever service my hand offered her, her heart turned its hostility on it).[187]

In dealing with the problems and abuses which he highlights, Wolfram employs a number of different methods to ameliorate or humanise the effects of this topos on women in particular. In the case of Orgeluse especially he presents a woman's resistance to the idea that a knight's wish to serve her should automatically leave her with no choice but to reward him

---

[182] Jaeger, *Love*, pp. 55f., 84.   [183] Riemer and Egert, *ABäG* 35 (1992), 78.
[184] Green, 'Homicide', pp. 47–50.   [185] Emmerling, *Geschlechterbeziehungen*, p. 272.
[186] Scheuble, *Sozialisation*, pp. 333f.   [187] See also *Perceval* 8561–75.

with her love and that she would be in the wrong if she did not conform to the system. Orgeluse thus insists on the independent choice which the convention denies her, and a similar resistance is offered by Itonje's steps to avert combat between Gawan and Gramoflanz.[188] Another method is for the element of reward or rather the commodification of woman which this implies to be excised from the motivation altogether, suggesting either altruism or other purposes on the part of the knight. Both these methods introduce the possibility of choice for the woman, or at least remove any trace of compulsion, an easing of her position which is taken further when the woman is shown taking the initiative and thereby revealing her willing acceptance or anticipation of the man's offer. Finally, amelioration of a woman's position can be achieved by introducing love into the relationship, by her for the man, by him for her, or preferably for each other. All this may amount to convenient solutions, but they betray the need to find a more acceptable motivation than the conventional topos, one which afforded the woman more independence and showed more concern for her interests. These methods must be illustrated in the following examples.

These examples present two forms of knightly service for a woman's love in Wolfram's work. Either the woman is regarded as a prize for the man's service (where the force of the convention leaves her little choice) or the woman is presented as a prize contested for by two men. We saw both these forms in Gottfried's account of events at the Irish court, where the steward conceives himself as Isolde's knight, serving her even against her will, but also as a contestant for her (under false colours) against Tristan's claim.[189] With Wolfram, as with Gottfried, these two forms cover different situations (the woman's relationship to one man or her position between two), but both agree in combining knighthood with love (or marriage) and in giving the woman little freedom of scope. It is this latter feature which Wolfram seeks to remedy.

The first form, woman as a reward for service, may be exemplified with three couples. The first, Gawan and the young girl Obilot, is apparently unproblematic in that Obilot, too young to know what is involved, accepts the convention of which she has heard talk and promises Gawan a reward (*lôn*) for his service of her (370, 1–7). That looks straightforward enough, but Wolfram underlines the fact that it is Obilot who takes the initiative here. Youthfully she recommends herself as worthy of service (370, 3), she decides on Gawan as the knight whose service she is to reward (352, 24–6) and is quite certain that Gawan is to serve her (358, 11: 'er sol dienst gein mir

[188] Brackert, 'Parzival', pp. 154f. [189] See above, pp. 135f.

kêren') for due reward (358, 12–14).[190] Using terms normally applied to the courtly lover and of which she has no true understanding, it is Obilot who makes the approach to Gawan, offers him *minne* before requesting service (369, 28–370, 3) and in effect subjects him to the moral blackmail to fall into line which the topos otherwise imposes on the woman.[191] This inversion of the convention, putting the man for once in the woman's position, is not meant to be taken seriously, given Obilot's youthful inexperience, but shows up the topos in an unexpected light.

The position with Obilot's elder sister, Obie, in her relationship with Meljanz is quite different, but is equally questioning of what is expected. With Chrétien, her counterpart demands of Meliant deeds of arms before he can enjoy her love and she thereby falls into line with what *amor et militia* demanded.[192] Wolfram's Obie acts differently, rebelling against the expectation (and pressure) of those at court who are commenting on her marriageable age (345, 22f.), no doubt with an eye to securing a suitable successor to her father.[193] Meljanz, as king of Liz and therefore the feudal superior of Obie's father (whom the court must have had in mind as a good match) presents such an opportunity when he asks her to reward his service with love (345, 27–9), as if the one were to follow automatically on the other (346, 22: 'genâde doch bîm dienste stêt' service is followed by favours).[194] Meljanz's fault in putting the cart before the horse (expecting reward or the promise of reward before service)[195] runs up against Obie's wish to retain some freedom of scope for herself.[196] She asks whether he has taken leave of his senses and claims for herself the right to judge if and when his knightly service is adequate, potentially putting off any reward for at least five years (345, 30–346, 14). The pressure against which Obie's pride rebels (the court's assumption that she should marry, Meljanz's expectation of an automatic reward) is taken two steps further. First, when he attempts to coerce Obie by reminding her of his royal authority over her father (346, 24–30) and then, as the background to Gawan's arrival at Bearosche, when he takes up arms against Obie's father as a means of forcing his will on her.[197] Against this assertion of royal and military authority, ultimately directed at her as a woman, Obie replies with a passionate declaration of her own freedom, great enough for any crown (347, 4: 'mîn vrîheit ist sô getân, / ieslîcher krône hôch genuoc' my freedom is high enough for any crown). Although the quarrelsome relationship between these two is eventually resolved in favour

---

[190] Christoph, *Couples*, pp. 108f.   [191] Buettner, *Gawan*, pp. 55–7.   [192] *Perceval* 4856–63.
[193] Christoph, *Couples*, pp. 99, 101, 105; Emmerling, *Geschlechterbeziehungen*, pp. 13, 31.
[194] Christoph, *Couples*, p. 100.   [195] *Ibid.*, p. 106.   [196] *Ibid.*, pp. 102f.   [197] *Ibid.*, p. 103.

of love in marriage (and throughout their quarrel we have been left in no doubt about Obie's feelings for Meljanz), enough is shown at the beginning to highlight the pressure to conform which is exerted against Obie and the sense of independence which leads her to rebel against coercion in either love or marriage.

This depiction of a woman's rebellion against social expectations is taken a decisive step further in the relationship between Gawan and Orgeluse, not least because it is a theme which pervades several Books. Orgeluse has been correctly interpreted in terms of her resistance to patriarchal norms of behaviour expected of a woman,[198] more decisively than was the case with Obie, but one reason for this is that as sovereign ruler of Logroys she is the only woman in *Parzival* who can uphold her political and military interests independently without needing a man, so that she is absolved from the obligation of *amor et militia* – the necessity to find a male protector.[199] How far removed she is from what is otherwise a woman's conventional position is shown by the fact that she takes the initiative in approaching Amfortas and Parzival[200] (not for protection, but for vengeance on Gramoflanz), not with the inexperience of Obilot towards Gawan, but as a woman enjoying full authority. This authority and the independence that lies behind it explain Orgeluse's warning, expressed more emphatically and frequently than Obie's to Meljanz, that Gawan is certainly not to expect any automatic reward for service of her.[201] This disjunction of service and reward, conventionally combined in the topos, is expressed when Gawan first encounters Orgeluse, for to his eager desire for love she responds by saying that any exploits of his in her service will not earn him love, but only disgrace as a reward (510, 9–14; 511, 17–19). On this Bumke has commented that Gawan does experience disgrace in the following encounters which could not have been foreseen by Orgeluse, so that Wolfram has stage-managed events so as to call knightly service of a woman into question.[202] Unlike Obilot, Orgeluse knows full well what is involved in service and reward and is aware of the reciprocity between the two stipulated by the topos, but her frequent disjunctions serve to deconstruct the convention from this woman's perspective. Unsurprisingly, Gawan clings optimistically to the convention, hoping that his obstinate service of Orgeluse will earn him her love, which it eventually does (as with Meljanz and Obie), if only at first as an assurance

---

[198] Emmerling, *Geschlechterbeziehungen*, pp. 139–41.
[199] Bumke, *ABäG* 38/39 (1994), 113; Emmerling, *Geschlechterbeziehungen*, pp. 142f.
[200] 617, 1–3; 619, 15–19.
[201] 509, 14; 510, 9–14, 28–30; 511, 3–10, 17–19. See also Dimpel, *ZfdPh* 120 (2001), 46.
[202] Bumke, *ABäG* 38/39 (1994), 111.

for the future (615, 3–7).[203] Even what might appear to be Gawan's supreme exploit at Schastel Marveile still does not qualify him as worthy of his lady. 'Orgeluse is not simply "booty" for the victorious knight'.[204] More so than any other woman character, she is not one to submit to male-dominated conventions.

The second aspect of *amor et militia*, woman as a prize fought over by men, can likewise be illustrated by three examples. In the first of these Gahmuret arrives at Patelamunt to find the woman ruler Belakane besieged by an army seeking vengeance for what they regard as her responsibility for the death of Isenhart. Although Gahmuret faces no single opponent, Belakane as an unmarried queen is in a vulnerable position, a potential prize for any knight strong enough to gain her hand and land by force. On arrival Gahmuret appears to conform to the convention in offering military service in exchange for a reward (17, 11: 'er bôt sîn dienst umbe guot, / als noch vil dicke ein rîter tuot' he offered his service for hire as many a knight still does), but this offer is made not to the woman, but to the inhabitants he first encounters. However, when he repeats his offer of service to Belakane personally it is in terms of helping her in her distress, with no mention of any recompense (24, 21–8).[205] If Gahmuret thus altruistically breaks loose from what is expected in knightly service for a woman's sake, Belakane for her part can be said to keep her distance from this convention and to be suspicious of it, for she has learnt of its dangers through the loss of Isenhart (26, 26–9).[206] In another detail, too (the introduction of love into the relationship of these two), Belakane fails to conform to the passive role conventionally imposed on the woman. The narrator grants her the initiative in being struck by Gahmuret's looks when they first meet and in feeling the pain of love (23, 22–8) and she seizes the initiative herself in love, as we shall see she also does in regard to marriage, for as the couple begin to feel attracted to each other (34, 16f.) she places herself at the disposal of her guest in whatever he may desire (34, 20–2). In granting Belakane this measure of independent action, but also in the couple's distance from what is expected of *amor et militia*, Wolfram exhibits his own distance from this topos.[207]

Parzival's encounter with Condwiramurs at Pelrapeire is a close echo of his father at Patelamunt, except that the woman is not simply besieged by an army, for the danger facing her is focused on the person of Clamide, seeking to gain her by force. Whereas Belakane was potentially a prize fought over by two men, Condwiramurs is that in actual fact, as she is in Chrétien's version where Clamadeu expects to have Blancheflor on defeating Perceval.[208] In such a situation Condwiramurs is badly in need of a protector against Clamide, pragmatic considerations could well force her to accept Parzival's service for her love as an escape from the immediate danger, while still being shuttled between two men. Clamide's siege serves the aim of forcing marriage on Condwiramurs, a prospect which she views with repugnance and to avoid which she is ready to contemplate suicide (194, 27–195, 1), as was Gottfried's Isolde in a similar position. Here too we are presented with a woman's perspective on the situation.

Having built up the case for a pragmatic decision, Wolfram allows none of this to come about. Whereas Chrétien has Perceval act in accordance with *amor et militia* by asking Blancheflor for her love as a reward (2103–5), the German counterpart acts like his father at Patelamunt. On arriving at Pelrapeire Parzival informs a young woman in Condwiramurs's retinue that he is ready to give what help he can, adding that a smile on greeting and no more than that will be his reward (182, 25: 'frowe, hie habt ein man / der iu dienet, ob ich kan. / iwer gruoz sol sîn mîn solt: / ich pin iu dienstlichen holt' Madam, here stands a man who will serve you if he can. A smile from you will be my reward. I am ready to serve you), a fact which is duly reported to Condwiramurs (189, 9f.). By not insisting on the element of pressure latent in the concept of service on behalf of a woman Parzival allows Condwiramurs what Clamide's action had denied her – the freedom to accept or reject, to make her own choice. When he then comes before Condwiramurs he simply asks her whether he can assist her in any way (195, 13: 'vrouwe, hilft iuch iemens trôst?'), adding that he will protect her against Clamide's henchman Kingrun (195, 27–196, 1), with no mention of any reward, not even a smile of greeting. As at Patelamunt, the sequence unfolds in the same direction: the couple are attracted to one another (186, 17–20; 188, 6–14) and, more emphatically than Belakane, Condwiramurs takes the initiative after Parzival's victory, choosing him as her husband in a combination of words with gesture (199, 26–8) expressive of her freely given *consensus*.[209] The deconstruction of *amor et militia* which this episode achieves is brought about by both participants. Condwiramurs refuses a compulsory marriage to Clamide and makes her own choice of Parzival, while Parzival offers help not tied to any automatic reward and gives Condwiramurs the chance of free choice.

Our last example, Gahmuret at the tournament of Kanvoleis, belongs to the context of service and reward only in a special, but most revealing sense,

---

[208] *Perceval* 2189.   [209] Christoph, *Couples*, p. 90.

taking very much further what we saw with Gawan and Obilot. In this episode Herzeloyde, a widowed queen after the death of Castis, is potentially in the same vulnerable position as Belakane was in fact and to meet this danger she arranges the tournament, offering herself as a prize to the victor, who is therefore well qualified to be her protector.[210] (The nature of the prize and the conditions of the tournament are unknown to Gahmuret when he participates.) We have here the familiar pattern of a woman put up as a prize to be fought over, with the significant difference that, although compelled by her situation, Herzeloyde takes the initiative in devising this answer to her difficulty. She also takes the initiative in other ways once the tournament has been set up. From the beginning she betrays her special interest in Gahmuret in her disappointment at his apparent reluctance to join in (69, 27f.), suggesting implicitly her preference for him as the victor (and therefore, unknown to him, her future husband).[211] As she speaks to herself on beholding Gahmuret in action she regards him as the victor (82, 3f.: 'doch waene et Gahmuretes tât / den hoesten prîs derworben hât' but I believe that Gahmuret's exploits have won the highest prize) long before the tournament proper, as distinct from the preliminaries, has even begun.[212]

The combination of Herzeloyde's initiative and choice with Gahmuret's ignorance of what the tournament involves leads to an ironic conclusion: in fighting for the prize at the tournament Gahmuret has unwittingly become Herzeloyde's prize, chosen by her.[213] Not content with that, Wolfram takes Gahmuret's subordination to a woman's decision a step further when he introduces the messengers of Amphlise, a recently widowed queen of France and Gahmuret's lady from earlier times, into the scene. Amphlise knows Gahmuret's qualities well enough to offer herself in marriage to him (77, 1–4), for she is now in the same precarious position as Herzeloyde. In making this offer she is another woman who takes the initiative, for she too has in effect chosen him as her knight at Kanvoleis (77, 8–10), in rivalry with Herzeloyde.[214] Despite his achievements in the tournament Gahmuret is here reduced to a passive status between two women who claim to control the issue and haggle over which of them deserves the prize. The tables are turned on what we might normally expect: instead of the woman, passive between two men who compete for her (Isolde at Dublin), Wolfram presents us with a man, passive between two women with rival claims. How Gahmuret's activity in the tournament is reduced to passivity is strikingly shown in the formulation of the verdict, settling the dispute between two

---

[210] *Ibid.*, p. 48.   [211] *Ibid.*, p. 45.   [212] *Ibid.*, pp. 46f.   [213] *Ibid.*, p. 46.   [214] *Ibid.*, p. 198.

queens in favour of Herzeloyde (96, 4: 'hât er den prîs hie genomn, / den sol diu küneginne hân' if he has won the prize here, the queen is to have him). In the first of these lines the subject is the knight Gahmuret who has won the prize, but in the following line Herzeloyde is the subject, while the object (*den*) is both the knight and the prize. In these two lines, as in the course of the whole tournament, a man has been manoeuvred into the position in which a woman usually found herself in feudal marriage policy and in the topos of *amor et militia*, commodified as a prize.[215]

One other passage reinforces this view. When Kaylet, Gahmuret's cousin, informs him of the terms of the tournament in which he has been acknowledged victor he also launches into praise of him for the many knights he has defeated (85, 12–86, 4). In embarrassment Gahmuret seeks to play this down, reproaching Kaylet for overpraising him (86, 5: 'Mîn frowe mac waenen daz du tobst, / sît du mich alsô verlobst' My lady will think that you are raving, if you overpraise me like this). The MHG verb *verloben* can mean 'to praise excessively', but also, like its modern equivalent, 'to betroth'. Aware now of the terms of the tournament, Gahmuret feels that with such praise on top of his victory the trap may be closing on him, that he is being married off.[216] This is confirmed by the next line with his complaint that he is being sold off (86, 7: 'dune maht mîn doch verkoufen niht' you will not be in a position to sell me), where the verb *verkoufen*, placing Gahmuret on a marriage market, recalls Isolde's complaint about marriage to Marke.[217] Kaylet's high praise of Gahmuret is what one would expect from a seller in such a market. In all this (the man as a prize, haggled over between two women, merchandise for sale) Gahmuret has been manipulated into the kind of situation in which women were liable to find themselves in patriarchal society. At the same time Wolfram has manoeuvred the men in his audience into the uncomfortable position of seeing for themselves, in the case of a male character with whom they might have every reason to sympathise, what being married off might be like for women in their society. With this theme of marriage we come in conclusion to a problem of central importance in Wolfram's work.

What importance Wolfram attached to marriage in his work is clear from a comparison with Chrétien. Although the French author treated it as a central problem in *Erec* his attention is directed elsewhere in *Perceval*, for all

---

[215] The independence shown by Herzeloyde is not entirely lost when after Gahmuret's death she retreats to Soltane. Although this is termed a wilderness (117, 9), she manages to construct for herself there an autonomous aristocratic manorial existence, complete with women servants and serfs to see to her needs, from which she sees to it that knighthood is excluded.

[216] Christoph, *Couples*, p. 49.   [217] See above, pp. 136f.

the fourteen betrothals or marriages presented or mentioned in the German work are additions by Wolfram to Chrétien, who has none of them.[218] Although Wolfram presents a view of marriage which, like his deconstruction of the chivalry topos, shows more concern for the position of women he realistically finds room, as did Hartmann and Gottfried, for numerous reflections of the very different practice of his day. These allow the audience to recognise their present condition, they depict the reality against which the author's counter-model is set up.

In agreement with medieval practice a woman can be given away in marriage by a ruler. It is probably meant to verge on the ludicrous when, as we draw nearer to the operetta-like happy ending of the work, Arthur marries off a number of women to men and is termed generous with ladies for that (730, 11: 'Artûs was frouwen milte'). However, the political calculations which could inform a ruler's decision in reality[219] are not absent from Wolfram's fictional world, since Arthur is thereby able to integrate non-Arthurian knights into his own sphere of influence and thus pacify them.[220] More commonly, though, a woman is given in marriage by a male kinsman, without apparent reference to her own wishes, as when Amfortas marries his sister Repanse de Schoye to Feirefiz (818, 18) or, in the secular world, other brothers dispose of their sisters in the same way (67, 26f.: the ruler of Gascôn and his sister Alize; 178, 16–19: Ehkunat and Mahaute).[221] What the narrator thinks of such practice by fathers is expressed directly in Wolfram's *Willehalm* (11, 19–24) in his rejection of parental control in arranging a marriage for the daughter in favour of granting her a free choice of partner,[222] but only indirectly in *Parzival* when Lyppaut, the father of Obie, talks not of choosing a husband *for* her, but of choosing *with* her (367, 24).

Matters are conducted just as patriarchally in the Grail realm, as we have so far seen only in the case of Repanse and Feirefiz, where the arrangement was settled amongst men (the woman remaining as silent as Enite with Hartmann).[223] Patriarchy is emphasised even further by the metaphysical dimension of Munsalvaesche when God himself plays a role as marriage-broker. Since only the Grail-king is allowed to marry (not by his own choice, but by God's: 478, 13f.), the sole possibility for Grail-knights is to be sent by God as rulers to lands without a lord (494, 7–14), as happens with

---

[218] Schumacher, *Auffassung*, p. 31; Wynn, *Parzival*, pp. 317f.   [219] See above, p. 24.
[220] Pratelidis, *Tafelrunde*, p. 168; Schu, *Abenteuer*, pp. 370f.
[221] Schumacher, *Auffassung*, pp. 21f., 33. This book is the best survey we have of Wolfram's view of marriage.
[222] *Ibid.*, p. 20; Schnell, *ZfdPh* 101 (1982), 357f.   [223] Scheuble, *Sozialisation*, p. 153, fn. 15.

Loherangrin.[224] No element of choice is present in his marriage to the princess of Brabant, either on his part (sent there by God) or for her in acknowledging God's will (824, 19, 24f., 28–30). Here, too, a pragmatic consideration is involved, for this arrangement is meant to produce future recruits for the Grail kingdom, unable to provide them from within (495, 1–6).[225] In this detail Munsalvaesche (or the divine command it follows) sees marriage as geared to the procreation of offspring and unconcerned with the personal feelings of the couple, just as feudal marriage practice and the Church regarded the primary purpose of wedlock as the provision of children.[226]

Schultz points out that gender relations in love service, where the man is meant to serve his lady, are reversed when they become husband and wife, for power now rests with him, 'thus restoring the man to the position that was thought to be his by nature'.[227] He cites the authority that now falls to Gawan on marrying Orgeluse (730, 16–19) and, amongst other examples, the dominance of Orilus over Jeschute. However, his comment that such is marriage in the extra-literary world, and such is marriage in *Parzival* ignores other features in Wolfram's depiction of marriage which will occupy us in the rest of this section and the author's overall intention to confront relations between the sexes, including marriage, in feudal society with a counter-model.

For perhaps the most detailed depiction of a truly patriarchal marriage we must return to the secular world of *Parzival*, to Orilus and Jeschute. We have already seen something of this husband's authority over his wife, extending to the right to punish on mere suspicion, unfounded at that. His authority is expressed by his role as Jeschute's *voget* (264, 4), her lord, protector and judge in one person and by the occurrence of terms like *gewalt* (264, 19), *gewaldic* (136, 13) and *gerihte* (136, 15). The narrator acknowledges that legally Orilus has every right to act in this way (264, 16–19), but the contrast he draws between Orilus's right (*reht*) to act thus and the injustice (*unreht*) which is inflicted on the innocent Jeschute suggests that the picture of patriarchal marriage hitherto presented is not Wolfram's last word on the subject.[228]

To see this we may turn first to three other examples of marriage which show a very different picture. They are the two marriages of Gahmuret and Parzival's marriage, relationships which we must now consider from an angle different from the chivalry topos. In each case the movement is away

[224] Schu, *Abenteuer*, p. 372.   [225] Pratelidis, *Tafelrunde*, pp. 168f.   [226] See above, pp. 21, 24, 25f.
[227] Schultz, *ZfdPh* 121 (2002), 355f.   [228] See above, pp. 186f.

from the possibility of a utilitarian, pragmatic motivation of marriage towards the personal experience of reciprocated love as an impetus to marriage, capable of mitigating the impersonality and compulsory element found in contemporary marriage practice.

The situation when Gahmuret encounters Belakane at Patelamunt has all the makings of a utilitarian union profitable to each party (she gains protection and he rulership over a land), but the dawning of love between them undoes this first impression completely.[229] We are not left long in doubt as to Gahmuret's emotions for Belakane (35, 2: 'in twanc doch ander nôt. / daz was diu strenge minne' he was troubled by something else, by the power of love; 20: 'in brâhte dicke in unmaht / diu swarze Moerinne' the black Moorish queen caused him many a swoon) as he finds it difficult to sleep after their first evening together. Belakane fares no better: her eyes cause her pain when she beholds Gahmuret, who succeeds in unlocking her heart (23, 22–6). More importantly, particular stress is laid on the reciprocity of their growing feelings. The glances they exchange with each other betray them (29, 6–8) and both their hearts are weighed down by love (34, 16: 'des herze truoc ir minnen last. / daz selbe ouch ir von im geschach' his heart bore the burden of love for her, as did hers for him), until at length *minne* unites them both in final consummation (44, 27–9). This continued stress on shared emotions before marriage and leading up to it is worlds removed from the impersonality and pragmatism with which women can otherwise be given in marriage with no concern for their wishes or feelings. The couple's marriage ritual is not described[230] (this may have been tricky between a Christian and a pagan), but that has the advantage that their sexual union amounts to what was recognised as a *consensus tacitus* on the part of both partners.[231] With that the woman's freedom of choice, largely ignored in feudal practice, is finally sealed.

Despite what we have seen of the unique reversal of expectations in the encounter of Gahmuret and Herzeloyde, their approach to marriage follows the same pattern as at Patelamunt. At the start utilitarian considerations seem to be present, especially in the widowed Herzeloyde's need for a tried protector, but again these fade more into the background as the theme of love comes to the fore.[232] The result is that for the woman political motives

---

[229] Wiegand, *Studien*, p. 33; Emmerling, *Geschlechterbeziehungen*, pp. 246f.

[230] Schumacher, *Auffassung*, p. 36.

[231] Emmerling, *Geschlechterbeziehungen*, p. 254, fn. 114. Cf. d'Avray, *Marriage*, p. 117, in more general terms: 'the sacramentality of marriage did not require a religious ritual, merely the exchange of consent'.

[232] Emmerling, *Geschlechterbeziehungen*, pp. 229, 248, 251.

are replaced by personal feelings for this one person. Because of the trap into which Gahmuret feels he has been manoeuvred he may be slower to feel love (as distinct from sexual interest) in Herzeloyde,[233] but that has for Wolfram the welcome result that priority can be given to the woman's feelings, so that the initiative she takes is in fact a narrative expression of her *consensus*. True to the conviction that love must be reciprocal, the author cannot avoid having Gahmuret fall in love, too, so that his successful tourneys are later seen as a token of the love of both of them (101, 20: 'ir zweier minne triwen jach' the love of these two was faithful). Belatedly the man may catch up emotionally with the woman, but again this has the advantage of giving priority to the woman's free choice of partner[234] (who fortunately for her is the victor at the tournament).

As in these last two cases, the situation in which Condwiramurs finds herself when Parzival arrives at Pelrapeire (an orphaned ruler, sorely besieged by a man attempting to seize her land and hand: 194, 18–25; 204, 7) is one to make utilitarian motives for marriage to the newcomer fully conceivable. Chrétien indeed follows this up by hinting at the political calculations made by Blancheflor in attempting to win Perceval to her side (2038–46), but these considerations have been dropped by Wolfram, both in the woman's behaviour (she is anything but another Laudine)[235] and in the readiness of Parzival to protect her without thought of reward. The contrast between Clamide and Parzival is revealing. The former's 'wooing' of Condwiramurs (184, 21: *bete*) takes the form of military compulsion, granting her no choice in the matter, but this attempted marriage by force is in contrast to the freedom Parzival allows her in not expecting a reward for his services and thereby implicitly giving her the right to choose her own marriage partner.[236] Insofar as Clamide's attempted compulsion reflects the woman's position in contemporary marriage policy (she has little choice in the matter), the contrast between the two men at Pelrapeire amounts to model and counter-model, to social practice and an alternative conception of marriage.[237] In rejecting Clamide's 'wooing' (177, 30–178, 1; 194, 27–195, 1) Condwiramurs has from the beginning insisted on her own choice, if only negatively, but this initiative is given a positive turn when after Parzival's defeat of Kingrun she takes him in her arms and expresses her wish to marry him (199, 26: 'in wirde niemer wîp / ûf erde decheines man, / wan den ich umbevangen hân' I shall never be the wife of any man on earth except the one I have embraced). The two also formally express their willingness to

---

[233] Wiegand, *Studien*, pp. 261, 266. [234] Emmerling, *Geschlechterbeziehungen*, pp. 231–3.
[235] *Ibid.*, pp. 299, 303, fn. 85. [236] Wiegand, *Studien*, pp. 38f. [237] *Ibid.*, p. 39.

marry (201, 19f.). That the love which grows between them is fully reciprocal is expressed simply and concisely at the close of Book IV (223, 7: 'er was ir liep, als was si im' he was dear to her, as she was to him).

The presence of love as a feature of these three case-studies is much more than a welcome amelioration of feudal marriages. Not merely is it the important factor motivating the conclusion of marriage, weakening or even ousting any impersonal considerations, it is also meant to inform marriage throughout. One of the ways in which Wolfram highlights this is to use the double formula describing love within marriage which we considered in *Erec*: *amîs und hêrre* sums up the husband as being also the lover of his wife. Chrétien's polemical use of the formula was perhaps occasioned by the novelty of the concept, but others who follow him use it more conventionally. Wolfram is one of those who avail themselves of it to convey the idea repeatedly that love and marriage are reconcilable for either sex.[238] Parzival recalls Condwiramurs as his *frowe unde wîp* (302, 7), who as his wife can also be termed his lover (738, 16: *friwendinne*). Orilus, as Jeschute's husband, is frequently termed her lover, *amîs* or *trût*,[239] and Obilot, speaking with God's approval (396, 19) and anticipating their forthcoming marriage, sees Obie as her husband's *amîe*, while she is to regard him 'zeim hêrren und zeim âmîs' (396, 14–17). After marriage to Orgeluse Gawan is termed her *âmîs* (728, 2) and conversely Itonje, eventually married to Gramoflanz, his *âmîe* (765, 13).

It would not be like Wolfram to leave things at that and be content with passing allusions. Whereas couples in *Perceval* are presented as lovers, but not as married, their counterparts with Wolfram take love with them into their marriage.[240] The note is struck already in the first two Books in which as many as seven love-relationships are sketched or referred to. Four of these issue in marriage, whilst this is made impossible for the other three only because of adverse circumstances.[241]

Other hints constantly remind us that love and marriage belong together. In recommending the example of Frimutel to Parzival, Trevrizent specifically refers to his loving his own wife (474, 14: 'der minnet sîn selbes wîp') and approves (468, 1–4) what Parzival tells him of his love for Condwiramurs (460, 9; 467, 27).[242] In each of these cases the phrasing is not 'his/my wife', but expressly 'his / my *own* wife' (*sîn / mîn selbes wîp*), as if dismissing the possibility of extramarital love. Parzival's assurance to Trevrizent in their

[238] Schumacher, *Auffassung*, pp. 108f.   [239] *Amîs*: 133, 10; 264, 10; 271, 19; 278, 8. *Trût*: 134, 21; 272, 8.
[240] Kolb, 'Vielfalt', pp. 245f.   [241] Emmerling, *Geschlechterbeziehungen*, p. 244.
[242] Schumacher, *Auffassung*, pp. 83f.

dialogue is amply borne out by the narrative action. He may be making an adjustment to Gawan's reputation as a lady-killer when he recommends him to a woman and her love in forthcoming combats (332, 10: 'dâ nem ein wîp für dich den strît … ir minn dich dâ behüete' let a woman take on the struggle in your stead … let her love protect you there). In his own case, however, the meaning of *wîp* is specified as 'wife' when, in the combat with his half-brother, Parzival draws inspiration from his love for Condwiramurs (743, 24: 'er dâht … / an sîn wîp die küneginne / unt an ir werden minne' he thought of his wife the queen and of her noble love).[243] The same focus on married love informs Wolfram's depiction of Parzival's trance before the drops of blood in the snow when lost in reverie and thoughts of his wife. True to his dismissal of marriage from his version Chrétien refers in his corresponding scene throughout to Perceval's *amie*.[244] In the German version we are told that Parzival fell into a love-trance (283, 14: 'er pflac der wâren minne' his love was true) and that this was brought about by his wife (283, 19: 'sölhe nôt fuogt im sîn wîp' his wife inflicted such distress on him). By being so specific in his use of *wîp* Wolfram shows up the difference between Parzival's position and the advice given to Gawan, but he also reveals his distance from Chrétien, both in his corresponding scene and, as Schumacher has shown, in his *Lancelot*.[245] In this other romance Lancelot also falls into a love-trance, but of course because of someone else's wife, Guinevere.

It is paradoxical that the combination of love with marriage is also presented in the relationship between two persons, Sigune and Schionatulander, who by human legal standards are not in fact married.[246] That may seem to equate them with the corresponding (unnamed) couple in Chrétien's version (referred to as unmarried: *ami*, 3440, and *amie*, 3610, respectively), but in his treatment of Sigune over four episodes, instead of one in the French text, Wolfram radically alters this. Schumacher has shown that, although no marriage can have taken place, nonetheless in Sigune's eyes, and she is confident in God's eyes, too, the dead Schionatulander is her husband (440, 8: 'er ist iedoch vor gote mîn man'). She can assert this because of her conviction that thoughts can be the equivalent of deeds (440, 9: 'ob gedanke wurken sulen diu werc') and make of her relationship with Schionatulander a marriage (440, 11: 'mîn ê'; 440, 13: 'der rehten ê'). This subjective view of her marriage is informed by her love for him. To 'der rehten ê' there corresponds 'rehter minne' (438, 5). Her love survives

---

[243] *Ibid.*, pp. 100–2.   [244] *Perceval* 4201, 4210, 4362, 4455.
[245] *Lancelot* 711–24; Schumacher, *Auffassung*, p. 110.
[246] Schumacher, *Auffassung*, pp. 49–60, 121f., 128–32, 178–80.

the death of her lover (141, 24: 'nu minne i'n alsô tôten' I love him, dead as he is). The faithfulness which for Wolfram is the hallmark of love (532, 10: 'reht minne ist wâriu triuwe') is hers in full measure (249, 24f.). Perhaps more emphatically than any legally acknowledged marriage in *Parzival*, Sigune's subjective view of her marriage is unthinkable without the love she bears Schionatulander.

Common to these examples of love–marriage, and absent from the arrangements for patriarchal marriages to which women are subjected and which Wolfram is shrewd enough to present as well, are the respect for the woman's attitude and the degree of choice she enjoys, whether this takes the form of an explicit agreement (*consensus*) or the suggestion that this is implied by the initiative which she herself shows, or by the love which she comes to feel for the man in question.[247] The importance attached by Wolfram to a woman's freedom of choice is the outstanding issue in this section and has been discussed by Schumacher against the background of the twelfth-century debate by canon lawyers as to whether *consensus* or *coitus*, consent or consummation, constituted marriage.[248] Examples of both occur in *Parzival*, where the latter, when freely chosen by both partners, is tantamount to *consensus tacitus*. In granting *consensus* this priority Wolfram once more agrees with the view of Hugh of Saint-Victor ('matrimonium non facit coitus, sed consensus').[249]

Bumke argues that Wolfram's audience was led to an awareness that the presentation of marriage in *Parzival* was in dispute with views on marriage in his day,[250] whether practised in feudal society or upheld by the clergy (subject to exceptions referred to above).[251] Schnell argues similarly, suggesting that within the wider framework of utilitarian marriages known to his audience the author has inserted a contrasting picture in which marriages are concluded for mutual love and attraction. Far from simply reflecting contemporary feudal practice, Wolfram rather speaks up against its impersonal pragmatism and neglect of love in marriage.[252] These views are more differentiated than and preferable to Scheuble's equation of Wolfram's picture with feudal practice and his outright denial of any model and counter-model conveyed in the work.[253] Those who judge Wolfram's attitude to women solely in terms of what they regard as his acceptance of various forms of violence against them, without taking into

---

[247] On love and *consensus* see d'Avray, *Marriage*, p. 16, fn. 68 (quoting Pacaut).
[248] Schumacher, *Auffassung*, pp. 36f., 60–4. Debate: Brundage, *Law*, pp. 236f., 262.
[249] *De B. Mariae virginitate, PL* 176, 858.   [250] Bumke, *Wolfram*, p. 115.
[251] See above, pp. 21f., 66f.   [252] Schnell, *ZfdPh* 101 (1982), 362f.
[253] Scheuble, *Sozialisation*, pp. 16, 103.

account his views on women's place in marriage (or his deconstruction of the chivalry topos with their interests in mind), deprive themselves of a highly relevant body of evidence.

With that criticism we may revert to the views referred to at the beginning of this chapter suggesting Wolfram's misogyny and now oppose to them dissenting voices in scholarship. Brackert maintains that Wolfram sees women and their concerns at the centre of the problem of chivalry[254] – with the implication that this is difficult to reconcile with misogyny and its marginalisation of women. Ernst goes somewhat further, drawing attention to the author's stand against abduction and rape perpetrated against women, his support of a sensitive wooing of women which respects their personality and the stress he places on their free will or *consensus* (here very much in sympathy with a growing body of clerical thought in the twelfth century).[255] Dallapiazza sees in the intimate partnership of marriage as presented in *Parzival* a counter-position adopted towards patriarchal practices, a view which is shared by Emmerling in her interpretation of women characters who question and resist those practices.[256] It is tempting to regard the debate on opposing views in modern scholarship (probably brought into being by the conjunction of model with counter-model which Scheuble would deny) as reflecting or continuing a discussion of the work and the issues it raised by a medieval audience which the author wished to stimulate. By putting forward both sides of the question he invites his audience to think further and adjudicate between them.

This chapter, concerned with Wolfram's *Parzival*, has taken Chrétien's version into account only insofar as the German text was affected. If this has yielded what I trust may be an overall picture of Wolfram's attitude to the relationship between the sexes, where does Chrétien stand in this?

That Chrétien, too, favoured the ideal of love in marriage (with the obvious advantage this meant for women) we have seen in his *Erec*, where it is Enide who expresses this from a woman's point of view, but it is also present, more categorically, in *Cligés*. The French author gives no more such references in his other works (least of all in *Lancelot* with its theme of adulterous love). After making his point in two earlier works there was no need for him to repeat it himself, although others followed his lead in France and Germany. To advocate a view of marriage so much more favourable to women's interests than contemporary practice in feudal society hardly suggests a misogynist. This is borne out by *Yvain*, where Chrétien goes

[254] Brackert, 'Parzival', p. 159.   [255] Ernst, 'Liebe', p. 231.
[256] Dallapiazza, 'Emotionalität', pp. 175f. Emmerling, *Geschlechterbeziehungen*, p. 139.

out of his way to undermine a possible antifeminine interpretation of Laudine's readiness to marry Yvain.[257]

But what position does Chrétien adopt in his *Perceval*? A number of points may clarify this.

- If Chrétien makes only a passing reference[258] to the dangers confronting women (widowed or orphaned) in feudal society, this could well be because, as with the theme of love in marriage, he had illustrated this before, both in *Yvain* (the precarious position of Laudine as a widow, Yvain's exploits on behalf of various women in distress) and in *Lancelot* (the custom of Logres).

- In *Perceval*, Chrétien is aware, like Wolfram, of the prevalence of male violence against women (military, disciplinary and sexual) and of women's victim status.[259] The German author may expand what is found in the French text,[260] and further emphasise its implications,[261] but this does not alter the fact that such details about women's plight are present in the French text, too.

- Chrétien had already composed a *roman à deux* in *Erec* and *Yvain*, and continued this in *Perceval* where, as with Wolfram, this is present in the case of Gauvain and women he encounters in successive episodes.

- Unlike Wolfram, Chrétien presents no married couples in *Perceval*, having already made his position polemically clear in two earlier works. What was new ground for Wolfram in *Parzival*, his first narrative work, was already 'old hat' for Chrétien, who had little reason to continue on this track.

- The outright rejections of negative generalisations critical of women in Wolfram's *Parzival* (in the case of Parzival and Amfortas) have no counterpart in the French work if only because it was discontinued before this point in the narrative. However, the case of *Yvain* (the defence of Laudine against a possible antifeminine charge) suggests that Chrétien is unlikely to have differed from Wolfram on this.

- What has occupied some space in this chapter, the German narrator's apparent antifeminism in his humorous remarks concerning women and his seemingly antifeminine generalisations, are all peculiar to Wolfram, with no counterpart in Chrétien.

- Wolfram may omit them from his version altogether, but two pointedly misogynous statements by characters in *Perceval* (Orguelleus, the *vavassour*)[262] are shown to rest on a misapprehension and cannot be taken as expressive of the French author's views.

---

[257] See above, pp. 81f.   [258] See above, p. 181.   [259] See above, pp. 182, 183f.
[260] See above, pp. 184f., 185f., 194.   [261] See above, p. 191.   [262] See above, pp. 200–2.

We still need, however, a full treatment of Chrétien's work at large (not merely his *Perceval*), considering his presentation of women and their relationship with men.

The fact that Wolfram often agrees with Chrétien or develops further what is implicit with him should not be taken as dismissive of Wolfram's own inventiveness. This is borne out by the German author's independent conclusion of *Parzival* beyond where Chrétien left off (adapting details from *Yvain* or Hartmann's *Iwein* to totally new ends), by the invention of Books I and II, by the expansion of the narrative's horizon to embrace the East (Gahmuret, Feirefiz, Priester Johannes), by the wholesale religious expansion of Book IX (Trevrizent) and not least by the expansion of the narrative concerning Sigune and Schionatulander far beyond what is found in Chrétien (even giving rise to a fragmentary work, *Titurel*, entirely Wolfram's creation). In different ways, with different degrees of originality and at different stages in their respective literary careers both authors, at least with regard to the theme of this book, were working in these two versions of the romance in much the same direction.

As was the case with *Erec* and *Tristan* we can only hypothesise about how men and women may have received *Parzival* and reacted to it in Wolfram's day. Men in a patriarchal society may have accepted without question the many episodes in which male authority over women and violence of various kinds against them are shown. As regards violence exercised between men the male members of the audience could equally have approved the way in which knightly combat serving a social function is not called into question,[263] but only if, like scholarship itself for some time, they concentrated on Parzival rather than Gawan, whose reservations about combat are more marked.[264] But there are also a number of details that must have been disturbing to conservative expectations. The emphasis placed on killing and death goes far beyond a mere reservation about knighthood, for the questioning of the chivalry topos strikes at the heart of a literary convention meant to harmonise the two concerns of *amor et militia* and the men in the audience are uncomfortably invited to look at things from a woman's point of view. Nor can they have always been happy to encounter a number of women characters who actively resist patriarchal assumptions or to see male authority diminished by the granting of free choice in marriage to women.

With women the reception of Wolfram's work is likely to have been much less ambiguous. More explicitly than with *Erec* and *Tristan* this romance is addressed to women too, is meant for them, especially in their

---

[263] Bumke, *Wolfram*, p. 122.   [264] Emmerling, *Geschlechterbeziehungen*, pp. 177–87.

role as potential readers. The fact that several women characters are granted considerable freedom of scope (more than Enite could ever dream of), even going as far as resistance to male expectations, surely made an appeal to women in the audience, as did the occasions when, in contrast to women characters, men are shown to have little self-knowledge and to be prone to reckless violence.[265] More than the other two authors we have considered Wolfram appeals to the interests of women and makes that appeal evident.

---

[265] Bumke, *ABäG* 38/39 (1994), 115f.; Lienert, 'Diskursivität', p. 243.

Conclusion

Throughout the texts considered in this book, Latin or vernacular, clerical or secular, there runs a common thread: there is no one medieval view of women, of the relationship between men and women in love and marriage, but as one might expect from human nature a plethora of views, changing over time according to circumstances and the different purposes for which a text may have been written. More commonly women are regarded negatively, but sometimes positively, so that there is no such thing as a universal misogyny in the Middle Ages. This has made it incumbent on us to recognise diverging voices and to listen to dissenting ones.

Already in the Bible and its multiform interpretations in the patristic and medieval periods opinions on these matters are far from coherent, but rather adopt different positions within a continuing discussion, amounting to a lasting ambivalence within Christian tradition about the place of women in the history of salvation. This ambivalence underlies the two episodes in Genesis, the creation of man and the Fall, which are the founding texts of medieval misogyny, for both also give rise to repeated attempts to qualify or deny their antifeminine implications and to argue for some measure of equality between the sexes. With regard to the specific question of marriage, which loomed large for the Church in the twelfth century, the problems posed as it sought to impose its views and authority on the lay world produced different solutions within the clerical world, for example whether it was *consensus* or consummation that constituted marriage. The ultimate victory of *consensus* as essential to marriage also brought about a clash with the practice of arranged marriages in feudal society, as did the Church's repeated attempts to make the divorce of an unwanted wife more and more difficult. The result was a variety of discordant voices both within the Church and in its dialogue with the lay world.

However persistent throughout the patristic and medieval periods discussion of these issues may have been, it is above all the diversity and contradictory nature of the twelfth century, most markedly its love of disputation, which makes it a turning point for our concern, as for so many others.[1] It was a period of uncertainty about the sacramental nature of marriage, about what actually constituted marriage and about its indissolubility. Gratian's attempt in his *Decretum* to resolve these differences in his own theory of marriage was not the last word in this debate, but the reconciliation attempted by him is testimony to the changes that had necessitated his attempt. The debate conducted by canonists and theologians also found literary expression in Latin on the nature of women. Marbod of Rennes has two chapters in his *Liber decem capitulorum*, one of which attacks women as unredeemably evil, but the other praises the idealised virtues of the good woman.[2] Andreas Capellanus follows Ovid's diptych (the effects of whose *Ars amatoria* are countered by his *Remedia amoris*) in turning the first two Books of *De amore* (presenting woman as the object of man's desire) on their head in the third, with its unrelieved depiction of woman's evil nature. However playful these literary exercises may have been, they exemplify the need to debate the questions which on another level altogether preoccupied canonists and theologians.

Within vernacular literature it is the romance, another innovation of the twelfth century and a genre that has been our theme in Part II, which continues this debate for the lay members of its audience. It does this by incorporating a number of different viewpoints (author, narrator, characters, each with its own voice) and juxtaposing them intertextually with voices from other works. What emerges is 'a plurality of discourses in dialogue with each other and other narratives'.[3] Sometimes the attempt may be made by romance authors to integrate these views expressly, as Gratian had endeavoured in canon law. This is not always the case, however, least of all in Wolfram's *Parzival*, for issues can sometimes be left unresolved and the debate open-ended.[4] This should not be dismissed as an author's abrogation of his duty to think his problems through, for it can also be an invitation to his audience to do precisely this for themselves, provoked to sharper thought by the discrepancy of the viewpoints presented. Rather than providing their audience with a ready-made answer (such as Thomasin von Zerclaere had advocated in his moralistic view of layman's reading)[5] these authors inculcate an awareness of problems and the need to ponder them for oneself. By being confronted with what is unresolved in the text

---

[1] Weimar, *Renaissance*; Southern, *Humanism*.
[2] Blamires, *Woman*, pp. 100–3, 228–32; *Case*, pp. 19f.
[3] Groos, 'Transpositions', p. 258; *Romancing*, p. x.   [4] Schu, *Abenteuer*, p. 119.
[5] *Welscher Gast* 1026–80.

the audience is invited to ask questions. The juxtaposition of different viewpoints in one work is a sure means of questioning one (or both) of them, but in any case inviting further thought, with the added advantage for the author of ensuring that his work would remain alive in his audience's minds as part of an ongoing discussion. The dialogic nature of a work which Groos, following Bakhtin, sees in *Parzival*[6] is meant to be extended beyond the work itself as a contribution to a contemporary debate, intensified in the twelfth century, about women and marriage, embracing other works and also to be conducted amongst the audience. The questioning which such a plurality of voices prompted was assisted by the fictional nature of the romances we have considered: their scope for invention enabled the authors to comment on what was given (in the society of their day and in texts which conformed to society's conventions) and to invite speculation on other possibilities, however utopian.[7] Merely to suggest other possibilities more favourable to women's status, to the kind of 'defence of women' outlined by Blamires, was enough to convert discourse about women into debate in which conflicting ideas could not be evaded.[8]

In this debate the authors we have been concerned with set up counter-models contrasting with the view of women and marriage which prevailed (but not exclusively) in their day, both in ecclesiastical circles and in lay society. These authors show that they are aware of the difficulties they face in doing this. In *Erec*, the first vernacular attempt in this direction, this is suggested, above all with Chrétien, by a shrewd awareness of the utopian nature of the precarious solution offered. In Gottfried's *Tristan* the concerted attempt in the excursus on women to subvert established clerical topoi critical of women illustrates more drastically the difficulty of rescuing a positive view of woman from a narrative dealing with adultery. In Wolfram's *Parzival* the defence of women can likewise not afford to ignore misogynous views which are inserted to complete the picture of the world depicted, but also so that they may be undermined.

None of these authors could simply exclude the views they were contesting and still remain plausible to listeners whom they wished to entertain alternative opinions. To attack traditional misogyny head-on would have been counter-productive and invited outright rejection, so that an indirect approach, subversive more by implication than by point-blank assertion, promised more. What long-term success this meant for their counter-models is another matter, however. Just as the discovery of vernacular fictionality by

---

[6] Groos, 'Transpositions', pp. 257–76; *Romancing*, pp. 17–20, 21–5, 95–118.
[7] Emmerling, *Geschlechterbeziehungen*, p. 4.   [8] Schnell, *Frauendiskurs*, p. 206.

these same authors was of short duration, giving way to historical literary interests in the thirteenth century, so does this incipient defence of women appear not to have been continued consistently in the romances that followed. In that sense the relatively short timespan covered in this book (1160–1220) can rightly be termed a 'privileged moment' in which new voices in a vernacular debate make themselves heard for the first time.

Bibliography

PRIMARY SOURCES

Works are listed here under the author, where known, or under the title of the work itself.

Abelard, *Historia calamitatum*, J. T. Muckle (ed.) *MSt* 12 (1950), 163–213

Ambrose, *De virginibus*, PL 16, 187–232

Andreas Capellanus, *De amore libri tres*, E. Trojel (ed.), Munich 1964

Annolied, E. Nellmann (ed.), Stuttgart 1986

Benoît de Sainte-Maure, *Roman de Troie*, L. Constans (ed.), Paris 1904ff.

Bruno, *Expositio in epistolas Pauli*, PL 153, 1–566

Chaucer, *The Clerk's Tale*, J. Winny (ed.), Cambridge 1968
    The Franklin's Prologue and Tale, A. C. Spearing (ed.), Cambridge 1966
    The Man of Law's Tale, in: *Works*, F. N. Robinson (ed.), London 1968, pp. 62–75
    Troilus and Criseyde, R. K. Root (ed.), Princeton 1954

Chrétien de Troyes, *Cligés*, A. Micha (ed.), Paris 1957
    Erec et Enide, W. Foerster (ed.), Halle 1934
    Lancelot, M. Roques (ed.), Paris 1963
    Perceval, K. Busby (ed.), Tübingen 1993
    Yvain, W. Foerster (ed.), Halle 1926

Christine de Pizan, *Livre de la Cité des Dames*. Since the edition of M. C. Curnow is available only in microfilm, references are to the translation by R. Brown-Grant, *The Book of the City of Ladies*, Harmondsworth 1999

Eadmer, *Historia novorum*, PL 159, 347–524

Eckhart, Meister, *Die deutschen Werke*, J. Quint (ed.), Stuttgart 1936–76

Eilhart von Oberg, *Tristrant*, F. Lichtenstein (ed.), Strassburg 1877

Freidank, *Bescheidenheit*, H. E. Bezzenberger (ed.), Halle 1872

Geoffrey of Monmouth, *Historia regum Britannie (Bern, Burgerbibliothek, MS 568)*, N. Wright (ed.), Cambridge 1985

Gilbertus Lunicensis, *De statu ecclesiae*, PL 159, 997–1004

Gislebert of Mons, *Chronicon Hanoniense*, L. Vanderkindere (ed.), Brussels 1904

Godefridi episcopi Ambianensis, Vita, AASS Nov. III, pp. 905–44

Gottfried von Strassburg, *Tristan*, P. Ganz (ed.), Wiesbaden 1978

Gratian, *Decretum*, E. Friedberg (ed.), Graz 1959

Guibert de Gembloux, *Epistolae*, A. Derolez (ed.), Turnhout 1988/89

Hali Meiðhad, B. Millett and J. Wogan-Browne (eds.), *Medieval English prose for women. Selections from the Katherine Group and 'Ancrene Wisse'*, Oxford 1992, pp. 2–43

Hartmann von Aue, *Erec*, A. Leitzmann and L. Wolff (eds.), revised K. Gärtner, Tübingen 2006

Iwein, G. F. Benecke and K. Lachmann (eds.), revised L. Wolff, Berlin 1968

Heinrich der Glichezare, *Reinhart Fuchs*, G. Baesecke (ed.), Halle 1925

Heinrich der Klausner, *Marienlegende*, K. Bartsch (ed.), *Mittelhochdeutsche Gedichte*, Stuttgart 1860, pp. 1–39

Heinrich von Freiberg, *Tristan*, A. Bernt (ed.), Halle 1906

Heinrich von Melk, *Das Priesterleben*, F. Maurer (ed.), *Die religiösen Dichtungen des 11. und 12. Jahrhunderts*, Tübingen 1970, III 258–301

Heinrich von Veldeke, *Eneasroman*, D. Kartschoke (ed.), Stuttgart 1986

Herbort von Fritzlar, *Liet von Troye*, G. K. Frommann (ed.), Quedlinburg 1837

Hermann, Bruder, *Leben der Gräfin Iolande von Vianden*, J. Meier (ed.), Breslau 1889

Hildegard von Bingen, *Liber divinorum operum*, A. Derolez and P. Dronke (eds.), Turnhout 1996

Scivias, A. Führkötter and A. Carlevaris (eds.), Turnhout 1978

Hrotsvitha von Gandersheim, *Gesta Ottonis*, H. Homeyer (ed.), *Opera*, Paderborn 1970, pp. 390–438

Hugh of Saint-Victor, *De B. Mariae virginitate*, PL 176, 857–76

De sacramentis, PL 176, 183–618

Summa sententiarum, PL 176, 41–174

Isidore of Seville, *Etymologiae*, W. M. Lindsay (ed.), Oxford 1910

Jean le Fèvre, *Livre de Leesce*, A.-G. Van Hamel (ed.), Paris 1892, 1905

Jerome, *Adversus Iovinianum*, PL 23, 222–354

John of Salisbury, *Policraticus*, C. C. I. Webb (ed.), Oxford 1909

Konrad von Würzburg, *Partonopier und Meliur*, K. Bartsch (ed.), Vienna 1871

Trojanischer Krieg, A. von Keller (ed.), Stuttgart 1858

Lamprecht von Regensburg, *Die Tochter Syon*, K. Weinhold (ed.), Paderborn 1880

Langmann, Adelheid, *Offenbarungen*, P. Strauch (ed.), Strassburg 1878

Love, Nicholas, *Mirrour of the blessed lyf of Jesu Christ*, L. F. Powell (ed.), Oxford 1908

Marbod of Rennes, *Epistolae*, PL 171, 1465–86

Marie de France, *Lanval*, J. Rychner (ed.), *Lais*, Paris 1966, pp. 72–92

Mechthild von Magdeburg, *Das fließende Licht der Gottheit*, G. Vollmann-Profe (ed.), Frankfurt 2003

Le Ménagier de Paris, J. Pichon (ed.), Paris 1846

Nibelungenlied, H. de Boor (ed.), Wiesbaden 1961

Ordericus Vitalis, *Historia ecclesiastica*, M. Chibnall (ed.), Oxford 1969–78

Otloh von St. Emmeram, *Liber de cursu spirituali*, PL 146, 139–242

Ottokar von Steiermark, *Österreichische Reimchronik*, MGH Deutsche Chroniken 5, 1/2

Ovid, *Ars amatoria*, J. H. Mozley (ed.), London 1962, pp. 11–175

Remedia amoris, J. H. Mozley (ed.), London 1962, pp. 178–233

Piramus, Denis, *La vie saint Edmund le rei*, H. Kjellman (ed.), Geneva 1974

Radulfus Glaber, *Historiae*, M. Prou (ed.), Paris 1886

Rudolf von Ems, *Alexander*, V. Junk (ed.), Leipzig 1928

Ruodlieb, F. P. Knapp (ed.), Stuttgart 1977

Rupert von Deutz, *De glorificatione Trinitatis*, *PL* 169, 14–202

Sachsenspiegel, Land- und Lehnrecht, K. A. Eckhardt (ed.), Hanover 1933

Seinte Margarete, B. Millett and J. Wogan-Browne (eds.), *Medieval English prose for women. Selections from the Katherine Group and 'Ancrene Wisse'*, Oxford 1992, pp. 44–85

Seuse, Heinrich, *Büchlein der ewigen Weisheit*, K. Bihlmeyer (ed.), *Heinrich Seuse. Deutsche Schriften*, Stuttgart 1907, pp. 196–325

Exemplar, ibid., pp. 1–554

Siegfried von Gorze, letter to Poppo von Stablo, W. von Giesebrecht (ed.), *Geschichte der deutschen Kaiserzeit*, Leipzig ⁵1885, pp. 714–8

Speculum humanae salvationis, J. Lutz and P. Perdrizet (eds.), Leipzig 1907

Sunder, Friedrich, *Gnaden-Leben*, S. Ringler (ed.), *Viten- und Offenbarungsliteratur in Frauenklöstern des Mittelalters*, Munich 1980, pp. 391–444

Thomas, *Roman de Tristan*, B. H. Wind (ed.), Geneva 1960

Thomasin von Zerclaere, *Der welsche Gast*, H. Rückert (ed.), Quedlinburg 1852

Ulrich von Lichtenstein, *Das Frauenbuch*, C. Young (ed.), Stuttgart, 2003

Ulrich von Türheim, *Tristan*, T. Kerth (ed.), Tübingen 1979

Virgil, *Aeneid*, R. A. B. Mynors (ed.), Oxford 1969

Wace, *Roman de Brut*, J. Weiss (ed.), Exeter 1999

Roman de Rou, A. J. Holden (ed.), Paris 1970–3

Walther von der Vogelweide, C. Cormeau (ed.), Berlin 1996

William of Malmesbury, *Gesta regum Anglorum*, W. Stubbs (ed.), London 1887

Historia novella, *PL* 179, 1391–1440

Wohunge of ure lauerd, W. Meredith Thompson (ed.), London 1958

SECONDARY SOURCES

Footnote references in this book give a key word (normally the first noun in the title), permitting recognition of the entry in the bibliography.

d'Alverny, M.-T., 'Comment les théologiens et les philosophes voient la femme', in: *La femme dans les civilisations des Xe–XIIIe siècles. Actes du colloque tenu à Poitiers les 23–25 septembre 1976* (Tirage à part des *Cahiers de Civilisation Médiévale* 20, 1977), pp. 15–39

Backes, S., *Von Munsalvaesche zum Artushof. Stellenkommentar zum fünften Buch von Wolframs Parzival (249, 1–279, 30)*, Herne 1999

Baldwin, J. W., 'Five discourses on desire: sexuality and gender in Northern France around 1200', *Speculum* 66 (1991), 797–819

The language of sex. Five voices from northern France around 1200, Chicago 1994

Aristocratic life in medieval France. The romances of Jean Renart and Gerbert de Montreuil, Baltimore 2000

Barstow, A. L., *Married priests and the reforming papacy. The eleventh-century debates*, New York 1982

Bennewitz, I., '"Darumb lieben Toechter / seyt nicht zu gar fürwitzig..." Deutschsprachige moralisch-didaktische Literatur des 13.–15. Jahrhunderts', in: E. Kleinau and C. Opitz (ed.), *Geschichte der Mädchen- und Frauenbildung* I, Frankfurt 1996, pp. 23–41

Benton, J. F., 'The court of Champagne as a literary centre', *Speculum* 36 (1961), 551–91

Bériou, N. and d'Avray, D. L., 'The image of the ideal husband in thirteenth-century France', in: N. Bériou and D. L. d'Avray (eds.), *Modern questions about medieval sermons. Essays on marriage, death, history and sanctity*, Spoleto 1994, pp. 31–69

Bernards, M., *Speculum virginum. Geistigkeit und Seelenleben der Frau im Hochmittelalter*, Cologne 1955

Berschin, W., 'Herrscher, "Richter", Ritter, Frauen: die Laienstände nach Bonizo', in: W. Van Hoecke and A. Welkenhuysen (eds.), *Love and marriage in the twelfth century*, Louvain 1981, pp. 116–29

Bezzola, R. R., *Les origines et la formation de la littérature courtoise en Occident (500–1200)*, Paris 1958–63

Blamires, A., *Woman defamed and woman defended. An anthology of medieval texts*, Oxford 1992

'Women and preaching in medieval orthodoxy, heresy, and saints' lives', *Viator* 26 (1995), 135–52

The case for women in medieval culture, Oxford 1997

'Paradox in the medieval gender doctrine of head and body', in: P. Biller and A. J. Minnis (eds.), *Medieval theology and the natural body*, York 1997, pp. 13–29

'Beneath the pulpit', in: C. Dinshaw and D. Wallace (eds.), *The Cambridge Companion to medieval women's writing*, Cambridge 2003, pp. 141–58

Bloch, R. H., *Medieval misogyny and the invention of Western romantic love*, Chicago 1991

The anonymous Marie de France, Chicago 2003

Blosen, H., 'Noch einmal: zu Enites Schuld in Hartmanns "Erec". Mit Ausblicken auf Chrétiens Roman und das Mabinogi von "Gereint"', *OL* 31 (1976), 81–109

Blumenfeld-Kosinski, R., 'Christine de Pizan and the misogynistic tradition', *RR* 81 (1990), 279–92

'Jean le Fèvre's *Livre de Leesce*: praise or blame of women?', *Speculum* 69 (1994), 705–25

Blumstein, A. K., *Misogyny and idealization in the courtly romance*, Bonn 1977

Bond, G. A., 'Composing yourself: Ovid's *Heroides*, Baudri of Bourgueil and the problem of persona', *Mediaevalia* 13 (1989), 83–117

The loving subject. Desire, eloquence, and power in Romanesque France, Philadelphia 1995

Brackert, H., '"der lac an riterschefte tôt". Parzival und das Leid der Frauen', in: *Ist zwîvel herzen nâchgebûr. Festschrift G. Schweikle*, Stuttgart 1989, pp. 143–63

Braun, W., *Studien zum Ruodlieb. Ritterideal, Erzählstruktur und Darstellungsstil*, Berlin 1962

Brooke, C. N. L., *The medieval idea of marriage*, Oxford 1991

Brundage, J. A., *Law, sex, and Christian society in medieval Europe*, Chicago 1990

Buettner, B. C., *Gawan in Wolfram's 'Parzival'*, Ph.D. dissertation, Cornell 1984

Bullough, V. L., 'Medieval medical and scientific views of women', *Viator* 4 (1973), 485–501

Bumke, J., *Wolframs Willehalm. Studien zur Epenstruktur und zum Heiligkeitsbegriff der ausgehenden Blütezeit*, Heidelberg 1959

Mäzene im Mittelalter. Die Gönner und Auftraggeber der höfischen Literatur in Deutschland 1150–1300, Munich 1979

'Liebe und Ehe in der höfischen Gesellschaft', in: R. Krohn (ed.), *Liebe als Literatur. Aufsätze zur erotischen Dichtung in Deutschland*, Munich 1983, pp. 25–45

Höfische Kultur. Literatur und Gesellschaft im hohen Mittelalter, Munich 1986

'Parzival und Feirefiz–Priester Johannes–Loherangrin. Der offene Schluß des "Parzival" von Wolfram von Eschenbach', *DVjs* 65 (1991), 236–64

'Geschlechterbeziehungen in den Gawanbüchern von Wolframs "Parzival"', *ABäG* 38/39 (1994), 105–21

Wolfram von Eschenbach. 7., völlig neu bearbeitete Auflage, Stuttgart 1997

Die Blutstropfen im Schnee. Über Wahrnehmung und Erkenntnis im 'Parzival' Wolframs von Eschenbach, Tübingen 2001

Bürkle, S., 'Weibliche Spiritualität und imaginierte Weiblichkeit. Deutungsmuster und -perspektiven frauenmystischer Literatur im Blick auf die Thesen Caroline Walker Bynums', *ZfdPh* 113 (1994), Sonderheft Mystik, 116–43

Literatur im Kloster. Historische Funktion und rhetorische Legitimation frauenmystischer Texte des 14. Jahrhunderts, Tübingen 1999

Burrow, J. A., *A reading of Sir Gawain and the Green Knight*, London 1965

Ricardian poetry. Chaucer, Gower, Langland and the Gawain poet, London 1971

Buschinger, D., 'Le viol dans la littérature allemande au moyen âge', in: D. Buschinger and A. Crépin (eds.), *Amour, mariage et transgressions au moyen âge*, Göppingen 1984, pp. 369–88

Bynum, C. W., *Jesus as mother. Studies in the spirituality of the High Middle Ages*, Berkeley 1982

Holy feast and holy fast. The religious significance of food to medieval women, Berkeley 1987

Fragmentation and redemption. Essays on gender and the human body in medieval religion, New York 1991

Cadden, J., *Meanings of sex difference in the Middle Ages. Medicine, science and culture*, Cambridge 1993

Cartlidge, N., *Medieval marriage. Literary approaches, 1100–1300*, Cambridge 1997

Chinca, M., *Gottfried von Strassburg. Tristan*, Cambridge 1997

Christoph, S. R., *Wolfram von Eschenbach's couples*, Amsterdam 1981

Combridge, R., *Das Recht im 'Tristan' Gottfrieds von Straßburg*, Berlin 1984

Coxon, S., 'Der Ritter und die Fährmannstochter. Zum schwankhaften Erzählen in Wolframs "Parzival"', *Wolfram-Studien* 17 (2002), 114–35

Dallapiazza, M., 'Emotionalität und Geschlechterbeziehung bei Chrétien, Hartmann und Wolfram', in: P. Schulze-Belli and M. Dallapiazza (eds.), *Liebe und Abenteuer im Artusroman des Mittelalters*, Göppingen 1990, pp. 167–84

d'Avray, D. L., *Medieval marriage. Symbolism and society*, Oxford 2005

Dimpel, F. M., 'Dilemmata: die Orgeluse-Gawan-Handlung im "Parzival"', *ZfdPh* 120 (2001), 39–59

Dinzelbacher, P., 'Das politische Wirken der Mystikerinnen in Kirche und Staat: Hildegard, Birgitta, Katharina', in: P. Dinzelbacher and D. R. Bauer (eds.), *Religiöse Frauenbewegung und mystische Frömmigkeit im Mittelalter*, Cologne 1988, pp. 265–302

'Rollenverweigerung, religiöser Aufbruch und mystisches Erleben mittelalterlicher Frauen', in: P. Dinzelbacher and D. R. Bauer (eds.), *Religiöse Frauenbewegung und mystische Frömmigkeit im Mittelalter*, Cologne 1988, pp. 1–58

'Die Gottesgeburt in der Seele und im Körper. Von der somatischen Konsequenz einer theologischen Metapher', in: T. Kornbichler and W. Maaz (eds.) *Variationen der Liebe. Historische Psychologie der Geschlechterbeziehung*, Tübingen 1995, pp. 94–128

Donahue, C., 'The policy of Alexander the Third's consent theory of marriage', in: S. Kuttner (ed.), *Proceedings of the Fourth International Congress of medieval canon law*, Vatican City 1976, pp. 251–79

Draesner, U., *Wege durch erzählte Welten. Intertextuelle Verweise als Mittel der Bedeutungskonstitution in Wolframs 'Parzival'*, Frankfurt 1993

Dronke, P., *Poetic individuality in the Middle Ages. New departures in poetry 1000–1150*, Oxford 1970

Duby, G., *Medieval marriage. Two models from twelfth-century France*, Baltimore 1978

The three orders. Feudal society imagined, Chicago 1980

The knight, the lady and the priest. The making of modern marriage in medieval France, London 1984

Duggan, C., 'Equity and compassion in papal marriage decretals to England', in: W. Van Hoecke and A. Welkenhuysen, (eds.) *Love and marriage in the twelfth century*, Louvain 1981, pp. 59–87

Edwards, C., *Wolfram von Eschenbach, Parzival*, Cambridge 2004

Eichholz, B., *Kommentar zur Sigune- und Ither-Szene im 3. Buch von Wolframs 'Parzival' (138, 9–161, 8)*, Stuttgart 1987

Elliott, D., *Spiritual marriage. Sexual abstinence in medieval wedlock*, Princeton NJ 1993

'Marriage', in: C. Dinshaw and D. Wallace (eds.), *The Cambridge Companion to medieval women's writing*, Cambridge 2003, pp. 40–57

Emmerling, S., *Geschlechterbeziehungen in den Gawan-Büchern des 'Parzival'. Wolframs Arbeit an einem literarischen Modell*, Tübingen 2003

Endres, R., 'Minderwertigkeit, Geltungsstreben und Gemeinschaftsgefühl in Texten Wolframs von Eschenbach', in: R. Krohn *et al.* (eds.), *Stauferzeit. Geschichte Literatur Kunst*, Stuttgart 1979, pp. 377–93

Erdmann, C., *Die Entstehung des Kreuzzugsgedankens*, repr. Stuttgart 1955

Ernst, U., 'Liebe und Gewalt im *Parzival* Wolframs von Eschenbach. Literatur-psychologische Befunde und mentalitätsgeschichtliche Begründungen', in: T. Ehlert (ed.), *Chevaliers errants, demoiselles et l'Autre: höfische und nachhöfische Literatur im europäischen Mittelalter*, Göppingen 1998, pp. 215–43

Fanous, S., 'Christina of Markyate and the double crown', in: S. Fanous and H. Leyser (eds.), *Christina of Markyate. A twelfth-century holy woman*, London 2005, pp. 53–78

Fenster, T. S. and Lees, C. A. (eds.), *Gender in debate from the early Middle Ages to the Renaissance*, New York 2002

Ferrante, J. M., *Woman as image in medieval literature. From the twelfth century to Dante*, New York 1975

  To the glory of her sex. Women's roles in the composition of medieval texts, Bloomington 1997

  '*Scribe quae vides et audis*. Hildegard, her language, her secretaries', in: D. Townsend and A. Taylor (eds.), *The tongue of the fathers. Gender and ideology in twelfth-century Latin*, Philadelphia 1998, pp. 102–35

Fisher, R., 'Erecs Schuld und Enitens Unschuld bei Hartmann', *Euphorion* 69 (1975), 160–74

  'Räuber, Riesen und die Stimme der Vernunft in Hartmanns und Chrétiens *Erec*', *DVjs* 60 (1986), 353–74

  '"Dô was doch sîn manheit schîn". How does Hartmann understand Erec's manliness?', *Mediaevistik* 14 (2001), 83–93

Fossier, R., 'La femme dans les sociétés occidentales', in: *La femme dans les civilisations des Xe–XIIIe siècles. Actes du colloque tenu à Poitiers les 23–25 septembre 1976* (Tirage à part des *Cahiers de Civilisation Médiévale* 20, 1977), pp. 3–14

Garnerus, G., *Parzivals zweite Begegnung mit dem Artushof. Kommentar zu Buch VI/1 von Wolframs Parzival (280, 1–312, 1)*, Herne 1999

Gaunt, S., *Gender and genre in medieval French literature*, Cambridge 1995

Gellinek, C., 'Marriage by consent in literary sources of Germany', *SG* 12 (1967), 557–79

Gillespie, V., 'The study of classical authors from the twelfth century to *c.* 1450', in: A. Minnis and I. Johnson (eds.), *The Cambridge history of literary criticism. II: The Middle Ages*, Cambridge 2005, pp. 145–235

Gillingham, J., 'Love, marriage and politics in the twelfth century', *FMLS* 25 (1989), 292–303

Gnädinger, L., *Hiudan und Petitcreiu. Gestalt und Figur des Hundes in der mittelalterlichen Tristandichtung*, Zürich 1971

Gold, P. S., *The lady and the virgin. Image, attitude, and experience in twelfth-century France*, Chicago 1985

Gössmann, E., 'Anthropologie und soziale Stellung der Frau nach Summen und Sentenzenkommentaren des 13. Jahrhunderts', in: A. Zimmermann (ed.),

Soziale Ordnungen im Selbstverständnis des Mittelalters. 1. Halbband, Berlin 1979, pp. 281–97

Gravdal, K., *Ravishing maidens. Writing rape in medieval French literature and law*, Philadelphia 1991

'Chrétien de Troyes, Gratian, and the medieval romance of sexual violence', *Signs* 17 (1991/2), 558–85

Green, D. H., 'Hartmann's ironic praise of Erec', *MLR* 70 (1975), 795–807

'On damning with faint praise in medieval literature', *Viator* 6 (1975), 117–69

'Alieniloquium. Zur Begriffsbestimmung der mittelalterlichen Ironie', in: H. Fromm *et al.* (eds.), *Verbum et Signum*, Munich 1975, pp. 119–59

'On recognising medieval irony', in: A. P. Foulkes (ed.), *The uses of criticism*, Bern 1976, pp. 11–55

'The king and the knight in the medieval romance', in: A. Stephens *et al.* (eds.), *Festschrift for Ralph Farrell*, Bern 1977, pp. 175–83

'Homicide and *Parzival*', in: D. H. Green and L. P. Johnson, *Approaches to Wolfram von Eschenbach*, Bern 1978, pp. 11–82

Irony in the medieval romance, Cambridge 1979

'The art of namedropping in Wolfram's "Parzival"', *Wolfram-Studien* 6 (1980), 84–150

The art of recognition in Wolfram's Parzival, Cambridge 1982

Medieval listening and reading. The primary reception of German literature 800–1300, Cambridge 1994

Women readers in the Middle Ages, Cambridge 2007

Groos, A., 'Dialogic transpositions: The Grail hero wins a wife', in: M. H. Jones and R. Wisbey (eds.), *Chrétien de Troyes and the German Middle Ages*, Cambridge 1993, pp. 257–76

Romancing the Grail. Genre, science, and quest in Wolfram's Parzival, Ithaca 1995

Grundmann, H., *Religiöse Bewegungen im Mittelalter. Untersuchungen über die geschichtlichen Zusammenhänge zwischen der Ketzerei, den Bettelorden und der religiösen Frauenbewegung im 12. und 13. Jahrhundert und über die geschichtlichen Grundlagen der deutschen Mystik*, Berlin 1935

Haas, A. M., *Parzivals tumpheit bei Wolfram von Eschenbach*, Berlin 1964

Hafner, S., *Maskulinität in der höfischen Erzählliteratur*, Frankfurt 2004

Hahn, G., *Walther von der Vogelweide. Eine Einführung*, Munich 1986

Hahn, I., *Raum und Landschaft in Gottfrieds Tristan. Ein Beitrag zur Werkdeutung*, Munich 1963

'Parzivals Schönheit. Zum Problem des Erkennens und Verkennens im "Parzival"', in: H. Fromm *et al.* (eds.), *Verbum und Signum*, Munich 1975, II 203–32

Hamburger, J. E., *The visual and the visionary. Art and female spirituality in late medieval Germany*, New York 1998

Hanning, R. W., *The individual in twelfth-century romance*, New Haven 1977

Hartmann, H., *Gahmuret und Herzeloyde. Kommentar zum zweiten Buch des Parzival Wolframs von Eschenbach*, Herne 2000

Hatto, A. T., *Gottfried von Strassburg, Tristan. With the surviving fragments of the Tristran of Thomas*, Harmondsworth 1960

Parzival. Wolfram von Eschenbach, Harmondsworth 1980

Head, T., 'The marriages of Christina of Markyate', in: S. Fanous and H. Leyser (eds.), *Christina of Markyate. A twelfth-century holy woman*, London 2005, pp. 116–37

Hermann, Bruder, *Leben der Gräfin Iolande von Vianden*, J. Meier (ed.), Breslau 1889

His, R., *Strafrecht des deutschen Mittelalters*, Leipzig 1920, 1935

Horowitz, J., 'La diabolisation de la sexualité dans la littérature du Graal au XIIIe siècle, le cas de la *Queste del Graal*', in: F. Wolfzettel (ed.), *Arthurian romance and gender. Masculin/féminin dans le roman arthurien médiéval. Geschlechterrollen im mittelalterlichen Artusroman*, Amsterdam 1995, pp. 238–50

Huber, C., *Gottfried von Straßburg: Tristan*, Berlin 2000

Huby, M., 'Hat Hartmann von Aue im *Erec* das Eheproblem neu gedeutet?', *RG* 6 (1976), 3–17

Jackson, W. T. H., *The anatomy of love. The Tristan of Gottfried von Strassburg*, New York 1971

Jaeger, C. S., *The origins of courtliness. Civilizing trends and the formation of courtly ideals 939–1210*, Philadelphia 1985

'Mark and Tristan: the love of medieval kings and their courts', in: W. McConnell (ed.), *'in hôhem prîse'. A Festschrift in honor of Ernst S. Dick*, Göppingen 1989, pp. 183–97

Ennobling love. In search of a lost sensibility, Philadelphia 1999

Jillings, L., 'The ideal of queenship in Hartmann's *Erec*', in: P. B. Grout *et al.* (ed.), *The legend of Arthur in the Middle Ages*, Cambridge 1983, pp. 113–28

Johnson, L. P., 'Parzival's beauty', in: D. H. Green and L. P. Johnson, *Approaches to Wolfram von Eschenbach. Five essays*, Bern 1978, pp. 273–94

'Gottfried von Strassburg: *Tristan*', in: B. Ford (ed.), *Medieval literature: The European inheritance*, Harmondsworth 1983, pp. 207–21

Jones, M. H., '*Durch schœnen list er sprach*: Empathy, pretence, and narrative point of view in Hartmann von Aue's "Erec"', in: M. Chinca *et al.* (eds.), *Blütezeit*, Tübingen 2000, pp. 291–307

Karg, I., *...sîn süeze sûrez ungemach... Erzählen von der Minne in Wolframs Parzival*, Göppingen 1993

Kasten, I., *Frauenlieder des Mittelalters. Zweisprachig*, Stuttgart 1990

Keck, A., *Die Liebeskonzeption der mittelalterlichen Tristanromane. Zur Erzähllogik der Werke Bérouls, Eilharts, Thomas und Gottfrieds*, Munich 1998

Keller, H. E., *My secret is mine. Studies on religion and eros in the German Middle Ages*, Louvain 2000

Kellermann, W., 'L'adaptation du roman d'Erec et Enide de Chrestien de Troyes par Hartmann von Aue', in: *Mélanges Jean Frappier*, Geneva 1970, I 509–22

Kesting, P., *Maria-Frouwe. Über den Einfluß der Marienverehrung auf den Minnesang bis Walther von der Vogelweide*, Munich 1965

Ketsch, P., *Frauen im Mittelalter. Bd. 2: Frauenbild und Frauenrechte in Kirche und Gesellschaft. Quellen und Materialien*, A. Kuhn (ed.), Düsseldorf 1984

Kinzel, K., 'Der begriff der *kiusche* bei Wolfram von Eschenbach', *ZfdPh* 18 (1886), 447–58

Kistler, R., *Heinrich von Veldeke und Ovid*, Tübingen 1993

Knapp, F. P., *Ruodlieb. Mittellateinisch und deutsch*, Stuttgart 1977

Köhler, R., 'Die Erde als jungfräuliche Mutter Adams', *Germania* 7 (1862), 476–80

Kolb, H., 'Vielfalt der *kiusche*. Eine bedeutungsgeschichtliche Studie zu Wolframs "Parzival"', in: H. Fromm *et al.* (eds.), *Verbum et Signum*, Munich 1975, pp. 233–46

Krohn, R., 'Erotik und Tabu in Gottfrieds "Tristan": König Marke', in: R. Krohn *et al.* (eds.), *Stauferzeit. Geschichte Literatur Kunst*, Stuttgart 1978, pp. 362–76 *Gottfried von Straßburg, Tristan. Band 3: Kommentar*, Stuttgart 1981

Krueger, R. L., *Women readers and the ideology of gender in Old French verse romance*, Cambridge 1993

Kullmann, D., 'Hommes amoureux et femmes raisonnables. *Erec et Enide* et la doctrine ecclésiastique du mariage', in: F. Wolfzettel (ed.), *Arthurian romance and gender. Masculin/féminin dans le roman arthurien médiéval. Geschlechterrollen im mittelalterlichen Artusroman*, Amsterdam 1995, pp. 119–29

Küsters, U. *Der verschlossene Gorten. Volkssprachlizhe Hohelieda – Auslegung und monastiche Lebensform im 12. Jahrhundert*, Düsseldorf 1985

Kuttner, U., *Das Erzählen des Erzählten. Eine Studie zum Stil in Hartmanns 'Erec' und 'Iwein'*, Bonn 1978

Labarge, M. W., *Women in medieval life*, London 2001

Lacy, N. J., *The craft of Chrétien de Troyes. An essay in narrative art*, Leiden 1980

Lähnemann, H., 'Tristan und der Sündenfall. Ein Theologumenon auf höfischen Abwegen', in: C. Huber and V. Millet (eds.), *Der Tristan Gottfrieds von Straßburg*, Tübingen 2002, pp. 221–42

Langer, O., *Christliche Mystik im Mittelalter. Mystik und Rationalisierung – Stationen eines Konflikts*, Darmstadt 2004

Leclercq, J., 'L'amour et le mariage vus par des clercs et des religieux, spécialement au XIIe siècle', in: W. Van Hoecke and A. Welkenhuysen, *Love and marriage in the twelfth century*, Louvain 1981, pp. 102–15

Lefay-Toury, M.-N., 'Roman breton et mythes courtois. L'évolution du personnage féminin dans les romans de Chrétien de Troyes', *CCM* 15 (1972), 193–293

Lejeune, R., 'Rôle littéraire d'Aliénor d'Aquitaine et de sa famille', *CN* 14 (1954), 5–57

Lewis, C. S., *The allegory of love. A study in medieval tradition*, London 1946

Leyser, H., *Medieval women. A social history of women in England 450–1500*, London 1996

Leyser, K. J., *Rule and conflict in early medieval society. Ottonian Saxony*, London 1979

Lienert, E., 'Zur Diskursivität der Gewalt in Wolframs "Parzival"', *Wolfram-Studien* 17 (2002), 223–45

Lot-Borodine, M., *De l'amour profane à l'amour sacré*, Paris 1961

Mann, J., *Apologies to women. Inaugural lecture*, Cambridge 1991
   Feminizing Chaucer, Cambridge 2002
McCash, J. H., 'Mutual love as a medieval ideal', in: K. Busby and E. Kooper (eds.), *Courtly literature. Culture and context*, Amsterdam 1990, pp. 429–38
McConeghy, P. M., 'Women's speech and silence in Hartmann von Aue's *Erec*', *PMLA* 102 (1987), 772–83
McCracken, P., *The romance of adultery. Queenship and sexual transgression in Old French literature*, Philadelphia 1998
McLaughlin, M. M., 'Peter Abelard and the dignity of women: twelfth-century "feminism" in theory and practice', in: *Pierre Abélard, Pierre le Vénérable. Les courants philosophiques, littéraires et artistiques en Occident au milieu du XIIe siècle. Abbaye de Cluny 2–9 juillet 1972*, Paris 1975, pp. 287–333
McNamara, J. A., 'The *Herrenfrage*. The restructuring of the gender system, 1050–1150', in: C. A. Lees (ed.), *Medieval masculinities. Regarding men in the Middle Ages*, Minneapolis 1994, pp. 3–29
Meissburger, G., *Tristan und Isold mit den weißen Händen. Die Auffassung der Minne, der Liebe und der Ehe bei Gottfried von Straßburg und Ulrich von Türheim*, Basel 1954
Mersmann, W., *Der Besitzwechsel und seine Bedeutung in den Dichtungen Wolframs von Eschenbach und Gottfrieds von Straßburg*, Munich 1971
Mertens, V., *Laudine. Soziale Problematik im Iwein Hartmanns von Aue*, Berlin 1978
   'Enide–Enite. Projektionen weiblicher Identität bei Chrétien und Hartmann', in: *Erec, ou l'ouverture du monde arthurien. Actes du Colloque du Centre d'Études Médiévales de l'Université de Picardie, Amiens 16–17 janvier 1993*, Greifswald 1993, pp. 61–74
   'Deutsche Literatur am Welfenhof', in: J. Luckhardt and F. Niehoff (ed.), *Heinrich der Löwe und seine Zeit. Herrschaft und Repräsentation der Welfen 1125–1235*, Munich 1995, II 204–12
Meyer, H., 'Die Eheschließung im "Ruodlieb" und das Eheschwert', *ZfRG (GA)* 52 (1932), 276–93
Minnis, A., *Magister amoris. The Roman de la Rose and vernacular hermeneutics*, Oxford 2001
Mohr, W., 'Parzivals ritterliche Schuld', in: *Wirkendes Wort. Sammelband II. Ältere deutsche Sprache und Literatur*, Düsseldorf 1962, pp. 196–208
   'Zu den epischen Hintergründen in Wolframs *Parzival*', in: *Mediaeval German studies presented to Frederick Norman*, London 1965, pp. 174–87
   'Wolframs Kyot und Guiot de Provins', in: W. Mohr, *Wolfram von Eschenbach. Aufsätze*, Göppingen 1979, pp. 152–69
Nellmann, E., *Wolframs Erzähltechnik. Untersuchungen zur Funktion des Erzählers*, Wiesbaden 1973
   Wolfram von Eschenbach. Parzival, Frankfurt 1994
Neudeck, O., 'Das Stigma des Anfortas. Zum Paradoxon der Gewalt in Wolframs "Parzival"', *IASL* 19 (1994), 52–75
Newman, B., *Sister of wisdom. St. Hildegard's theology of the feminine*, Aldershot 1987

From virile woman to WomanChrist. Studies in medieval religion and literature, Philadelphia 1995

Nolan, B., *Chaucer and the tradition of the roman antique*, Cambridge 1992

Noltze, H., *Gahmurets Orientfahrt. Kommentar zum ersten Buch von Wolframs 'Parzival'* (4, 27–58, 26), Würzburg 1995

Noonan, J. T., 'Power to choose', *Viator* 4 (1973), 419–34

Ohly, F., *Hohelied-Studien. Grundzüge einer Geschichte der Hoheliedauslegung des Abendlandes bis um 1200*, Wiesbaden 1958

Okken, L., *Kommentar zum Tristan-Roman Gottfrieds von Straßburg. 1. Band*, Amsterdam 1984

Ormrod, W. M., 'Knights of Venus', *MÆ* 73 (2004), 290–305

Owen, D. D. R., 'Theme and variations: sexual aggression in Chrétien de Troyes', *FMLS* 21 (1985), 376–86

Owst, G. R., *Literature and pulpit in medieval England*, Cambridge 1933

Palmer, N. F., review of S. Ringler, *Viten- und Offenbarungsliteratur in Frauenklöstern des Mittelalters*, *PBB* 107 (1985), 467–73

'The Middle High German vocabulary of shame in its literary context. A study of *blûc, blûkeit, biulîche*', in: J. L. Flood *et al.* (eds.), *Das unsichtbare Band der Sprache*, Stuttgart 1993, pp. 57–84

Paterson, L. M., *The world of the troubadours. Medieval Occitan society, c.1100–c.1300*, Cambridge 1993

Payen, J. C., 'La "mise en roman" du mariage dans la littérature française des XIIe et XIIIe siècles: de l'évolution idéologique à la typologie des genres', in: W. Van Hoecke and A. Welkenhuysen (ed.), *Love and marriage in the twelfth century*, Louvain 1981, pp. 219–35

Pérennec, R., 'Adaptation et société: l'adaptation par Hartmann d'Aue du roman de Chrétien de Troyes, Erec et Enide', *EG* 28 (1973), 289–303

'Les fautes d'Enide. Culpabilité féminine et association conjugale', in: S. Hartmann and C. Lecouteux (eds.), *Deutsch-französische Germanistik*, Göppingen 1984, pp. 69–105

Recherches sur le roman arthurien en vers en Allemagne aux XIIe et XIIIe siècles. Deuxième partie: 'Lanzelet', 'Le Conte du Graal', 'Parzival', Göppingen 1984

Peters, U., 'Frauenliteratur im Mittelalter? Überlegungen zur Trobairitzpoesie, zur Frauenmystik und zur feministischen Literaturbetrachtung', *GRM* 38 (1988), 35–56

Platelle, H., 'Le problème du scandale: les nouvelles modes masculines aux XIe et XIIe siècles', *RBPH* 53 (1975), 1071–96

Power, E., *Medieval women*, Cambridge 2000

Pratelidis, K., *Tafelrunde und Gral. Die Artuswelt und ihr Verhältnis zur Gralswelt im 'Parzival' Wolframs von Eschenbach*, Würzburg 1994

Pratt, K., 'Adapting Enide: Chrétien, Hartmann, and the female reader', in: M. H. Jones and R. Wisbey (eds.), *Chrétien de Troyes and the German Middle Ages*, Cambridge 1993, pp. 67–84

Putter, A., 'Arthurian literature and the rhetoric of "effeminacy"', in: F. Wolfzettel (ed.), *Arthurian romance and gender. Masculin/féminin dans le roman arthurien médiéval. Geschlechterrollen im mittelalterlichen Artusroman*, Amsterdam 1995, pp. 34–49

Sir Gawain and the Green Knight and French Arthurian romance, Oxford 1995

Quast, B., 'Getriuwiu wandelunge. Ehe und Minne in Hartmanns "Erec"', *ZfdA* 122 (1993), 162–80

Ranke, F., *Tristan und Isold*, Munich 1925

Rassow, P., 'Zum Kampf um das Eherecht im 12. Jahrhundert', *MIÖG* 58 (1950), 310–16

Reinitzer, H., 'Über Beispielfiguren im *Erec*', *DVjs* 50 (1976), 597–639

Reuvekamp-Felber, T., *Volkssprache zwischen Stift und Hof. Hofgeistliche in Literatur und Gesellschaft des 12. und 13. Jahrhunderts*, Cologne 2003

Riddy, F., 'Nature, culture and gender in *Sir Gawain and the Green Knight*', in: F. Wolfzettel (ed.), *Arthurian romance and gender. Masculin/féminin dans le roman arthurien médiéval, Geschlechterrollen im mittelalterlichen Artusroman*, Amsterdam 1995, pp. 215–25

Rieger, D., 'Le motif du viol dans la littérature de la France médiévale entre norme courtoise et réalité courtoise', *CCM* 31 (1988), 241–67

Riemer, W. and Egert, E., 'Deconstructing an established ideal: Wolfram von Eschenbach's criticism of the *Minneaventiure* system in *Parzival*', *ABäG* 35 (1992), 65–86

Roth, D., 'Mittelalterliche Misogynie – ein Mythos? Die antiken *molestiae nuptiarum* im *Adversus Iovinianum* und ihre Rezeption in der lateinischen Literatur des 12. Jahrhunderts', *AfK* 80 (1998), 39–66

Ruberg, U., *Beredtes Schweigen in lehrhafter und erzählender deutscher Literatur des Mittelalters. Mit kommentierter Erstedition spätmittelalterlicher Lehrtexte über das Schweigen*, Munich 1978

Rubin, M., *Corpus Christi. The eucharist in late medieval culture*, Cambridge 1991

Ruh, K., *Meister Eckhart. Theologe, Prediger, Mystiker*, Munich 1985

Geschichte der abendländischen Mystik. Dritter Band. Die Mystik des deutschen Predigerordens und ihre Grundlegung durch die Hochscholastik, Munich 1996

Salzer, A., *Die Sinnbilder und Beiworte Mariens in der deutschen Literatur und lateinischen Hymnenpoesie des Mittelalters. Mit Berücksichtigung der patristischen Literatur. Eine literatur-historische Studie*, Darmstadt 1967

Sargent-Baur, B. N., 'Erec's Enide: "sa fame ou s'amie"?', *RPh* 33 (1980), 373–87

Saunders, C., 'A matter of consent: Middle English romance and the law of *raptus*', in: N. J. Menuge (ed.), *Medieval women and the law*, Woodbridge 2003, pp. 105–24

Schausten, M., *Erzählwelten der Tristangeschichte im hohen Mittelalter. Untersuchungen zu den deutschsprachigen Tristanfassungen des 12. und 13. Jahrhunderts*, Munich 1999

Scheuble, R., *mannes manheit, vrouwen meister. Männliche Sozialisation und Formen der Gewalt gegen Frauen im Nibelungenlied und in Wolframs von Eschenbach Parzival*, Frankfurt 2005

Schirmer, W. F. and Broich, U., *Studien zum literarischen Patronat im England des 12. Jahrhunderts*, Cologne 1962

Schirok, B., 'Zu den Akrosticha in Gottfrieds "Tristan". Versuch einer kritischen und weiterführenden Bestandsaufnahme', *ZfdA* 113 (1984), 188–213

Schmid, E., *Familiengeschichten und Heilsmythologie. Die Verwandtschaftsstrukturen in den französischen und deutschen Gralromanen des 12. und 13. Jahrhunderts*, Tübingen 1986

'Spekulationen über das Band der Ehe in Chrétiens und Hartmanns Erec-Roman', in: D. Klein (ed.), *Vom Mittelalter zur Neuzeit*, Wiesbaden 2000, pp. 109–27

'*Der maere wildenaere*. Oder die Angst des Dichters vor der Vorlage', *Wolfram-Studien* 17 (2002), 95–113

Schmolke-Hasselmann, B., *Der arthurische Versroman von Chrestien bis Froissart. Zur Geschichte einer Gattung*, Tübingen 1980

Schnell, R., 'Ovids *Ars amatoria* und die höfische Minnetheorie', *Euphorion* 69 (1975), 132–59

Andreas Capellanus. Zur Rezeption des römischen und kanonischen Rechts in De Amore, Munich 1982

'Gottfrieds Tristan und die Institution der Ehe', *ZfdPh* 101 (1982), 334–69

'Literatur als Korrektiv sozialer Realität. Zur Eheschliessung in mittelalterlichen Dichtungen', in: M. Gosman and J. van Os (ed.), *Non nova, sed nove*, Groningen 1984, pp. 225–38

'Der Frauenexkurs in Gottfrieds Tristan (V. 17858–18114). Ein kritischer Kommentar', *ZfdPh* 103 (1984), 1–26

Causa Amoris, Liebeskonzeption und Liebesdarstellung in der mittelalterlichen Literatur, Bern 1985

'Geschlechtergeschichte, Diskursgeschichte und Literaturgeschichte. Eine Studie zu konkurrierenden Männerbildern in Mittelalter und Früher Neuzeit', *FMS* 32 (1998), 307–64

'Die Frau als Gefährtin (*socia*) des Mannes. Eine Studie zur Interdependenz von Textsorte, Adressat und Aussage', in: R. Schnell (ed.), *Geschlechterbeziehungen und Textfunktionen. Studien zu Eheschriften der Frühen Neuzeit*, Tübingen 1998, pp. 119–70

Frauendiskurs, Männerdiskurs, Ehediskurs. Textsorten und Geschlechterkonzepte in Mittelalter und Früher Neuzeit, Frankfurt 1998

Sexualität und Emotionalität in der vormodernen Ehe, Cologne 2002

'Die höfische Kultur des Mittelalters zwischen Ekel und Ästhetik', *FMS* 39 (2005), 1–100

Schnyder, M., 'Frau, Rubin und "âventiure". Zur "Frauenpassage" im *Parzival*-Prolog Wolframs von Eschenbach (2, 23–3, 24)', *DVjs* 72 (1995), 1–17

Scholz, M. G., *Walther von der Vogelweide*, Stuttgart 1999

Hartmann von Aue. Erec, Frankfurt 2004

Schreiner, K., 'Marienverehrung, Lesekultur, Schriftlichkeit. Bildungs- und frömmigkeitsgeschichtliche Studien zur Auslegung und Darstellung von "Mariä Verkündigung"', *FMS* 24 (1990), 314–68

Schu, C., *Vom erzählten Abenteuer zum Abenteuer des Erzählens. Überlegungen zur Romanhaftigkeit von Wolframs Parzival*, Frankfurt 2002

Schulenburg, J. T., 'Female sanctity: public and private roles, ca. 500–1100', in: M. Erler and M. Kowaleski (eds.), *Women and power in the Middle Ages*, Atlanta GA 1988, pp. 102–25

Forgetful of their sex. Female sanctity and society ca. 500–1100, Chicago 1998

Schultz, J. A., 'Love service, masculine anxiety and the consolation of fiction in Wolfram's "Parzival"', *ZfdPh* 121 (2002), 342–64

Schulze, U., 'Âmîs unde man. Die zentrale Problematik in Hartmanns "Erec"', *PBB* 105 (1983), 14–47

Schumacher, M., *Die Auffassung der Ehe in den Dichtungen Wolframs von Eschenbach*, Heidelberg 1967

Shahar, S., *The fourth estate. A history of women in the Middle Ages*, London 2003

Sheehan, M. M., 'Choice of marriage partner in the Middle Ages: development and mode of application of a theory of marriage', *SMRH* 1 (1978), 3–33

Sieverding, N., *Der ritterliche Kampf bei Hartmann und Wolfram. Seine Bewertung im Erec und Iwein und in den Gahmuret- und Gawan-Büchern des Parzival*, Heidelberg 1985

Smits, K., 'Enite als christliche Ehefrau', in: K. Smits *et al.* (eds.), *Interpretation und Edition deutscher Texte des Mittelalters*, Berlin 1981, pp. 13–25

Sosna, A., *Fiktionale Identität im höfischen Roman um 1200: 'Erec', 'Iwein', 'Parzival', 'Tristan'*, Stuttgart 2003

Southern, R. W., *Western society and the Church in the Middle Ages*, London 1990

Scholastic humanism and the unification of Europe (2 vols), Oxford 1995, 2001

Spearing, A. C., *The Franklin's Prologue and Tale from the Canterbury Tales of Geoffrey Chaucer*, Cambridge 1966

The Gawain-poet. A critical study, Cambridge 1970

Stadler, H., 'Die Sünderin Eva aus frauenmystischer Sicht: zur Genesis-Auslegung Mechthilds von Magdeburg', in: A. M. Haas and I. Kasten (eds.), *Schwierige Frauen – schwierige Männer in der Literatur des Mittelalters*, Bern 1999, pp. 201–20

Stafford, P., *Queens, concubines and dowagers. The king's wife in the early Middle Ages*, London 1998

Stone, L., *The family, sex, and marriage in England, 1500–1800*, Harmondsworth 1979

Thali, J., *Beten – Schreiben – Lesen. Literarisches Leben und Marienspiritualität im Kloster Engelthal*, Tübingen 2003

Thiébaux, M., *Dhuoda, Handbook for her warrior son. Liber manualis*, Cambridge 1998

Tomasek, T., *Die Utopie im 'Tristan' Gotfrids von Straßburg*, Tübingen 1985

Urscheler, A., *Kommunikation in Wolframs 'Parzival'. Eine Untersuchung zu Form und Funktion der Dialoge*, Bern 2002

Vauchez, A., *La sainteté en Occident aux derniers siècles du moyen âge d'après les procès de canonisation et les documents hagiographiques*, Rome 1981

Volfing, A., 'Welt ir nu hoeren fürbaz? On the function of the Loherangrin episode in Wolfram von Eschenbach's *Parzival* (V. 824, 1–826, 30)', *PBB* 126 (2004), 65–84

Wagner, W., 'Die Gestalt der jungen Isolde in Gottfrieds *Tristan*', *Euphorion* 67 (1973), 52–9

Wand, C., *Wolfram von Eschenbach und Hartmann von Aue. Literarische Reaktionen auf Hartmann im 'Parzival'*, Herne 1989

Wapnewski, P., *Die Lyrik Wolframs von Eschenbach. Edition, Kommentar, Interpretation*, Munich 1972

Watson, N., '"Yf wommen be double naturelly": remaking "woman" in Julian of Norwich's revelation of love', *Exemplaria* 8 (1996), 1–34

'Conceptions of the word: the mother tongue and the incarnation of God', *NML* 1 (1997), 85–124

Weigand, R., 'Liebe und Ehe bei den Dekretisten des 12. Jahrhunderts', in: W. Van Hoecke and A. Welkenhuysen (eds.), *Love and marriage in the twelfth century*, Louvain 1981, pp. 41–58

Weimar, P., *Die Renaissance der Wissenschaften im 12. Jahrhundert*, Zürich 1981

Wenzel, H., 'Fernliebe und Hohe Minne. Zur räumlichen und zur sozialen Distanz in der Minnethematik', in: R. Krohn (ed.), *Liebe als Literatur. Aufsätze zur erotischen Dichtung in Deutschland*, Munich 1983, pp. 187–208

Wessel, F., *Probleme der Metaphorik und der Minnemetaphorik in Gottfrieds von Straßburg 'Tristan und Isolde'*, Munich 1984

Wiegand, H. E., *Studien zur Minne und Ehe in Wolframs 'Parzival' und Hartmanns Artusepik*, Berlin 1972

Wind, B. H., *Thomas. Les fragments du roman de Tristan. Poème du XIIe siècle*, Paris 1960

Windeatt, B. A., *Geoffrey Chaucer. Troilus and Criseyde*, Oxford 1998

Wisbey, R., 'Wunder des Orients in der "Wiener Genesis" und in Wolframs "Parzival"', in: L. P. Johnson *et al.* (eds.), *Studien zur frühmittelhochdeutschen Literatur*, Berlin 1974, pp. 180–214

'Living in the presence of the past: Exemplary perspectives in Gottfried's *Tristan*', in: A. Stevens and R. Wisbey (eds.), *Gottfried von Strassburg and the medieval Tristan Legend*, Cambridge 1990, pp. 257–76

Wogan-Browne, J., *Saints' lives and women's literary culture c.1150–1300. Virginity and its authorization*, Oxford 2001

Yeandle, D. N., 'Herzeloyde: problems of characterization in Book III of Wolfram's *Parzival*', *Euphorion* 75 (1981), 1–28

Commentary on the Soltane and Jeschute episodes in Book III of Wolfram von Eschenbach's Parzival (116, 5–138, 8), Heidelberg 1984

Young, C., 'The construction of gender in *Willehalm*', in: M. H. Jones and T. McFarland (eds.), *Wolfram's 'Willehalm'. Fifteen essays*, Rochester NY 2002, pp. 249–69

Ulrich von Liechtenstein. Das Frauenbuch. Mittelhochdeutsch/Neuhochdeutsch, Stuttgart 2003

Zimmermann, G., *Kommentar zum VII. Buch von Wolfram von Eschenbachs 'Parzival'*, Göppingen 1974

Index

CAMBRIDGE STUDIES IN MEDIEVAL LITERATURE